PENGUIN  C

# THE KORAN

Born in Baghdad, N. J. Dawood came to England as an Iraq State Scholar in 1945 and graduated from London University. In 1959 he founded The Arabic Advertising & Publishing Co Ltd, London (ARADCO), which is now one of the major producers of Arabic typesetting outside the Middle East. His translation of *Tales from the Thousand and One Nights* was first published as Penguin No. 1001 in 1954 and has since been printed in over twenty various formats and editions. It is now available as a Penguin Audiobook.

He is best known for his translation of the Koran, the first in contemporary English, which was published as a Penguin Classic in 1956 and has since sold over one million copies. An illustrated hardback edition of the Koran was published by Allen Lane in 1978. In the present edition the translation has been completely revised, an index has been added and the arrangement of the *sūrahs* follows the traditional sequence. This translation is also available in a parallel English–Arabic edition published by Penguin Books.

As well as contributing book reviews and articles on literary subjects to the national press, N. J. Dawood has retold for children two selections from *The Arabian Nights*, published in the Puffin Classics in 1989. He has edited and abridged *The Muqaddimah of Ibn Khaldūn* (Princeton University Press), translated numerous technical works into Arabic, written and spoken radio and film commentaries and contributed to specialized English–Arabic dictionaries.

# THE
# KORAN

TRANSLATED WITH NOTES BY
N. J. DAWOOD

PENGUIN BOOKS

PENGUIN BOOKS

Published by the Penguin Group
Penguin Books Ltd, 80 Strand, London WC2R ORL, England
Penguin Group (USA) Inc., 375 Hudson Street, New York, New York 10014, USA
Penguin Group (Canada), 90 Eglinton Avenue East, Suite 700, Toronto, Ontario, Canada M4P 2Y3
(a division of Pearson Penguin Canada Inc.)
Penguin Ireland, 25 St Stephen's Green, Dublin 2, Ireland (a division of Penguin Books Ltd)
Penguin Group (Australia), 250 Camberwell Road, Camberwell,
Victoria 3124, Australia (a division of Pearson Australia Group Pty Ltd)
Penguin Books India Pvt Ltd, 11 Community Centre,
Panchsheel Park, New Delhi – 110 017, India
Penguin Group (NZ), 67 Apollo Drive, Mairangi Bay, Auckland 1310, New Zealand
(a division of Pearson New Zealand Ltd)
Penguin Books (South Africa) (Pty) Ltd, 24 Sturdee Avenue, Rosebank, Johannesburg 2196, South Africa

Penguin Books Ltd, Registered Offices: 80 Strand, London WC2R ORL, England

www.penguin.com

English translation first published in Penguin Classics 1956
First revised edition 1959
Second revised edition 1966
Third revised edition 1968
Fourth revised edition 1974
Fifth revised edition following the traditional sequence of *sūrahs*,
published 1990
Reprinted with revisions 1993
Reprinted with minor revisions 1994
Reprinted with minor revisions and additional notes 1995
Reprinted with further revisions and additional notes 1997
Reprinted with minor revisions, 1999
Reprinted with minor revisions, 2003
This 50th anniversary edition published with further revisions 2006

15

Copyright © N. J. Dawood, 1956, 1959, 1966, 1968, 1974, 1990, 1993, 1997, 1999, 2003, 2006
All rights reserved

The moral right of the translator has been asserted

Printed in England by Clays Ltd, St Ives plc
Set in Lasercomp Garamond

ISBN-13: 978-0-140-44920-4

# CONTENTS

# CONTENTS

# CONTENTS

# CONTENTS

# INTRODUCTION

THE KORAN[1] is the earliest and by far the finest work of Classical Arabic prose. For Muslims it is the infallible Word of God, a transcript of a tablet preserved in heaven, revealed to the Prophet Muḥammad by the Angel Gabriel. Except in the opening verses and some few passages in which the Prophet or the Angel speaks in the first person, the speaker throughout is God.[2]

The posthumous son of 'Abdullāh bin 'Abd al-Muṭṭalib, of the tribe of Quraysh, Muḥammad was born in Mecca about the year A.D. 570. His mother Āminah died when he was still a child, and he was brought up by his grandfather and then by his uncle Abū Ṭālib. As a youth he travelled with the trading caravans from Mecca to Syria, and at the age of twenty-five married Khadījah, daughter of Khuwailid, a rich widow fifteen years his senior. Meanwhile he had acquired a reputation for honesty and wisdom, and had come under the influence of Jewish and Christian teachings.

Long before Muḥammad's call, Arabian paganism was showing signs of decay. At the Ka'bah the Meccans worshipped not only Allāh, the supreme Semitic God, but also a number of female deities whom they regarded as the daughters of Allāh. Among these were Al-Lāt, Al-'Uzzā, and Manāt, who represented the Sun, Venus, and Fortune respectively. Impressed by Jewish and Christian monotheism,

---

1. The Arabic name (Qur'ān) means 'The Recital.'

2. God speaks in the first person plural, which often changes to the first person singular or the third person singular in the course of the same sentence.

I

a number of theists, or spiritual fundamentalists, known as ḥanīfs had already rejected idolatry for an ascetic religion of their own. Muḥammad appears to have been influenced by them. It was his habit to retire to a cave in the mountains in order to give himself up to solitary prayer and meditation. According to Muslim tradition, one night in Ramaḍān about the year 610, as he was asleep or in a trance, the Angel Gabriel came to him and said: 'Recite!' He replied: 'What shall I recite?' The order was repeated three times, until the Angel himself said:

'Recite in the name of your Lord who created, created man from clots of blood.

'Recite! Your Lord is the Most Bountiful One, who by the pen taught man what he did not know.'

When he awoke, these words, we are told, seemed to be 'inscribed upon his heart'.

Muḥammad, who disclaimed power to perform miracles, firmly believed that he was the messenger of God, sent forth to confirm previous scriptures. God had revealed His will to the Jews and the Christians through chosen apostles, but they disobeyed God's commandments and divided themselves into sects. The Koran accuses the Jews of corrupting the Scriptures and the Christians of worshipping Jesus as the son of God, although He had expressly commanded them to worship none but Him. Having thus gone astray, they must be brought back to the right path, to the true religion preached by Abraham. This was Islām – absolute submission or resignation to the will of God.

The Koran preaches the oneness of God and emphasizes divine mercy and forgiveness. God is almighty and all-knowing, and though compassionate towards His creatures He is stern in retribution. He enjoins justice and fair dealing, kindness to orphans and widows, and charity to the poor. The most important duties of the Muslim are faith in God and His apostle, prayer, almsgiving, fasting, and (if possible) pilgrimage to the Sacred House at Mecca, built by Abraham for the worship of the One God.

The Koranic revelations followed each other at brief

intervals and were at first committed to memory by professional remembrancers. During Muḥammad's lifetime verses were written on palm-leaves, stones, and any material that came to hand. Their collection was completed during the caliphate of 'Umar, the second Caliph, and an authorized version was established during the caliphate of 'Uthmān, his successor (644–56). To this day this version is regarded by believers as the authoritative Word of God. But, owing to the fact that the kufic script in which the Koran was originally written contained no indication of vowels or diacritical points, variant readings are recognized by Muslims as of equal authority.

In preparing the contents of the Koran for book-form its editor or editors followed no chronological sequence. Its chapters were arranged generally in order of length, the longest coming first and the shortest last. Attempts have been made by Noldeke, Grimme, Rodwell, and Bell to arrange the chapters in chronological order, but scholars are agreed that a strictly chronological arrangement is impossible without dissecting some of the chapters into scattered verses, owing to the inclusion of revelations spoken in Medina in chapters begun several years earlier in Mecca.

In preparing this translation it has been my aim to present the modern reader with an intelligible version of the Koran in contemporary English. The translation, first published in 1956, has now been completely revised in the light of a life-long study of the style and language of the Koran and has been brought as close to the original as English grammar and idiom will allow. Basic changes include 'God' instead of 'Allah', 'Lord of the Universe', instead of 'Lord of the Creation' and 'alms levy' instead of 'alms tax'.

It is acknowledged that the Koran is not only one of the most influential books of prophetic literature but also a literary masterpiece in its own right. In adhering to a rigidly literal rendering of Arabic idioms, previous translations have, in my opinion, practically failed to convey both the meaning and the rhetorical grandeur of the original. It

3

ought to be borne in mind that the Koran contains many statements which, if not recognized as altogether obscure, lend themselves to more than one interpretation. I have taken pains to reproduce these ambiguities wherever they occur, and have provided explanatory footnotes in order to avoid turning the text into an interpretation rather than a translation. Throughout this rendering the standard commentaries of Al-Zamakhsharī, Al-Baiḍāwī and Al-Jalālayn have been closely followed.

Here a word should also be said about the cryptic Arabic letters which head certain chapters of the Koran. Various theories have been put forward by Muslim and Western scholars to explain their meaning, but none of them is satisfactory. The fact is that no one knows what they stand for. Traditional commentators dismiss them by saying 'God alone knows what He means by these letters.'

In the foregoing paragraphs I have endeavoured to confine myself to a bare outline of the facts regarding the genesis of the Koran and its subsequent preservation. It is the text itself that matters; and the reader should be allowed to approach it with a free and unprejudiced mind.

*London, 1989*                    N. J. D.

This translation of the Koran, first published in 1956, has since undergone at least eight major revisions over the years. This 50th anniversary edition strives more tenaciously than ever before to combine accuracy with clarity and respect for the English language.

*London, 2006*                    N. J. D.

# NOTE TO THE GENERAL READER

It is recognized that reading the *sūrahs* in their traditional sequence – as presented in this translation – is not essential for an adequate understanding of the Koran. Readers approaching the Koran for the first time may therefore find it helpful to begin with the shorter and more poetic chapters, such as those describing the Day of Judgement, Paradise and Hell (e.g. 'The Cessation' and 'The Merciful') and those with biblical themes (e.g. 'Mary' and 'Joseph') in the second half of the book, before attempting the much longer and often more complex chapters in the first half (e.g. 'The Cow' and 'The Table'), which presuppose familiarity with events in the early days of Islam.

# CHRONOLOGICAL TABLE OF THE MAIN EVENTS IN THE LIFE OF MUḤAMMAD

| | |
|---|---|
| *c.* 570 | Birth of Muḥammad (his father having died a few months earlier) |
| 576 | Death of his mother Āminah |
| 595 | Marriage to Khadījah |
| *c.* 610 | Beginning of Call |
| 615 | Flight of his followers to Ethiopia |
| 619 | Death of Khadījah |
| 620 | Muḥammad's reputed 'Night Journey' from Mecca to Jerusalem, and thence to the Seventh Heaven |
| 622 | The *Hijra* (Flight or Migration) of Muḥammad and his followers to Medina, and beginning of the Muslim Era |
| 624 | Battle of Badr: the Quraysh defeated by the Muslims |
| 625 | Battle of Uḥud: the Muslims defeated |
| 626 | The Jewish tribe of al-Naḍīr crushed and expelled |
| 627 | 'The War of the Ditch' – the Meccans' expedition against the Muslims in Medina. Attackers driven off |
| 627 | The Jewish tribe of Qurayẓah raided by Muḥammad |
| 628 | The Treaty of Ḥudaybiyya; truce with the Quraysh, who recognize Muḥammad's right to proselytize without hindrance |

7

629        The Jews of Khaybar put to the sword. Muḥammad sends letters and messengers to the Kings of Persia, Yemen, and Ethiopia and the Emperor Heraclius, inviting them to accept Islām

630        Truce broken by the Quraysh. Mecca taken by Muḥammad – the entire population converted, and the Kaʿbah established as the religious centre of Islām

631        'The Year of Embassies' – Islām accepted by the Arabian tribes

632        Muḥammad's Farewell Pilgrimage to Mecca

632, 8 June    Death of Muḥammad, three months after his return to Medina

# THE EXORDIUM

## IN THE NAME OF GOD
## THE COMPASSIONATE
## THE MERCIFUL

*Praise be to God, Lord of the Universe,*
*The Compassionate, the Merciful,*
*Sovereign of the Day of Judgement!*
*You alone we worship, and to You alone*
*we turn for help.*
*Guide us to the straight path,*
*The path of those whom You have favoured,*
*Not of those who have incurred Your wrath,*
*Nor of those who have gone astray.*

\*

# THE COW

*In the Name of God, the Compassionate, the Merciful*

ALIF *lām mīm*. This Book is not to be doubted. It is a guide 2:1
for the righteous, who believe in the unseen and are
steadfast in prayer; who give in alms[1] from what We gave
them; who believe in what has been revealed to you[2] and
what was revealed before you, and have absolute faith in the
life to come. These are rightly guided by their Lord; these
shall surely triumph.

As for the unbelievers, it is the same whether or not you
forewarn them; they will not have faith. God has set a seal
upon their hearts and ears; their sight is dimmed and
grievous punishment awaits them.

There are some who declare: 'We believe in God and the
Last Day,' yet they are no true believers. They seek to
deceive God and those who believe in Him: but they
deceive none save themselves, though they may not perceive
it. There is a sickness in their hearts which God has 2:10
aggravated: they shall be sternly punished for the lies they
ever told.

When they are told: 'You shall not do evil in the land,'
they reply: 'Surely we are doing only what is good.' But it is
they who are the evil-doers, though they may not perceive it.

And when they are told: 'Believe as the people believe,' they
reply: 'Are we to believe as fools believe?' It is they who are
the fools, if they but knew it!

When they meet the faithful, they declare: 'We, too, are
believers.' But when alone with their devils they say to
them: 'We follow none but you: we were only mocking.'
God will mock them and keep them long in sin, ever
straying from the right path.

Such are those that barter guidance for error: they profit
nothing, nor are they on the right path. They are like one 2:17
who kindled a fire, but as soon as it lit up all around him

---

1. Or 'give to the cause'.    2. Muḥammad.

11

God put it out and left him in darkness: they do not see.
2:18 Deaf, dumb, and blind, they will never return to the right
path.

Or like those who, beneath a dark storm-cloud charged
with thunder and lightning, thrust their fingers into their
ears at the sound of every thunder-clap for fear of death
(God thus encompasses the unbelievers). The lightning
almost snatches away their sight: whenever it flashes upon
them they walk on, but as soon as it darkens they stand still.
Indeed, if God pleased, He could take away their hearing
and their sight: God has power over all things.

You people! Serve your Lord, who has created you and
those who have gone before you, so that you may guard
yourselves against evil; who has made the earth a bed for
you and the sky a dome, and has sent down water from the
sky to bring forth fruits for your sustenance. Do not
knowingly set up other gods beside God.

2:23    If you doubt what We have revealed to Our servant,
produce one chapter comparable to it. Call upon your
idols to assist you, if what you say be true. But if you fail
(as you are sure to fail), then guard yourselves against
the Fire whose fuel is men and stones, prepared for the
unbelievers.

Proclaim good tidings to those who have faith and do
good works. They shall dwell in gardens watered by running
streams: whenever they are given fruit to eat they will say:
'This is what we used to eat before,' for they shall be given
the like. Wedded to chaste spouses, they shall abide therein
for ever.

God does not disdain to make comparison with a gnat
or with a larger creature. The faithful know that it is the
truth from their Lord, but the unbelievers ask: 'What could
God mean by this comparison?'

By such comparisons God confounds many and enlightens
many. But He confounds none except the evil-doers, who
2:27 break His covenant after accepting it, and put asunder what
He has bidden to be united, and perpetrate corruption in
the land. These will surely be the losers.

How can you deny God? Did He not give you life when  2:28
you were dead, and will He not cause you to die and then
restore you to life? Will you not return to Him at last? He
created for you all that the earth contains; then, ascending
to the sky, He fashioned it into seven heavens. He has knowledge of all things.

When your Lord said to the angels: 'I am placing on the
earth one that shall rule as My deputy,' they replied: 'Will
You put there one that will do evil and shed blood, when
we have for so long sung Your praises and sanctified Your
name?'

He said: 'I know what you know not.'

He taught Adam the names of all things and then set
them before the angels, saying: 'Tell Me the names of these,
if what you say be true.'

'Glory be to You,' they replied, 'we have no knowledge  2:32
except that which You have given us. You alone are all-
knowing and wise.'

Then said He: 'Adam, tell them their names.' And when
Adam had named them, He said: 'Did I not tell you that I
know the secrets of the heavens and the earth, and know all
that you reveal and all that you conceal?'

And when We said to the angels: 'Prostrate yourselves
before Adam,' they all prostrated themselves except Satan,
who in his pride refused and became an unbeliever.

We said: 'Adam, dwell with your wife in Paradise and
eat of its fruits to your hearts' content wherever you will.
But never approach this tree or you shall both become transgressors.'

But Satan lured them thence and brought about their
banishment. 'Get you down,' We said, 'and be enemies to
each other. The earth will for a while provide your dwelling and your sustenance.'

Then Adam received commandments from his Lord, and
his Lord relented towards him. He is the Relenting One,
the Merciful.

'Get you down hence, all,' We said. 'When My guidance  2:38
is revealed to you, those that follow My guidance shall have

2:39 nothing to fear or to regret; but those that deny and reject Our revelations shall be the inmates of the Fire, and there shall they abide for ever.'

Children of Israel, remember the favour I have bestowed upon you. Keep your covenant, and I will be true to Mine. Dread My power. Have faith in My revelations, which confirm your Scriptures, and do not be the first to deny them. Do not sell My revelations for a paltry price; fear Me. Do not confound truth with falsehood, nor knowingly conceal the truth. Attend to your prayers, render the alms levy, and kneel with those who kneel. Would you enjoin righteousness on men and forget it yourselves? Yet you read the Scriptures. Have you no sense?

Fortify yourselves with patience and with prayer. This may indeed be an exacting discipline, but not to the devout, who know that they will meet their Lord and that to Him they will return.

2:47 Children of Israel, remember the favour I have bestowed upon you, and that I exalted you above the nations. Guard yourselves against the day on which no soul shall stand for another: when no intercession shall be accepted for it, no ransom be taken from it, no help be given it.

Remember how We delivered you from Pharaoh's people, who had oppressed you cruelly, slaying your sons and sparing only your daughters. Surely that was a great trial by your Lord. We parted the sea for you and, taking you to safety, drowned Pharaoh's men before your very eyes. We made a tryst with Moses for the fortieth night, and in his absence you took up the calf and thus committed evil. Yet after that We pardoned you, so that you might give thanks.

We gave Moses the Scriptures and knowledge of right
2:54 and wrong, so that you might be rightly guided. Moses said to his people: 'You have wronged yourselves, my people, in worshipping the calf. Turn in penitence to your Creator and slay the culprits among you. That will be best for you in your Creator's sight.' And He relented towards you. He is the Relenting One, the Merciful.

When you said to Moses: 'We will not believe in you 2:55 until we see God with our own eyes,' the thunderbolt struck you while you were looking on. Then We revived you from your stupor, so that you might give thanks.

We caused the clouds to draw their shadow over you and sent down for you manna and quails,[1] saying: 'Eat of the good things We have given you.' Indeed, they[2] did not wrong Us, but they wronged themselves.

'Enter this city,' We said, 'and eat where you will to your hearts' content. Make your way reverently through the gates, saying: "We repent." We shall forgive you your sins and bestow abundance on the righteous.' But that which they were told the wrongdoers replaced with other words; and We let loose on the wrongdoers a scourge from heaven as punishment for their misdeeds.

When Moses requested water for his people We said to him: 'Strike the Rock with your staff.' Thereupon twelve springs gushed from the Rock, and each tribe knew their drinking-place. We said: 'Eat and drink of that which God has provided and do not foul the land with evil.'

'Moses,' you[2] said, 'we will no longer put up with this 2:61 monotonous diet. Call on your Lord to give us some of the varied produce of the earth, green herbs and cucumbers, corn and lentils and onions.'[3]

'What!' he answered. 'Would you exchange that which is good for what is worse? Go back to some city. There you will find all you have asked for.'

Shame and misery were stamped upon them[2] and they incurred the wrath of God; because they disbelieved God's signs and slew the prophets unjustly; because they were rebels and transgressors.

Believers, those who follow the Jewish Faith, Christians, and Sabaeans – whoever believes in God and the Last Day and does what is right – shall be rewarded by their Lord; they have nothing to fear or to regret.

We made a covenant with you[2] and raised the Mount 2:63

---

1. Cf. Exodus xvi.　　2. The Israelites.　　3. Cf. Numbers xi, 5.

above you, saying: 'Grasp fervently what We have given you, and bear in mind its precepts, that you may guard 2:64 yourselves against evil.' Yet after that you turned away, and but for God's grace and mercy you would have surely been among the lost.

You have heard of those of you that broke the Sabbath. We said to them: 'You shall be changed into detested apes.' We made their fate an example to their own generation and to those who followed them, and a lesson to the righteous.

When Moses said to his people: 'God commands you to sacrifice a cow,' they replied: 'Are you trifling with us?'

'God forbid that I should be so foolish!' he rejoined.

'Call on your Lord,' they said, 'to make known to us what kind of cow she shall be.'

He replied: 'Your Lord says: "Let her be neither an old cow nor a young heifer, but in between." Do, therefore, as you are bidden.'

'Call on your Lord,' they said, 'to make known to us what her colour shall be.'

He replied: 'Your Lord says: "Let the cow be yellow, a rich yellow, pleasing to those that see it."'

2:70 'Call on your Lord,' they said, 'to make known to us the exact type of cow she shall be; for to us cows look all alike. If God wills we shall be rightly guided.'

Moses replied: 'Your Lord says: "Let her be a healthy cow, not worn out with ploughing the earth or watering the field; a cow free from any blemish."'

'Now you have told us all,' they answered. And they slaughtered a cow, after they had nearly declined to do so.

And when you slew a man and then fell out with one another concerning him, God made known what you concealed. We said: 'Strike him with a part of it.' Thus God restores the dead to life and shows you His signs, that you may grow in understanding.

2:74 Yet after that your hearts became as hard as rock or even harder; for from some rocks rivers take their course: some break asunder and water gushes from them: and others tumble down through fear of God. God is not unaware of what you do.

Do you[1] then hope that they will believe in you, when 2:75 some of them have already heard the Word of God and knowingly perverted it, although they understood its meaning?

When they meet the faithful they declare: 'We, too, are believers.' But when alone they say to each other: 'Must you declare to them what God has revealed to you? They will only dispute with you about it in your Lord's presence. Have you no sense?'

Do they not know that God has knowledge of all that they conceal and all that they reveal?

There are illiterate men among them who, ignorant of the Scriptures, know of nothing but wishful fancies and vague conjecture. Woe betide those that write the scriptures with their own hands and then declare: 'This is from God,' in order to gain some paltry end. Woeful shall be their fate, because of what their hands have written, because of what they did!

They declare: 'The Fire will never touch us – except for a 2:80 few days.' Say: 'Did God make you such a promise – God will not break His promise – or do you assert of God what you know not?'

Truly, those that commit evil and become engrossed in sin shall be the inmates of the Fire; there shall they abide for ever. But those that have faith and do good works are the heirs of Paradise; there shall they abide for ever.

When We made a covenant with the Israelites We said: 'Serve none but God. Show kindness to your parents, to your kinsfolk, to orphans, and to the destitute. Exhort men to righteousness. Attend to your prayers and render the alms levy.' But you all broke your covenant except a few, and paid no heed.

And when We made a covenant with you We said: 'You 2:84 shall not shed your kinsmen's blood or turn them out of

---

1. The believers are here addressed.

their dwellings.' To this you consented and bore witness.

2:85 Yet there you were, slaying your own kinsfolk, and turning a number of them out of their dwellings, and helping each other against them with sin and aggression; though had they come to you as captives, you would have ransomed them. Surely their expulsion was unlawful. Can you believe in one part of the Scriptures and deny another?

Those of you that act thus shall be rewarded with disgrace in this world and with grievous punishment on the Day of Resurrection. God is never heedless of what you do.

Such are they who buy the life of this world at the price of the life to come. Their punishment shall not be mitigated, nor shall they be helped.

To Moses We gave the Scriptures and after him We sent other apostles. We gave Jesus son of Mary veritable signs and strengthened him with the Holy Spirit. Will you then scorn each apostle whose message does not suit your fancies, charging some with imposture and slaying others?

2:88 They say: 'Our hearts are sealed.' But God has cursed them for their unbelief. They have but little faith.

And now that a Book confirming their own has come to them from God, they deny it, although they know it to be the truth and have long prayed for help against the unbelievers. God's curse be upon the infidels! Evil is that for which they have bartered away their souls. To deny God's own revelation, grudging that He should reveal His bounty to whom He chooses from among His servants! They have incurred God's most inexorable wrath. Ignominious punishment awaits the unbelievers.

When they are told: 'Believe in what God has revealed,' they reply: 'We believe in what was revealed to *us*.' But they deny what has since been revealed, although it is the truth, corroborating their own scriptures.

Say: 'Why did you kill the prophets of God, if you are
2:92 true believers? Moses came to you with veritable signs, but in his absence you worshipped the calf and committed evil.'

18

When We made a covenant with you and raised the 2:93
Mount above you, saying: 'Grasp fervently what We have
given you and hear Our commandments,' you[1] replied: 'We
hear but disobey.'

For their unbelief they were made to drink down the calf
into their hearts.[2] Say: 'Evil is that to which your faith
prompts you if you are indeed believers.'

Say: 'If God's Abode of the Hereafter is for yourselves
alone, to the exclusion of all others, then wish for death if
your claim be true!'

But they will never wish for death, because of what they
did; for God knows the evil-doers. Indeed, you will find
they love this life more than other men: more than the
pagans do. Each one of them would love to live a thousand
years.

But even if their lives were indeed prolonged, that will
surely not save them from Our scourge. God is watching
all their actions.

Say: 'Whoever is an enemy of Gabriel' (who has by
God's grace revealed to you[3] the Koran as a guide and
joyful tidings for the faithful, confirming previous scriptures) 'whoever is an enemy of God, His angels, or His 2:98
apostles, or of Gabriel or Michael, will surely find that God
is the enemy of the unbelievers.'

We have sent down to you clear revelations: none will
deny them except the evil-doers. What! Whenever they
make a covenant, must some of them cast it aside? Most of
them are unbelievers.

And now that an apostle has come to them from God
confirming their own Scriptures, some of those to whom
the Scriptures were given cast off the Book of God over
their backs as though they know nothing and accept what 2:102
the devils tell of Solomon's kingdom. Not that Solomon
was an unbeliever: it is the devils who are unbelievers. They
teach men witchcraft and that which was revealed to the
angels Hārūt and Mārūt in Babylon. Yet they never instruct

1. Lit., they.    2. Cf. Exodus xxxii, 20.    3. Muḥammad.

19

any man without saying to him beforehand: 'We have been sent to tempt you; do not renounce your faith.' From these two, they learn a charm by which they can create discord between husband and wife, although they can harm none with what they learn except by God's leave. They learn, indeed, what harms them and does not profit them; yet they know full well that anyone who engaged in that traffic would have no share in the life to come. Vile is that for which they have sold their souls, if they but knew

2:103 it! Had they embraced the Faith and kept from evil, far better for them would God's reward have been, if they but knew it.

Believers, do not say *Rā'inā*, but say *Unzurnā*.¹ Take heed; woeful punishment awaits the unbelievers.

The unbelievers among the People of the Book, and the pagans, resent that any blessings should have been sent down to you from your Lord. But God chooses whom He will for His mercy. God's grace is infinite.

2:106 If We abrogate a verse or cause it to be forgotten, We will replace it by a better one or one similar. Did you not know that God has power over all things? Did you not know that it is God who has sovereignty over the heavens and the earth, and that there is none besides God to protect or help you?

Would you rather demand of your Apostle that which was once demanded of Moses? He that barters faith for unbelief has surely strayed from the right path.

2:109 Many among the People of the Book wish, through envy, to lead you back to unbelief, now that you have embraced the Faith and the truth has been made plain to them. Forgive them and bear with them until God makes known His will. God has power over all things.

1. These words mean 'Listen to us' and 'Look upon us' respectively; but in Judaeo-Arabic the sound of the first conveys the sense, 'Our evil one'. Arabian Jews used the expression as a derisive pun.

Attend to your prayers and render the alms levy. What- 2:110
ever good you do shall be recompensed by God. God is
watching all your actions.

They declare: 'None shall enter Paradise but Jews and
Christians.' Such are their wishful fancies. Say: 'Let us have
your proof, if what you say be true.' Indeed, those that
submit to God and do good works shall be recompensed
by their Lord: they shall have nothing to fear or to
regret.

The Jews say the Christians are misguided, and the Christians say it is the Jews who are misguided. Yet they both
read the Scriptures. And the ignorant say the same of both.
God will on the Day of Resurrection judge their disputes.

Who is more wicked than the men who seek to destroy
the mosques of God and forbid His name to be mentioned
in them, when it behoves these men to enter them with fear
in their hearts? They shall be held up to shame in this world,
and in the world to come grievous punishment awaits them.

To God belongs the east and the west. Whichever way 2:115
you turn there is the face of God. He is omnipresent and all-
knowing.

They say: 'God has begotten a son.' Glory be to Him!
His is what the heavens and the earth contain; all is
obedient to Him. Creator of the heavens and the earth!
When He decrees a thing, He need only say 'Be,' and it is.

The ignorant ask: 'Why does God not speak to us or give
us a sign?' The same demand was made by those before
them: their hearts are all alike. But to those whose faith is
firm We have already revealed Our signs.

We have sent you forth to proclaim the truth and to give
warning. You shall not be questioned about the heirs of Hell.

You will please neither the Jews nor the Christians unless
you follow their faith. Say: 'God's guidance is the only
guidance.' And if after all the knowledge you have been
given you yield to their desires, there shall be none to help
or protect you from the wrath of God. Those to whom We 2:121
have given the Book, and who read it as it ought to be read,
truly believe in it; those that deny it will surely be the losers.

2:122   Children of Israel, remember the favour I have bestowed upon you, and that I exalted you above the nations. Guard yourselves against a day on which no soul shall stand for another: when no ransom shall be accepted from it, no intercession avail it, no help be given it.

When his Lord put Abraham to the proof by enjoining on him certain commandments and Abraham fulfilled them, He said: 'I have appointed you a leader of mankind.'

'And what of my descendants?' asked Abraham.

'My covenant,' said He, 'does not apply to the evil-doers.'

We made the House[1] a resort and a sanctuary for mankind, saying: 'Make the place where Abraham stood a house of worship.' We enjoined Abraham and Ishmael to cleanse Our House for those who walk round it, who meditate in it, and who kneel and prostrate themselves.

'Lord,' said Abraham, 'make this a secure land and bestow plenty upon its people, those of them that believe in God and the Last Day.'

'As for those that do not,' He answered, 'I shall let them live awhile, and then shall drag them to the scourge of the Fire: an evil fate.'

2:127   Abraham and Ishmael built the House and dedicated it, saying: 'Accept this from us, Lord. You are the One that hears all and knows all. Lord, make us submissive to You; make of our descendants a community that will submit to You. Teach us our rites of worship and turn to us with mercy; You are the Forgiving One the Merciful. Lord, send forth to them an apostle of their own who shall declare to them Your revelations, and shall instruct them in the Book and in wisdom, and shall purify them of sin. You are the Mighty, the Wise One.'

Who but a foolish man would renounce the faith of Abraham? We chose him in this world, and in the world to
2:131   come he shall abide among the righteous. When his Lord said to him: 'Submit,' he answered: 'I have submitted to the Lord of the Universe.'

---

1. The Ka'bah at Mecca.

Abraham enjoined the faith on his children, and so did 2:132
Jacob, saying: 'My children, God has chosen for you
the true faith. Do not depart this life except in full
submission.'

Were you present when death came to Jacob? He said to
his children: 'What will you worship when I am gone?'
They replied: 'We will worship your God and the God of
your forefathers Abraham and Ishmael and Isaac: the One
God. To Him we will submit.'

That community has passed away. Theirs is what they did
and yours what you have done. You shall not be questioned
about their actions.

They say: 'Accept the Jewish or the Christian faith and
you shall be rightly guided.'

Say: 'By no means! We believe in the faith of Abraham,
the upright one. He was no idolater.'

Say: 'We believe in God and that which has been revealed 2:136
to us; in what was revealed to Abraham, Ishmael, Isaac,
Jacob, and the tribes; to Moses and Jesus and the other
prophets by their Lord. We make no distinction among any
of them, and to Him we submit.'

If they accept your faith, they shall be rightly guided; if
they reject it, they shall surely be in schism. Against them
God is your all-sufficient defender. He hears all and knows
all.

We take on God's own dye. And who has a better dye
than God's? Him will we worship.

Say: 'Would you dispute with us about God, who is our
Lord and your Lord? We shall both be judged by our
works. To Him alone we are devoted.

'Do you claim that Abraham, Ishmael, Isaac, Jacob, and
the tribes, were all Jews or Christians?' Say: 'Who knows
better, you or God? Who is more wicked than the man
who hides a testimony he has received from God? God is
never heedless of what you do.'

That community has passed away. Theirs is what they did 2:141
and yours what you have done. You shall not be questioned
about their actions.

2:142 The foolish will ask: 'What has made them turn away from their *qiblah*?'[1]

Say: 'The East and the West are God's. He guides whom He will to the right path.'

Thus have We made you a just community, so that you may testify against mankind and that your own Apostle may testify against you. We decreed your former *qiblah* only in order that We might know the Apostle's true adherents and those who were to disown him. It was indeed a hard test, but not to those whom God has guided. God's aim was not to make your faith fruitless. He is compassionate and merciful to men.

2:144 Many a time have We seen you[2] turn your face towards the sky. We will make you turn towards a *qiblah* that will please you. Turn your face towards the Holy Mosque; wherever you[3] be, turn your faces towards it.

Those to whom the Scriptures were given know this to be the truth from their Lord. God is never heedless of what they do. But even if you gave them every proof they would not accept your *qiblah*, nor would you accept theirs; nor would any of them accept the *qiblah* of the other. If, after all the knowledge you have been given, you yield to their desires, then you will surely become an evil-doer.

Those to whom We gave the Scriptures know Our apostle as they know their own sons. But some of them deliberately conceal the truth. This is the truth from your Lord: therefore never doubt it.

Each one has a goal towards which he turns. But wherever you are, emulate one another in good works. God will bring you all before Him. God has power over all things.

2:149 Whichever way you depart, face towards the Holy Mosque. This is surely the truth from your Lord. God is never heedless of what you do.

1. The direction which the Muslim faces in prayer. At first the believers were ordered to turn towards Jerusalem, afterwards to Mecca.

2. Muḥammad.

3. The faithful.

Whichever way you depart, face towards the Holy 2:150
Mosque: and whever you are, face towards it, so that people
will have no cause to reproach you, except the evil-doers
among them. Have no fear of them; fear Me, so that I may
perfect My favour to you and that you may be rightly
guided.

Thus have We sent forth to you an apostle of your own
who will recite to you Our revelations and purify you of
sin, who will instruct you in the Book and in wisdom and
teach you that of which you had no knowledge. Remember
Me, then, and I will remember you. Give thanks to Me and
never deny Me.

Believers, fortify yourselves with patience and with prayer.
God is with those that are patient. Do not say that those
slain in the cause of God are dead. They are alive, but you
are not aware of them.

We shall test your steadfastness with fear and famine,
with loss of property and life and crops. Give good news to
those who endure with fortitude; who in adversity say: 'We 2:156
belong to God, and to Him we shall return.' On such men
will be God's blessing and mercy; such men are rightly
guided.

Ṣafā and Marwa[1] are two of God's beacons. It shall be no
offence for the pilgrim or the visitor to the Sacred House to
walk around them. He that does good of his own accord shall
be recompensed by God. God has knowledge of all things.

Those that hide the clear proofs and the guidance We
have revealed to mankind after We had proclaimed them in
the Scriptures shall be cursed by God and cursed by those
who invoke damnation; except those that repent and mend
their ways and make known the truth. Towards them I shall
relent. I am the Relenting One, the Merciful. But the
infidels who die unbelievers shall incur the curse of God,
the angels, and all mankind. Under it they shall remain for 2:162
ever; their punishment shall not be mitigated, nor shall they
be reprieved.

1. Two hills near Mecca, held in reverence by pagan Arabs.

2:163  Your God is one God. There is no god but Him. He is the Compassionate, the Merciful.

In the creation of the heavens and the earth; in the alternation of night and day; in the ships that sail the ocean with cargoes beneficial to men; in the water which God sends down from the sky and with which He revives the earth after its death, dispersing over it all manner of beasts; in the disposal of the winds, and in the clouds that are driven between sky and earth: surely in these there are signs for rational men.

Yet there are some who worship idols, bestowing on them the adoration due to God (though the love of God is stronger in the faithful). But when they face their punishment the wrongdoers will learn that might is God's alone, and God is stern in retribution. When they face their punishment those who were followed will disown their followers, and the bonds which now unite them will break asunder. Those who followed them will say: 'Could we but live again, we would disown them as they have now disowned us.'

Thus will God show them their own works. They shall sigh with remorse, but shall never emerge from the Fire.

2:168  You people! Eat of what is lawful and wholesome on the earth and do not walk in Satan's footsteps, for he is your inveterate foe. He enjoins on you evil and lewdness, and bids you assert about God what you know not.

When they are told: 'Follow what God has revealed,' they reply: 'We will follow what our fathers practised,' even though their fathers understood nothing and had no guidance.

The unbelievers are like beasts which, call out to them as one may, can hear nothing but a shout and a cry. Deaf, dumb, and blind, they understand nothing.

Believers, eat of the wholesome things with which We have provided you and give thanks to God, if it is Him you worship.

2:173  He has forbidden you carrion, blood, and the flesh of swine; also any flesh that is consecrated other than in the name of God. But whoever is driven by necessity, intending neither to sin nor to transgress, shall incur no guilt. God is forgiving and merciful.

Those that suppress any part of the Scriptures which God 2:174 has revealed in order to gain some paltry end shall swallow nothing but fire into their bellies. On the Day of Resurrection God will neither speak to them nor purify them. Woeful punishment awaits them.

Such are those that barter guidance for error and forgiveness for punishment. How steadfastly they seek the Fire! That is because God has revealed the Book with the truth; those that disagree about it are in extreme schism.

Righteousness does not consist in whether you face towards the East or the West. The righteous man is he who believes in God and the Last Day, in the angels and the Book and the prophets; who, though he loves it dearly, gives away his wealth to kinsfolk, to orphans, to the destitute, to the traveller in need and to beggars, and for the redemption of captives; who attends to his prayers and renders the alms levy; who is true to his promises and steadfast in trial and adversity and in times of war. Such are the true believers; such are the God-fearing.

Believers, retaliation is decreed for you in bloodshed: a 2:178 free man for a free man, a slave for a slave, and a female for a female. He who is pardoned by his aggrieved brother shall be prosecuted according to usage and shall pay him a liberal fine. This is a merciful dispensation from your Lord. He that transgresses thereafter shall be sternly punished.

Men of understanding! In retaliation you have a safeguard for your lives; perchance you will guard yourselves against evil.

It is decreed that when death approaches, those of you that leave property shall bequeath it equitably to parents and kindred. This is a duty incumbent on the righteous. He that alters a will after hearing it shall be accountable for his crime. God hears all and knows all.

He that suspects an error or an injustice on the part of a 2:182 testator and brings about a settlement among the parties incurs no guilt. God is forgiving and merciful.

2:183    Believers, fasting is decreed for you as it was decreed for those before you; perchance you will guard yourselves against evil. Fast a certain number of days, but if any one among you is ill or on a journey, let him fast a similar number of days later; and for those that cannot[1] endure it there is a penance ordained: the feeding of a poor man. He that does good of his own accord shall be well rewarded; but to fast is better for you, if you but knew it.

In the month of Ramaḍān the Koran was revealed, a book of guidance for mankind with proofs of guidance distinguishing right from wrong[2]. Therefore whoever of you is present in that month let him fast. But he who is ill or on a journey shall fast a similar number of days later on.

God desires your well-being, not your discomfort. He desires you to fast the whole month so that you may magnify God and render thanks to Him for giving you His guidance.

2:186    If My servants question you about Me, tell them that I am near. I answer the prayer of the suppliant when he calls to Me; therefore let them answer My call and put their trust in Me, that they may be rightly guided.

It is now lawful for you to lie with your wives on the night of the fast; they are a comfort to you as you are to them. God knew that you were deceiving yourselves. He has relented towards you and pardoned you. Therefore you may now lie with them and seek what God has ordained for you. Eat and drink until you can tell a white thread from a black one in the light of the coming dawn. Then resume the fast till nightfall and do not approach them, but stay at your prayers in the mosques.

These are the bounds set by God: do not approach them. Thus He makes known His revelations to mankind that they may guard themselves against evil.

2:188    Do not devour one another's property by unjust means,

---

1. Thus Al-Jalālayn; the negative being understood. Alternatively: '. . . and for those well able to fast there is a penance ordained.'
2. Alternatively: '. . . with proofs of guidance and *salvation*.'

nor bribe the judges with it in order that you may wrongfully and knowingly usurp other people's possessions.

They question you about the phases of the moon. Say: 2:189 'They are seasons fixed for the people and for the pilgrimage.'

Righteousness does not consist in entering your dwellings from the back.[1] The righteous man is he that fears God. Enter your dwellings by their doors and fear God, so that you may prosper.

Fight for the sake of God those that fight against you, but do not attack them first. God does not love aggressors.

Slay them wherever you find them. Drive them out of the places from which they drove you. Idolatry is more grievous than bloodshed. But do not fight them within the precincts of the Holy Mosque unless they attack you there; if they attack you put them to the sword. Thus shall the unbelievers be rewarded: but if they mend their ways, know that God is forgiving and merciful.

Fight against them until idolatry is no more and God's 2:193 religion reigns supreme. But if they desist, fight none except the evil-doers.

A sacred month for a sacred month: sacred things too are subject to retaliation. If anyone attacks you, attack him as he attacked you. Have fear of God, and know that God is with the righteous.

Give generously for the cause of God and do not with your own hands cast yourselves into destruction. Be charitable; God loves the charitable.

Make the pilgrimage and visit the Sacred House for His 2:196 sake. If you cannot, send such offerings as you can afford and do not shave your heads until the offerings have reached their destination. But if any of you is ill or suffers from an ailment of the head, he must do penance either by fasting or by almsgiving or by offering a sacrifice.

If in peacetime anyone among you combines the visit with the pilgrimage, he must offer such gifts as he can afford; but

---

1. It was the custom of pagan Arabs, on returning from pilgrimage, to enter their homes from the back.

if he lacks the means let him fast three days during the pilgrimage and seven when he has returned; that is, ten days in all. That is incumbent on him whose family are not present at the Holy Mosque. Have fear of God: know that God is stern in retribution.

2:197 Make the pilgrimage in the appointed months. He that intends to perform it in those months must abstain from sexual intercourse, obscene language, and acrimonious disputes while on pilgrimage. God is aware of whatever good you do. Provide well for yourselves: the best provision is piety. Fear Me, then, you that are endowed with understanding.

It shall be no offence for you to seek the bounty of your Lord. When you come down from 'Arafāt[1] remember God as you approach the sacred monument. Remember Him that gave you guidance when you were in error. Then go out from the place whence the pilgrims will go out and implore the forgiveness of God. God is forgiving and merciful. And when you have fulfilled your sacred duties, remember God as you remember your forefathers or with deeper reverence.

There are some who say: 'Lord, give us abundance in this 2:201 world.' These shall have no share in the world to come. But there are others who say: 'Lord, give us what is good both in this world and in the world to come, and keep us from the torment of the Fire.' These shall have a share, according to what they did. Swift is God's reckoning.

Give glory to God on the appointed days. He that departs on the second day incurs no sin, nor does he who stays on longer, if he truly fears God. Have fear of God, then, and know that you shall all be gathered before Him.

There are some whose views on this life please you: they even call on God to vouch for that which is in their hearts; whereas in fact they are the deadliest of your 2:205 opponents. No sooner do they leave you than they hasten to do evil in the land, destroying crops and cattle. God does not love evil.

1. Near Mecca.

When they are told: 'Have fear of God,' vanity carries 2:206 them off to sin. Sufficient for them shall be Hell, an evil resting-place.

But there are others who would give away their lives in order to find favour with God. God is compassionate to His servants.

Believers, submit all of you to God and do not walk in Satan's footsteps; he is your inveterate foe. If you lapse after the veritable signs that have been shown to you, know that God is mighty and wise.

Are they waiting for God to come down to them in the shadow of a cloud, with all the angels? Their fate will have been settled then. To God shall all things return.

Ask the Israelites how many conspicuous signs We gave them. He that tampers with the gift of God after it is bestowed on him shall find that God is stern in retribution.

For the unbelievers the life of this world is decked with all manner of temptations. They scoff at the faithful, but those that fear God shall be above them on the Day of Resurrection. God gives unstintingly to whom He will.

People were once but one community. Then God sent 2:213 forth prophets to give them good news and to warn them, and with these He sent down the Book with the Truth, that it might serve as arbiter in the disputes of men. (None disputed it save those to whom it was given, and that was through envy of one another, after veritable signs had been vouchsafed them.) So God guided by His will those who believed in the truth which had been disputed. God guides whom He will to a straight path.

Did you suppose that you would go to Paradise untouched by the suffering which was endured by those before you? Affliction and adversity befell them; and so shaken were they that each apostle, and those who shared his faith, cried out: 'When will God's help come?' God's help is ever near.

They will ask you about almsgiving. Say: 'Whatever you 2:215 bestow in charity must go to parents and to kinsfolk, to the orphans and to the destitute and to the traveller in need. God is aware of whatever good you do.'

2:216 Fighting is obligatory for you, much as you dislike it. But you may hate a thing although it is good for you, and love a thing although it is bad for you. God knows, but you know not.

They ask you about the sacred month. Say: 'To fight in this month is a grave offence; but to debar others from the path of God, to deny Him, and to expel His worshippers from the Holy Mosque, is far more grave in His sight. Idolatry is more grievous than bloodshed.'

They will not cease to fight against you until they force you to renounce your faith – if they are able. But whoever of you recants and dies an unbeliever, his works shall come to nothing in this world and in the world to come. Such men shall be the tenants of the Fire, wherein they shall abide for ever.

Those that have embraced the Faith, and those that have fled their land and fought for the cause of God, may hope for God's mercy. God is forgiving and merciful.

2:219 They ask you about drinking and gambling. Say: 'There is great harm in both, although they have some benefits for the people; but their harm is far greater than their benefit.'

They ask you what they should give in alms. Say: 'What you can spare.' Thus God makes plain to you His revelations so that you may reflect upon this world and the here-after.

They question you concerning orphans. Say: 'To deal justly with them is best. If you mix their affairs with yours, remember they are your brothers. God knows the unjust from the just. If God pleased, He could afflict you. God is mighty and wise.'

2:221 You shall not wed pagan women, unless they embrace the Faith. A believing slave-girl is better than an idolatress, although she may please you. Nor shall you wed idolaters, unless they embrace the Faith. A believing slave is better than an idolater, although he may please you. These call you to the Fire; but God calls you, by His will, to Paradise and to forgiveness. He makes plain His revelations to mankind, so that they may take heed.

They ask you about menstruation. Say: 'It is an indisposi- 2:222
tion. Keep aloof from women during their menstrual periods and do not approach them until they are clean again; when they are clean, have intercourse with them whence God enjoined you. God loves those that turn to Him in penitence and strive to keep themselves clean.'

Women are your fields: go, then, into your fields whence you please. Do good works and fear God. Bear in mind that you shall meet Him. Give good tidings to the believers.

Do not make God, when you swear by Him, a means to prevent you from dealing justly, from guarding yourselves against evil, and from making peace among people. God knows all and hears all. God will not call you to account for that which is inadvertent in your oaths. But He will take you to task for that which is intended in your hearts. God is forgiving and lenient.

Those that renounce their wives on oath must wait four 2:226
months. If they change their minds, God is forgiving and merciful; but if they decide to divorce them, know that God hears all and knows all.

Divorced women must wait, keeping themselves from men, three menstrual courses. It is unlawful for them, if they believe in God and the Last Day, to hide what God has created in their wombs: in which case their husbands would do well to take them back, should they desire reconciliation.

Women shall with justice have rights similar to those exercised against them, although men have a status above women. God is mighty and wise.

Divorce[1] may be pronounced twice, and then a woman 2:229
must be retained in honour or allowed to go with kindness. It is unlawful for husbands to take from them anything they have given them, unless both fear that they may not be able to keep within the bounds set by God; in which case it shall be no offence for either of them if the wife redeems herself.

1. Revocable divorce, or the renunciation of one's wife on oath.

These are the bounds set by God; do not transgress them. Those that transgress the bounds of God are wrongdoers.

2:230 If a man divorces[1] his wife, he cannot remarry her until she has wedded another man and been divorced by him; in which case it shall be no offence for either of them to return to the other, if they think that they can keep within the bounds set by God.

Such are the bounds of God. He makes them plain to men of knowledge.

When you have renounced your wives and they have reached the end of their waiting period, either retain them in honour or let them go with kindness. But you shall not retain them in order to harm them or to wrong them. Whoever does this wrongs his own soul.

Do not trifle with God's revelations. Remember the favour God has bestowed upon you, and the Book and the wisdom He has revealed for your instruction. Fear God and know that God has knowledge of all things.

If a man has renounced his wife and she has reached the end of her waiting period, do not prevent her from remarrying her husband if they have come to an honourable agreement. This is enjoined on every one of you who believes in God and the Last Day; it is more honourable for you and more chaste. God knows, but you know not.

2:233 Mothers shall give suck to their children for two whole years if the father wishes the sucking to be completed. They must be maintained and clothed in a reasonable manner by the child's father. None should be charged with more than one can bear. A mother should not be allowed to suffer on account of her child, nor should a father on account of his child. The same duties devolve upon the father's heir. But if, after consultation, they choose by mutual consent to wean the child, they shall incur no guilt. Nor shall it be any offence for you if you prefer to have a nurse for your children, provided that you pay her what you promise,

1. By pronouncing the formula 'I divorce you' for the third time.

according to usage. Have fear of God and know that God is cognizant of all your actions.

Widows shall wait, keeping themselves apart from men, 2:234 for four months and ten days after their husbands' death. When they have reached the end of their waiting period, it shall be no offence for you to let them do whatever they choose for themselves, provided that it is decent. God is cognizant of all your actions.

It shall be no offence for you openly to propose marriage to such women or to cherish them in your hearts. God knows that you will remember them. Do not arrange to meet them in secret, and if you do, speak to them honourably. But you shall not consummate the marriage before the end of their waiting period. Know that God has knowledge of all your thoughts. Therefore take heed and bear in mind that God is forgiving and lenient.

It shall be no offence for you to divorce your wives 2:236 before the marriage is consummated or the dowry settled. Provide for them with fairness; the rich man according to his means and the poor man according to his. This is binding on righteous men. If you divorce them before the marriage is consummated, but after their dowry has been settled, give them the half of their dowry, unless they or the husband agree to waive it. But it is more proper that the husband should waive it. Do not forget to show kindness to each other. God observes your actions.

Attend regularly to your prayers, including the middle prayer, and stand up with all devotion before God. When you are exposed to danger pray on foot or while riding; and when you are restored to safety remember God, as He has taught you what you did not know.

You shall bequeath your widows a year's maintenance without causing them to leave their homes; but if they leave of their own accord, no blame shall be attached to you for any course they may deem reasonable to pursue. God is mighty and wise. Reasonable provision shall also be made 2:241 for divorced women. That is incumbent on righteous men.

2:242   Thus God makes known to you His revelations that you may grow in understanding.

Consider those that fled their homes in their thousands for fear of death. God said to them: 'You shall perish,' and then He brought them back to life. Surely God is bountiful to mankind, but most men do not give thanks.

Fight for the cause of God and bear in mind that God hears all and knows all.

Who will grant God a generous loan? He will repay him many times over. God gives in scant measure and abundantly. To Him shall you be recalled.

Have you not heard of what the leaders of the Israelites demanded of one of their prophets after the death of Moses? 'Raise up for us a king,' they said, 'and we will fight for the cause of God.'

He replied: 'What if you refuse, when ordered so to fight?'

'Why should we refuse to fight for the cause of God,' they said, 'when we have been driven from our dwellings and our children?'

But when at last they were ordered to fight, they all refused, except a few of them. God knows the evil-doers.

2:247   Their prophet said to them: 'God has appointed Saul to be your king.' But they replied: 'Should he be given the kingship, when we are more deserving of it than he? Besides, he is not rich at all.'

He said: 'God has chosen him to rule over you and made him grow in wisdom and in stature. God gives His sovereignty to whom He will. God is munificent and all-knowing.'

2:248   Their prophet also said to them: 'The advent of the Ark shall be the portent of his reign. Therein shall be tranquillity[1] from your Lord, and the relics which the House of Moses and the House of Aaron left behind. It will be borne by the angels. That will be a sign for you, if you are true believers.'

1. This is the meaning of the Arabic word *sakīnah*, which, however, may well be related to *shekhinah* (the Holy Presence) in the Old Testament.

And when Saul marched out with his army, he said: 'God 2:249
will put you to the proof at a certain river. He that drinks
from it shall cease to be my soldier, but he that does not
drink from it, or contents himself with a taste of it in the
hollow of his hand, shall fight by my side.'[1]

But they all drank from it, except a few of them. And
when Saul had crossed the river with those who shared his
faith, they said: 'We have no power this day against Goliath
and his warriors.'

But those of them who believed that they would meet
God replied: 'Many a small band has, by God's grace,
vanquished a mighty army. God is with those who endure
with fortitude.'

When they met Goliath and his warriors they cried: 2:250
'Lord, fill our hearts with steadfastness. Make us firm of
foot and help us against the unbelievers.'

By God's will they routed them. David slew Goliath,[2] and
God bestowed on him sovereignty and wisdom and taught
him what He pleased. Had God not defeated some by the
might of others, the earth would have been utterly corrupted. But God is bountiful to mankind.

Such are God's revelations. We recite them to you in
all truth, for you are one of Our emissaries. Of these
emissaries We have exalted some above others. To some God
spoke directly; others He raised to a lofty status. We gave
Jesus son of Mary indisputable signs and strengthened
him with the Holy Spirit. Had God pleased, those who
succeeded them would not have fought against one another
after the veritable signs had been given them. But they
disagreed among themselves; some had faith and others had
none. Yet had God pleased they would not have fought
against one another. God does what He will.

Believers, bestow in alms a part of what We have given 2:254
you before that day arrives when commerce and friendship
and intercession shall be no more. Truly, it is the unbelievers
who are unjust.

1. Cf. Judges vii.     2. I Samuel xvii.

2:255   God: there is no god but Him, the Living, the Eternal
One. Neither slumber nor sleep overtakes Him. His is
what the heavens and the earth contain. Who can intercede
with Him except by His permission? He knows what is
before and behind men. They can grasp only that part of
His knowledge which He wills. His throne is as vast as
the heavens and the earth, and the preservation of both
does not weary Him. He is the Exalted, the Immense
One.

There shall be no compulsion in religion. True guidance
is now distinct from error. He that renounces idol-worship
and puts his faith in God shall grasp a firm handle that
will never break. God hears all and knows all.

God is the Patron of the faithful. He leads them from
darkness to the light. As for the unbelievers, their patrons
are false gods, who lead them from light to darkness. They
are the heirs of the Fire and shall abide in it for ever.

2:258   Have you not heard of him who argued with Abraham
about his Lord because God had bestowed sovereignty
upon him? Abraham said: 'My Lord is He who has the
power of life and death.'

'I, too,' replied the other, 'have the power of life and
death.'

'God brings up the sun from the east,' said Abraham.
'Bring it up yourself from the west.'

The unbeliever was confounded. God does not guide the
evil-doers.

2:259   Or of him, who, when passing by a ruined and desolate
city, remarked: 'How can God give life to this city, now
that it is dead?' Thereupon God caused him to die, and after
a hundred years brought him back to life.

'How long have you lingered?' asked God.

'A day,' he replied, 'or part of a day.'

'Know, then,' said God, 'that you have stayed away a
hundred years. Yet look at your food and drink: they have
not rotted. And look at your ass. We will make you a sign
for the people: see how We will raise the bones and clothe
them with flesh.'

And when it had all become manifest to him, he said: 'Now I know that God has power over all things.'

When Abraham said: 'Show me, Lord, how You will 2:260 raise the dead,' He replied: 'Have you no faith?'

'Yes,' said Abraham, 'but just to reassure my heart.'

'Take four birds,' said He, 'draw them to you, and cut their bodies to pieces. Scatter them over the mountain-tops, then call them back. They will come swiftly to you. Know that God is mighty and wise.'

Those that give their wealth for the cause of God can be compared to a grain of corn which brings forth seven ears, each bearing a hundred grains. God gives abundance to whom He will; God is munificent and all-knowing.

Those that give their wealth for the cause of God and do not follow their almsgiving with taunts and insults shall be rewarded by their Lord; they shall have nothing to fear or to regret.

A kind word with forgiveness is better than charity 2:263 followed by insult. God is self-sufficient and gracious.

Believers, do not mar your almsgiving with taunts and mischief-making, like those who spend their wealth only to impress people and believe neither in God nor in the Last Day. Such men are like a rock covered with earth: a shower falls upon it and leaves it hard and bare. They shall gain nothing from their works. God does not guide the unbelievers.

But those that give away their wealth from a desire to please God and to reassure their own souls are like an orchard on a hill-side: if a shower falls upon it, it yields up twice its normal produce; and if no rain falls, it is watered by the dew. God takes cognizance of all your actions.

Would any one of you, being a man well-advanced in age 2:266 with helpless children to support, wish to have his orchard – an orchard planted with palm-trees, vines and all manner of fruits, and watered by running streams – blasted and consumed by a fiery whirlwind?

Thus God makes plain to you His revelations, so that you may give thought.

2:267　Believers, give in alms from the wealth you have lawfully earned and from that which We have brought out of the earth for you; not worthless things which you yourselves would but reluctantly accept. Know that God is self-sufficient and glorious.

Satan threatens you with poverty and enjoins lewdness on you. But God promises you His forgiveness and His bounty. God is munificent and all-knowing.

He gives wisdom to whom He will; and he that receives the gift of wisdom is rich indeed. Yet none but men of sense bear this in mind.

Whatever alms you give and whatever vows you make are known to God. The evil-doers shall have none to help them.

To be charitable in public is good, but to give alms to the poor in private is better and will atone for some of your sins. God has knowledge of all your actions.

2:272　It is not for you to guide them. God gives guidance to whom He will.

Whatever alms you give shall rebound to your own advantage, provided that you give them for the love of God. And whatever alms you give shall be repaid to you in full: you shall not be wronged.

As for those needy men who, being wholly preoccupied with fighting for the cause of God, cannot travel the land in quest of trading ventures: the ignorant take them for men of wealth on account of their modest behaviour. But you can recognize them by their look – they never importune people for alms. Whatever alms you give are known to God.

Those that give alms by day and by night, in private and in public, shall be rewarded by their Lord. They shall have nothing to fear or to regret.

2:275　Those that live on usury shall rise up before God like men whom Satan has demented by his touch; for they claim that trading is no different from usury. But God has permitted trading and made usury unlawful. He that has received an admonition from his Lord and mended his ways may keep his previous gains; God will be his judge. Those that turn back shall be the inmates of the Fire, wherein they shall abide for ever.

God has laid His curse on usury and blessed almsgiving 2:276 with increase. God bears no love for the impious and the sinful.

Those that have faith and do good works, attend to their prayers and render the alms levy, will be rewarded by their Lord and will have nothing to fear or to regret.

Believers, have fear of God and waive what is still due to you from usury, if your faith be true; or war shall be declared against you by God and His apostle. If you repent, you may retain your principal, suffering no loss and causing loss to none.

If your debtor be in straits, grant him a delay until he can discharge his debt; but if you waive the sum as alms it will be better for you, if you but knew it.

Fear the day when you shall all return to God; when every soul shall be paid back for what it did. None shall be wronged.

Believers, when you contract a debt for a fixed period, put it 2:282 in writing. Let a scribe write it down for you with fairness; no scribe should refuse to write as God has taught him. Therefore let him write; and let the debtor dictate, fearing God his Lord and not diminishing the sum he owes. If the debtor be an ignorant or feeble-minded person, or one who cannot ditate, let his guardian dictate for him in fairness. Call in two male witnesses from among you, but if two men cannot be found, then one man and two women whom you judge fit to act as witnesses; so that if either of them make an error, the other will remind her. Witnesses must not refuse if called upon to give evidence. So do not fail to put your debts in writing, be they small or large, together with the date of payment. This is more just in the sight of God; it ensures accuracy in testifying and is the best way to remove all doubt. But if the transaction be a bargain concluded on the spot, it is no offence for you if you do not put it into writing.

See that witnesses are present when you barter with one another, and let no harm be done to either scribe or witness. If you harm them you will commit a transgression. Have fear of God; God teaches you, and God has knowledge of all things.

2:283 If you are travelling the road and a scribe cannot be found, then let pledges be given. If any one of you entrusts another with a pledge, let the trustee restore the pledge to its owner; and let him fear God, his Lord.

You shall not withhold testimony; sinful is the heart of him who withholds it. God has knowledge of all your actions.

To God belongs all that the heavens and the earth contain. Whether you reveal your thoughts or hide them, God will bring you to account for them. He will forgive whom He will and punish whom He pleases; God has power over all things.

The Apostle believes in what has been revealed to him by his Lord, and so do the faithful. They all believe in God and His angels, His scriptures, and His apostles: We discriminate against none of His apostles. They say: 'We hear and obey. Grant us Your forgiveness, Lord; to You shall all return.
2:286 God does not charge a soul with more than it can bear. It shall be requited for whatever good and whatever evil it has done. Lord, do not be angry with us if we forget or lapse into error. Lord, do not lay on us a burden such as You laid on those before us. Lord, do not charge us with more than we can bear. Pardon us, forgive us our sins, and have mercy upon us. You alone are our Protector. Give us victory over the unbelievers.'

# THE 'IMRANS

*In the Name of God, the Compassionate, the Merciful*

3:1 A L I F *lām mīm*. God! There is no god but Him, the Living, the Ever-existent One.

He has revealed to you the Book with the Truth, confirming the scriptures which preceded it; for He has already

revealed the Torah and the Gospel for the guidance of 3:4
mankind, and the distinction between right and wrong.

Those that deny God's revelations shall be sternly punished; God is mighty and capable of revenge. Nothing on
earth or in heaven is hidden from God. It is He who shapes
your bodies in your mothers' wombs as He pleases. There is
no god but Him, the Mighty, the Wise One.

It is He who has revealed to you the Book. Some of its
verses are precise in meaning – they are the foundation of
the Book – and others ambiguous. Those whose hearts are
infected with disbelief observe the ambiguous part, so as to
create dissension by seeking to explain it. But no one knows
its meaning except God. Those who are well-grounded in
knowledge say: 'We believe in it: it is all from our Lord. But
only the wise take heed. Lord, do not cause our hearts to go 3:8
astray after You have guided us. Grant us mercy through
Your own grace; You are the munificent Giver. Lord, You
will surely gather all mankind upon a day that will indubita-
bly come. God will not break His promise.'

As for the unbelievers, neither their riches nor their
children will in the least save them from God's wrath. They
shall become the fuel of the Fire. They are like Pharaoh's
people and those before them; they denied Our revelations,
and God smote them in their sin. God is stern in
retribution.

Say to the unbelievers: 'You shall be overthrown and
driven into Hell – an evil resting-place!'

Indeed, there was a sign for you in the two armies which
met on the battlefield.[1] One was fighting for the cause of
God, the other being a host of unbelievers. The faithful saw
with their very eyes that they were twice their own number.
But God strengthens with His aid whom He will. Surely in
that there was a lesson for the discerning.

Men are tempted by the lure of women and offspring, of 3:14
hoarded treasures of gold and silver, of splendid horses,

---

1. In the Battle of Badr. There were 319 Muslims and 1,000
Meccans.

cattle, and plantations. These are the enjoyments of this life, but far better is the return to God.

3:15 Say: 'Shall I tell you of better things than these, with which the righteous shall be rewarded by their Lord? Gardens watered by running streams, where they shall dwell for ever: spouses of perfect chastity: and grace from God.'

God is watching His servants, those who say: 'Lord, we believe in You: forgive us our sins and keep us from the torment of the Fire'; who are steadfast, sincere, obedient, and charitable; and who implore forgiveness at break of day.

God bears witness that there is no god but Him, and so do the angels and the sages. He is the Executor of Justice, the Only God, the Mighty, the Wise One.

3:19 The only true faith in God's sight is Islām. Those to whom the Scriptures were given disagreed among themselves, through insolence, only after knowledge had been vouchsafed them. He that denies God's revelations should know that swift is God's reckoning.

If they argue with you, say: 'I have submitted to God and so have those that follow me.'

To those who were given the Scriptures and to the Gentiles say: 'Will you submit to God?' If they become Muslims they shall be rightly guided; if they pay no heed, then your only duty is to warn them. God is watching all His servants.

Those that deny God's revelations and slay the prophets unjustly and kill those among the people who preach fair dealing – warn them of a woeful scourge. Their works shall come to nothing in this world and in the world to come, and there shall be none to help them.

Do but consider those who have received a portion of the Scriptures. When they are called on to accept the judgement of God's Book, some turn their backs and pay no heed. For they declare: 'We shall endure the Fire for a few days only.' In their religion they are deceived by their own lies.

3:25 What will they do when We gather them all together

upon a day which is sure to come, when every soul will be given what it has earned with no injustice?

Say: 'Lord, Sovereign of all sovereignty, You bestow 3:26 sovereignty on whom You will and take it away from whom You please; You exalt whomever You will and abase whomever You please. In Your hand lies all that is good; You have power over all things. You cause the night to pass into the day, and the day to pass into the night; You bring forth the living from the dead and You bring forth the dead from the living. You give without stint to whom You will.'

Let not believers make friends with infidels in preference to the faithful – he that does this has nothing to hope for from God – except in self-defence. God admonishes you to fear Him: for to God shall all return.

Say: 'Whether you hide what is in your hearts or reveal it, 3:29 it is known to God. He knows all that the heavens and the earth contain; God has power over all things.'

The day will surely come when each soul will be confronted with whatever good it did. As for its evil deeds, it will wish they were a long way off. God admonishes you to fear Him. God is compassionate towards His servants.

Say: 'If you love God, follow me. God will love you and forgive you your sins. God is forgiving and merciful.'

Say: 'Obey God and the Apostle.' If they pay no heed, then, surely, God does not love the unbelievers.

God exalted Adam and Noah, Abraham's descendants and the descendants of 'Imrān[1] above the nations. They were the offspring of one another. God hears all and knows all.

Remember the words of 'Imrān's[2] wife. 'Lord,' she said, 'I dedicate to Your service that which is in my womb. Accept it from me. You alone hear all and know all.'

And when she was delivered of the child, she said: 'Lord, 3:36 I have given birth to a daughter' – God well knew of what she was delivered: the male is not like the female – 'and

1. Amram, the father of Moses and Aaron, (Exodus xi, 20).
2. 'Imrān is also the name given in the Koran to Mary's father.

have called her Mary. Protect her and all her descendants from Satan, the Accursed One.'

3:37 Her Lord graciously accepted her. He made her grow a goodly child and entrusted her to the care of Zacharias.

Whenever Zacharias visited her in the Shrine he found that she had food with her. 'Mary,' he said, 'where is this food from?'

'It is from God,' she answered. 'God gives without measure to whom He will.'

Thereupon Zacharias prayed to his Lord, saying: 'Lord, grant me of Your own grace upright descendants. You hear all prayers.'

And as he stood praying in the Shrine, the angels called out to him, saying: 'God bids you rejoice in the birth of John, who shall confirm the Word of God. He shall be princely and chaste, a prophet and a righteous man.'

3:40 'Lord,' said Zacharias, 'how shall I have a son when I am now overtaken by old age and my wife is barren?'

'Such is the will of God,' He replied. 'He does what He pleases.'

'Lord,' said he, 'vouchsafe me a sign.'

'For three days and three nights,' He replied, 'you shall not speak to people except by signs. Remember your Lord always; give glory to Him evening and morning.'

And remember the angels' words to Mary. They said:[1] 'God has chosen you. He has made you pure and exalted you above womankind. Mary, be obedient to your Lord; bow down and worship with the worshippers.'

This is an account of a divine secret. We reveal it to you.[2] You were not present when they cast lots to see which of them should have charge of Mary; nor were you present when they argued about her.

The angels said to Mary: 'God bids you rejoice in a Word from Him. His name is the Messiah, Jesus son of Mary. He shall be noble in this world and in the world to come, 3:46 and shall be one of those who are favoured. He shall preach

---

1. Cf. Luke i, 26–38.    2. Muḥammad.

46

to people in his cradle and in the prime of manhood, and shall lead a righteous life.'

'Lord,' she said, 'how can I bear a child when no man has touched me?' 3:47

He replied: 'Even thus. God creates whom He will. When He decrees a thing He need only say: "Be," and it is. He will instruct him in the Scriptures and in wisdom, in the Torah and in the Gospel, and send him forth as an apostle to the Israelites. He will say: "I bring you a sign from your Lord. From clay I will make for you the likeness of a bird. I shall breathe into it and, by God's leave, it shall become a living bird. By God's leave I shall heal the blind man and the leper, and raise the dead to life. I shall tell you what to eat and what to store up in your houses. Surely that will be a sign for you, if you are true believers. I come to confirm the Torah which preceded me and to make lawful for you some of the things you are forbidden. I bring you a sign from your Lord: therefore fear God and obey me. God is my Lord and your Lord: therefore serve Him. That is a straight path."' 3:51

When Jesus observed that they had no faith, he said: 'Who will help me in the cause of God?'

The disciples replied: 'We are God's helpers. We believe in God. Bear witness that we submit to Him. Lord, we believe in Your revelations and follow the apostle. Count us among Your witnesses.'

They contrived, and God contrived. God is the supreme Contriver. God said: 'Jesus, I am about to claim you back and lift you up to Me. I shall take you away from the unbelievers and exalt your followers above them till the Day of Resurrection. Then to Me you shall all return and I shall judge your disputes. The unbelievers shall be sternly punished in this world and in the world to come: there shall be none to help them. As for those that have faith and do good works, they shall be given their reward in full. God does not love the evil-doers.'

This revelation, and this wise admonition, We recite to you. Jesus is like Adam in the sight of God. He created him 3:59 from dust and then said to him: 'Be,' and he was.

3:60 This is the truth from your Lord: therefore do not doubt it. To those that dispute with you concerning him after the knowledge you have received, say: 'Come, let us gather our sons and your sons, our wives and your wives, our people and your people. We will then pray and call down the curse of God on every liar.'

This is the whole truth. There is no god but God. Surely it is God who is the Mighty, the Wise One.

If they pay no heed, God knows the evil-doers.

Say: 'People of the Book, let us come to an agreement: that we will worship none but God, that we will associate none with Him, and that none of us shall set up mortals as deities besides God.'

If they turn away, say: 'Bear witness, then, that we submit to God.'

People of the Book, why do you argue about Abraham when both the Torah and the Gospel were not revealed till after him? Have you no sense?

3:66 Indeed, you have argued about things of which you have some knowledge. Must you now argue about that of which you know nothing at all? God knows, but you know not.

Abraham was neither Jew nor Christian. He was an upright man, one who submitted to God. He was no idolater. Surely the men who are nearest to Abraham are those who follow him, this Prophet, and the true believers. God is the guardian of the faithful. Some of the People of the Book wish to mislead you; but they mislead none but themselves, though they may not perceive it.

People of the Book! Why do you deny God's revelations when you know that they are true?

People of the Book! Why do you confound the true with the false, and knowingly hide the truth?

Some of the People of the Book say to one another: 'Believe in that which is revealed to the faithful in the morning and deny it in the evening, so that they may
3:73 themselves abandon their faith. Believe in none except those that follow your own religion.' (Say: 'The only guidance is the guidance of God!') 'Do not believe that anyone will be

given the like of that which you were given, or that they will ever dispute with you in your Lord's presence.'

Say: 'Grace is in the hands of God: He bestows it on whom He will. God is munificent and all-knowing. He is 3:74 merciful to whom He will. God's grace is infinite.'

Among the People of the Book there are some who, if you trust them with a heap of gold, will return it to you intact; and there are others who, if you trust them with one dinar, will not hand it back unless you demand it with importunity. For they say: 'We are not bound to keep faith with Gentiles.' Thus they deliberately say of God what is untrue. Indeed, those that keep faith and guard themselves against evil know that God loves the righteous.

Those that sell the covenant of God and their own oaths for a paltry price shall have no share in the world to come. God will neither speak to them, nor look at them, nor purify them on the Day of Resurrection. Woeful punishment awaits them.

And there are some among them who twist their tongues 3:78 when quoting the Scriptures, so that you may think it from the Scriptures, whereas it is not from the Scriptures. They say: 'This is from God,' whereas it is not from God. Thus they knowingly ascribe falsehood to God.

No mortal whom God has given the Scriptures and whom He has endowed with judgement and prophethood would say to people: 'Worship me instead of God.' But rather: 'Be devoted servants of God, for you have taught and studied the Scriptures.' Nor would he enjoin you to serve the angels and the prophets as your gods; for would he enjoin you to be unbelievers after you have submitted to God?

When God made His covenant with the prophets, He said: 'Here are the Scriptures and the wisdom which I have given you. An apostle will come forth to confirm them. Believe in him and help him. Will you affirm this and accept the burden I have laid on you in these terms?'

They replied: 'We will affirm it.'

'Then bear witness,' He said, 'and I will bear witness with you. He that hereafter rebels is a transgressor.' 3:82

3:83    Are they seeking a religion other than God's, when every soul in the heavens and the earth has submitted to Him, willingly or by compulsion? To Him shall they return.

Say: 'We believe in God and what is revealed to us; in that which was revealed to Abraham and Ishmael, to Isaac and Jacob and the tribes; and in that which their Lord gave Moses and Jesus and the prophets. We discriminate against none of them. To Him we have surrendered ourselves.'

He that chooses a religion other than Islām, it will not be accepted from him and in the world to come he will surely be among the losers.

How will God guide those who lapse into unbelief after embracing the Faith and acknowledging the Apostle as true, and after receiving veritable proofs? God does not guide the evil-doers. Their reward will be the curse of God, the angels, and all mankind; under it they shall abide for ever. Their punishment shall not be mitigated, nor shall they be

3:89    reprieved; except those who afterwards repent and mend their ways, for God is forgiving and merciful.

But those that recant after accepting the true faith and grow in unbelief, their repentance shall not be accepted. These are the truly erring ones.

As for those that recant and die unbelievers, no ransom shall be accepted from them: be it as much gold as would fill the entire earth. Woeful punishment awaits them, and none shall help them.

You shall never be truly righteous until you give in alms what you dearly cherish. The alms you give are known to God.

All food was lawful to the Israelites except what Israel forbade himself before the Torah was revealed. Say: 'Bring the Torah and read it, if what you say be true.'

Those that after this invent falsehoods about God are great transgressors.

Say: 'God has declared the truth. Follow the faith of Abraham. He was an upright man, no idolater.'

3:96    The first temple ever to be built for mankind was that at

Bakkah,[1] a blessed site, a beacon for the nations. In it 3:97 there are veritable signs and the spot where Abraham stood. Whoever enters it is safe. Pilgrimage to the House is a duty to God for all who can make the journey. As for the unbelievers, God can surely do without them.

Say: 'People of the Book, why do you deny the revelations of God? God bears witness to all your actions.'

Say: 'People of the Book, why do you debar believers from the path of God and seek to make it crooked when you have witnessed all? God is never heedless of what you do.'

Believers, if you yield to a group from among those who were given the Book, they will turn you back from faith to unbelief. But how can you disbelieve when God's revelations are recited to you and His own Apostle is in your midst? He that holds fast to God shall be guided to a straight path.

Believers, fear God as you rightly should, and when 3:102 death comes, die true Muslims. Cling one and all to the faith of God and let nothing divide you. Remember the favour God has bestowed upon you: how, after your enmity, He united your hearts, so that you are now brothers through His grace; and how He delivered you from the abyss of fire when you stood on the very brink of it. Thus God makes plain to you His revelations, so that you may be rightly guided.

Let there become of you a community that shall call for righteousness, enjoin justice, and forbid evil. Such men will surely triumph.

Do not follow the example of those who became divided and opposed to one another after veritable proofs had been given them. Grievous punishment awaits them on the day when some faces will be bright with joy and others blackened. The black-faced sinners will be asked: 'Did you recant after embracing the true Faith? Taste then Our scourge, for you were unbelievers!' As for those whose faces will be bright, they shall abide for ever in God's mercy.

Such are God's revelations; We recite them to you in all truth. God desires no injustice to mankind. His is all that the 3:109

1. Another name for Mecca.

heavens and the earth contain. To God shall all things return.

3:110 You are the noblest community ever raised up for mankind. You enjoin justice and forbid evil. You believe in God.

Had the People of the Book accepted the Faith, it would surely have been better for them. Some are true believers, but most of them are evil-doers.

If they harm you, they can cause you but little hurt; and if they fight against you they will turn their backs and run away. Then there shall be none to help them. Ignominy shall attend them wherever they are found, unless they make a covenant with God or with man. They have incurred the wrath of God and have been utterly humbled: because they disbelieved God's revelations and slew the prophets unjustly; and because they were rebels and transgressors.

3:113 Yet they are not all alike. There are among the People of the Book some upright men who all night long recite the revelations of God and worship Him; who believe in God and the Last Day; who enjoin justice and forbid evil and vie with each other in good works. These are righteous men: whatever good they do, its reward shall not be denied them. God well knows the righteous.

As for the unbelievers, neither their riches nor their children shall in the least protect them from God's scourge. They are the heirs of the Fire, and there they shall remain for ever. The wealth they spend in this world is like a freezing wind that smites the tillage of men who have wronged themselves, laying it waste. God is not unjust to them; they are unjust to their own souls.

3:118 Believers, do not make friends with any but your own people. They will spare no pains to corrupt you. They desire nothing but your ruin. Their hatred is evident from what they utter with their mouths, but greater is the hatred which their breasts conceal.

We have made plain to you Our revelations. Strive to understand them.

See how you love them and they do not love you. You 3:119
believe in the entire Book.

When they meet you they say: 'We, too, are believers.'
But when alone, they bite their finger-tips with rage. Say:
'May you perish in your rage! God has knowledge of your
innermost thoughts.'

When you are blessed with good fortune they grieve: but
when evil befalls you they rejoice. If you persevere and
guard yourselves against evil, their machinations will never
harm you. God has knowledge of all their actions.

Remember when you¹ left your people at an early hour to
lead the faithful to their battle-posts.² God heard all and knew
all. Two of your battalions became faint-hearted, but God
was their protector. In God let the faithful put their trust.

God had already given you victory at Badr when you
were helpless. Therefore have fear of God. Perhaps you will
give thanks.

You said to the believers: 'Is it not enough that your Lord
should send down three thousand angels to help you?'

Yes! If you have patience and guard yourselves against 3:125
evil, God will send to your aid five thousand angels
splendidly accoutred, if they suddenly attack you.

God designed this to be but good news for you, so that
your hearts might be comforted (victory comes only from
God, the Mighty, the Wise One) and that He might cut off
the flank of the unbelievers or put them to flight, that they
might withdraw utterly defeated.

It is no concern of yours whether He will forgive or punish
them. They are wrongdoers. His is all that the heavens and
the earth contain. He pardons whom He will and punishes
whom He pleases. God is forgiving and merciful.

Believers, do not live on usury, doubling your wealth
many times over. Have fear of God, that you may prosper.
Guard yourselves against the Fire, prepared for unbelievers. 3:131

1. Muḥammad.
2. The allusion is to the Battle of Uḥud, in which the Muslims
were defeated by the Quraysh of Mecca.

3:132 Obey God and the Apostle that you may find mercy. Vie with each other to earn the forgiveness of your Lord and a Paradise as vast as heaven and earth, prepared for the righteous: those who give alms alike in prosperity and in adversity; who curb their anger and forgive their fellow men (God loves the charitable); who, if they commit evil or wrong their souls, remember God and seek forgiveness for their sins (for who but God can forgive sins?) and do not knowingly persist in their misdeeds. These shall be rewarded with forgiveness from their Lord and with gardens watered by running streams, where they shall dwell for ever. Blessed is the reward of those who do good works.

Numerous were the cults that came and went before you. Roam the world and see what was the fate of those who disbelieved.

This is a declaration to mankind: a guide and an admonition to the righteous. Take heart and do not despair. Have faith and you shall triumph.

3:140 If you have suffered a defeat, so did the enemy. We alternate these vicissitudes among mankind so that God may know the true believers and choose martyrs from among you (God does not love the evil-doers); and that God may test the faithful and annihilate the infidels.

Did you suppose that you would enter Paradise before God has proved the men who fought for Him and endured with fortitude? You used to wish for death before you met it, and now you have seen what it is like. Muḥammad is no more than an apostle: other apostles have passed away before him. If he die or be slain, will you recant? He that recants will do no harm to God. But God will recompense the thankful.

No one dies unless God wills. The term of every life is fixed. He that desires the reward of this world shall have it; and he that desires the reward of the life to come shall have it also. We will surely recompense the thankful.

Many large armies have fought by the side of their prophet. They were never daunted by what befell them on the path of God: they neither weakened nor cringed 3:147 abjectly. God loves the steadfast. Their only words were:

'Lord, forgive us our sins and our excesses; make us firm of foot and give us victory over the unbelievers.' Therefore God gave them the reward of this life, and the glorious 3:148 recompense of the life to come; God loves the righteous.

Believers, if you yield to the infidels they will drag you back to unbelief and you will return headlong to perdition. But God is your protector. He is the best of helpers.

We will put terror into the hearts of the unbelievers. They serve other deities besides God for whom He has revealed no sanction. The Fire shall be their home; evil indeed is the dwelling of the evil-doers.

God fulfilled His pledge to you when, by His leave, you defeated them. But afterwards your courage failed you; discord reigned among you and you disobeyed the Apostle after he had brought you within sight of what you wished for. Some chose this world; others chose the world to come. He allowed you to be defeated in order to test you. But now He has forgiven you, for God is gracious to the faithful.

Remember how you fled in panic while the Apostle at 3:153 your rear was calling out to you. Therefore He paid you back with sorrow for every vexation. [He has now forgiven you] so that you might not grieve for what you missed or what befell you. God is cognizant of all your actions.

Then, after sorrow, He let peace fall upon you – a sleep which overtook some, while others lay troubled by their own fancies, thinking unjust and foolish thoughts about God.

'Have we any say in the matter?' they ask.

Say to them: '*All* is in the hands of God.'

They conceal in their minds what they do not disclose to you.

They complain: 'Had we had any say in the matter, we should not have been slain here.'

Say to them: 'Had you stayed in your homes, those of you who were destined to be slain would have gone to their graves nevertheless; for it was God's will to test your faith and courage. God has knowledge of your innermost thoughts.'

Those of you who ran away on the day the two 3:155

armies met[1] must have been seduced by Satan on account of some evil they had done. But now God has pardoned them; God is forgiving and gracious.

3:156 Believers, do not follow the example of the infidels, who say of their brothers when they meet death abroad or in battle: 'Had they stayed with us they would not have died, nor would they have been killed.' God will cause them to regret their words. It is God who ordains life and death. God has knowledge of all your actions.

If you should die or be slain in the cause of God, His forgiveness and His mercy would surely be better than all the riches they amass. If you should die or be slain, before God shall you all be gathered.

It was thanks to God's mercy that you[2] dealt so leniently with them. Had you been cruel or hard-hearted, they would have surely deserted you. Therefore pardon them and implore God to forgive them. Take counsel with them in the conduct of affairs; and when you are resolved, put your trust in God. God loves those that are trustful.

3:160 If God helps you, none can overcome you. If He abandons you, who then can help you? Therefore in God let the faithful put their trust.

No prophet would rob his followers; for anyone that steals shall on the Day of Resurrection bring with him that which he has stolen. Then shall every soul be paid what it has earned: none shall be wronged.

Can the man who seeks to please God be compared to him who has incurred His wrath? Hell shall be his home, evil his fate.

Varied are the rewards of God. God is cognizant of all their actions.

3:164 God has surely been gracious to the faithful in sending them an apostle of their own to declare to them His revelations, to purify them, and to instruct them in the Book and in wisdom; for before that they were in monstrous error.

1. In the Battle of Uḥud.　　2. Muḥammad.

When a disaster befell you after you had yourselves 3:165 inflicted losses twice as heavy, you exclaimed: 'Whose fault was that?'

Say to them: 'It was your own fault. God has power over all things. The misfortune which befell you when the two armies met was ordained by God, so that He might know the true believers and know the hypocrites.'

When they were told: 'Come, fight for the cause of God and defend yourselves,' they replied: 'If only we could fight, we would surely come with you.'

On that day they were nearer unbelief than faith. Their words belied their intentions: but God knew their secret thoughts. Such were the men who, as they sat at home, said of their brothers: 'Had they listened to us, they would not have been slain.'

Say to them: 'Ward off death from yourselves, then, if what you say be true!'

Never think that those who were slain in the cause of 3:169 God are dead. They are alive, and well provided for by their Lord; pleased with His gifts and rejoicing that those they left behind, who have not yet joined them, have nothing to fear or to regret; rejoicing in God's grace and bounty. God will not deny the faithful their reward.

As for the men who after their defeat answered the call of God and the Apostle, those of them that do what is right and keep from evil shall be richly recompensed. They are those who, on being told: 'Your enemies have mustered a great force against you: fear them,' grew more tenacious in their faith and replied: 'God's help is all-sufficient for us. He is the best protector.'

Thus did they earn God's grace and bounty, and no harm befell them. For they had striven to please God, and God's bounty is infinite.

It is Satan that prompts men to fear his followers. But have no fear of them. Fear Me, if you are true believers. Do not grieve for those that quickly renounce their faith. In no 3:176 way will they harm God. God intends to give them no share in the hereafter. Grievous punishment awaits them.

3:177    Those that barter their faith for unbelief will in no way harm God. Woeful punishment awaits them.

Let not the unbelievers think that We prolong their days for their own good. We give them respite only so that they may commit more grievous sins. Shameful punishment awaits them.

It was not God's aim to leave the faithful in their present plight, but only to separate the evil from the good. Nor was God to reveal to you what is hidden. But God chooses those of His apostles whom He will. Therefore have faith in God and His apostles, for if you have faith and guard yourselves against evil, your recompense shall be rich indeed.

Never let those who hoard the wealth which God has bestowed on them out of His bounty think it good for them: indeed it is an evil thing for them. The riches they have hoarded shall become their fetters on the Day of Resurrection. It is God who will inherit the heavens and the earth. God is cognizant of all your actions.

God has heard the words of those who said: 'God is poor, but we are rich.' Their words We will record, and their slaying of the prophets unjustly. We shall say: 'Taste now the torment of the Conflagration. Here is the reward of your misdeeds. God is not unjust to His servants.'

3:183    To those that declare: 'God has commanded us to believe in no apostle unless he brings down fire to consume an offering,' say: 'Other apostles before me have come to you with veritable signs and worked the miracle you asked for. Why did you slay them, if what you say be true?'

If they reject you, other apostles have been rejected before you, although they came with veritable signs, psalms, and the light-giving Scriptures.

Every soul shall taste death. You shall receive your rewards only on the Day of Resurrection. Whoever is spared the Fire and is admitted to Paradise will surely triumph; for the life of this world is nothing but a fleeting vanity.

3:186    You shall be sorely tried in the matter of your possessions and your persons, and will hear much that is hurtful from those who were given the Scriptures before you, and from the pagans. But if you endure with fortitude and guard yourselves against evil, you will surely triumph.

When God made a covenant with those to whom the 3:187 Scriptures were given He said: 'Proclaim these to mankind and do not suppress them.' But they cast the Scriptures over their backs and sold them for a paltry price. Evil was their bargain.

Never think that those who rejoice in their misdeeds and wish to be praised for what they have not done – never think they will escape the scourge. Woeful punishment awaits them.

God has sovereignty over the heavens and the earth. God has power over all things.

In the creation of the heavens and the earth, and in the alternation of night and day, there are signs for men of sense; those that remember God when standing, sitting, and lying down, and reflect on the creation of the heavens and the earth, saying: 'Lord, You have not created this in vain. Glory be to You! Save us from the torment of the Fire. Lord, those whom You will cast into the Fire You will put 3:192 to eternal shame: none will help the evil-doers. Lord, we have heard someone calling to the true faith, saying: "Believe in your Lord," and we believed. Lord, forgive us our sins and remove from us our evil deeds and make us die with the righteous. Lord, grant us what You promised through Your apostles, and do not hold us up to shame on the Day of Resurrection. You never break Your promise.'

Their Lord answers them, saying: 'I will deny no man or woman among you the reward of their labours. You are the offspring of one another.'

Those that fled their homes or were expelled from them, and those that suffered persecution for My sake and fought and were slain: I shall forgive them their sins and admit them to gardens watered by running streams, as a recompense from God; God dispenses the richest recompense.

Do not be deceived by the fortunes of the unbelievers in the land. Their prosperity is brief. Hell shall be their home, 3:197

3:198 an evil resting-place. As for those that fear their Lord, theirs shall be gardens watered by running streams in which they will abide for ever, and a goodly welcome from God. God's recompense is surely better for the righteous.

Some there are among the People of the Book who truly believe in God, and in what has been revealed to you and what was revealed to them. They humble themselves before God and do not sell God's revelations for a trifling price. These shall be rewarded by their Lord. Swift is God's reckoning.

3:200 Believers, be patient and forebear. Stand firm in your faith and fear God, so that you may triumph.

# WOMEN

*In the Name of God, the Compassionate, the Merciful*

4:1 YOU PEOPLE! Have fear of your Lord, who created you from a single soul. From that soul He created its spouse, and through them He bestrewed the earth with countless men and women.

Fear God, in whose name you plead with one another, and honour the mothers who bore you. God is ever watching you.

Give orphans the property which belongs to them. Do not exchange their valuables for worthless things or cheat them of their possessions; for this would surely be a grievous sin. If you fear that you cannot treat orphans[1] with fairness, then you may marry other women who seem good to you: two, three, or four of them. But if you fear that you cannot maintain equality among them, marry one only or any slave-girls you may own. This will make it easier for you to avoid injustice.

Give women their dowry as a free gift; but if they choose to make over to you a part of it, you may regard it as lawfully yours.

4:5 Do not give the feeble-minded the property with which

---

1. Orphan girls.

God has entrusted you for their support; but maintain and clothe them with its proceeds, and speak kind words to them.

Put orphans to the test until they reach a marriageable 4:6 age. If you find them capable of sound judgement, hand over to them their property, and do not deprive them of it by squandering it before they come of age.

Let not the rich guardian touch the property of his orphan ward; and let him who is poor use no more than a fair portion of it for his own advantage.

When you hand over to them their property, call in some witnesses; sufficient is God's accounting of your actions.

Men shall have a share in what their parents and kinsmen leave; and women shall have a share in what their parents and kinsmen leave: whether it be little or much, they shall be legally entitled to a share.

If relatives, orphans, or needy men are present at the division of an inheritance, give them, too, a share of it, and speak kind words to them.

Let those who are solicitous about the welfare of their young children after their own death take care not to wrong orphans. Let them fear God and speak for justice.

Those that devour the property of orphans unjustly, 4:10 swallow fire into their bellies; they shall burn in a mighty conflagration.

God has thus enjoined you concerning your children:

A male shall inherit twice as much as a female. If there be more than two girls, they shall have two-thirds of the inheritance; but if there be one only, she shall inherit the half. Parents shall inherit a sixth each, if the deceased have a child; but if he leave no child and his parents be his heirs, his mother shall have a third. If he have brothers, his mother shall have a sixth after payment of any legacy he may have bequeathed or any debt he may have owed.

You may wonder whether your parents or your children are more beneficial to you. But this is the law of God; surely God is all-knowing and wise.

You shall inherit the half of your wives' estate if they die 4:12

childless. If they leave children, a quarter of their estate shall be yours after payment of any legacy they may have bequeathed or any debt they may have owed.

Your wives shall inherit one quarter of your estate if you die childless. If you leave children, they shall inherit one-eighth, after payment of any legacy you may have bequeathed or any debt you may have owed.

If a man or a woman leave neither children nor parents and have a brother or a sister, they shall each inherit one-sixth. If there be more, they shall equally share the third of the estate, after payment of any legacy he may have bequeathed or any debt he may have owed, without prejudice to the rights of the heirs. That is a commandment from God. God is all-knowing, and gracious.

4:13 Such are the bounds set by God. He that obeys God and His apostle shall dwell for ever in gardens watered by running streams. That is the supreme triumph. But he that defies God and His apostle and transgresses His bounds, shall be cast into a Fire wherein he will abide for ever. Shameful punishment awaits him.

If any of your women commit a lewd act, call in four witnesses from among yourselves against them; if they testify to their guilt confine them to their houses till death overtakes them or till God finds another way for them.

4:16 If two men among you commit a lewd act, punish them both. If they repent and mend their ways, let them be. God is forgiving and merciful.

God forgives those who commit evil in ignorance and then quickly turn to Him in penitence. God will pardon them. God is all-knowing and wise. But He will not forgive those who do evil and, when death comes to them, say: 'Now we repent!' Nor those who die unbelievers: for them We have prepared a woeful scourge.

4:19 Believers, it is unlawful for you to inherit the women of your deceased kinsmen against their will, or to bar them from re-marrying, in order that you may force them to give up a part of what you have given them, unless they be guilty of a proven lewd act. Treat them with kindness; for even if you dislike them, it may well be that you dislike a thing which God has meant for your own abundant good.

If you wish to replace one wife with another, do not take 4:20 from her the dowry you have given her even if it be a talent of gold. That would be improper and grossly unjust; for how can you take it back when you have lain with each other and entered into a firm contract?

You shall not marry the women whom your fathers married: all previous such marriages excepted. That was an evil practice, indecent and abominable.

Forbidden to you are your mothers, your daughters, your sisters, your paternal and maternal aunts, the daughters of your brothers and sisters, your foster-mothers, your foster-sisters, the mothers of your wives, your step-daughters who are in your charge, born of the wives with whom you have lain (it is no offence for you to marry your step-daughters if you have not consummated your marriage with their mothers), and the wives of your own begotten sons. You are also forbidden to take in marriage two sisters at one and the same time: all previous such marriages excepted. Surely God is forgiving and merciful. Also married women, except 4:24 those whom you own as slaves. Such is the decree of God. All women other than these are lawful for you, provided you court them with your wealth in modest conduct, not in fornication. Give them their dowry for the enjoyment you have had of them as a duty; but it shall be no offence for you to make any other agreement among yourselves after you have fulfilled your duty. Surely God is all-knowing and wise.

If any one of you cannot afford to marry a free believing 4:25 woman, let him marry a slave-girl who is a believer (God best knows your faith: you are born one of another). Marry them with the permission of their masters and give them their dowry in all justice, provided they are honourable and chaste and have not entertained other men. If after marriage they commit adultery, they shall suffer half the penalty inflicted upon free adulteresses. Such is the law for those of you who fear to commit sin: but if you abstain, it will be better for you. God is forgiving and merciful.

4:26    God desires to make this known to you and to guide you along the paths of those who have gone before you, and to turn to you with mercy. God is all-knowing and wise.

God wishes to forgive you, but those who follow their own appetites wish to see you stray grievously into error. God wishes to lighten your burdens, for man was created weak.

Believers, do not consume your wealth among yourselves in vanity, but rather trade with it by mutual consent.

Do not kill yourselves. God is merciful to you, but he that does that through wickedness and injustice shall be burned in fire. That is easy enough for God.

If you avoid the enormities you are forbidden, We shall pardon your misdeeds and usher you in with all honour. Do not covet the favours by which God has exalted some among you above others. Men shall be rewarded according to their deeds, and women shall be rewarded according to their deeds. Rather implore God to bestow on you His gifts. Surely God has knowledge of all things.

To every parent and kinsman We have appointed heirs who will inherit from them. As for those with whom you have entered into agreements, let them, too, have their share. Surely God bears witness to all things.

4:34    Men have authority over women because God has made the one superior to the other, and because they spend their wealth to maintain them. Good women are obedient. They guard their unseen parts because God has guarded them. As for those from whom you fear disobedience, admonish them, forsake them in beds[1] apart, and beat them. Then if they obey you, take no further action against them. Surely God is high, supreme.

If you fear a breach between a man and his wife, appoint an arbiter from his people and another from hers. If they wish to be reconciled, God will bring them together again. Surely God is all-knowing and wise.

4:36    Serve God and associate none with Him. Show kindness to parents and kindred, to orphans and to the destitute, to

1. or *bedrooms*.

near and distant neighbours, to those that keep company with you, to the traveller in need, and to the slaves you own. God does not love arrogant and boastful men, who are themselves tight-fisted and enjoin others to be tight-fisted; who con- 4:37 ceal the riches which God of His bounty has bestowed upon them (We have prepared a shameful punishment for the unbelievers); and who spend their wealth only to impress people, believing neither in God nor in the Last Day. He that chooses Satan for his friend, an evil friend has he.

What harm could befall them if they believed in God and the Last Day and gave in alms from that which God bestowed on them? Surely God knows them.

God will wrong none by as much as the weight of an atom. A good deed He will repay twofold. Of His own bounty He will bestow a rich recompense.

How will it be when We produce a witness from each community and call upon you to testify against them? On that day those who disbelieved and disobeyed the Apostle will wish that they were levelled with the dust; they shall hide nothing from God.

Believers, do not approach your prayers when you are 4:43 drunk, but wait till you can grasp the meaning of your words; nor when you are unclean – unless you are travelling the road – until you have washed yourselves. If you are sick or on a journey, or if, when you have relieved yourselves or had intercourse with women, you can find no water, take some clean sand and rub your faces and your hands with it. Gracious is God and forgiving.

Consider those to whom a portion of the Scriptures was given. They purchase error for themselves and wish to see you go astray. But God best knows your enemies. Sufficient is God to protect you, and sufficient is God to help you.

Among those who follow the Jewish Faith are some who 4:46 take words out of their context and say:[1] 'We hear, but disobey. May you be bereft of hearing! *Rā'inā!*' – thus distorting the phrase with their tongues and reviling the true faith. But if

1. To Muḥammad.

they said: 'We hear and obey: hear us and *Unzurnā*,'¹ it would be better and more proper for them. God has cursed them in their unbelief. They have no faith, except a few of them.

4:47 You to whom the Scriptures were given! Believe in that which We have revealed, confirming your own scriptures, before We obliterate your faces and turn them backward, or lay Our curse on you as We laid it on the Sabbath-breakers. What God ordains shall be accomplished.

God will not forgive those who serve other gods besides Him; but He will forgive whom He will for other sins. He that serves other gods besides Him is guilty of a heinous sin.

Have you seen those who think themselves pure? God purifies whom He will. They shall not be wronged by as much as the husk of a date-stone.

See how they invent falsehoods about God. This in itself is a most grievous sin.

4:51 Consider those to whom a portion of the Scriptures was given. They believe in idols and false gods and say of the infidels: 'These are better guided than the believers.' These are they on whom God has laid His curse. He who is cursed by God has none to help him.

Will they have a share in the Kingdom? If so, they will not give others so much as the speck on a date-stone.

Do they envy others what God has of His bounty given them? We gave Abraham's descendants scriptures and prophethood, and an illustrious kingdom. Some believe in him,² but others reject him. Sufficient scourge is the fire of Hell.

4:56 Those that deny Our revelations We will burn in fire. No sooner will their skins be consumed than We shall give them other skins, so that they may truly taste the scourge. Surely God is mighty and wise.

---

1. The words mean 'Listen to us' and 'Look upon us' respectively; but in Judaeo-Arabic the sound of the first conveys the sense, 'Our evil one'. Arabian Jews used the expression as a derisive pun.
2. Muḥammad.

As for those that have faith and do good works, We shall 4:57
admit them to gardens watered by running streams, where,
wedded to chaste spouses, they shall abide for ever. To a
cool shade We shall admit them.

God commands you to hand back your trusts to their
rightful owners, and, when you pass judgement among
people, to judge with fairness. Noble is that to which God
exhorts you. Surely God hears all and observes all.

Believers, obey God and obey the Apostle and those in
authority among you. Should you disagree about anything
refer it to God and the Apostle, if you truly believe in God
and the Last Day. This will in the end be better and more
just.

Mark those who profess to believe in what has been
revealed to you and what was revealed before you. They
seek the judgement of the devil, although they were bidden
to deny him. Satan would lead them far into error.

When they are told: 'Come to be judged by that 4:61
which God has revealed and by the Apostle,' you see the
hypocrites turn a deaf ear to you. But how would it be if
some disaster befell them on account of what their hands
committed? They would come to you swearing by God that
they desired nothing but amity and conciliation. But God
knows what their hearts conceal. Let them be. Admonish
them and sternly rebuke them.

We sent forth apostles so that men should do their
bidding by God's leave. If, when they wronged themselves,
they had come to you imploring God's pardon, and if the
Apostle had sought of God forgiveness for them, they
would have found God forgiving and merciful.

But they will not – I swear by your Lord – they will not
be true believers until they seek your arbitration in their
disputes. Then they will not doubt the justice of your
verdicts and will submit to you entirely.

Had We commanded them, saying: 'Lay down your 4:66
lives,' or 'Flee from your country,' only a few would have
complied. Yet, had they done what they were admonished
to do, it would have been better for them and their faith

4:67 would have been strengthened. We would have bestowed on them of Our grace a rich recompense and guided them to a straight path.

He that obeys God and the Apostle shall dwell with the prophets and the saints, the martyrs and the righteous men whom God has favoured. Gracious companions will be those.

Such is the bounty of God. Sufficient is God's infinite knowledge.

Believers, be ever on your guard. March in detachments or in one body. Someone among you is sure to lag behind, so that if a disaster befell you, he would say: 'God has been gracious to me; I was not present with them.' But if, by God's grace, you were successful, he would surely say, as though there was no friendship between you and him: 'Would that I had been with them! I should have won a great victory.'

Let those who would exchange the life of this world for the hereafter, fight for the cause of God; whoever fights for the cause of God, whether he dies or triumphs, on him We shall bestow a rich recompense.

4:75 And how should you not fight for the cause of God, and for the helpless old men, women, and children[1] who say: 'Deliver us, Lord, from this city of wrongdoers; send forth to us a guardian from Your presence; send to us from Your presence one that will help us'?

The true believers fight for the cause of God, but the infidels fight for the devil. Fight then against the friends of Satan. Satan's cunning is weak indeed.

4:77 Mark those who were told: 'Lay down your arms; recite your prayers and render the alms levy.' When they were ordered to fight, some of them feared man as much as they feared God or even more. 'Lord,' they said, 'why do You bid us fight? Could you not give us a brief respite?'

Say: 'Trifling are the pleasures of this life. Better is the life to come for those who would keep from evil. You shall not

---

1. In Mecca.

be wronged by as much as the husk of a date-stone.
Wherever you be, death will overtake you: though you put 4:78
yourselves in lofty towers.'

When they are blessed with good fortune, they say: 'This
is from God.' But when evil befalls them, they say: 'It was
your[1] fault.'

Say to them: 'All is from God!'

What has come over these men that they can hardly
understand a word?

Whatever good befalls you,[2] it is from God: and whatever
ill from yourself.

We have sent you forth as an apostle to mankind. God is
your all-sufficient witness.

He that obeys the Apostle obeys God. As for those that
pay no heed, know then that We have not sent you to be
their keeper.

They promise to obey you: but as soon as they leave
you a number of them plot in secret to do otherwise.
God takes note of all their plots. Therefore let them be,
and put your trust in God. God is your all-sufficient
guardian.

Will they not ponder on the Koran? If it had not come 4:82
from God, they could have surely found in it many contradictions.

When they hear any news, good or bad, they at once
make it known to all; whereas if they reported it to the
Apostle and to the men in charge, those who sought news
could learn it from them. But for God's grace and mercy, all
but a few of you would have followed Satan.

Therefore fight for the cause of God. You are accountable
for none but yourself. Rouse the faithful: perchance God
will overthrow the might of the unbelievers. Mightier is
God and more terrible is His punishment.

He that mediates in a good cause shall gain by his 4:85
mediation; but he that mediates in a bad cause shall be held
accountable for its evil. God surely controls all things.

1. Muḥammad's.    2. Man.

69

4:86    If a man greets you, let your greeting be better than his –
or at least return his greeting. God surely keeps count of all
things.

God: there is no god but Him. He will surely gather you
all together on the Day of Resurrection: that day is not to be
doubted. And who has a truer word than God?

Why are you thus divided concerning the hypocrites,
when God Himself has cast them off on account of their
misdeeds? Would you guide those whom God has confounded? He whom God confounds you cannot guide.

They would have you disbelieve as they themselves have
disbelieved, so that you may be all alike. Do not befriend
them until they have fled their homes in the cause of God.
If they desert you, seize them and put them to death
wherever you find them. Look for neither friends nor
helpers among them except those who seek refuge with
your allies or come over to you because their hearts forbid
them to fight against you or against their own people. Had
God pleased, He would have given them power over you,
so that they would have taken arms against you. Therefore,
if they keep away from you and cease their hostility and
offer you peace, God bids you not to harm them.

4:91    Others you will find who seek security from you as well
as from their own people. Whenever they are called back to
sedition they plunge into it headlong. If these do not keep
their distance from you, if they neither offer you peace nor
cease their hostilities against you, lay hold of them and kill
them wherever you find them. Over such men We give you
absolute authority.

4:92    It is unlawful for a believer to kill another believer,
accidents excepted. He that accidentally kills a believer must
free one Muslim slave and pay blood-money to the family of
the victim, unless they choose to give it away in alms. If the
victim be a Muslim from a hostile tribe, the penalty is the
freeing of one Muslim slave. But if the victim be a member
of an allied tribe, then blood-money must be paid to his
family and a Muslim slave set free. He that lacks the means
must fast two consecutive months. Such is the penance

imposed by God: God is all-knowing and wise.

He that kills a believer by design shall burn in Hell for 4:93 ever. He shall incur the wrath of God, who will lay His curse on him and prepare for him a mighty scourge.

Believers, show discernment when you go to fight for the cause of God, and do not say to those that offer you peace: 'You are not believers,' – seeking the chance booty of this world; for with God there are abundant gains. Such was your custom in days gone by, but now God has bestowed on you His grace. Therefore show discernment; God is cognizant of all your actions.

The believers who stay at home – apart from those that suffer from a grave disability – are not the equals of those who fight for the cause of God with their goods and their persons. God has exalted the men who fight with their goods and their persons above those who stay at home. God has promised all a good reward; but far richer is the recompense of those who fight for Him: ranks of His own bestowal, forgiveness, and mercy. Surely God is forgiving and merciful.

The angels will ask those whom they claim back while 4:97 steeped in sin: 'What were you doing?' 'We were oppressed in the land,' they will reply. They will say: 'Was not the earth of God spacious enough for you to fly for refuge?' Hell shall be their home: an evil fate.

As for the helpless men, women, and children who have neither the strength nor the means to escape, God may pardon them: surely God pardons and forgives.

He that leaves his home in the cause of God shall find many a refuge in the land and great abundance. He that leaves his dwelling to fight for God and His apostle and is then overtaken by death shall be recompensed by God. Surely God is forgiving and merciful.

It is no offence for you to shorten your prayers when travelling the road if you fear that the unbelievers may attack you. The unbelievers are your inveterate foe.

When you (Prophet) are with the faithful, conducting 4:102 their prayers, let one party of them rise up to pray with you, armed with their weapons. After making their prostrations, let them withdraw to the rear and then let another party who have not prayed come forward and pray with you; and let these also be on their guard, armed with their weapons. It would much please the unbelievers if you neglected your arms and your baggage, so that they could swoop upon you with one assault. But it is no offence for you to lay aside your arms when overtaken by heavy rain or stricken with an illness, although you must be always on your guard. God has prepared a shameful punishment for the unbelievers.

4:103     When your prayers are ended, remember God standing, sitting, and lying down. Attend regularly to your prayers so long as you are safe: for prayer is a duty incumbent on the faithful, to be conducted at appointed hours.

Seek out the enemy relentlessly. If you have suffered, they too have suffered: but you at least hope to receive from God what they cannot hope for. God is all-knowing and wise.

We have revealed to you the Book with the Truth, so that you may arbitrate among men by that which God has shown you. You shall not plead for traitors. Implore God's forgiveness: God is ever forgiving and merciful. Nor shall you plead for those who betray their own souls; God does not love the treacherous or the sinful.

4:108     They seek to hide themselves from men, but they cannot hide themselves from God. He is with them when they utter in secret what does not please Him: God has knowledge of all their actions.

Yes, you may plead for them in this life, but who will plead for them with God on the Day of Resurrection? Who will be their defender?

He that does evil or wrongs his own soul and then seeks God's pardon, will find God forgiving and merciful.

He that commits sin commits it against his own soul. God is all-knowing and wise.

He that commits an offence or a crime and charges an innocent man with it, shall bear the guilt of calumny and gross injustice.

4:113     But for God's grace and mercy you would have been led astray by some among them. They lead astray none but themselves, nor can they do you any harm.

God has revealed to you the Book and His wisdom and taught you what you did not know before. God's goodness to you has been great indeed.

There is no virtue in much of their counsel: only in his who 4:114 enjoins charity, kindness, and peace among men. He that does this to please God, on him We shall bestow a rich recompense.

He that disobeys the Apostle after Our guidance has been revealed to him, and follows a path other than that of the faithful, shall be given what he has chosen. We will burn him in the fire of Hell: an evil end.

God will not forgive idolatry. He will forgive whom He will all other sins. He that serves other gods besides God has strayed far indeed.

Rather than to Him, they pray but to females: they pray but to a rebellious Satan. God has laid His curse on Satan, for he had said: 'I shall entice a number of Your servants and lead them astray. I shall arouse in them vain desires and order them to slit the ears of cattle. I shall order them to tamper with God's creation.' Indeed, he that chooses Satan rather than God for his protector ruins himself beyond redemption.

He makes promises and stirs up in them vain desires; 4:120 Satan makes them promises only to deceive them. Hell shall be their home: from it they shall find no refuge.

As for those that have faith and do good works, We shall admit them to gardens watered by running streams, and there shall they abide for ever. Such is God's true promise: and who has a truer word than God?

It shall not be in accordance with your wishes, nor shall it be as the People of the Book desire. He that does evil shall be requited with evil: he shall find none besides God to protect or help him. But the believers who do good works, both men and women, shall enter Paradise. They shall not suffer the least injustice.

And who has a nobler religion than he who submits to 4:125 God, does what is right, and follows the faith of saintly Abraham, whom God chose to be His friend?

4:126     To God belongs all that the heavens and the earth contain. God encompasses all things.

They consult you concerning women. Say: 'God has instructed you about them, and so have the verses proclaimed to you in the Book, concerning the orphan girls whom you deny their lawful rights and refuse to marry; also regarding helpless children. He has instructed you to deal justly with orphans. God has knowledge of all the good you do.'

If a woman fear ill-treatment or desertion on the part of her husband, it shall be no offence for them to seek a mutual agreement, for agreement is best. People are prone to avarice. But if you do what is right and guard yourselves against evil, know then that God is cognizant of all your actions.

Try as you may, you cannot treat all your wives impartially. Do not set yourself altogether against any of them, leaving her, as it were, in suspense. If you do what is right and guard yourselves against evil, you will find God forgiving and merciful. If they separate, God will compensate both out of His own abundance: God is munificent and wise.

4:131     To God belongs all that the heavens and the earth contain. We exhort you, as We have exhorted those to whom the Book was given before you, to fear God. If you deny Him, know that to God belongs all that the heavens and the earth contain. God is self-sufficient and worthy of praise.

To God belongs all that the heavens and the earth contain. God is the all-sufficient guardian. If He pleased, He could destroy you all, you people! and replace you by other men. This God has the power to do.

Let the man who seeks the reward of this life know that it is God who dispenses the reward of both this life and the life to come. He hears all and sees all.

4:135     Believers, conduct yourselves with justice and bear true witness before God, even though it be against yourselves, your parents, or your kinsfolk. Be they rich or poor, God knows better about them both. So do not be led by passion, lest you swerve from the truth. If you distort your testimony or decline to give it, know that God is cognizant of all your actions.

Believers, have faith in God and His apostle, in the Book 4:136 He has revealed to His apostle, and in the Scriptures He formerly revealed. He that denies God, His angels, His Scriptures, His apostles, and the Last Day has strayed far.

Those who accept the Faith and then renounce it, who again embrace it and again deny it and grow in unbelief – God will neither forgive them nor rightly guide them.

Give warning to the hypocrites that woeful punishment awaits them: those who choose the unbelievers rather than the faithful for their friends. Are they seeking glory at their hands? Surely all glory belongs to God.

He has instructed you in the Book that when you hear God's revelations being denied or ridiculed you must not sit and listen to them until they engage in other talk, or else you shall yourselves become like them. God will surely gather in Hell the hypocrites and the unbelievers all.

They watch your fortunes closely. If God grants you a 4:141 victory, they say: 'Did we not stand on your side?' And if it be the unbelievers' turn, they say to them: 'Were we not mightier than you, and did we not protect you from the faithful?'

God will judge between you on the Day of Resurrection. God will not let the unbelievers triumph over the faithful.

The hypocrites seek to deceive God, but it is He who deceives them. When they rise to pray, they stand up sluggishly: they pray only to be seen by people and remember God but little, wavering between this and that and belonging neither to these nor those. You cannot guide the man whom God has confounded.

Believers, do not choose the infidels rather than the faithful for your friends. Would you give God clear evidence against yourselves?

The hypocrites shall be cast into the lowest depths of the Fire: there shall be none to help them. But those who 4:146 repent and mend their ways, who hold fast to God and are sincere in their devotion to God – they shall be numbered with the faithful, and the faithful shall be richly rewarded by God.

4:147     And why should God punish you if you render thanks to Him and truly believe in Him? God will surely recompense your labours, for He knows them all.

God does not love harsh words, except when uttered by a man who is truly wronged. God hears all and knows all. Whether you do good openly or in private, whether you forgive an injustice – God is forgiving and all-powerful.

Those that deny God and His apostles, and those that draw a line between God and His apostles, saying: 'We believe in some, but deny others,' – thus seeking a middle way – these indeed are the unbelievers. For the unbelievers We have prepared a shameful punishment.

As for those that believe in God and His apostles and discriminate against none of them, they shall be recompensed by Him. God is forgiving and merciful.

4:153     The People of the Book ask you to bring down for them a book from heaven. Of Moses they demanded a harder thing than that. They said to him: 'Show us God distinctly.' And for their wickedness the thunderbolt smote them. They worshipped the calf after clear signs had been revealed to them; yet We forgave them that, and bestowed on Moses clear authority.

When We made a covenant with them We raised the Mount above them and said: 'Enter the gates in adoration. Do not break the Sabbath.' We took from them a solemn covenant. But they broke their covenant, denied the revelations of God, and killed the prophets unjustly. They said: 'Our hearts are sealed.'

It is God who has sealed their hearts, on account of their unbelief. They have no faith, except a few of them.

They denied the truth and uttered a monstrous falsehood 4:157 against Mary. They declared: 'We have put to death the Messiah, Jesus son of Mary, the apostle of God.' They did not kill him, nor did they crucify him, but they thought they did.[1]

---

1. Or, literally, 'he was made to resemble another for them'.

Those that disagreed about him were in doubt concerning him; they knew nothing about him that was not sheer conjecture; they did not slay him for certain. God lifted him up to 4:158 Him; God is mighty and wise. There is none among the People of the Book but will believe in him before his death; and on the Day of Resurrection he will bear witness against them.

Because of their iniquity, We forbade those who followed the Jewish Faith wholesome things which were formerly allowed them; because time after time they have debarred others from the path of God; because they practise usury – although they were forbidden it – and cheat people of their possessions. Woeful punishment have We prepared for those that disbelieve. But those of them that have deep learning, and those that truly believe in what has been revealed to you and what was revealed before you; who attend to their prayers and render the alms levy and have faith in God and the Last Day – on these We shall bestow a rich recompense.

We have revealed Our will to you as We revealed it to 4:163 Noah and to the prophets who came after him; as We revealed it to Abraham, Ishmael, Isaac, Jacob, and the tribes; to Jesus, Job, Jonah, Aaron, Solomon and David, to whom We gave the Psalms. Of some apostles We have already told you, but there are others of whom We have not yet spoken (God spoke directly to Moses): apostles who brought good news to mankind and admonished them, so that they might have no plea against God after their coming. God is mighty and wise.

God bears witness, by that which He has revealed to you, that He revealed it with His knowledge; and so do the angels. There is no better witness than God.

Those that disbelieve and debar others from the path of God have strayed far into error. God will not forgive those who disbelieve and act unjustly; nor will He guide them to any path other than the path of Hell, wherein they shall abide for ever. Surely that is easy enough for God.

You people! The Apostle has brought you the Truth 4:170 from your Lord. Have faith and it shall be well with you. If you disbelieve, know that to God belongs all that the heavens and the earth contain. God is all-knowing and wise.

4:171     People of the Book,[1] do not transgress the bounds of your religion. Speak nothing but the truth about God. The Messiah, Jesus son of Mary, was no more than God's apostle and His Word which He cast to Mary: a spirit from Him. So believe in God and His apostles and do not say: 'Three.' Forbear, and it shall be better for you. God is but one God. God forbid that He should have a son! His is all that the heavens and the earth contain. God is the all-sufficient protector. The Messiah does not disdain to be a servant of God, nor do the angels who are nearest to Him. Those who through arrogance disdain His service shall all be brought before Him.

4:173     As for those that have faith and do good works, God will bestow on them their rewards and enrich them from His own abundance. But those who are scornful and proud He will sternly punish, and they will find none besides God to protect or help them.

You people! You have received clear evidence from your Lord. We have sent down to you a glorious light. Those that believe in God and hold fast to Him He will admit to His mercy and His grace; He will guide them to Him along a straight path.

4:176     They seek your guidance. Say: 'Thus God instructs you regarding those that die childless and without living parents. If a man die childless and he have a sister, she shall inherit the half of his estate. If a woman die childless, her brother shall be her sole heir. If a childless man have two sisters, they shall inherit two-thirds of his estate; but if he have both brothers and sisters, the share of each male shall be that of two females.'

Thus God makes plain to you His precepts so that you may not err. God has knowledge of all things.

---

1. Christians.

# THE TABLE

*In the Name of God, the Compassionate, the Merciful*

BELIEVERS, BE true to your obligations. It is lawful for 5:1
you to eat the flesh of all beasts other than that which is
hereby announced to you. Game is forbidden while you are
on pilgrimage. God decrees what He will.

Believers, do not violate the rites of God, or the sacred
month, or the offerings or their ornaments, or those that
repair to the Sacred House seeking their Lord's grace and
pleasure. Once your pilgrimage is ended, you shall be free to
go hunting.

Do not allow your hatred for those who would debar
you from the Holy Mosque to lead you into sin. Help
one another in what is good and pious, not in what is
wicked and sinful. Have fear of God; God is stern in retribution.

You are forbidden carrion, blood, and the flesh of swine; 5:3
also any flesh dedicated to any other than God. You are
forbidden the flesh of strangled animals and of those beaten
or gored to death; of those killed by a fall or mangled by
beasts of prey (unless you make it clean by giving the death-
stroke yourselves); also of animals sacrificed to idols.

You are forbidden to settle disputes by consulting the
Arrows. That is a pernicious practice.

The unbelievers have this day abandoned all hope of
vanquishing your religion. Have no fear of them: fear Me.

This day I have perfected your religion for you and
completed My favour to you. I have chosen Islām to be
your faith.

He that is constrained by hunger to eat of what is
forbidden, not intending to commit sin, will find God
forgiving and merciful.

They ask you what is lawful for them. Say: 'All whole- 5:4
some things are lawful for you, as well as that which you
have taught the birds and beasts of prey to catch, training
them as God has taught you. Eat of what they catch for

you, pronouncing upon it the name of God. And have fear of God: swift is God's reckoning.'

5:5　All wholesome things have this day been made lawful for you. The food of those to whom the Book was given[1] is lawful for you, and yours for them.

Lawful for you are the believing women and the free women from among those who were given the Book before you, provided that you give them their dowries and live in honour with them, neither committing fornication nor taking them as mistresses.

He that denies the Faith shall gain nothing from his labours. In the world to come he will surely be among the losers.

Believers, when you rise to pray wash your faces and your hands as far as the elbow, and wipe your heads and your feet to the ankle. If you are unclean, cleanse yourselves. But if you are sick or on a journey, or if, when you have just relieved yourselves or had intercourse with women, you can find no water, take some clean sand and rub your faces and your hands with it. God does not wish to burden you; He seeks only to purify you and to perfect His favour to you, so that you may give thanks.

5:7　Remember God's favour to you, and the covenant with which He bound you when you said: 'We hear and obey.' Have fear of God. God knows the innermost thoughts of men.

Believers, fulfil your duties to God and bear true witness. Do not allow your hatred for other men to turn you away from justice. Deal justly; that is nearer to true piety. Have fear of God; God is cognizant of all your actions.

God has promised those that have faith and do good works forgiveness and a rich reward. As for those who disbelieve and deny Our revelations, they are the heirs of Hell.

5:11　Believers, remember the favour which God bestowed upon you when He restrained the hands of those who sought to harm you. Have fear of God. In God let the faithful put their trust.

---

1. The Jews (but not the Christians).

God made a covenant with the Israelites and raised 5:12
among them twelve chieftains. God said: 'I shall be with
you. If you attend to your prayers and render the alms levy;
if you believe in My apostles and assist them and give God a
generous loan, I shall forgive you your sins and admit you
to gardens watered by running streams. But he that hereafter
denies Me shall stray from the right path.'

But because they broke their covenant We laid on them
Our curse and hardened their hearts. They have tampered
with words out of their context and forgotten much of what
they were enjoined. You will ever find them deceitful,
except for a few of them. But pardon them and bear with
them. God loves those who do good.

With those who said they were Christians We made a
covenant also, but they too have forgotten much of what
they were exhorted to do. Therefore We stirred among
them enmity and hatred, which shall endure till the Day of
Resurrection, when God will declare to them all that they
have done.

People of the Book! Our apostle has come to reveal to 5:15
you much of what you have hidden of the Scriptures, and to
forgive you much. A light has come to you from God and a
glorious Book, with which God will guide to the paths of
peace those that seek to please Him; He will lead them by
His will from darkness to the light; He will guide them to a
straight path.

They do blaspheme, who declare: 'God is the Messiah,
the son of Mary.' Say: 'Who could prevent God, if He so
willed, from destroying the Messiah, the son of Mary, his
mother, and all the people of the earth? God has sovereignty
over the heavens and the earth and all that lies between
them. He creates what He will; and God has power over all
things.'

The Jews and the Christians say: 'We are the children of 5:18
God and His loved ones.' Say: 'Why then does He punish
you for your sins? Surely you are mortals of His own
creation. He forgives whom He will and punishes whom He
pleases. God has sovereignty over the heavens and the earth
and all that lies between them. All shall return to Him.'

5:19     People of the Book! Our apostle has come to you with revelations after an interval which saw no apostles, lest you say: 'No one has come to give us good news or to warn us.' Now someone has come to give you good news and to warn you. God has power over all things.

Bear in mind the words of Moses to his people. He said: 'Remember, my people, the favour which God has bestowed upon you. He has raised up prophets among you, made you kings, and given you that which He has given to no other nation. Enter, my people, the holy land which God has assigned for you. Do not turn back, and thus lose all.'

'Moses,' they replied, 'a race of giants dwells in this land. We will not set foot in it till they are gone. As soon as they are gone we will enter.'

Thereupon two God-fearing men whom God had favoured said: 'Go in to them through the gates, and when you have entered you shall surely be victorious. In God put your trust, if you are true believers.'

5:24     But they replied: 'Moses, we will not go in so long as *they* are in it. Go, you and your Lord, and fight. Here we will stay.'

'Lord,' cried Moses, 'I have none but myself and my brother. Keep us apart from the iniquitous people.'

He replied: 'They shall be forbidden this land for forty years, during which time they shall wander homeless on the earth. Do not grieve for the iniquitous people.'

Recount to them in all truth the story of Adam's two sons: how they each made an offering, and how the offering of the one was accepted while that of the other was not. One said: 'I will surely kill you.' The other replied: 'God accepts offerings only from the righteous. If you stretch your hand to kill me, I shall not stretch mine to slay you; for I fear God, Lord of the Universe. I would rather you should add your sin against me to your other sins and thus become an inmate of the Fire. Such is the recompense of the unjust.'

5:30     His soul prompted him to slay his brother; he slew him

and thus became one of the lost. Then God sent down a 5:31
raven, which clawed the earth to show him how to bury the
naked corpse of his brother. 'Alas!' he cried. 'Have I not
strength enough to do as this raven has done and so bury
my brother's naked corpse?' And he repented.

That was why We laid it down for the Israelites that
whoever killed a human being, except as punishment for
murder or other villainy in the land, shall be deemed as
having killed all mankind; and that whoever saved a human
life shall be deemed as having saved all mankind.

Our apostles brought them veritable proofs: yet many
among them, even after that, did prodigious evil in the
land.

Those that make war against God and His apostle and
spread disorder in the land shall be slain or crucified or have
their hands and feet cut off on alternate sides, or be
banished from the land. They shall be held up to shame in
this world and sternly punished in the hereafter: except
those that repent before you reduce them. For you must
know that God is forgiving and merciful.

Believers, have fear of God and seek the right path to 5:35
Him. Fight valiantly for His cause, so that you may
triumph.

As for the unbelievers, if they offered all that the earth
contains and as much besides to redeem themselves from
the torment of the Day of Resurrection, it shall not be
accepted from them. Woeful punishment awaits them.

They will strive to get out of the Fire, but get out of it
they shall not. Lasting punishment awaits them.

As for the man or woman who is guilty of theft, cut off
their hands to punish them for their crimes. That is the
punishment enjoined by God. God is mighty and wise.
But whoever repents after committing evil, and mends his
ways, shall be pardoned by God. God is forgiving and
merciful.

Did you not know that God has sovereignty over the 5:40
heavens and the earth? He punishes whom He will and
forgives whom He pleases. God has power over all things.

5:41     Apostle, do not grieve for those who plunge headlong into unbelief; those who say with their tongues: 'We believe,' but have no faith in their hearts, and those of the Jewish Faith who listen to lies and listen to others who have not come to you. They tamper with words out of their context and say: 'If this be given you, accept it; if not, then beware!'

You cannot help a man if God intends to try him. Those whose hearts God does not intend to purify shall be held up to shame in this world, and in the world to come grievous punishment awaits them.

They listen to falsehoods and practise what is unlawful. If they come to you, give them your judgement or avoid them. If you avoid them, they can in no way harm you; but if you do act as their judge, judge them with fairness. God loves those that deal justly.

But how will they come to you for judgement when they already have the Torah which enshrines God's own judgement? Soon after, they will turn their backs: they are no true believers.

5:44     We have revealed the Torah, in which there is guidance and light. By it the prophets who submitted to God judged the Jews, and so did the rabbis and the divines, according to God's Book which had been committed to their keeping and to which they themselves were witnesses.

Have no fear of man; fear Me, and do not sell My revelations for a paltry sum. Unbelievers are those who do not judge according to God's revelations.

We decreed for them a life for a life, an eye for an eye, a nose for a nose, an ear for an ear, a tooth for a tooth, and a wound for a wound. But if a man charitably forbears from retaliation, his remission shall atone for him. Transgressors are those that do not judge according to God's revelations.

After them We sent forth Jesus son of Mary, confirming the Torah already revealed, and gave him the Gospel, in which there is guidance and light, corroborating what was revealed before it in the Torah: a guide and an ad-
5:47 monition to the righteous. Therefore let those who follow the Gospel judge according to what God has revealed

therein. Evil-doers are those that do not judge according to God's revelations.

And to you We have revealed the Book with the truth. It 5:48 confirms the Scriptures which came before it and stands as a guardian over them. Therefore give judgement among men according to God's revelations, and do not yield to their whims or swerve from the truth made known to you.

We have ordained a law and assigned a path for each of you. Had God pleased, He could have made of you one community: but it is His wish to prove you by that which He has bestowed upon you. Vie with each other in good works, for to God shall you all return and He will resolve your differences for you.

Pronounce judgement among them according to God's revelations and do not be led by their desires. Take heed lest they turn you away from a part of that which God has revealed to you. If they reject your judgement, know that it is God's wish to scourge them for their sins. A great many of mankind are evil-doers.

Is it pagan laws that they wish to be judged by? Who is a better judge than God for men whose faith is firm?

Believers, take neither the Jews nor the Christians for 5:51 your friends. They are friends with one another. Whoever of you seeks their friendship shall become one of their number. God does not guide the wrongdoers.

You see the faint-hearted hastening to woo them. They say: 'We fear lest a change of fortune should befall us.' But it may well be that when God grants you victory or makes known His will, they will regret their secret plans. Then will the faithful say: 'Are these the men who solemnly swore by God that they would stand by you?' Their works will come to nothing and they will lose all.

Believers, if any among you renounce the Faith, God will 5:54 replace them by others who love Him and are loved by Him, who are humble towards the faithful and stern towards the unbelievers, zealous for God's cause and fearless of man's censure. Such is the grace of God: He bestows it on whom He will. God is munificent and all-knowing.

5:55    Your only protectors are God, His apostle, and the faithful: those who attend to their prayers, render the alms levy, and kneel down in worship. Those who seek the protection of God, His apostle, and the faithful must know that God's followers are sure to triumph.

Believers, do not seek the friendship of the infidels and those who were given the Book before you, who have made of your religion a jest and a diversion. Have fear of God, if you are true believers. When you call them to pray, they treat their prayers as a jest and a diversion. This is because they are devoid of understanding.

Say: 'People of the Book, is it not that you hate us only because we believe in God and in what has been revealed to us and to others before, and because most of you are evil-doers?'

Say: 'Shall I tell you who will receive a worse reward from God? Those whom God has cursed and with whom He has been angry, transforming them into apes and swine, and those who serve the devil. Worse is the plight of these, and they have strayed farther from the right path.'

5:61    When they came to you they said: 'We are believers.' Indeed, infidels they came and infidels they departed. God knew best what they concealed.

You see many among them vie with one another in sin and wickedness and practise what is unlawful. Evil is what they do.

Why do their rabbis and divines not forbid them to blaspheme or to practise what is unlawful? Evil indeed are their doings.

5:64    The Jews say: 'God's hand is chained.' May their own hands be chained! May they be cursed for what they say! By no means. His hands are both outstretched: He bestows as He will.

That which is revealed to you from your Lord will surely increase the wickedness and unbelief of many of them. We have stirred among them enmity and hatred, which will endure till the Day of Resurrection. Whenever they kindle the fire of war, God puts it out. They spread evil in the land, but God does not love the evil-doers.

If the People of the Book accept the true faith and keep 5:65 from evil, We will pardon them their sins and admit them to the gardens of delight. If they observe the Torah and the Gospel and what has been revealed to them from their Lord, they shall enjoy abundance from above and from beneath.

There are some among them who are righteous men; but there are many among them who do nothing but evil.

Apostle, proclaim what has been revealed to you from your Lord; if you do not, you will surely fail to convey His message. God will protect you from all people. God does not guide the unbelievers.

Say: 'People of the Book, you will attain nothing until you observe the Torah and the Gospel and that which has been revealed to you from your Lord.'

That which has been revealed to you from your Lord will surely increase the wickedness and unbelief of many of them. But do not grieve for the unbelievers.

Believers, those who follow the Jewish Faith, Sabaeans and Christians – whoever believes in God and the Last Day and does what is right – shall have nothing to fear or to regret.

We made a covenant with the Israelites and sent forth 5:70 apostles among them. But whenever an apostle came to them with a message that did not suit their inclinations, some they accused of lying and others they put to death. They thought no punishment would follow: they were blind and deaf. Then God turned to them in mercy, but many again were blind and deaf. God is ever watching their actions.

They do blaspheme, that say: 'God is the Messiah, the son of Mary.' For the Messiah himself said: 'Children of Israel, serve God, my Lord and your Lord.' He that worships other deities besides God, God will deny him Paradise, and the Fire shall be his home. None shall help the evil-doers.

They do blaspheme, that say: 'God is one of three.' There is but one God. If they do not desist from so saying, those of them that disbelieve shall be sternly punished.

Will they not turn to God in penitence and seek forgive- 5:74 ness of Him? God is forgiving and merciful.

5:75    The Messiah, the son of Mary, was no more than an apostle: other apostles passed away before him. His mother was a saintly woman. They both ate earthly food.

See how We make plain to them Our revelations. See how they ignore the truth.

Say: 'Will you serve instead of God that which can neither harm nor help you? God is He who hears all and knows all.'

Say: 'People of the Book! Do not transgress the bounds of truth in your religion. Do not yield to the desires of those who have erred before; who have led many astray and have themselves strayed from the even path.'

Those of the Israelites who disbelieved were cursed by David and Jesus son of Mary, because they rebelled and committed evil. Nor did they censure themselves for any wrong they did. Evil were their deeds.

You see many among them making friends with unbelievers. Evil is that to which their souls prompt them. They have incurred the wrath of God and shall endure eternal torment. Had they believed in God and the Prophet and that which has been revealed to him, they would not have befriended them. But many of them are evil-doers.

5:82    You will find that the most implacable of people in their enmity to the faithful are the Jews and the pagans, and that the nearest in affection to them are those who say: 'We are Christians.' That is because there are priests and monks among them; and because they are free from pride.

When they listen to that which was revealed to the Apostle, you see their eyes fill with tears as they recognize its truth. They say: 'Lord, we believe. Count us among the witnesses. Why should we not believe in God and in the truth that has come down to us? Why should we not hope our Lord will admit us among the righteous?' And for their words God has rewarded them with gardens watered by running streams, where they shall dwell for ever. Such is the recompense of the righteous. But those that disbelieve and deny Our revelations shall become the inmates of Hell.

5:87    Believers, do not forbid the wholesome things which

God made lawful for you. Do not transgress; God does not love the transgressors. Eat of the lawful and wholesome 5:88 things which God has given you. Have fear of God, in whom you do believe.

God will not punish you for that which is inadvertent in your oaths. But He will take you to task over the oaths which you solemnly swear. The penalty for a broken oath is the feeding of ten needy men with such food as you normally offer to your own people; or the clothing of ten needy men; or the freeing of a slave. He that cannot afford any of these must fast three days. In this way you shall expiate your broken oaths. Therefore be true to that which you have sworn. Thus God makes plain to you His revelations, so that you may give thanks.

Believers, wine and games of chance, idols and divining 5:90 arrows, are abominations devised by Satan. Avoid them, so that you may prosper. Satan seeks to stir up enmity and hatred among you by means of wine and gambling, and to keep you from the remembrance of God and from your prayers. Will you not abstain from them?

Obey God, and obey the Apostle. Beware; if you pay no heed, know that Our apostle's duty is only to give clear warning.

In regard to any food they may have eaten, no blame shall be attached to those that have embraced the Faith and done good works so long as they fear God and believe in Him and do good works; so long as they fear God and believe in Him; so long as they fear God and do good works. God loves the charitable.

Believers, God will put you to the proof by means of the game which you can catch with your hands or with your spears, so that He may know those who fear Him in their hearts. He that transgresses hereafter shall be sternly punished.

Believers, kill no game while on pilgrimage. He that kills 5:95 game by design shall present, as an offering to the Ka'bah, an animal equivalent to the one he killed, to be determined by two just men among you; or he shall, in expiation, either feed the poor or fast, so that he may taste the evil consequences of his deed. God has forgiven what is past; but if anyone relapses into wrongdoing God will avenge Himself on him: God is mighty and capable of revenge.

5:96    Lawful for you is what you catch from the sea and the sustenance it provides; a wholesome food, for you and for the seafarer. But you are forbidden the game of the land while you are on pilgrimage. Have fear of God, before whom you shall all be assembled.

God has made the Ka'bah, the Sacred House, the sacred month, and the sacrificial offerings with their ornaments, eternal values for mankind; so that you may know God has knowledge of all that the heavens and the earth contain; that God has knowledge of all things.

Know that God is stern in retribution, and that God is forgiving and merciful.

The Apostle's duty is but to give warning. God knows all that you conceal and all that you reveal.

Say: 'Good and evil are not alike, even though the abundance of evil may tempt you. Have fear of God, you men of understanding, so that you may triumph.'

5:101    Believers, do not ask questions about things which, if made known to you, would only pain you; but if you ask them when the Koran is being revealed, they shall be made plain to you. God will pardon you for this; God is forgiving and gracious. Other men inquired about them before you, only to disbelieve them afterwards.

God demands neither a *bahirah*, nor a *sa'ibah*, nor a *wasilah*, nor a *hami*.[1] The unbelievers invent falsehoods about God. Most of them are lacking in judgement.

When they are told: 'Come to that which God has revealed, and to the Apostle,' they reply: 'Sufficient for us is the faith we inherited from our fathers,' even though their fathers knew nothing and were not rightly guided.

5:105    Believers, you are accountable for none but yourselves; he that strays cannot harm you if you are on the right

---

1. Names given by pagan Arabs to sacrificial animals offered at the Ka'bah.

path. To God shall you all return, and He will declare to you what you have done.

Believers, when death approaches you, let two just men 5:106 from among you act as witnesses when you make your testament; or two men from another tribe if the calamity of death overtakes you while you are travelling the land. Detain them after prayers, and if you doubt their honesty, let them swear by God: 'We will not sell our testimony for any price even to a kinsman. We will not hide the testimony of God; for we should then be evil-doers.' If both prove dishonest, replace them by another pair from among those immediately concerned, and let them both swear by God, saying: 'Our testimony is truer than theirs. We have told no lies, for we should then be wrongdoers.' Thus will they be more likely to bear true witness or to fear that the oaths of others may contradict theirs. Have fear of God and be obedient. God does not guide the evil-doers.

One day God will gather all the apostles and ask them: 'How were you received?' They will reply: 'We have no knowledge. You alone know what is hidden.' God will say: 5:110 'Jesus son of Mary, remember the favour I bestowed on you and on your mother: how I strengthened you with the Holy Spirit, so that you preached to people in your cradle and in the prime of manhood; how I instructed you in the Book and in wisdom, in the Torah and in the Gospel; how by My leave you fashioned from clay the likeness of a bird and breathed into it so that, by My leave, it became a living bird; how, by My leave, you healed the blind man and the leper, and by My leave restored the dead to life; how I protected you from the Israelites when you had come to them with clear signs: when those of them who disbelieved declared: "This is but plain sorcery"; how, when I enjoined the disciples to believe in Me and in My apostle, they replied: "We believe; bear witness that we submit."'

'Jesus son of Mary,' said the disciples, 'can your Lord send down to us from heaven a table spread with food?'

He replied: 'Have fear of God, if you are true believers.'

'We wish to eat of it,' they said, 'so that we may reassure 5:113

our hearts and know that what you said to us is true, and that we may be witnesses of it.'

5:114 'Lord,' said Jesus son of Mary, 'send down to us from heaven a table spread with food, that it may mark a feast for the first of us and the last of us: a sign from You. Give us our sustenance; You are the best provider.'

God replied: 'I am sending one to you. But whoever of you disbelieves hereafter shall be punished as no man will ever be punished.'

Then God will say: 'Jesus son of Mary, did you ever say to the people: "Worship me and my mother as gods besides God?"'

'Glory be to You,' he will answer, 'I could never have claimed what I have no right to. If I had ever said so, You would have surely known it. You know what is in my mind, but I know not what is in Yours. You alone know what is hidden. I told them only what You bade me. I said: "Serve God, my Lord and your Lord." I watched over 5:117 them while living in their midst, and ever since You took me to Yourself, You have been watching them. You are the witness of all things. If You punish them, they surely are Your servants; and if You forgive them, surely You are mighty and wise.'

God will say: 'This is the day when their truthfulness will benefit the truthful. They shall for ever dwell in gardens watered by running streams. God is pleased with them, and they are pleased with Him. That is the supreme triumph.'

God has sovereignty over the heavens and the earth and 5:120 all that they contain. He has power over all things.

# CATTLE

*In the Name of God, the Compassionate, the Merciful*

PRAISE BE to God, who has created the heavens and the 6:1 earth and ordained darkness and light. Yet the unbelievers set up other gods as equals with their Lord.

It was He who created you from clay. Then He decreed a

term for you in this world and another specified by Him. Yet you are still in doubt.

He is God in the heavens and on earth. He has knowledge 6:3 of all that you conceal and all that you reveal. He knows what you do.

Yet every time a revelation comes to them from their Lord, they pay no need to it. Thus do they deny the truth when it is declared to them: but they shall learn the consequences of their scorn.

Can they not see how many generations We have destroyed before them? We had made them more powerful in the land than yourselves,[1] sent down for them abundant water from the sky and gave them rivers that rolled at their feet. Yet because they sinned We destroyed them all and raised up other generations after them.

If We sent down to you a Book inscribed on real parchment and they touched it with their own hands, the unbelievers would still assert: 'This is but plain sorcery.'

They ask: 'Why has no angel been sent down to him?' If 6:8 We had sent down an angel, their fate would have been sealed and they would have never been reprieved. If We had made him an angel, We would have given him the semblance of a man, and would have thus added to their confusion.

Other apostles have been laughed to scorn before you. But those that scoffed at them were felled by the very scourge they had derided.

Say: 'Roam the earth and see what was the fate of those that disbelieved.'

Say: 'To whom belongs all that the heavens and the earth contain?' Say: 'To God. He has decreed mercy for Himself, and will gather you all on the Day of Resurrection: a day not to be doubted. Those who have forfeited their souls will never have faith.'

His is whatever takes its rest in the night or in the day. He hears all and knows all. Say: 'Should I take any but God 6:14

1. The Meccans.

for my Defender? Creator of the heavens and the earth, He gives nourishment to all and is nourished by none.'

Say: 'I was commanded to be the first to submit. You shall serve no other god besides Him.'

6:15 Say: 'I will never disobey my Lord, for I fear the torment of a fateful day.'

He who is spared that day shall have received His mercy. That is the glorious triumph.

If God afflicts you with an evil, none can remove it but He; and if He blesses you with good fortune, know that He has power over all things.

He reigns supreme over His servants. He alone is wise and all-knowing.

Say: 'What counts most in testimony?'

Say: 'God is my witness and your witness. This Koran has been revealed to me that I may thereby warn you and all whom it may reach. Will you really testify there are other gods besides God?'

Say: 'I will testify to no such thing!'

Say: 'He is but one God. I disown the gods you serve besides Him.'

6:20 Those to whom We have given the Scriptures[1] know him as they know their own children. But those who have forfeited their souls will never have faith.

Who is more wicked than the man who invents a falsehood about God or denies His revelations? The wrong-doers shall never prosper.

On the day We gather them all together We shall say to the pagans: 'Where are your idols now, those whom you claimed to be your gods?' They will have no case to argue, but will only say: 'By God, our Lord, we have never worshipped idols.'

You shall see how they will deceive themselves and how the deities of their own invention will forsake them.

6:25 Some of them listen to you. But We have cast veils over their hearts and made them hard of hearing lest they

---

1. Christians and Jews.

understand your words. They will believe in none of Our signs, even if they see them, one and all.

When they come to argue with you the unbelievers say: 'This is nothing but fables of the ancients.' They forbid it and distance themselves from it. They ruin none but themselves, though they do not perceive it. 6:26

If you could see them when they are set before the Fire! They will say: 'Would that we could return! Then we would not deny the revelations of our Lord and would be true believers.' Indeed, that which they concealed before will manifest itself to them.

But if they were sent back, they would return to that which they have been forbidden. They are surely lying.

They declare: 'There is no other life but this; nor shall we ever be raised to life again.'

If you could see them when they are set before their Lord! He will say: 'Is this not real?' 'Yes, by our Lord,' they will reply, and He will say: 'Taste then Our scourge, the reward of your unbelief!'

Lost indeed are those who deny they will ever meet God. When the Hour of Doom overtakes them unawares, they will exclaim: 'Alas, we have neglected much in our lifetime!' And they shall bear their burdens on their backs. Evil are the burdens they shall bear. 6:31

The life of this world is but a sport and a diversion. Surely better is the life to come for those that fear God. Will you not understand?

We know too well that what they say grieves you. It is not you that they are disbelieving; the evil-doers deny God's own revelations. Other apostles have been denied before you. But they patiently bore with disbelief and persecution until Our help came down to them: for none can change the decrees of God. You have already heard of those apostles.

If you find their aversion hard to bear, seek if you can a chasm in the earth or a ladder to the sky by which you may bring them a sign. Had God pleased He would have given them guidance, one and all. Do not be foolish, then. 6:35

6:36 Those that can hear will surely answer. As for the dead, God will bring them back to life. Then to Him shall they return.

They ask: 'Why was no sign sent down to him from his Lord?'

Say: 'God is well able to send down a sign.' But most of them are ignorant men.

All the beasts that roam the earth and all the birds that soar on high are but communities like your own. We have left out nothing in the Book. Before their Lord they shall be gathered all.

Deaf and dumb are those that deny Our revelations: they blunder about in darkness. God confounds whom He will, and guides to the right path whom He pleases.

Say: 'Do but consider. When God's scourge smites you and the Hour of Doom suddenly overtakes you, will you call on any but God to help you? Answer me, if you are truthful! No, on Him alone you will call; and, if He please, He will relieve your affliction. Then you will forget your idols.'

6:42 We sent forth apostles before you to other nations, and afflicted them with calamities and misfortunes so that they might humble themselves. If only they humbled themselves when Our scourge overtook them! But their hearts hardened, and Satan made their deeds seem fair to them.

And when they had clean forgotten Our admonition We granted them all that they desired; but just as they were rejoicing in what they were given, We suddenly smote them and they were plunged into utter despair. Thus were the evildoers annihilated. Praise be to God, Lord of the Universe!

Say: 'Do but consider: if God took away your hearing and your sight and set a seal upon your hearts, could any but God restore them to you?'

See how We make plain to them Our revelations. And yet they turn away.

Say: 'Do but consider: if the scourge of God overtook you unawares or predictably, would any perish but the transgressors?'

6:48 We send forth apostles only to proclaim good news

and to give warning. Those that believe in them and mend their ways shall have nothing to fear or to regret. But those that deny Our revelations shall be punished for their 6:49 misdeeds.

Say: 'I do not tell you that I possess God's treasures or know what is hidden, nor do I claim to be an angel. I follow only that which is revealed to me.'

Say: 'Are the blind and the seeing equal? Can you not think?'

Warn those who dread to be assembled before their Lord that they have no guardian or intercessor besides Him, so that they may guard themselves against evil. Do not drive away those that call on their Lord morning and evening, seeking only to gain His favour. You are in no way accountable for them, nor are they in any way accountable for you. If you dismiss them, you shall yourself become an evil-doer.

Thus have We made some among them a means for testing others, so that they should say: 'Are these the men whom God favours among us?' But does not God best know the thankful?

When those that believe in Our revelations come to you, 6:54 say: 'Peace be upon you. Your Lord has decreed mercy for Himself. If any one among you commits evil through ignorance and then repents and mends his ways, he will find God forgiving and merciful.'

Thus do We make plain Our revelations, so that the path of the wicked may be laid bare.

Say: 'I am forbidden to serve the gods whom you invoke besides God.'

Say: 'I will not yield to your wishes, for then I would have strayed and ceased to be on the right path.'

Say: 'I have received veritable proofs from my Lord, yet you deny Him. I have no power to hasten that which you challenge; judgement is for God only. He declares the truth and is the best of arbiters.'

Say: 'Had I the power to hasten that which you challenge, 6:58 our dispute would be ended. But God best knows the evil-

6:59 doers. He has the keys of all that is hidden: none knows them but He. He has knowledge of all that land and sea contain: every leaf that falls is known to Him. There is no grain in the darkest bowels of the earth, nor anything green or sear, but is recorded in a glorious Book.

'It is He that claims you back by night, knowing what you have done by day, and then rouses you up to fulfil your allotted span of life. Then to Him shall you return, and He will then declare to you all that you have done.

'He reigns supreme over His servants. He sends forth guardians who watch over you and claim your souls without fail when death overtakes you. Then are all men restored to God, their true Lord. His is the Judgement, and most swift is His reckoning.'

Say: 'Who delivers you from the perils of land and sea, when you call out to Him humbly and in secret, saying: "Save us, and we will be truly thankful!"?'

Say: 'God delivers you from them, and from all afflictions. Yet you worship idols.'

6:65 Say: 'He has power to let loose His scourge upon you from above your heads and from beneath your feet, and to divide you into discordant factions, causing the one to suffer at the hands of the other.'

See how We make plain Our revelations, that they may understand them.

Your people have rejected this[1] although it is the very truth. Say: 'I am not your keeper. The time will come when every prophecy shall be fulfilled, and you shall learn.'

When you see those that scoff at Our revelations, withdraw from them till they engage in other talk. Should Satan cause you to forget this, take leave of the wrongdoers as soon as you remember. Those that fear God are in no way accountable for them. We remind them only so that they may guard themselves against evil.

6:70 Avoid those that treat their faith as a sport and a diversion and are seduced by the life of this world. Admonish them

1. The Koran.

with this lest their souls be damned by their own sins. They have no guardian or intercessor besides God: and though they offer every ransom, it shall not be accepted from them. Such are those that are damned by their own sins. Scalding water shall they drink and be sternly punished for their unbelief.

Say: 'Are we to call on idols which can neither help nor 6:71 harm us? Are we to turn upon our heels after God has guided us, like him who, being bewitched by devils in the land, blunders along perplexed, although his friends call him to the right path, shouting: "Come this way!"?'

Say: 'God's guidance is the only guidance. We are commanded to submit to the Lord of the Universe, to pray, and to fear Him. Before Him shall you be gathered all.'

It was He who created the heavens and the earth in all truth. On the day when He says: 'Be,' it shall be. His word is the truth. All sovereignty shall be His on the day when the trumpet is sounded. He has knowledge of the unknown and the manifest. He alone is wise and all-knowing.

Tell of Abraham, who said to Azar, his father: 'Will you worship idols as your gods? Surely you and all your people are in palpable error.'

Thus did We show Abraham the kingdom of the heavens 6:75 and the earth, so that he might become a firm believer.

When night drew its shadow over him, he saw a star. 'That,' he said, 'is surely my God.'

But when it faded in the morning light, he said: 'I will not worship gods that fade.'

When he beheld the rising moon, he said: 'That is my God.' But when it set, he said: 'If my Lord does not guide me, I shall surely go astray.'

Then, when he beheld the sun shining, he said: 'That must be my God: it is the largest.'

But when it set, he said to his people: 'I disown your idols. I will turn my face to Him who has created the 6:79 heavens and the earth, and will live a righteous life. I am no idolater.'

6:80　His people argued with him. He said: 'Will you argue with me about God, who has given me guidance? I do not fear your idols, unless my Lord so willed. My Lord has knowledge of all things. Will you not be warned? And how should I fear your idols when you yourselves are not afraid of serving idols not sanctioned by God? Which of us is more deserving of salvation? Tell me, if you know the truth. Those that have faith and do not taint their faith with wrongdoing shall surely earn salvation, while they follow the right path.'

Such was the argument with which We furnished Abraham against his people. We raise whom We will to an exalted rank. Your Lord is wise and all-knowing.

We gave him Isaac and Jacob and guided both as We had guided Noah before them. Among his descendants were David and Solomon, Job and Joseph and Moses and Aaron (thus do we reward the righteous); Zacharias and John, Jesus and Elias (all were upright men); and Ishmael, Elisha, Jonah and Lot. All these We exalted above the nations as We exalted some of their fathers, their children, and their brothers. We chose them and guided them to a straight path.

6:88　Such is God's guidance; He bestows it on those of His servants whom He chooses. Had they served other gods besides Him, their labours would have been vain indeed.

On those men We bestowed the Scriptures, wisdom, and prophethood. If these are denied by this generation, We will entrust them to others who will not deny them.

Those were the men whom God guided. Follow then their guidance and say: 'I demand of you no recompense for this. It is but an admonition to all mankind.'

6:91　They have no true notion of God's glory, those that say: 'God has never revealed anything to a mortal.'

Say: 'Who, then, revealed the Scriptures which Moses brought down, a light and a guide for mankind? You have transcribed them on scraps of paper, declaring some and suppressing much, though now you have been taught what neither you nor your fathers knew before.'

Say: 'God!' Then leave them to amuse themselves with foolish chatter.

This is a blessed Book which We have revealed, confirm- 6:92 ing what came before it, that you may warn the mother city[1] and those that dwell around her. Those who believe in the life to come will believe in it and be steadfast in their prayers.

Who is more wicked than the man who invents a falsehood about God, or says: 'This was revealed to me,' when nothing was revealed to him? Or the man who says: 'I can reveal the like of what God has revealed'?

Could you but see the wrongdoers when death over-whelms them! With hands outstretched, the angels will say: 'Yield up your souls. You shall be rewarded with the scourge of shame this day, for you have said of God what is untrue and scorned His revelations. And now you have returned to Us, alone as We created you at first, leaving behind all that We bestowed on you. Nor do We see with you your intercessors, those whom you claimed to be God's equals. Broken are the ties which bound you, and that which you presumed has failed you.'

It is God who splits the seed and the fruit-stone. He 6:95 brings forth the living from the dead, and the dead from the living. Such is God. How then can you turn away?

He kindles the light of dawn. He has ordained the night for rest and the sun and the moon for reckoning. Such is the ordinance of the Mighty One, the All-knowing.

It is He that has created for you the stars, so that they may guide you in the darkness of land and sea. We have made plain Our revelations to men of knowledge.

It was He that created you from a single being and furnished you with a dwelling and a resting-place. We have made plain Our revelations to men of understanding.

It is He who sends down water from the sky with which 6:99 We bring forth the buds of every plant. From these We bring forth green foliage and close-growing grain, palm-trees

---

1. Mecca.

laden with clusters of dates, vineyards and olive groves, and pomegranates alike and different. Behold their fruits when they ripen. Surely in these there are signs for true believers.

6:100 Yet they regard the jinn as God's equals, though He Himself created them, and in their ignorance ascribe to Him sons and daughters. Glory be to Him! Exalted be He above their imputations!

Creator of the heavens and the earth. How should He have a son when He had no consort? He created all things, and He has knowledge of all things.

Such is God, your Lord. There is no god but Him, the Creator of all things. Therefore serve Him. Of all things He is the Guardian.

No mortal eyes can see Him, though He sees all eyes. He is benign and all-knowing.

Momentous portents have come to you from your Lord. He that sees them shall himself have much to gain, but he who is blind to them shall lose much indeed. I[1] am not your keeper.

6:105 Thus do We make plain Our revelations, that they may say: 'You[1] have studied deep,' and that this may become clear to men of knowledge. Therefore follow what has been revealed to you from your Lord. There is no god but Him. Avoid the pagans. Had God pleased, they would not have worshipped idols. We have not made you their keeper, nor are you their guardian.

Do not revile[2] the idols which they invoke besides God, lest in their ignorance they revile God with rancour. Thus have We made the actions of each community seem pleasing to itself. To their Lord shall they return, and He will declare to them what they have done.

6:109 They solemnly swear by God that if a sign be given them they would believe in it. Say: 'Signs are only vouchsafed by God.' And how can you tell that if a sign be given them they will indeed believe in it?

1. Muḥammad.    2. These words are addressed to the believers.

We will turn away their hearts and eyes from the Truth  6:110
since they refused to believe in it at first. We will let them
blunder about in their wrongdoing.

If We sent the angels down to them, and caused the dead
to speak with them, and ranged all things in front of them,
they would still not believe, unless God willed otherwise.
But most of them are ignorant men.

Thus have We assigned for every prophet an enemy: the
devils among men and jinn, who inspire each other with
vain and varnished falsehoods. But had your Lord pleased,
they would not have done so. Therefore leave them to their
own inventions, so that the hearts of those who have no
faith in the life to come may be inclined to what they say
and, being pleased, persist in their sinful ways.

Should I[1] seek a judge other than God when it is He who
has revealed the Book for you with all its precepts? Those
to whom We gave the Scriptures know that it is the truth
revealed by your Lord. Therefore have no doubts.

Perfected are the words of your Lord in truth and justice.
None can change His words. He hears all and knows all.

If you obeyed the greater part of those on earth, they  6:116
would lead you away from God's path. They follow
nothing but idle fancies and preach nothing but falsehoods.
Surely your Lord is best aware of those who stray from His
path, as He best knows the rightly guided.

Eat only of that which has been consecrated in the name
of God, if you truly believe in His revelations. And why
should you not eat of that which has been consecrated in
God's name when He has made plain to you what He
forbade you, except when you are constrained?

Many are those that are misled through ignorance by
their desires: surely your Lord best knows the transgressors.

Sin neither openly nor in secret. Those that commit sin
shall be punished for their sins.

Therefore do not eat of that which has not been con-  6:121
secrated in the name of God; for that is sinful.

1. Muḥammad.

103

The devils will teach their votaries to argue with you. If you obey them, you shall yourselves become idolaters.

6:122 Can the dead man whom We have raised to life, and given a light to walk with among people, be compared to him who is in darkness from which he will never emerge? Thus do their deeds seem fair to the unbelievers.

We have placed in every city arch-transgressors who scheme within its walls. But they scheme only against themselves, though they may not perceive it. When a sign is revealed to them they say: 'We will not believe in it unless we are given that which God's apostles have been given.' But God knows best whom to entrust with His message.

God will humiliate the transgressors and mete out to them grievous punishment for their scheming.

If God intends to guide a man, He opens his bosom to Islām. But if He pleases to confound him, He makes his bosom small and narrow as though he were climbing up to the sky. Thus shall God lay the scourge on the unbelievers.

Such is the path of your Lord: a straight path. We have made plain Our revelations to thinking men. They shall dwell in peace with their Lord. He will give them His protection as recompense for what they do.

6:128 On the day He assembles them all together, He will say: 'Jinn, you have seduced mankind in great numbers.' And their votaries among mankind will say: 'Lord, we have enjoyed each other's fellowship. But now we have reached the end of the appointed term which You decreed for us.'

He will say: 'The Fire shall be your home, and there shall you remain for ever unless God ordain otherwise.' Your Lord is wise and all-knowing.

Thus do We give the wicked sway over each other as punishment for their misdeeds.

6:130 Then He will say: 'Jinn and men! Did there not come to you apostles of your own who proclaimed to you My revelations and warned you of this day?'

They will reply: 'We bear witness against our own souls.' Indeed, the life of this world has seduced them. They will testify against themselves that they were unbelievers.

Nor would your Lord destroy the nations without just 6:131
cause and due warning. They shall be rewarded according
to their deeds. Your Lord is never heedless of what they do.

Your Lord is the Self-sufficient One, the Merciful. He
can destroy you if He wills and replace you with whom He
pleases, just as He raised you from the offspring of other
nations.

That which you are promised is sure to come. Escape it
you shall not.

Say: 'Do all that is in your power, my people, and I will do
what is in mine. You shall learn who is to gain the recompense of the Hereafter. The wrongdoers shall not triumph.'

They set aside for God a share of their produce and of
their cattle, saying: 'This is for God' – so they pretend –
'and this for our idols.' Their idols' share does not reach
God, but the share of God is wholly given to their idols.
How ill they judge!

Their idols have induced many pagans to kill their 6:137
children, seeking to ruin them and to confuse them in their
faith. Had God pleased they would not have done so.
Therefore leave them to their false inventions.

They say: 'These animals and these crops are forbidden.
None may eat of them save those whom we permit.' So they
assert. And there are other beasts which they prohibit men
from riding, and others over which they do not pronounce
the name of God, thus committing a sin against Him. He
will punish them for their invented lies.

They also say: 'The offspring of these animals is lawful
for our males but forbidden to our females.' But if it is still-
born, they all partake of it! God will punish them for that
which they impute to Him. He is wise and all-knowing.

Losers are those that in their ignorance have wantonly
slain their own children and made unlawful what God has
given them, inventing falsehoods about God. They have
gone astray and are not guided.

It is He who brings gardens into being: creepers and 6:141
upright trees, the palm and all manner of crops, olives, and
pomegranates alike and different. Eat of these fruits when

they ripen and give away what is due of them upon the harvest day. But you shall not be prodigal; He does not love the prodigal.

6:142 Of the beasts you have, some are for carrying burdens and others for slaughter. Eat of that which God has given you and do not walk in Satan's footsteps; he is your inveterate foe.

He has given you eight kinds of livestock. Take first a pair of sheep and a pair of goats. Say: 'Of these, has He forbidden you the males, the females, or their offspring? Answer me, if you are men of truth.' Then a pair of camels and a pair of cattle. Say: 'Of these, has He forbidden you the males, the females, or their offspring? Were you present when God gave you these commandments?'

Who is more wicked than the man who in his ignorance invents a lie about God to mislead mankind? God does not guide the wrongdoers.

Say: 'I find nothing in what has been revealed to me that for-
6:145 bids people to eat of any food except carrion, running blood, and the flesh of swine – for these are unclean – and any flesh that has been profanely consecrated to gods other than God. But whoever is driven by necessity, intending neither to sin nor to transgress, will find your Lord forgiving and merciful.'

We forbade the Jews all animals with undivided hoofs and the fat of sheep and oxen, except what is on their backs and intestines and what is mixed with their bones. Such is the penance We imposed on them for their misdeeds. What We declare is true. If they disbelieve in you, say: 'All-encompassing is the mercy of your Lord: but His punishment cannot be warded off from sinful men.'

6:148 The idolaters will say: 'Had God pleased, neither we nor our fathers would have served other gods besides Him; nor would we have declared anything unlawful.' In like manner did those who have gone before them deny the Truth until they felt Our scourge.

Say: 'Have you any evidence you can put before us? You believe in nothing but conjecture and follow nothing but falsehoods.'

Say: 'God alone has the conclusive proof. Had He so 6:149
pleased He would have guided you all.'

Say: 'Bring me those witnesses of yours who can testify
that God has forbidden this.' If they so testify, do not testify
with them, nor yield to the wishes of those that deny Our
revelations, disbelieve in the life to come, and set up other
gods as equals with their Lord.

Say: 'Come, I will tell you what your Lord has made
binding on you: that you shall serve no other gods besides
Him; that you shall show kindness to your parents; that you
shall not kill your children because you cannot support
them (We provide for you and for them); that you shall not
commit lewd acts, whether openly or in secret; and that you
shall not kill – for that is forbidden by God – except for a
just cause. Thus God exhorts you, that you may grow in
wisdom.'

Do not tamper with the property of orphans, but strive
to improve their lot until they reach maturity. Give just
weight and full measure; We never charge a soul with more
than it can bear. Speak for justice, even if it affects your
own kinsmen. Be true to the covenant of God. Thus He
exhorts you, so that you may take heed.

This path of Mine is straight. Follow it and do not follow 6:153
other paths, for they will lead you away from Him. He thus
exhorts you, so that you may guard yourselves against evil.

To Moses We gave the Scriptures, a perfect code for the
righteous with precepts about all things, a guide and a
benison, so that they might believe in meeting their Lord.
And now We have revealed this Book truly blessed.
Observe it and keep from evil, so that you may find mercy
and not say: 'The Scriptures were revealed only to two
communities[1] before us; we have no knowledge of what
they read'; or: 'Had the Scriptures been revealed to us we 6:157
would have been better guided than they.'

A veritable sign has now come to you from your Lord, a
guide and a benison. And who is more wicked than the man

---

1. Jews and Christians.

who denies the revelations of God and turns away from them? Those that turn away from Our revelations shall be sternly punished for their indifference.

6:158 Are they waiting for the angels or your Lord to come down to them, or for a sign from your Lord to be given them? On the day when a sign from your Lord is given them, faith shall not avail the soul that had no faith before or did not put its faith to good uses.

Say: 'Wait if you will; we too are waiting.'

Have nothing to do with those who have split up their religion into sects. God will call them to account and declare to them what they have done.

He that does a good deed shall be repaid tenfold; but he that does evil shall be rewarded only with evil. None shall be wronged.

Say: 'My Lord has guided me to a straight path, to an upright religion, to the faith of saintly Abraham, who was no idolater.'

Say: 'My prayers and my devotions, my life and my death, are all for God, Lord of the Universe: He has no peer. Thus am I commanded, being the first of the Muslims.'

Say: 'Should I seek any but God for my Lord, when He is the Lord of all things? Each man shall reap the fruits of his own deeds: no soul shall bear another's burden. In the end to your Lord shall you return, and He will resolve your disputes for you.'

6:165 He has given you the earth for your heritage and exalted some of you in rank above others, so that He might prove you with His gifts. Swift is your Lord in retribution; yet is He forgiving and merciful.

# THE HEIGHTS

*In the Name of God, the Compassionate, the Merciful*

7:1 ALIF *lām mīm ṣād*. This Book has been revealed to you – let not your heart be troubled about it – so that you may thereby give warning and admonish the faithful.

Observe that which is brought down to you[1] from your 7:3
Lord and follow no other masters besides Him. But you
seldom take warning.

How many cities have We destroyed! In the night Our
scourge fell upon them, or at midday, when they were
drowsing.

And when Our scourge fell upon them, their only cry
was: 'We have indeed been wicked men.'

We will surely question those to whom the messengers
were sent, and We will question the messengers themselves.
With knowledge We will recount to them what they have
done, for We were never away from them.

On that day all shall be weighed with justice. Those
whose good deeds weigh heavy in the scales shall triumph,
but those whose deeds are light shall lose their souls,
because they have denied Our revelations.

We have given you power in the land and provided you
with a livelihood: yet you are seldom thankful.

We created you and gave you form. Then We said to the 7:11
angels: 'Prostrate yourselves before Adam.' They all prostrated themselves except Satan, who refused to prostrate
himself.

'Why did you not prostrate yourself when I commanded
you?' He asked.

'I am nobler than he,' he replied. 'You created me from
fire, but You created him from clay.'

He said: 'Get you down hence! This is no place for your
contemptuous pride. Away with you! Humble shall you
henceforth be.'

He replied: 'Reprieve me till the Day of Resurrection.'

'You are reprieved,' said He.

'Because You have led me into sin,' he declared, 'I will
waylay Your servants as they walk on Your straight path,
then spring upon them from the front and from the rear, 7:17
from their right and from their left. Then You will find the
greater part of them ungrateful.'

---

1. The Meccans.

7:18 'Begone!' He said. 'A despicable outcast you shall hence-forth be. As for those that follow you, I shall fill Hell with you all.'

To Adam He said: 'Dwell with your wife in Paradise, and eat of any fruit you please; but never approach this tree or you shall both become transgressors.'

But Satan tempted them, so that he might reveal to them their shameful parts, which they had never seen before. He said: 'Your Lord has forbidden you to approach this tree only to prevent you from becoming angels or immortals.' Then he swore to them that he would give them friendly counsel.

Thus did he cunningly seduce them. And when they had eaten of the tree, their shame became visible to them, and they both covered themselves with the leaves of the garden.

Their Lord called out to them, saying: 'Did I not forbid you to approach that tree, and did I not say to you that Satan was your inveterate foe?'

They replied: 'Lord, we have wronged our souls. Pardon us and have mercy on us, or we shall surely be among the lost.'

7:24 He said: 'Get you down hence, and may your descendants be enemies to each other. The earth will for a while provide your dwelling and your comforts. There you shall live and there shall you die, and thence shall you be raised to life.'

Children of Adam! We have given you clothes to cover your shameful parts, and garments pleasing to the eye; but the finest of all these is the robe of piety.

That is one of God's revelations. Perchance they will take heed.

Children of Adam! Let not Satan tempt you, as he seduced your parents out of Paradise. He stripped them of their garments to reveal to them their shameful parts. He and his minions see you whence you cannot see them. We have made the devils guardians over the unbelievers.

7:28 When they commit a lewd act, they say: 'This is what our fathers used to do. God enjoined it.'

Say: 'God does not enjoin lewdness. Would you tell of God what you know not?'

Say: 'My Lord has ordered you to act justly. Turn to Him 7:29
wherever you kneel in prayer and call on Him with true
devotion. Even as He created you, so shall you return.'

Some He has guided and some He has justly left in error;
for they chose the devils for their protectors instead of God
and deemed themselves on the right path.

Children of Adam, dress well when you attend your
mosques. Eat and drink, but avoid excess. He does not love
the intemperate.

Say: 'Who has forbidden you to wear the decent clothes or to
eat the good things which God has provided for His servants?'

Say: 'These are for the enjoyment of the faithful in the life
of this world [though shared by others]; but they shall be
theirs alone on the Day of Resurrection.'

Thus do We make plain Our revelations to men of
knowledge.

Say: 'My Lord has forbidden all lewd acts, whether overt
or disguised, sin, and wrongful oppression; He has forbidden you to worship what He did not sanction, or to tell of
God what you know not.'

A space of time is fixed for every nation; when their hour 7:34
is come, not for one moment shall they hold it back, nor can
they go before it.

Children of Adam, when apostles of your own come to
proclaim to you My revelations, those that take warning
and mend their ways will have nothing to fear or to regret;
but those that deny and scorn Our revelations shall be the
heirs of the Fire, wherein they shall remain for ever.

Who is more wicked than the man who invents a
falsehood about God or denies His revelations? Such men
shall have their destined share, and when Our angels come
to claim back their souls they shall say: 'Where are your
idols now, those whom you invoked besides God?' 'They
have forsaken us,' they will answer, and will confess that
they were unbelievers.

He will say: 'Enter the Fire and join the communities of 7:38
jinn and men that have gone before you.'

As it enters, every community will curse the one that went

before it, and when all are gathered there, the last of them will say of the first: 'These, Lord, have led us astray. Let their punishment be doubled in the Fire.'

He will answer: 'All shall be doubly punished, although you may not know it.'

7:39 Then the first will say to the last: 'You were no better than we. Taste the penalty of your misdeeds.'

For those that have denied and scorned Our revelations the gates of heaven shall not be opened; nor shall they enter Paradise until the camel shall pass through the eye of a needle. Thus shall We reward the guilty.

Hell shall be their couch, and sheets of fire shall cover them. Thus shall We reward the evil-doers.

As for those that have faith and do good works – We never charge a soul with more than it can bear – they are the heirs of Paradise, and there they shall abide for ever.

We shall take away all hatred from their hearts. Rivers will roll at their feet and they shall say: 'Praise be to God who has guided us hither. Had He not given us guidance we would have strayed from the right path. Our Lord's apostles have surely preached the truth.' And a voice will cry out to them, saying: 'This is the Paradise which you have earned with your labours.'

7:44 Then the heirs of Paradise will cry out to the inmates of the Fire: 'What our Lord promised we have found to be true. Have you, too, found the promise of your Lord to be true?'

'Yes,' they will answer, and a herald will cry out among them: 'Cursed are the evil-doers who have debarred others from the path of God and sought to make it crooked, and who had no faith in the life to come.'

A barrier will divide them, and on the Heights there will be men who recognize each one by his look. To those in Paradise they shall say: 'Peace be upon you!' But they shall not yet enter, though they long to be there.

And when they turn their eyes towards the inmates of the Fire they will cry: 'Lord, do not cast us among these wicked 7:48 people!' Then, those on the Heights will say to men they recognize by their looks: 'Nothing have your riches or your

scornful pride availed you. Are these the men who you 7:49
swore would never earn God's mercy?'

[And again turning to the blessed they will say:] 'Come in
to Paradise. You have nothing to fear or to regret.'

The damned will cry out to the blessed: 'Give us some
water, or some of that which God has given you.' But the
blessed will reply: 'God has forbidden both to the unbelievers, who made their religion a diversion and an idle
sport, and who were seduced by their earthly life.'

On that day We will forget them as they forgot they
would ever meet that day: for they denied Our revelations.

We have bestowed on them a Book which We imbued
with knowledge, a guide and a blessing to true believers.
Are they waiting but for its fulfilment? On the day it is
fulfilled, those that have forgotten it will say: 'Our Lord's
apostles have surely preached the truth before. Will no one
plead on our behalf? Could we but live our lives again, we
would not do as we have done.' They shall forfeit their
souls, and that which they devised will fail them.

Your Lord is God, who created the heavens and the earth 7:54
in six days and then ascended the throne. He throws the
veil of night over the day. Swiftly they follow one another.
And the sun and the moon and the stars – all subservient to
His will. His is the creation, His the command. Blessed be
God, Lord of the Universe!

Pray to your Lord with humility and in secret. He does
not love the transgressors.

Do not corrupt the earth after it has been purged of evil.
Pray to Him with fear and hope; His mercy is within reach
of the righteous.

He sends forth the winds as harbingers of His mercy, and
when they have gathered up a heavy cloud, We drive it on
to some dead land and let the water fall upon it, bringing
forth all manner of fruit. Thus will We raise the dead to life.
Perchance you will take heed.

Good soil yields fruit by God's will. But poor and scant 7:58
are the fruits which spring from barren soil. Thus do We
make plain Our revelations to those who render thanks.

7:59     Long ago, We sent forth Noah to his people. He said: 'Serve God, my people, for you have no god but Him. Beware the torment of a fateful day.'

But the elders of his people said: 'We can see that you are in palpable error.'

'I am not in error, my people,' he replied. 'I am sent forth by the Lord of the Universe to make known to you my Lord's will and to give you friendly counsel, for I know of God what you know not. Do you think it strange that an admonition should come to you from your Lord through a mortal like yourselves, and that He should warn you, so that you may keep from evil and be shown mercy?'

They denied him. So We saved him and all who were with him in the ark, and drowned those that denied Our revelations. Surely they were blind men.

And to the tribe of 'Ād We sent their kinsman Hūd. He said: 'Serve God, my people, for you have no god but Him. Will you not guard yourselves against evil?'

The unbelievers among the elders of his tribe said: 'We can see you are a foolish man, and, what is more, we think that you are lying.'

7:67     'Foolish I am not, my people,' he replied. 'I am sent forth by the Lord of the Universe to make known to you His will and to give you honest counsel. Do you think it strange that an admonition should come to you from your Lord through a mortal like yourselves and that he should warn you? Remember that He has made you the heirs of Noah's people and endowed you with greater power than He has given to other men. Remember God's favours, so that you may prosper.'

They said: 'Would you have us serve God only and renounce the gods which our fathers worshipped? Bring down the scourge you threaten us with, if what you say be true.'

7:71     He answered: 'Your Lord's punishment and wrath have already visited you. Would you dispute with me about mere names which you and your fathers have invented, and for which God has revealed no sanction? Wait if you will; I too am waiting.'

We delivered him and those who were with him through 7:72 Our mercy, and annihilated those that disbelieved Our revelations. They were unbelievers all.

And to Thamūd We sent their kinsman Ṣāliḥ. He said: 'Serve God, my people, for you have no god but Him. A veritable proof has come to you from your Lord. Here is God's she-camel: a sign for you. Leave her to graze at will in God's own land and do not molest her, lest a woeful scourge should take you. Remember, He has made you the heirs of 'Ād, and provided you with dwellings in the land. You have built mansions on its plains and hewed out houses on the mountains. Remember God's favours and do not corrupt the earth with wickedness.'

The haughty elders of his people said to the believers who were oppressed: 'Do you really believe that Ṣāliḥ is sent forth from his Lord?'

They answered: 'We believe in the message he has been sent with.'

The haughty elders said: 'We deny all that you believe in.' 7:76 They slaughtered the she-camel and defied the commandment of their Lord, saying to Ṣāliḥ: 'Bring down the scourge you threaten us with, if you truly are an apostle.'

Thereupon the earthquake felled them, and when morning came they were crouching lifeless in their dwellings. He left them, saying: 'I conveyed to you, my people, the message of my Lord and gave you good counsel; but you had no love for those who give good counsel.'

And Lot, who said to his people: 'Will you persist in these lewd acts which no other nation has committed before you? You lust after men instead of women. Truly, you are a degenerate people.'

His people's only answer was: 'Banish them from your city. They are men who would keep themselves chaste.'

We delivered him and all his kinsfolk, except his wife, who stayed behind, and let loose a shower upon them. 7:84 Consider the fate of the evil-doers.

7:85     And to Midian, their kinsman Shu'aib. He said: 'Serve God, my people, for you have no god but Him. A veritable sign has come to you from your Lord. Give just weight and measure and do not defraud others of their possessions. Do not corrupt the land after it has been purged of evil. That is best for you, if you are true believers.

'Do not squat in every highway, threatening and debarring from the path of God those who believe in Him, and seeking to make that path crooked. Remember how He multiplied you when you were few in number. Consider the fate of the evil-doers.

'If there are some among you who believe in my message and others who disbelieve it, be patient till God shall judge between us. He is the best of judges.'

The haughty elders of his tribe said: 'Return to our fold, Shu'aib, or we will banish you from our city, you and all your followers.'

'Even though we are unwilling?' he replied. 'If we returned
7:89   to the faith from which God has delivered us, we should be false to God; nor can we turn to it again except by the will of God, our Lord. Our Lord encompasses all things with His knowledge, and in God we have put our trust. Lord, judge rightly between us and our people; You are the best of judges.'

But the infidel chieftains said to their people: 'If you follow Shu'aib, you shall indeed be losers.'

Thereupon the earthquake felled them, and when morning came they were crouching lifeless in their dwellings, as if those that spurned Shu'aib had never lived there. Those that spurned Shu'aib were themselves the losers.

He left them, saying: 'I conveyed to you, my people, the messages of my Lord and gave you good counsel. How can I grieve for an unbelieving people?'

Whenever We sent a prophet to a city We afflicted its people with calamities and misfortunes so that they might
7:95   abase themselves. Then We changed adversity to good fortune, so that when they had multiplied they said: 'Our fathers also had their sorrows and their joys.' And in their heedlessness We suddenly smote them.

Had the people of those cities believed and kept from 7:96
evil, We would have showered upon them blessings from
heaven and earth. But they disbelieved, and We punished
them for their misdeeds.

Were the people of those cities secure from Our power
when it overtook them in the night while they were sleeping?

Were the people of those cities secure from Our power
when it overtook them in the morning at their play?

Did they feel themselves secure from God's cunning?
None feels secure from God's cunning except the losers.

Is it not plain to the present generation that if We
pleased, We could punish them for their sins and set a seal
upon their hearts, leaving them bereft of hearing?

We have recounted to you the history of those nations.
Their apostles came to them with veritable proofs, yet they
persisted in their unbelief. Thus God seals up the hearts of
the unbelievers.

We found the larger part of them untrue to their 7:102
commitments; indeed, We found the larger part of them
immersed in evil.

After those We sent forth Moses with Our signs to
Pharaoh and his chieftains, but they too disbelieved them.
Consider the fate of the evil-doers.

Moses said: 'Pharaoh, I am an apostle from the Lord of
the Universe, and may tell nothing of God but what is true.
I bring you a clear sign from your Lord. Let the Children of
Israel depart with me.'

He answered: 'If you have brought a sign, show it to us.'

Moses threw down his staff, and thereupon it changed to
a veritable serpent. Then he drew out his hand, and it
was white to all who saw it.

The elders of Pharaoh's people said: 'This man is a skilful
sorcerer who seeks to drive you from your land. What
would you have us do?'

Others said: 'Put them off awhile, him and his brother,
and send forth heralds to the cities to summon every 7:112
skilful sorcerer to your presence.'

7:113　　The sorcerers came to Pharaoh. They said: 'Shall we be rewarded if we win?'

'Yes,' he answered. 'And you shall become my favoured friends.'

They said: 'Moses, will you first throw, or shall we?'

'Throw,' he replied.

And when the magicians threw, they bewitched the people's eyes and terrified them by a display of mighty sorcery.

Then We signalled to Moses: 'Now throw down your staff.' And thereupon it swallowed up their false devices.[1]

Thus did the truth prevail, and all their doings proved vain. Pharaoh and his men were defeated and put to shame, and the enchanters prostrated themselves, saying: 'We believe in the Lord of the Universe, the Lord of Moses and Aaron.'

Pharaoh said: 'Do you dare believe in Him before I give you leave? This is a plot you have contrived to turn the people out of their city. But you shall learn. I will cut off your hands and feet on alternate sides and then crucify you all!'

7:125　　They replied: 'We shall surely return to our Lord. You would punish us only because we believed in the signs of our Lord when they were shown to us. Lord, give us patience and let us die in submission.'

The elders of Pharaoh's nation said: 'Will you allow Moses and his people to perpetrate corruption in the land and to forsake you and your gods?'

He replied: 'We will put their sons to death[2] and spare only their daughters. We shall yet triumph over them.'

Moses said to his people: 'Seek help in God and be patient. The earth is God's; He gives it to those of His servants whom He chooses. Happy shall be the lot of the righteous.'

7:129　　They replied: 'We were oppressed before you came to us, and oppressed we still remain.'

He said: 'Your Lord will perchance destroy your enemies and make you rulers in the land. Then He will see how you conduct yourselves.'

1. Cf. Exodus vii, 11ff.　　2. Cf. Exodus i, 22.

We afflicted Pharaoh's people with dearth and famine so  7:130
that they might take heed. When good things came their
way, they said: 'It is our due,' but when evil befell them
they ascribed it to Moses and his people. Yet it was God
who had ordained their ills, though most of them did not
know it.

They said: 'Whatever miracles you work to enchant us,
we will not believe in you.'

So We plagued them with floods and locusts, with lice
and frogs and blood: clear miracles, yet they scorned them
all, for they were a wicked nation.

And when each plague smote them, they said: 'Moses,
pray to your Lord for us: invoke the promise He has made
you. If you lift the plague from us, we will believe in you
and let the Israelites go with you.'

But when We had lifted the plague from them and the
appointed time had come, they broke their promise. So We
took vengeance on them and drowned them in the sea, for
they had denied Our signs and paid no heed to them.

We gave the persecuted people dominion over the eastern  7:137
and the western lands which We had blessed. Thus was
your Lord's gracious word fulfilled for the Israelites,
because they had endured with fortitude; and We destroyed
the edifices and the towers of Pharaoh and his people.

We led the Israelites across the sea, and they came upon a
people who worshipped idols which they had. They said to
Moses: 'Make us a god just like the gods they have.'

Moses replied: 'You are indeed an ignorant people. That
which they follow is doomed, and all their works are vain.
Am I to seek for you a deity other than God, when He has
exalted you above the nations? We delivered you from
Pharaoh's people, who had oppressed you cruelly, putting
your sons to death and sparing only your daughters. Surely
that was a great trial by your Lord.'

We promised Moses thirty nights, to which We added ten  7:142
nights more: so that the appointment with his Lord was
after forty nights.

Moses said to his brother Aaron: 'Take my place among

my people. Do what is right and do not follow the path of the wrongdoers.'

7:143　And when Moses came at the appointed time and His Lord communed with him, he said: 'Lord, reveal Yourself to me, that I may look upon You.'

He replied: 'You shall never see Me. But look upon the Mountain; if it remains firm upon its base, then only shall you see Me.'

And when his Lord revealed Himself to the Mountain, He levelled it to dust. Moses fell down senseless, and, when he recovered, said: 'Glory be to You! I turn to You in penitence, being the first of the believers.'

He replied: 'Moses, I have chosen you of all people to make known My messages and My commandments. Take therefore what I have given you, and be thankful.'

We inscribed for him upon the Tablets all manner of precepts, and instructions concerning all things, and said to him: 'Observe these steadfastly, and enjoin your people to observe what is best in them. I shall show you the home of
7:146　the wicked. I will turn away from My signs those who lord it in the land with arrogance and injustice, so that even if they witness each and every sign they shall deny them. If they see the right path, they shall not walk upon it: but if they see the path of error, they shall choose it for their path; because they disbelieved Our signs and paid no heed to them.

'Vain are the deeds of those who disbelieve in Our signs and in the life to come. Shall they not be rewarded according only to their deeds?'

In his absence the people of Moses made a calf from their ornaments, an image with a hollow sound. Did they not see that it could neither speak to them nor give them guidance? Yet they worshipped it and thus committed evil.

But when they repented and realized that they had sinned they said: 'If our Lord does not have mercy on us and pardon us, we shall surely be among the lost.'

7:150　And when Moses returned to his people, angry and sorrowful, he said: 'Evil is the thing you did in my absence! Would you hasten the retribution of your Lord?'

He threw down the Tablets and, seizing his brother by the hair, dragged him closer.

'Son of my mother,' cried Aaron, 'the people overpowered me and almost did me to death. Do not let my enemies gloat over me; do not number me among the wrongdoers.'

'Lord,' said Moses, 'forgive me and forgive my brother. 7:151 Admit us to Your mercy, for, of all those that show mercy, You are the most merciful.'

Those that worshipped the calf incurred the anger of their Lord and disgrace in this life. Thus shall We reward those who fabricate falsehoods. As for those that do evil but later repent and have faith, they shall find your Lord forgiving and merciful.

When his anger was allayed, Moses took up the Tablets, upon which was inscribed a pledge of guidance and of mercy to those that fear their Lord. He chose from among his people 7:155 seventy men[1] for Our appointment and, when the earth shook beneath their feet, said: 'Had it been Your will, Lord, You could have destroyed them long ago, and myself too. But would You destroy us because of what the fools among us did? That trial was ordained by You, to confound whom You willed and to guide whom You pleased. You alone are our guardian. Forgive us and have mercy on us: You are the noblest of those who forgive. Ordain for us what is good, both in this life and in the hereafter. To You alone we turn.'

He replied: 'I will visit My scourge upon whom I please: yet My mercy encompasses all things. I will show mercy to those that keep from evil and give alms, and to those that in Our signs believe; to those that shall follow the Apostle – 7:157 the Unlettered[2] Prophet – whom they shall find described to them in the Torah and the Gospel. He will enjoin righteousness upon them and forbid them to do evil. He will make good things lawful to them and prohibit all that is foul. He will relieve them of their burdens and of the shackles that weigh upon them. Those that believe in him and honour him, those that aid him and follow the light sent down with him, shall surely triumph.'

1. Cf. Exodus xxiv 1, 9.     2. The word can also mean 'gentile'.

7:158    Say:[1] 'You people! I am God's emissary to you all. He has
sovereignty over the heavens and the earth. There is no god
but Him. He ordains life and death. Therefore have faith in
God and His apostle, the Unlettered Prophet, who believes
in God and His commandments. Follow him so that you
may be rightly guided.'

Yet among the people of Moses there are some who
preach the truth and act justly.

We divided them into twelve tribes, each a whole
community. And when his people demanded drink of him,
We revealed our Will to Moses, saying: 'Strike the rock
with your staff.' Thereupon twelve springs gushed from the
rock and each tribe knew its drinking-place.

We caused the clouds to draw their shadow over them
and sent down for them manna and quails, saying: 'Eat of
the wholesome things We have given you.' Indeed they did
Us no wrong, but they wronged themselves.

7:161    When they were told: 'Dwell in this town, and eat of
whatever you please; pray for forgiveness and enter the
gates adoring: We will forgive you your sins and bestow
abundance on the righteous,' – the wrongdoers among
them replaced what they were told with other words; and
We let loose on them a scourge from heaven as punishment
for their misdeeds.

Ask them about the town which overlooked the sea and
what befell its people when they broke the Sabbath. On
their Sabbath the fish appeared before them floating on the
water, but on week-days they never came near them. Thus
did We tempt them because they had done wrong.

When some asked: 'Why do you admonish a people
whom God will destroy or sternly punish?' they replied: 'So
that we may be free from blame in the sight of your Lord,
and that they may guard themselves against evil.' Therefore,
when they forgot the warning they were given, We delivered
those who had warned them against evil, and sternly
7:166    punished the wrongdoers for their misdeeds. And when

1. These words are addressed to Muḥammad.

122

they scornfully persisted in their forbidden ways, We said to them: 'Turn into detested apes.'

Then your Lord declared that He would raise against 7:167 them others who would oppress them cruelly till the Day of Resurrection. Swift is the retribution of your Lord, yet is He forgiving and merciful.

We dispersed them through the earth in multitudes – some were righteous men, others were not – and tested them with blessings and misfortunes so that they might return to the right path. Then others succeeded them who inherited the Book and took to the vanities of this nether life. 'We shall be forgiven,' they said. And if such vanities came their way once more, they would again indulge in them.

Are they not committed in the Scriptures, which they have studied well, to tell nothing of God but what is true? Surely the world to come is a better prize for those that keep from evil. Have you no sense?

As for those that strictly observe the Scriptures and are 7:170 steadfast in prayer, We shall not deny the righteous their reward.

When We suspended the Mountain over them as though it were a shadow (they feared that it was falling down on them) We said: 'Hold fast to that which We have given you and bear in mind what it contains, so that you may keep from evil.'

Your Lord brought forth descendants from the loins of Adam's children, and made them testify against themselves. He said: 'Am I not your Lord?' They replied: 'We bear witness that You are.' This He did, lest you should say on the Day of Resurrection: 'We had no knowledge of that,' or: 'Our forefathers were, indeed, idolaters; but will You destroy us, their descendants, on account of what the followers of falsehood did?'

Thus do We make plain Our revelations so that they may return to the right path.

Tell them of the man to whom We vouchsafed Our signs and who turned away from them: how Satan pursued him and he was led astray. Had it been Our will, We would have 7:176

exalted him through Our signs: but he clung to this earthly life and succumbed to his desires. He was like the dog which pants if you chase it away, but pants still if you leave it alone. Such are those that deny Our revelations. Recount to them these parables, so that they may take thought.

7:177 Evil is the tale of those that denied Our revelations and were unjust to their own souls.

The man whom God guides is rightly guided; but those whom He confounds will surely lose out.

We have predestined for Hell numerous jinn and men. They have hearts they cannot comprehend with; they have eyes they cannot see with; and they have ears they cannot hear with. They are like beasts – indeed, they are more misguided. Such are the heedless.

God has the Most Excellent Names. Call on Him by His Names and keep away from those that pervert them. They shall receive their due for their misdeeds.

Among those whom We created there are some who give true guidance and act justly. As for those that deny Our revelations, We will lead them step by step to ruin, whence 7:183 they cannot tell; for though I bear with them, My stratagem is sure.

Has it never occurred to them that their compatriot[1] is no madman, but one who gives plain warning? Will they not ponder upon the kingdom of the heavens and the earth, and all that God created, to see whether their hour is not drawing near? And in what other revelation will they believe, those that deny this?

None can guide those whom God confounds. He leaves them blundering about in their sinful ways.

7:187 They ask you about the Hour of Doom: when will it come? Say: 'None but my Lord has knowledge of it.[2] None but He shall reveal it – at the appointed time. A fateful hour shall it be, both in the heavens and on earth. It will but suddenly overtake you.'

They will put questions to you as though you were privy

1. Muḥammad.    2. Cf. Mark xiii, 32.

to it. Say: 'None but God has knowledge of it, though most are unaware of this.'

Say: 'I have not the power to acquire benefits or to avert 7:188 evil from myself, except by the will of God. Had I possessed knowledge of what is hidden, I would have availed myself of much that is good and no harm would have touched me. But I am no more than one who gives warning and good news to true believers.'

It was He who created you from a single being. From that being He created his spouse, so that he might find comfort in her. And when he had lain with her, she conceived, and for a time her burden was light. She carried it with ease, but when it grew heavy, they both cried to God their Lord: 'Grant us a goodly child and we will be truly thankful.'

Yet when He had granted them a goodly child, they set up other gods besides Him in return for what He gave them. Exalted be God above their idols!

Will they worship those which can create nothing, but are themselves created? They cannot help them, nor can 7:192 they help themselves.

If you call them to the right path they will not follow you. It is the same whether you call to them or hold your peace.

Those whom you invoke besides God are, like yourselves, His servants. Call on them, and let them answer you, if what you say be true!

Have they feet to walk with? Have they hands to hold with? Have they eyes to see with? Have they ears to hear with?

Say: 'Call on your false gods and scheme against me. Give me no respite. My guardian is God, who has revealed the Book. He is the guardian of the righteous. Those to whom you pray besides Him cannot help you, nor can they help themselves.'

If you call them to the right path, they will not hear you. 7:198 You find them looking towards you, but they cannot see you.

7:199 Show forgiveness, speak for justice, and avoid the ignorant. If Satan tempts you, seek refuge in God; He hears all and knows all.

If those that guard themselves against evil are tempted by Satan, they have but to remember; and they shall see the light. As for their brothers, they shall be kept long in error, nor shall they ever desist.

When you have no verse to recite to them, they say: 'Have you not yet invented one?' Say: 'I follow only what is revealed to me by my Lord. This Book is a veritable proof from your Lord, a guide and a blessing to true believers.'

When the Koran is recited, listen to it in silence so that you may be shown mercy. Remember your Lord deep in your soul with humility and reverence, and without ostentation: in the morning and in the evening; and do not be negligent.

7:206 Those who dwell with your Lord do not disdain His service. They give glory to Him and prostrate themselves before Him.

# THE SPOILS[1]

*In the Name of God, the Compassionate, the Merciful*

8:1 THEY ASK you about the spoils. Say: 'The spoils belong to God and the Apostle. Therefore have fear of God and end your disputes. Obey God and His apostle, if you are true believers.'

The true believers are those whose hearts are filled with awe at the mention of God, and whose faith grows stronger as they listen to His revelations. They are those who put their trust in their Lord, pray steadfastly, and give in alms from what We gave them. Such are the true believers. They will be exalted and forgiven by their Lord, and a generous provision shall be made for them.

8:5 Your Lord bade you leave your home to fight for justice,

---

1. Of the Battle of Badr, A.D. 624.

but some of the faithful were reluctant. They argued with  8:6
you about the truth that had been revealed, as though they
were being led to certain death while they looked on.

God promised you victory over one of the two bands,
but it was your wish to take possession of the one that was
unarmed.[1] God wished to vindicate the truth by His words
and to rout the unbelievers, so that He might vindicate
the truth and render falsehood vain, though the wrongdoers
wished otherwise.

When you prayed to your Lord for help, He answered: 'I
am sending to your aid a thousand angels in their ranks.' By
this good news God sought to reassure your hearts, for
victory comes only from God; God is mighty and wise.

You were overcome by sleep, a token of His protection.
He sent down water from the sky to cleanse you and to
purify you of Satan's filth, to strengthen your hearts and to
steady your footsteps.

God revealed His will to the angels, saying: 'I shall be  8:12
with you. Give courage to the believers. I shall cast terror
into the hearts of the infidels. Strike off their heads, strike
off the very tips of their fingers!'

That was because they defied God and His apostle. He
that defies God and His apostle shall be sternly punished by
God. We said to them: 'Taste this. The scourge of the Fire
awaits the unbelievers.'

Believers, when you encounter the infidels on the march,
do not turn your backs to them in flight. If anyone on that
day turns his back to them, except for tactical reasons, or to
join another band, he shall incur the wrath of God and Hell
shall be his home: an evil fate.

It was not you, but God, who slew them. It was not you  8:17

1. Muḥammad's plan was to attack an unarmed caravan belonging to the Quraysh of Mecca on its way from Syria to that city. An
army of Meccans marched to its assistance. Some of the Muslims
wished to attack the caravan, others the Meccan army. Muḥammad's forces, only 319 strong, routed the Meccans, who were
nearly 1,000 in number.

who smote them: God smote them so that He might richly reward the faithful. God hears all and knows all. Even so; 8:18 God will surely frustrate the designs of the unbelievers.

If you[1] were seeking a judgement, now has a judgement come to you. If you desist, it will be best for you. If you resume your war against the faithful, We will return to their assistance, and your forces, superior though they be in number, shall avail you nothing: for God is with the faithful.

Believers, obey God and His apostle, and do not forsake him, now that you have heard all. Do not be like those who say: 'We hear,' but pay no heed to what they hear.

The meanest beasts in God's sight are those that are deaf, dumb, and devoid of reason. Had God perceived any virtue in them, He would have surely endowed them with hearing. But even if He had made them hear, they would have turned away and refused to listen.

Believers, obey God and the Apostle when he calls you to that which gives you life. Know that God stands between man and his heart, and that in His presence you shall all be assembled.

8:25 Guard yourselves against temptation. The wrongdoers among you are not the only men who will be tempted. Know that God's punishment is stern.

Remember, when you were few in number and persecuted in the land, ever fearing the onslaught of the people, how He gave you shelter. He made you strong with His help and provided you with wholesome things, so that you might give thanks.

Believers, do not betray God and the Apostle, nor knowingly betray your trust. Know that your children and your worldly goods are but a temptation, and that God's recompense is great.

Believers, if you fear God He will grant you salvation and cleanse you of your sins and forgive you. The bounty of God is great.

8:30 Remember how the unbelievers plotted against you.[2]

1. The Meccans.        2. Muḥammad.

They sought to take you captive or to have you slain or banished. They schemed – but God also schemed. God is most profound in His machinations.

Whenever Our revelations are recited to them, they say: 8:31 'We have heard them. If we wished, we could say the like. They are but fables of the ancients.'

They also say: 'Lord, if this be Your revealed truth, rain down upon us stones from heaven or send some dreadful scourge to punish us.'

But God would not punish them while you were present in their midst. Nor would He punish them if they sought forgiveness.

Yet it is but just that He should punish them; for they have debarred others from the Sacred Mosque, although they have no right to be its guardians. Its only guardians are those that fear God, though most of them do not know it.

Their prayers at the Sacred House are nothing but whistling and clapping of hands. 'Taste then the scourge, because you disbelieved.'

The unbelievers expend their riches in debarring others 8:36 from the path of God. Thus they dissipate their wealth: but they shall rue it, and in the end be overthrown. The unbelievers shall into Hell be driven.

God will separate the wicked from the just. He will heap all the wicked one upon another and then cast them into Hell. These will surely be the losers.

Tell the unbelievers that if they mend their ways their past shall be forgiven; but if they persist in sin, let them reflect upon the fate of bygone nations.

Make war on them until idolatry shall cease and God's religion shall reign supreme. If they desist, God is cognizant of all their actions; but if they pay no heed, know then that God will protect you. He is the noblest Helper and the noblest Protector.

Know that one-fifth of your spoils shall belong to God, the 8:41 Apostle, the Apostle's kinsfolk, the orphans, the destitute, and the traveller in need: if you truly believe in God and what We revealed to Our servant on the day of victory, the day when the two armies met. God has power over all things.

8:42 You were encamped on this side of the valley and the unbelievers on the farther side, with the caravan below. Had they offered battle, you would have surely declined; but God sought to accomplish what He had ordained, so that, by a clear sign, he that was destined to perish might die, and he that was destined to live might survive. God hears all and knows all.

God made them appear to you in a dream as a small band. Had He showed them to you as a great army, your courage would have failed you and discord would have triumphed in your ranks. But this God spared you. He knows your innermost thoughts.

And when you met them, He made each appear to the other few in number, that God might accomplish what He had ordained. To God shall all things return.

Believers, when you meet their army stand firm and pray
8:46 fervently to God, so that you may triumph. Obey God and His apostle and do not dispute with one another, lest you lose courage and your resolve weaken. Have patience: God is with those that are patient.

Do not be like those who left their homes elated with insolence and vainglory. They debar others from the path of God: but God has knowledge of all their actions.

Satan made their foul deeds seem fair to them. He said: 'No man shall conquer you this day. I shall be at hand to help you.' But when the two armies came within sight of each other, he took to his heels, saying: 'I am done with you, for I can see what you cannot. I fear God. God's punishment is stern.'

The hypocrites, and those whose hearts were tainted, said: 'Their religion has deceived them.' But he that puts his trust in God shall find God mighty and wise.

8:50 If you could see the angels when they carry off the souls of the unbelievers! They shall strike them on their faces and their backs, saying: 'Taste the torment of the Conflagration!

This is the punishment for what your hands committed.' 8:51
God is not unjust to His servants.

Like Pharaoh's people and those before them, they
disbelieved God's revelations. Therefore God will smite
them for their sins. Mighty is God and stern His retribution.

God does not change the blessings He has bestowed
upon a people until they change what is in their hearts. God
hears all and knows all.

Like Pharaoh's people and those before them, they
disbelieved their Lord's revelations. Therefore We will
destroy them for their sins even as We drowned Pharaoh's
people. They were wicked all.

The basest creatures in the sight of God are the faithless
who will not believe; those who time after time violate their
treaties with you and have no fear of God. If you capture
them in battle discriminate between them and those that
follow them, so that their followers may take warning.

If you fear treachery from any of your allies, you may
fairly retaliate by breaking off your treaty with them. God
does not love the treacherous.

Let not the unbelievers think that they will ever get 8:59
away. They have not the power so to do. Muster against
them all the men and cavalry at your command, so that you
may strike terror into the enemy of God and your enemy,
and others besides them who are unknown to you but
known to God. All that you give in the cause of God shall
be repaid to you. You shall not be wronged.

If they incline to peace, make peace with them, and put
your trust in God. It is surely He who hears all and knows
all. Should they seek to deceive you, God is all-sufficient
for you. He has made you strong with His help and rallied
the faithful round you, making their hearts one. If you had
given away all the riches of the earth, you could not have so
united them: but God has united them. He is mighty and
wise.

Prophet, God is your strength, and the faithful who
follow you.

Prophet, rouse the faithful to arms. If there are twenty 8:65

steadfast men among you, they shall vanquish two hundred; and if there are a hundred, they shall rout a thousand unbelievers, for they are devoid of understanding.

8:66    God has now lightened your burden, for He knows that you are weak. If there are a hundred steadfast men among you, they shall vanquish two hundred; and if there are a thousand, they shall, by God's will, defeat two thousand. God is with those that are steadfast.

A prophet may not take captives until he has fought and triumphed in the land. You[1] seek the chance gain of this world, but God desires for you the world to come. God is mighty and wise. Had there not been a previous writ from God, you would have been sternly punished for what you took. Enjoy therefore the good and lawful things which you have gained in war, and fear God. God is forgiving and merciful.

Prophet, say to those you have taken captive: 'If God finds goodness in your hearts, He will give you that which is better than what has been taken from you, and He will forgive you. God is forgiving and merciful.'

8:71    But if they seek to betray you, know they have already betrayed God. Therefore He has made you triumph over them. God is all-knowing and wise.

Those that have embraced the Faith and fled their homes, and fought for the cause of God with their wealth and with their persons; and those that have sheltered them and helped them, shall be as friends to each other.

Those that have embraced the Faith, but have not left their homes, shall in no way become your friends until they have done so. But if they seek your help in the cause of the true Faith, it is your duty to assist them, except against a people with whom you have a treaty. God is cognizant of all your actions.

8:73    The unbelievers give aid and comfort to each other. If you fail to do likewise, there will be disorder in the land and great corruption.

1. Muḥammad's followers.

Those that have embraced the Faith and fled their homes and fought for the cause of God, and those that have sheltered them and helped them – they are the true believers. Forgiveness and a gracious provision await them.

Those that have since embraced the Faith and fled their 8:75 homes and fought with you – they too are your brothers; although according to the Book of God those who are bound by ties of blood are nearest to one another. God has knowledge of all things.

# REPENTANCE[1]

A DECLARATION of immunity from God and His apostle 9:1 to the idolaters with whom you have made agreements:

For four months you shall go unmolested in the land. But know that you shall not escape God's judgement, and that God will humble the unbelievers.

A proclamation to the people from God and His apostle on the day of the greater pilgrimage:

God and His apostle are under no obligation to the idolaters. If you repent, it shall be well with you; but if you pay no heed, know that you shall not be immune from God's judgement.

Proclaim a woeful punishment to the unbelievers, except to those idolaters who have honoured their treaties with you in every detail and aided none against you. With these keep faith, until their treaties have run their term. God loves the righteous.

When the sacred months[2] are over slay the idolaters 9:5 wherever you find them. Arrest them, besiege them, and lie in ambush everywhere for them. If they repent and take to

1. This is the only chapter in the Koran which does not begin with the invocation 'In the Name of God, etc.' Traditional commentators regard it as a continuation of 'The Spoils'.

2. Shawwāl, Dhūl-Qu'adah, Dhūl-Ḥajjah, and Muḥarram.

prayer and render the alms levy, allow them to go their way. God is forgiving and merciful.

9:6 If an idolater seeks asylum with you, give him protection so that he may hear the Word of God, and then convey him to safety. For the idolaters are ignorant men.

God and His apostle repose no trust in idolaters, save those with whom you have made treaties at the Sacred Mosque. So long as they keep faith with you, keep faith with them. God loves the righteous.

How can you trust them? If they prevail against you, they will respect neither agreements nor ties of kindred. They flatter you with their tongues, but their hearts reject you. Most of them are evil-doers.

They sell God's revelations for trifling gain and debar others from His path. Evil is what they do. They break faith with the believers and set at nought all ties of kindred. Such are the transgressors.

If they repent and take to prayer and render the alms levy, they shall become your brothers in the Faith. Thus do We make plain Our revelations to men of knowledge.

9:12 But if, after coming to terms with you, they break their oaths, and revile your faith, make war on the leaders of unbelief – for no oaths are binding with them – so that they may desist.

Will you not fight against those who have broken their oaths and conspired to banish the Apostle? They were the first to attack you. Do you fear them? Surely God is more deserving of your fear, if you are true believers.

Make war on them: God will chastise them at your hands and humble them. He will grant you victory over them and heal the spirit of the faithful. He will take away all rancour from their hearts: God shows mercy to whom He pleases. God is all-knowing and wise.

Did you imagine you would be forsaken before God has had time to know those of you who have fought valiantly and served none but God, His Apostle and the faithful? God is cognizant of all your actions.

9:17 It ill becomes the idolaters to visit the mosques of God, for they are unbelievers, self-confessed. Vain shall be their works, and in the Fire they shall abide for ever.

None should visit the mosques of God except those who 9:18 believe in God and the Last Day, attend to their prayers and render the alms levy and fear none but God. These shall be rightly guided.

Do you pretend that he who gives a drink to the pilgrims and pays a visit to the Sacred Mosque is as worthy as the man who believes in God and the Last Day, and fights for God's cause? These are not held equal by God. God does not guide the wrongdoers.

Those that have embraced the Faith, and left their homes, and fought for God's cause with their wealth and with their persons, are held in higher regard by God. It is they who shall triumph. Their Lord has promised them mercy from Himself, and His pleasure and gardens of eternal bliss where they shall dwell for ever. God's recompense is great indeed.

Believers, do not befriend your fathers or your brothers if they choose unbelief in preference to faith. Wrongdoers are those that befriend them.

Say: 'If your fathers, your sons, your brothers, your 9:24 wives, your tribes, the property you have acquired, the merchandise you fear may not be sold, and the homes you love, are dearer to you than God, His apostle and the struggle for His cause, then wait until God shall fulfil His decree. God does not guide the evil-doers.'

God has aided you on many a battlefield. In the Battle of Hunain[1] you set great store by your numbers, but they availed you nothing: the earth, for all its vastness, seemed to close in upon you, and you turned your backs and fled. Then God caused His tranquillity[2] to descend upon His apostle 9:26 and the faithful: He sent to your aid invisible warriors and sternly punished the unbelievers. Thus were the infidels rewarded.

---

1. Fought in A.D. 630. The Muslim army was 12,000 strong, the Meccans 4,000.

2. See footnote, p. 36.

9:27    Yet God will show mercy to whom He will. God is forgiving and merciful.

Believers, know that the idolaters are unclean. Let them not approach the Sacred Mosque after this year is ended. If you fear poverty, God, if He pleases, will enrich you through His own bounty. God is all-knowing and wise.

Fight against such of those to whom the Scriptures were given as believe in neither God nor the Last Day, who do not forbid what God and His apostle have forbidden, and do not embrace the true Faith, until they pay tribute out of hand and are utterly subdued.

The Jews say Ezra is the son of God, and the Christians say the Messiah is the son of God. Such are the words they utter with their mouths, by which they emulate the infidels of old. God confound them! How perverse they are!

9:31    They make of their clerics and their monks, and of the Messiah, the son of Mary, Lords besides God; though they were ordered to serve one God only. There is no god but Him. Exalted be He above those they deify besides Him!

They would extinguish the light of God with their mouths: but God seeks only to perfect His light, though the infidels abhor it.

It is He who has sent forth His apostle with guidance and the True Faith that he may exalt it above all religion, though the idolaters abhor it.

Believers, many are the clerics and the monks who defraud the people of their possessions and debar them from the path of God. To those that hoard up gold and silver and do not spend it in God's cause, proclaim a woeful punishment. The day will surely come when their treasures shall be heated in the fire of Hell, and their foreheads, sides, and backs branded with them. They will be told: 'These are the riches which you hoarded. Taste then what you were hoarding.'

9:36    God ordained the months twelve in number when He created the heavens and the earth. Of these, four are sacred, according to the true Faith. Therefore do not sin against yourselves by violating them. But you may fight against the idolaters in all these months, since they themselves fight against you in all of them. Know that God is with the righteous.

The postponement of sacred months is a grossly impious 9:37 practice, in which the unbelievers are misguided. They allow it one year and forbid it in the next, so that they may make up for the months which God has sanctified, thus making lawful what God has forbidden. Their foul acts seem fair to them: God does not guide the unbelievers.

Believers, why is it that when you are told: 'March in the cause of God,' you linger slothfully in the land? Are you content with this life in preference to the life to come? Few indeed are the blessings of this life, compared with those of the life to come.

If you do not go to war, He will punish you sternly, and will replace you by other men. You will in no way harm Him: for God has power over all things.

If you do not help him,[1] God did help him when he was 9:40 driven out by the unbelievers with one other.[2] In the cave he said to his companion: 'Do not despair, God is with us.' God caused His tranquillity[3] to descend upon him and sent to his aid warriors invisible to you, so that He brought low the unbelievers' design: supreme is God's design. God is mighty and wise.

Whether unarmed or well-equipped, march on and fight for the cause of God, with your wealth and with your persons. This will be best for you, if you but knew it.

Had the gain been immediate or the journey short, they 9:42 would have followed you:[4] but the distance seemed too far to them. Yet they will swear by God: 'Had we been able, we would have marched with you.' They bring ruin upon themselves. God knows that they are surely lying.

1. Muḥammad.
2. Abū-Bakr, later the first of the Rightly-guided Caliphs.
3. See footnote, p. 36.
4. Muḥammad.

9:43    God forgive you! Why did you give them leave to stay behind before you knew those who spoke the truth from those who invented false excuses?

Those that believe in God and the Last Day will not beg you to exempt them from fighting with their wealth and with their persons. God best knows the righteous. Only those seek exemption who disbelieve in God and the Last Day, and whose hearts are filled with doubt. Because they doubt, they waver.

Had they intended to set forth, they would have prepared themselves for war. But God was loth to let them go, and held them back. They were bidden to stay with those who stayed behind.

Had they taken the field with you, they would have only added to your burden. They would have wormed their way through your ranks, seeking to sow discord among you: and among you there were some who would have been willing listeners. God knows the evil-doers.

9:48    They had sought before this to sow dissension, and hatched plots against you. But in the end the truth prevailed and the will of God triumphed, much as they disliked it.

Some of them say: 'Give us leave to stay behind, and do not expose us to temptation.' Surely they have already succumbed to temptation. Hell shall engulf the unbelievers.

If you meet with success, it grieves them; but if a disaster befalls you, they say: 'We have taken our precautions.' And they turn away, rejoicing.

Say: 'Nothing will befall us except what God has ordained. He is our Guardian. In God let the faithful put their trust.'

Say: 'Are you waiting for anything to befall us except victory or martyrdom? We are waiting for God's scourge to smite you, direct from Him or at our hands. Wait if you will; we too are waiting.'

9:53    Say: 'Whether you give willingly or with reluctance, your offerings shall not be accepted from you; for you are wicked men.'

Their offerings shall not be accepted from them because 9:54 they have denied God and His apostle. They pray half-heartedly and begrudge their contributions.

Let neither their riches nor their children rouse your envy. Through these God seeks to punish them in this life, so that their souls shall depart while still in unbelief.

They swear by God that they are believers like you. Yet they are not. They are afraid of you. If they could find a shelter or a cave, or any hiding-place, they would run in frantic haste to seek refuge in it.

There are some among them who speak ill of you[1] concerning the distribution of alms. If a share is given them, they are contented: but if they receive nothing, they grow resentful.

Would that they were satisfied with what God and His apostle have given them, and said: 'God is all-sufficient for us. God will provide for us from His own abundance, and so will His apostle. To God we will submit.'

Alms shall be only for the poor and the destitute, for those 9:60 that are engaged in the management of alms and those whose hearts are sympathetic to the Faith, for the freeing of slaves and debtors, for the advancement of God's cause, and for the traveller in need. That is a duty enjoined by God. God is all-knowing and wise.

And there are others among them who speak ill of the Prophet, saying: 'He believes everything he hears.' Say: 'He hears only what is good for you. He believes in God and puts his trust in the faithful. He is a blessing to the true believers among you. Those that wrong the Apostle of God shall be sternly punished.'

They swear in the name of God in order to please you. But it is more just that they should please God and the Apostle, if they are true believers.

Are they not aware that the man who defies God and His 9:63

---

1. Muḥammad.

139

apostle shall abide for ever in the fire of Hell? That surely is the supreme humiliation.

9:64 The hypocrites are afraid lest a Chapter be revealed to them, telling them what is in their hearts. Say: 'Scoff if you will; God will surely bring to light what you are dreading.'

If you question them, they will say: 'We were only jesting and making merry.' Say: 'Would you mock God, His revelations, and His apostle? Make no excuses. You have renounced the faith after embracing it. If We pardon some of you, We will punish others, for they are guilty men.'

Be they men or women, the hypocrites are all alike. They enjoin what is evil, forbid what is just, and tighten their fists. They forgot God, so God forgot them. Surely the hypocrites are evil-doers.

God has promised the hypocrites, both men and women, and the unbelievers, the fire of Hell. They shall abide in it for ever: a sufficient recompense. The curse of God is upon them; lasting torment awaits them.

9:69 Your ways are like the ways of those who have gone before you. They were mightier than you, and were blessed with greater riches and more children. Like them, you have enjoyed your earthly lot and, like them, you have engaged in idle talk. But vain were their works in this life, and vain they shall be in the life to come. These will surely be the losers.

Have they not heard the histories of those who have gone before them? The fate of Noah's people and of Thamūd and 'Ād; of Abraham's people and the people of Midian and the Ruined Cities? Their apostles showed them veritable signs. God did not wrong them, but they wronged themselves.

The true believers, both men and women, are friends to one another. They enjoin what is just and forbid what is evil; they attend to their prayers, and render the alms levy, and obey God and His apostle. On these God will have mercy. God is mighty and wise.

9:72 God has promised the men and women who believe in

Him gardens watered by running streams, in which they shall abide for ever: goodly mansions in the gardens of Eden: and, what is more, they shall have grace in God's sight. That is the supreme triumph.

Prophet, make war on the unbelievers and the hypocrites 9:73 and deal rigorously with them. Hell shall be their home: an evil fate.

They swear by God that they said nothing. Yet they uttered the word of unbelief and renounced Islām after embracing it. They sought to do what they could not attain. Yet they had no reason to be spiteful; except perhaps because God and His apostle had enriched them through His bounty. If they repent, it will indeed be better for them; but if they pay no heed, God will sternly punish them, both in this world and in the world to come. They shall have none on earth to protect or help them.

Some pledged themselves, saying: 'If God is bountiful to us, we will give alms and live like righteous men.' But when God had bestowed His favours on them they tightened their fists and, turning their backs, hurried away. He has 9:77 caused hypocrisy to reign in their hearts till the day they meet Him, because they have been untrue to the pledge they gave Him and because of the lies they told.

Are they not aware that God knows what they conceal and what they talk about in secret? That God knows what is hidden? As for those that taunt the believers who give freely, and deride those who give according to their means, God will deride them. Woeful punishment awaits them.

It is the same whether or not you beg forgiveness for them. If seventy times you beg forgiveness for them, God will not forgive them, for they have denied God and His apostle. God does not guide the evil-doers.

Those that stayed at home were glad that they were left 9:81 behind by God's apostle, for they had no wish to fight for the cause of God with their wealth and with their persons. They said to each other: 'Do not go to war, the heat is fierce.'

Say to them: 'More fierce is the heat of Hell-fire!' Would that they understood!

9:82    They shall laugh but little and shed many tears. Thus shall they be rewarded for their misdeeds.

If God brings you back in safety and some of them ask leave to march with you, say: 'You shall not march with me, nor shall you fight with me against an enemy. You chose to stay at home on the first occasion; therefore you shall now stay with those who will remain behind.'

You shall not pray for any of their dead, nor shall you attend their burial. For they denied God and His apostle and remained sinners to the last.

Let neither their riches nor their children rouse your envy. Through these God seeks to punish them in this life, so that their souls shall depart while still in unbelief

Whenever a Chapter was revealed, saying: 'Believe in God and fight alongside His apostle,' the rich among them excused themselves to you, saying: 'Leave us with those who are to stay behind.'

9:87    They were content to be with those who stayed behind: a seal was set upon their hearts, leaving them bereft of understanding. But the Apostle and the men who shared his faith fought with their goods and with their persons. These shall be rewarded with good things. These shall surely prosper. God has prepared for them gardens watered by running streams, in which they shall abide for ever. That is the supreme triumph.

Some Arabs of the desert turned up with excuses, begging leave to stay behind; while those who denied God and His apostle remained idle at home. A woeful scourge shall fall on those of them that disbelieved.

It shall be no offence for the disabled, the sick, and those lacking the means to stay behind: if they are true to God and His apostle. The righteous shall not be blamed: God is forgiving and merciful. Nor shall those be blamed who, when they came to you demanding conveyances to the battle-front and you could find none to carry them, went away in tears grieving that they had not the means to contribute.

9:93    The offenders are those that seek exemption although they are men of wealth. They are content to be with those who stay behind. God has set a seal upon their hearts; they are devoid of knowledge.

When you return to them they will come up to you with 9:94 excuses. Say: 'Make no excuses: we will not believe you. God has revealed to us the truth about you. God and His apostle will watch your actions. Then you shall return to Him who knows alike the unknown and the manifest, and He will declare to you what you have done.'

When you return they will appeal to you in God's name to let them be. So let them be: they are unclean. Hell shall be their home, the punishment for their misdeeds.

They will swear to you in order to gain your acceptance. But if you accept them, God will not accept the evil-doers.

The desert Arabs surpass others in unbelief and hypocrisy, and have more cause to be ignorant of the laws which God has revealed to His apostle. But God is all-knowing and wise.

Some desert Arabs regard what they give as a compulsory fine and wait for some misfortune to befall you. May ill-fortune befall them! God hears all and knows all.

Yet there are others among the desert Arabs who 9:99 believe in God and the Last Day, and regard what they give as a means of bringing them close to God and to the Apostle's prayers. Indeed, closer they shall be brought; God will admit them to His mercy. God is forgiving and merciful.

As for those who led the way, the first of the *muhājirīn*[1] and the *anṣār*,[2] and those who nobly followed them, God is pleased with them and they are pleased with Him. He has prepared for them gardens watered by running streams, where they shall dwell for ever. That is the supreme triumph.

Some of the desert Arabs around you are hypocrites, and 9:101 so are some of the citizens of Madīnah, who are indeed fanatical in their hypocrisy. You do not know them, but We

---

1. Muḥammad's early followers who fled with him to Medina.
2. Muḥammad's supporters in Medina.

know them well. Twice We will chastise them: then shall they return to a grievous torment.

9:102 Others there are who have confessed their sins; their good works had been intermixed with evil. Perchance God will turn to them in mercy. God is forgiving and merciful. Take alms from them, so that they may thereby be cleansed and purified, and pray for them: for your prayers will give them comfort. God hears all and knows all.

Do they not know that God accepts the repentance of His servants and takes their alms, and that God is the Forgiving One, the Merciful?

Say: 'Do as you will. God will behold your works, and so will His apostle and the faithful; then shall you return to Him who knows alike the unknown and the manifest, and He will declare to you all that you have done.'

There are yet others who must await God's decree. He will either punish or pardon them. God is all-knowing and wise.

9:107 And there are those who built a mosque from mischievous motives, to spread unbelief and disunite the faithful, in expectation of him[1] who had made war on God and His apostle. They swear that their intentions were good, but God bears witness that they are lying. You shall not set foot in it. It is more fitting that you should pray in a mosque founded on piety from the very first. There you shall find men who would keep themselves pure. God loves those that purify themselves.

Who is a better man, he who founds his house on the fear of God and His good pleasure, or he who builds on the brink of a crumbling precipice, so that his house will fall with him into the fire of Hell? God does not guide the wrongdoers.

9:110 The edifice which they have built shall ever inspire their hearts with doubt, until their hearts are cut in pieces. God is all-knowing and wise.

1. Abū 'Āmir.

God has purchased from the faithful their lives and 9:111
worldly goods, and in return has promised them the Garden.
They will fight for the cause of God, they will slay and be
slain. Such is the true promise which He has made them in
the Torah, the Gospel and the Koran. And who is more
true to his pledge than God? Rejoice then in the bargain
you have made. That is the supreme triumph.

Those that repent and those that serve and praise Him;
those that fast and those that kneel and prostrate themselves;
those that enjoin justice, forbid evil, and observe the
commandments of God [shall be richly recompensed].
Proclaim the good tidings to the faithful.

It is not for the Prophet or the believers to beg forgiveness
for idolaters, even though they be related to them, after it
has become manifest that they have earned the punishment
of Hell. Abraham prayed for his father only to fulfil a
promise he had made him. But when he realized he was an
enemy of God, he disowned him. Yet Abraham was a
compassionate and tender-hearted man.

Nor will God confound men after He has given them 9:115
guidance until He has made plain to them all that they
should avoid. God has knowledge of all things.

God has sovereignty over the heavens and the earth; He
ordains life and death. You have none besides God to
protect or help you.

God turned in mercy to the Prophet, the *muhājirīn* and
the *anṣār*, who stood by him in the hour of adversity,
when some were on the point of losing heart. He turned to
them in mercy. He took pity on them and was merciful.
And to the three who had been left behind. So despondent
were they that the earth, for all its vastness, and their own
souls, seemed to close in upon them. They knew there was
no refuge from God except in Him. Therefore He turned to
them in mercy, so that they might repent. God is the
Forgiving One, the Merciful.

Believers, have fear of God and stand with those who
uphold the cause of truth. No cause have the people of 9:120
Madīnah and the desert Arabs who dwell around them to

forsake God's apostle or to jeopardize his life so as to safeguard their own; for they do not expose themselves to thirst or hunger or to any ordeal for the sake of God, nor do they take any step which may provoke the unbelievers, nor do they inflict any loss on an enemy, but shall be noted down for them as a good deed: God will not deny the 9:121 righteous their reward. Each sum they give, be it small or large, and each valley they traverse, shall be noted down, so that God may requite them for their noblest deeds.

It is not right that all the faithful should go to war at once. A band from each community should stay behind to instruct themselves in religion and to admonish their men when they return, so that they may take heed.

Believers, make war on the infidels who dwell around you. Deal firmly with them. Know that God is with the righteous.

9:124 Whenever a Chapter is revealed, some of them ask: 'Whose faith will this increase?' It will surely increase the believers' faith and give them joy. As for those whose hearts are tainted, it will add uncleanness to their uncleanness, so that they shall die while still in unbelief.

Do they not see how every year they were afflicted once or twice? Yet they neither repent nor take warning. Whenever a Chapter is revealed, they glance at each other, asking: 'Is anyone watching you?' Then they turn away. God has turned away their hearts, for they are senseless men.

There has now come to you an apostle of your own, one who grieves at your sinfulness and cares for you; one who is benevolent and merciful to true believers.

If they pay no heed, say: 'God is all-sufficient for me. 9:129 There is no god but Him. In Him I have put my trust. He is the Lord of the Glorious Throne.'

# JONAH

*In the Name of God, the Compassionate, the Merciful*

ALIF *lām rā'*. These are the verses of the Wise Book: Does 10:1
it seem strange to people that We revealed Our will to a
mortal from among themselves, saying: 'Give warning to
the people, and proclaim good tidings to the faithful: their
endeavours shall be rewarded by their Lord'?

The unbelievers say: 'This man[1] is a skilled enchanter.'
Yet your Lord is God, who in six days created the heavens
and the earth and then ascended the throne, ordaining all
things. None has power to intercede for you, except him
who has received His sanction. Such is God, your Lord:
therefore serve Him. Will you not take heed?

To Him shall you all return: God's promise shall be
fulfilled. He brings the Creation into being and will then
restore it, so that He may justly recompense those who have
believed in Him and done good works. As for the unbelievers, scalding water shall they drink, and for their
unbelief woeful punishment awaits them.

It was He that gave the sun his brightness and the moon 10:5
her light, ordaining her phases that you may learn to
compute the seasons and the years. God created them only
to manifest the Truth. He makes plain His revelations to
men of knowledge.

In the alternation of night and day, and in all that God has
created in the heavens and the earth, there are signs for
righteous men.

Those who entertain no hope of meeting Us, being
pleased and contented with the life of this world, and those
who pay no heed to Our revelations, shall have the Fire as
their home in requital for their deeds.

As for those that believe and do good works, God will
guide them through their faith. Rivers will run at their feet
in the Gardens of Delight. Their prayer will be: 'Glory be to 10:10
You, Lord!' and their greeting: 'Peace!' 'Praise be to God,

1. Muḥammad.

147

Lord of the Universe' will be the burthen of their plea.

10:11 Had God hastened the punishment of people as they would hasten their reward, their fate would have been sealed. Therefore We leave those who entertain no hope of meeting Us to their wrongdoing, ever straying from the right path.

When misfortune befalls man, he prays to Us lying on his side, sitting, or standing on his feet. But as soon as We relieve his affliction he pursues his former ways, as though he never prayed for Our help. Thus their foul deeds seem fair to the transgressors.

We destroyed generations before your time on account of the wrongs they did; their apostles came to them with veritable signs, but they would not believe. Thus shall We reward the guilty. Then We made you their successors in the land, so that We might observe how you would conduct yourselves.

When Our clear revelations are recited to them, those who entertain no hope of meeting Us say to you: 'Give us a different Koran, or change it.'

Say: 'It is not for me to change it of my own accord. I follow only what is revealed to me, for I fear, if I disobey my Lord, the punishment of a fateful day.'

10:16 Say: 'Had God pleased, I would never have recited it to you, nor would He have made you aware of it. A whole lifetime I dwelt among you before its coming. Will you not understand?'

Who is more wicked than the man who invents a falsehood about God or denies His revelations? Truly, the evil-doers shall not triumph.

They worship idols that can neither harm nor help them, and say: 'These will intercede for us with God.'

Say: 'Do you presume to tell God of what He knows to exist neither in the heavens nor on earth?' Glory be to Him! Exalted be He above the gods they serve besides Him!

10:19 There was a time when mankind were but one community. Then they disagreed among themselves: and but for a Word from your Lord, long since decreed, their differences would have been firmly resolved.

And they ask: 'Why has no sign been sent down to him 10:20 by his Lord?'

Say: 'God alone has knowledge of what is hidden. Wait if you will: I too am waiting.'

No sooner do We show mercy to people after some misfortune has afflicted them than they begin to scheme against Our revelations. Say: 'More swift is God's scheming. Our angels are recording your intrigues.'

It is He who guides them by land and sea. They embark: and as the ships set sail, rejoicing in a favourable wind, a raging tempest overtakes them. Billows surge upon them from every side and they fear they are encompassed by death. They pray to God with all fervour, saying: 'Deliver us from this peril and we will be truly thankful.'

Yet when He does deliver them, they perpetrate corruption in the land and act unjustly.

You people! It is your own souls that you are corrupting. Take your enjoyment in this life: to Us shall you then return, and We will declare to you all that you have done.

This present life is like the rich garment with which 10:24 the earth adorns itself when watered by the rain We send down from the sky. Crops, sustaining man and beast, grow luxuriantly: but, as the earth's tenants begin to think themselves its masters, down comes Our scourge upon it, by night or by day, laying it waste, as though it did not blossom but yesterday. Thus do We make plain Our revelations to thoughtful men.

God invites you to the Home of Peace. He guides whom He will to a straight path. Those that do good works shall have a good reward, and more besides. Neither blackness nor misery shall overcast their faces. They are the heirs of Paradise, wherein they shall abide for ever.

As for those that have done evil, evil shall be rewarded with evil. Misery will oppress them (they shall have none to protect them from God), as though patches of the night's own darkness veiled their faces. They are the heirs of the Fire, wherein they shall abide for ever.

On the day We assemble them all together, We shall 10:28

149

say to the idolaters: 'Keep to your places, you and your idols!' We will separate them one from another, and then their idols will say to them: 'It was not us that you 10:29 worshipped. Sufficient is God as our witness, and your witness. Nor were we aware of your worship.'

Thereupon each soul will know what it has done. They shall be sent back to God, their true Lord, and the idols they invented will forsake them.

Say: 'Who provides for you from heaven and earth? Who has endowed you with sight and hearing? Who brings forth the living from the dead, and the dead from the living? Who ordains all things?'

They will reply: 'God.'

Say: 'Will you not take heed, then? Such is God, your true Lord. That which is not true must needs be false. How then can you turn away?'

Thus is the Word of your Lord made good about the evil-doers. They will not believe.

Say: 'Can any of your idols bring the Creation into being, and then restore it?' Say: 'God brings the Creation into being, and will then restore it. How is it that you are 10:35 so misled?'

Say: 'Can any of your idols give guidance to the truth?' Say: 'God gives guidance to the truth. Who is more worthy to be followed: He that can give guidance to the truth, or he that cannot and is himself in need of guidance? What has come over you that you so judge?'

Most of them follow nothing but mere conjecture. But conjecture is in no way a substitute for truth. God is cognizant of all their actions.

This Koran could not have been devised by any but God. It confirms what was revealed before it and fully explains the Scriptures. It is beyond doubt from the Lord of the Universe.

If they say: 'He invented it himself,' say: 'Bring me one chapter like it. Call on whom you may besides God to help you, if what you say be true!'

10:39 Indeed, they disbelieve what they cannot grasp, for

they have not yet seen its prophecy fulfilled. Likewise did those before them disbelieve. But see what was the end of the wrongdoers.

Some believe in it, while others do not. But your Lord 10:40 best knows the evil-doers.

If they disbelieve you, say: 'My deeds are mine and your deeds are yours. You are not accountable for my actions, nor am I accountable for what you do.'

Some of them listen to you. But can you make the deaf hear you, incapable as they are of understanding?

Some of them look upon you. But can you show the way to the blind, bereft as they are of sight?

Indeed, in no way does God wrong people, but people wrong themselves.

The day will come when He will gather them all together, as though they had sojourned in this world but for an hour. They will acquaint themselves with each other. They shall lose out, those who denied they would ever meet God and did not follow the right path.

Whether We let you glimpse in some measure the scourge We threaten them with, or call you back to Us before We smite them, to Us they shall return. God will then be witness to all their actions.

An apostle is sent to each community. When their apostle 10:47 comes, justice is done among them; they are not wronged.

They ask: 'When will this promise be fulfilled, if what you say be true?'

Say: 'I have no control over any harm or benefit to myself, except by the will of God. A space of time is fixed for each community; when their time is come, not for one hour shall they delay: nor can they go before it.'

Say: 'Do but consider. Should His scourge fall upon you in the night or by the light of day, what punishment would the guilty hasten? Will you believe in it when it does overtake you, although it was your wish to hurry it on?'

Then will the wrongdoers be told: 'Feel the everlasting 10:52 torment! Shall you not be rewarded according only to your deeds?'

10:53    They ask you if it is true. Say: 'Yes, by the Lord, it is certainly true! And you shall not escape.'

To redeem himself then, each sinner would gladly give all that the earth contained if he possessed it. When they behold the scourge, they will repent in secret. But judgement shall be fairly passed upon them; they shall not be wronged.

Surely to God belongs all that the heavens and the earth contain. Surely the promise of God is true, though most of them may not know it. It is He who ordains life and death, and to Him shall you be recalled.

You people! An admonition has come to you from your Lord, a cure for the mind, a guide and a blessing to true believers.

Say: 'In the grace and mercy of God let them rejoice, for these are better than the worldly riches they amass.'

Say: 'Do but consider the provision God has sent down for you. Some of it you pronounced unlawful and some, lawful.' Say: 'Was it God who gave you His leave, or do you invent falsehoods about God?'

10:60    What will they think, those who invent falsehoods about God, on the Day of Resurrection? God is bountiful to men: yet most of them do not give thanks.

You shall engage in no affair, you shall recite no verse from the Koran, you shall commit no act, but We will witness it. Not an atom's weight in earth or heaven escapes your Lord, nor is there any object smaller or greater, but is recorded in a glorious book.

Surely the servants of God have nothing to fear or to regret. Those that have faith and keep from evil shall rejoice both in this world and in the world to come: the words of God shall never change. That is the supreme triumph.

Let their words not grieve you. All glory belongs to God. He alone hears all and knows all.

Surely to God belong all who dwell in the heavens and on earth. Those that serve other gods besides God follow nothing but idle fancies and preach nothing but falsehoods.

10:67    He it is who has ordained the night for you to rest in and given the day its light for you to see with. Surely in this there are signs for prudent men.

They say: 'God has begotten a son.' God forbid! Self-sufficient is He. His is all that the heavens and the earth contain. Surely for this you have no sanction. Would you say of God what you know not? 10:68

Say: 'Those that invent falsehoods about God shall not prosper. They may take their ease in this life, but to Us they shall then return, and for their unbelief We will make them taste the grievous torment.'

Recount to them the tale of Noah. He said to his people: 'If it offends you, my people, that I should dwell in your midst and preach to you God's revelations (for in God I have put my trust), muster all your idols and decide on your course of action. Do not intrigue in secret. Execute your judgement and give me no respite. If you turn away from me, remember I demand of you no recompense. Only God will reward me. I am commanded to be one of those who shall submit to Him.'

But they disbelieved him. Therefore We saved Noah and those who were with him in the ark, so that they survived, and drowned the others who denied Our revelations. Consider the fate of those who were forewarned.

After him We sent apostles to their descendants. They showed them veritable signs, but they persisted in their unbelief. Thus do We seal up the hearts of the transgressors. 10:74

Then We sent forth Moses and Aaron with Our signs to Pharaoh and his nobles. But they responded with scorn, for they were wicked men. When the truth had come to them from Us, they declared: 'Surely this is but plain sorcery.'

Moses replied: 'Is this what you say of the Truth when it has come to you? Is this sorcery? Sorcerers shall never prosper.'

They said: 'Have you come to turn us away from the faith of our fathers, so that you two may lord it over the land? We will never believe in the pair of you.'

Then Pharaoh said: 'Bring every learned sorcerer to my presence.' 10:79

10:80    And when the sorcerers attended, Moses said to them: 'Cast down what you wish to cast.' And when they had thrown, he said: 'The sorcery that you have wrought, God will surely bring to nothing. He does not bless the work of those who do evil. By His words He vindicates the truth, much as the guilty may dislike it.'

Few of his[1] people believed in Moses, for they feared the persecution of Pharaoh and his nobles. Surely Pharaoh was a tyrant in the land, a man of rampant wickedness.

Moses said: 'If you believe in God, my people, and have surrendered yourselves to Him, in Him alone then put your trust.'

They replied: 'In God we have put our trust. Lord, do not let us suffer at the hands of wicked men. Deliver us, through Your mercy, from the unbelievers.'

We revealed Our will to Moses and his brother, saying: 'Build houses in Egypt for your people and make your homes places of worship. Conduct prayers and give good tidings to the faithful.'

10:88    'Lord,' said Moses, 'You have bestowed on Pharaoh and his nobles splendour and riches in this life, so that they may stray from Your path. Lord, destroy their riches and harden their hearts, so that they shall persist in unbelief until they face the woeful scourge.'

He replied: 'Your prayer shall be answered. Follow the straight path and do not walk in the footsteps of ignorant men.'

We led the Israelites across the sea, and Pharaoh and his legions pursued them with wickedness and spite. But as he was drowning, Pharaoh cried: 'Now I believe no god exists except the God in whom the Israelites believe. To Him I give up myself.'

'Only now! But before this you were a rebel and a wrongdoer. We shall today save your body, so that you may become a sign for all posterity: for a great many of mankind do not heed Our signs.'

10:93    We settled the Israelites in a secure land and provided

---

1. Pharaoh's.

them with wholesome things. Nor did they disagree among themselves until knowledge was given them. Your Lord will on the Day of Resurrection judge their differences.

If you doubt what We have revealed to you, ask those 10:94 who have read the Scriptures before you. The truth has come to you from your Lord: therefore do not doubt it. Nor shall you deny the revelations of God, for then you will surely be among the lost.

Those for whom the word of your Lord shall be fulfilled will not have faith, even if they be given every sign, until they face the woeful scourge. Were it otherwise, every community, had it believed, would have profited from its faith. But it was so only with Jonah's people. When they believed, We spared them the penalty of disgrace in this life and suffered them to take their ease a while. Had your Lord pleased, all the people of the earth would have believed in Him, one and all. Would you then force people to have faith?

None can have faith except by God's leave. He will visit His scourge upon the senseless.

Say: 'Behold what the heavens and the earth contain!' But neither signs nor warnings will avail the unbelievers.

What can they wait for but the fate of those who have 10:102 gone before them? Say: 'Wait if you will; I too am waiting.'

We shall save Our apostles and the true believers. It is but just that We should save the faithful.

Say: 'You people! Doubt my religion if you will, but never will I worship those that you worship besides God. I worship God, who will reclaim you all: for I am thus commanded to be a believer. I was bidden: "Dedicate yourself to the Faith in all uprightness and serve none besides God. You shall not pray to idols which can neither help nor harm you, for if you do, you will become a wrongdoer. If God afflicts you with a misfortune, none can remove it but He; and if He bestows on you a favour, none can withhold His bounty. He is bountiful to whom He will. He is the Forgiving One, the Merciful."'

Say: 'You people! The truth has come to you from your 10:108 Lord. He that follows the right path follows it for his own good, and he that strays does so at his own peril. I am not your keeper.'

10:109    Observe what is revealed to you, and have patience till God make known His judgement. He is the best of judges.


# HŪD

*In the Name of God, the Compassionate, the Merciful*

11:1 ALIF *lām rā'*. A Book, whose verses are perfected and then made plain, from Him who is wise and all-knowing:

Serve none but God. I am sent to you from Him to warn you and to give good tidings.

Seek forgiveness of your Lord and turn to Him in penitence. A goodly provision He will make for you for an appointed term, and will bestow His grace on each that has merit. But if you pay no heed, then beware the torment of a fateful day. To God shall you all return. He has power over all things.

They cover up their breasts to conceal their thoughts from Him. But when they put on their garments, does He not know what they conceal and what they reveal? He knows their innermost thoughts.

11:6    There is not a creature on the earth but God provides its sustenance. He knows its dwelling and its resting-place. All is recorded in a glorious book.

Throned above the waters, He made the heavens and the earth in six days, to find out which of you shall best acquit himself.

When you[1] say: 'After death you shall be raised to life,' 11:8 the unbelievers declare: 'It is but plain sorcery.' And if We put off their punishment till an appointed time, they ask: 'Why is it delayed?'

On the day it overtakes them, they shall not be immune from it. The terrors at which they scoffed will encompass them.

1. Muhammad.

If We show man Our mercy and then withhold it from 11:9
him, he yields to despair and becomes ungrateful. And if
after adversity We let him taste good fortune, he says:
'Gone are my sorrows from me,' and grows jubilant and
boastful.

Not so the steadfast who do good works. Forgiveness
and a rich recompense await them.

You may chance to omit a part of what is revealed to you
and be distressed because they say: 'Why has no treasure
been sent down to him? Why has no angel come with him?'

But you are only to give warning. God is the guardian of
all things. If they say: 'He has invented it[1] himself,' say to
them: 'Produce ten invented chapters like it. Call on whom
you will among your idols, if what you say be true. But if
they fail you, know that it is revealed with God's knowledge,
and that there is no god but Him. Will you then accept
Islām?'

Those that desire the life of this world with all its finery 11:15
shall be rewarded for their deeds in their own lifetime: they
shall not be given less. They are those who in the world to
come shall have earned nothing but the Fire. Fruitless are
their deeds, and vain are all their works.

Are they to be compared to those that have received a
revelation from their Lord, recited by a witness from Him
and heralded by the Book of Moses, a guide and a blessing?
These have faith in it, but the factions who deny it shall be
consigned to the Fire. Therefore do not doubt it. It is the
truth from your Lord: yet most people have no faith.

And who is more wicked than the man who invents a
falsehood about God? Such men shall be brought before
their Lord, and witnesses will say: 'These are they who lied
about their Lord.'

God's curse is on the wrongdoers, who debar others
from the path of God and seek to make it crooked, and who
deny the life to come. These shall not be impregnable in the 11:20
land; there is none to protect them besides God. Their

1. The Koran.

punishment shall be doubled, for they could neither hear nor see.

11:21 Such are those who shall forfeit their souls. Their false devices will forsake them, and in the life to come they will assuredly lose most.

As for those that have faith and do good works and humble themselves before their Lord, they are the heirs of Paradise, and there they shall abide for ever.

The two are like the blind and the deaf compared with those that can see and hear. Are the two equal? Will you not take heed?

We sent forth Noah to his people. He said: 'I have come to warn you plainly. Serve none but God. Beware the torment of a woeful day.'

The unbelieving elders of his people said: 'We see you as but a mortal like ourselves. Nor can we see you being followed by any but the lowliest of our men, those who are rash and undiscerning. We see no superior merit in you: indeed we think that you are lying.'

11:28 He said: 'Consider, my people! If my Lord has revealed to me His will and bestowed on me a favour of His own, though it be hidden from you, can we compel you to accept it against your will? I seek of you no recompense for this, my people; for none but God can reward me. Nor will I drive away the faithful, for they will surely meet their Lord. But I can see that you are ignorant men. And were I to drive them away, my people, who would protect me from God? Will you not take heed?

'I do not say to you that I possess God's treasures, nor have I knowledge of what is hidden. I do not claim to be an angel, nor do I say to those whom your eyes disdain that God will not be bountiful to them – God knows best what is in their hearts – for then I should become a wrongdoer.'

'Noah,' they replied, 'you have argued with us, and argued to excess. Bring down the scourge you threaten us with, if what you say be true!'

He said: 'God will bring it down upon you if He pleases: 11:34 nor shall you be immune. My counsel will not profit you if God intends to confound you, willing though I am to offer you counsel. He is your Lord, and to Him shall you return.'

If they declare: 'He has invented it himself,' say: 'If I have 11:35 indeed invented it, then may I be punished for my sin! I am innocent of yours.'

God's will was revealed to Noah, saying: 'None of your people will believe in you save those who already believe. Do not grieve at what they do. Build the ark under Our watchful eyes, and with Our inspiration. You shall not plead with Me for those who have done wrong: they shall assuredly be drowned.'

So he built the ark. And whenever the elders of his people passed by him they jeered at him. He said: 'If you mock us, we shall mock you just as you mock us. You shall learn who will be seized by a scourge that shall humiliate him, and be smitten by a scourge everlasting.'

And when Our will was done and water welled out from the Oven, We said to Noah: 'Take into the ark a pair from every species, your kinsfolk (except for those already doomed), and all the true believers.' But none except a few believed with him.

'Embark,' said Noah. 'In the name of God it shall set sail 11:41 and cast anchor. Surely my Lord is forgiving and merciful.'

And as the ark moved on with them amid the mountainous waves, Noah cried out to his son, who stood apart: 'Embark with us, my child. Do not remain with the unbelievers!'

He replied: 'I shall seek refuge in a mountain, which will protect me from the flood.'

Noah cried: 'None shall be secure today from the judgement of God but those who shall enjoy His mercy!' And thereupon the billows rolled between them, and Noah's son was drowned.

A voice cried out: 'Earth, swallow up your waters. Heaven, cease your rain!' The floods abated, and His will was done. The ark came to rest upon Al-Jūdī, and a voice declared: 'Gone are the evil-doers.'

Noah called out to his Lord, saying: 'Lord, my son was 11:45

my own flesh and blood. Your promise was surely true. You are the most just of judges.'

11:46 'Noah,' He replied, 'he was no kinsman of yours: he had acted unjustly. Do not question Me about things you know nothing of. I admonish you lest you become an ignorant man.'

'I seek refuge in You, Lord, for asking You about things I know nothing of,' said Noah. 'Forgive me and have mercy on me, or I shall surely be among the lost.'

'Noah,' He replied, 'go ashore in peace. Our blessings are upon you and on *some* of the descendants of those that are with you. As for the others, We will suffer them to take their ease awhile and will then visit upon them a woeful scourge.'

That which We have now revealed to you is secret history: it was unknown to you and to your people. Have patience; the righteous shall have a joyful end.

To 'Ād We sent their kinsman Hūd. He said: 'Serve God, my people; you have no god but Him. False are your inventions. I demand of you no recompense, my people, for none can reward me except my Creator. Will you not understand?

11:52 'My people, seek forgiveness of your Lord and turn to Him in penitence. He will send from the sky abundant rain upon you; He will add strength to your strength. Do not turn away from Him with wrongdoing.'

They replied: 'Hūd, you have given us no proof. We will not forsake our gods at your behest, nor will we believe in you. We can only suppose that our gods have afflicted you with evil.'

He said: 'God is my witness, and you are my witnesses too: I disown your idols. Scheme against me if you will, and give me no respite. I have put my trust in God, my Lord and your Lord. There is not a living creature on the earth whose destiny He does not govern. Straight is the path of my Lord.

'If you pay no heed, I have made known to you my message, and my Lord will replace you by other men. You will in no way harm Him. My Lord is watching over all things.'

11:58 And when Our judgement came to pass, We delivered

Hūd through Our mercy, together with those who shared his faith. We delivered them from a horrifying scourge.

Such were 'Ād. They denied the revelations of their 11:59 Lord, disobeyed His apostles, and did the bidding of every headstrong reprobate. Cursed were they in this world, and cursed they shall be on the Day of Resurrection.

'Ād denied their Lord. Gone are 'Ād, the people of Hūd.

And to Thamūd We sent their kinsman Ṣāliḥ. He said: 'Serve God, my people; you have no god but Him. It was He who brought you into being from the earth and gave you means to dwell upon it. Seek forgiveness of Him, and turn to Him in penitence. My Lord is near at hand and answers all.'

'Ṣāliḥ,' they replied, 'great were the hopes we placed in you. Would you now forbid us to serve the gods our fathers worshipped? Truly, we strongly doubt the faith to which you call us.'

He said: 'Do but consider, my people! If my Lord has revealed to me His will and bestowed on me His grace, who would protect me from God if I rebelled against Him? You would surely aggravate my ruin.

'My people, here is God's she-camel, a sign for you. 11:64 Leave her to graze at will in God's own land, and do not molest her lest an instant scourge should fall upon you.'

Yet they slew her. He said: 'You have but three days to take your ease in your dwellings. This prophecy shall not prove false.'

And when Our judgement came to pass, We delivered Ṣāliḥ through Our mercy from the ignominy of that day, together with those who shared his faith. Mighty is your Lord and all-powerful. The Cry took the evil-doers, and when morning came they were crouching lifeless in their dwellings, as though they had never prospered there.

Thamūd denied their Lord. Gone are the people of Thamūd.

Our messengers came to Abraham with good news. They said: 'Peace!' 'Peace!' he answered, and hastened to bring them a roasted calf. But when he saw their hands being 11:70 withheld from it, he mistrusted them and was afraid of them. They said: 'Have no fear. We are sent forth to the people of Lot.'

11:71 His wife, who was standing by, laughed.[1] We bade her rejoice in Isaac, and in Jacob after Isaac.

'Alas!' she replied. 'How shall I bear a child when I am old and my husband is well-advanced in years? This is indeed a strange thing.'

They replied: 'Do you marvel at the ways of God? May God's mercy and blessings be upon you, dear hosts! Worthy of praise is He and glorious.'

And when fear left him as he pondered the good news, Abraham pleaded with Us for the people of Lot. Abraham was gracious, tender-hearted, and devout.

We said: 'Abraham, plead no more. Your Lord's will must needs be done. Irrevocable is the scourge which shall smite them.'

And when Our messengers came to Lot, he grew anxious about them, for he was powerless to offer them protection. 'This is indeed a day of woe,' he said.

His people, long addicted to evil practices, came running 11:78 towards him. 'My people,' he said, 'here are my daughters:[2] surely they are more wholesome to you. Fear God, and do not shame me by insulting my guests. Is there not one right-minded man among you?'

They replied: 'You know we have no need of your daughters. You know full well what we are seeking.'

He cried: 'Would that I had strength enough to overcome you, or could find refuge in some mighty man!'

They said: 'Lot, we are the emissaries of your Lord: they shall not touch you. Depart with your kinsfolk in the dead of night and let none of you turn back, except your wife. She shall suffer the fate of the others. In the morning their hour will come. Is not the morning near?'

And when Our judgement came to pass, We turned their city upside down and let loose upon it a shower of clay-11:83 stones bearing the tokens of your Lord. The punishment of the unjust was not far off.

1. Cf. Genesis xviii, 12.　　2. Cf. Genesis xix, 8.

And to the people of Midian We sent their kinsman 11:84
Shu'aib. He said: 'Serve God, my people; you have no god
but Him. Do not give short weight or measure. Prosperous
though you are, beware the torment of a fateful day!

'My people, give just weight and measure in all fairness.
Do not defraud people of their possessions, nor shall you
corrupt the land with evil. Better for you is God's recompense, if you are true believers. I am not your keeper.'

'Shu'aib,' they replied, 'did your prayers teach you that we
should renounce the gods of our fathers and not conduct
our affairs in the manner we pleased? Truly, you are a wise
and gracious man!'

He said: 'Do but consider, my people! If my Lord has
revealed to me His will and bestowed on me a gracious gift,
should I not guide you? I do not wish to argue with you, only
to practise what I forbid you. I seek only to reform you:
as far as I am able. Nor can I succeed without God's help.
In Him I have put my trust and to Him I turn in penitence.

'Let your dispute with me not bring upon you the
doom which overtook the peoples of Noah, Hūd, and Ṣāliḥ;
nor is it long since the tribe of Lot was punished. Seek
forgiveness of your Lord and turn to Him in penitence.
Merciful and loving is my Lord.'

They replied: 'Shu'aib, much of what you say we cannot 11:91
comprehend. We know how weak you are in our midst. But
for your tribe, we should have stoned you. You shall on no
account prevail against us.'

He said: 'My people, have you more regard for my tribe
than for God? Dare you turn your backs upon Him? My
Lord has knowledge of all your actions. Do what you will,
my people, and so will I. You shall learn who will be
punished and held up to shame, and who is lying. Wait if
you will; I too am waiting.'

And when Our judgement came to pass We delivered
Shu'aib through Our mercy, together with those who
shared his faith. The Cry took the evil-doers, and when
morning came they were crouching lifeless in their dwellings, as though they had never prospered there. Like 11:95
Thamūd, gone are the people of Midian.

11:96    We sent forth Moses with Our signs and with clear authority to Pharaoh and his nobles. But they followed the behests of their master; misguided were Pharaoh's behests. He shall stand at the head of his people on the Day of Resurrection, and shall lead them into the Fire. Evil is the place they shall be led to.

A curse followed them in this world, and a curse shall follow them on the Day of Resurrection. Evil is the gift they shall receive.

We have recounted to you the annals of these communities: some have survived, while others have ceased to be. We did not wrong them, but they wronged themselves. The gods they called on besides God availed them nothing: and when your Lord's will was done, they only added to their ruin.

Such was the scourge your Lord visited upon the nations while they sinned. Harrowing and relentless is His scourge.

Surely in this there is a sign for him that dreads the torment in the Hereafter. That will be a day on which all people shall come together. That shall be a fateful day.

11:104    We shall defer it only to its appointed hour. And when that day arrives, no man shall speak but by His leave. Some shall be damned, and others shall be blessed. The damned shall be cast into the Fire, where, groaning and wailing, they shall abide as long as the heavens and the earth endure, unless your Lord ordain otherwise: your Lord shall accomplish what He will. As for the blessed, they shall abide in Paradise as long as the heavens and the earth endure, unless your Lord ordain otherwise. Theirs shall be an endless recompense.

Have no doubt as to what they worship. They serve the idols which their fathers served before them. We shall requite them in full measure.

We gave the Book to Moses, but differences arose about it. And but for a Word from your Lord, already decreed, their fate would have long been sealed. Yet they strongly doubt this.

Your Lord will surely reward all according to their deeds.
11:112  He has knowledge of all their actions. Follow then the

straight path as you are bidden, together with those who have repented with you, and do not transgress. He is watching all your actions.

Put no trust in the wrongdoers, lest the Fire should touch 11:113 you. None but God can protect or help you.

Attend to your prayers morning and evening, and in the night-time too. Good deeds shall make amends for sins. That is an admonition for thoughtful men. Therefore have patience; God will not deny the righteous their reward.

Were there, among the generations that have gone before you, any upright men who preached against evil, except the few We delivered from among them? The wrongdoers pursued their worldly pleasures and thus became guilty. Your Lord would not have ruined those towns, without just cause, had their inhabitants been righteous men.

Had your Lord pleased, He would have united all mankind in one community. They are still at odds, except for those to whom your Lord has shown mercy. To this end He has created them. The word of your Lord shall be fulfilled: 'I will fill Hell with jinn and humans all.'

We recount to you the histories of these apostles to put courage into your heart. Through them the Truth shall be revealed to you, with precepts and admonitions for the faithful.

Say to the infidels: 'Do whatever lies within your power, and so shall we. Wait if you will; we too are waiting.'

God alone has knowledge of what the heavens and the 11:123 earth conceal; to Him all things shall be referred. Serve Him, and put your trust in Him. Your Lord is never heedless of what you do.

# JOSEPH

*In the Name of God, the Compassionate, the Merciful*

ALIF *lām rā*'. These are the verses of the Glorious Book. 12:1 We have revealed the Koran in the Arabic tongue so that you may grow in understanding.

12:3     In revealing this Koran We will recount to you the best of narratives, though before it you were heedless.

Joseph said to his father: 'Father, I dreamt of eleven stars and the sun and the moon; I saw them prostrate themselves before me.'

'My son,' he replied, 'say nothing of this dream to your brothers, lest they plot evil against you: Satan is the sworn enemy of man. Even thus shall you be chosen by your Lord. He will teach you to interpret visions, and will perfect His favour to you and to the house of Jacob, as He perfected it to your forefathers Abraham and Isaac before you. Your Lord is all-knowing and wise.'

Surely in Joseph and his brothers there are signs for doubting men.

They said to each other: 'Surely Joseph and his brother are dearer to our father than ourselves, though we are many. Truly, our father is much mistaken. Let us slay Joseph, or cast him away in some far-off land, so that we may have no rivals in our father's love, and after that be honourable men.'

12:10     One of the brothers said: 'Do not slay Joseph; but, if you must, rather cast him into a dark pit. Some caravan will take him up.'

They said to their father: 'Why do you not trust us with Joseph? Surely we wish him well. Send him with us tomorrow, that he may play and enjoy himself. We will take good care of him.'

He replied: 'It would much grieve me to let him go with you; for I fear lest the wolf should eat him when you are off your guard.'

They said: 'If the wolf could eat him despite our number, then we should surely be lost!'

And when they took him with them, they resolved to cast him into a dark pit. We revealed to him Our will, saying: 'You shall tell them of all this when they will not know you.'

At nightfall they returned weeping to their father. They
12:17   said: 'We went off to compete together, and left Joseph

with our packs. The wolf devoured him. But you will not believe us, though we speak the truth.' And they showed 12:18 him their brother's shirt, stained with false blood.

'No!' he cried. 'Your souls have tempted you to evil. Sweet patience! God alone can help me bear the loss you speak of.'

And a caravan passed by, who sent their water-bearer to the pit. And when he had let down his pail, he cried: 'Rejoice! A boy!'

They concealed him as part of their merchandise. But God knew what they did. They sold him for a trifling price, for a few pieces of silver. They cared nothing for him.

The Egyptian who bought him said to his wife: 'Be kind to him. He may prove useful to us, or we may adopt him as our son.'

Thus We established Joseph in the land, and taught him to interpret dreams. God has power over all things, though most may not know it. And when he reached maturity We bestowed on him wisdom and knowledge. Thus do We reward the righteous.

His master's wife attempted to seduce him. She bolted the 12:23 doors and said: 'Come!'

'God forbid!' he replied. 'My lord has treated me with kindness. Wrongdoers shall never prosper.'

She made for him, and he himself would have succumbed to her had he not seen a sign from his Lord. Thus did We shield him from wantonness, for he was one of Our faithful servants.

They both rushed to the door. She tore his shirt from behind. And at the door they met her husband.

She cried: 'Shall not the man who wished to violate your wife be thrown into prison or sternly punished?'

Joseph said: 'It was she who attempted to seduce me.'

'If his shirt is torn from the front,' said one of her people, 'she is speaking the truth and he is lying. If it is torn from behind, then he is speaking the truth, and she is lying.'

And when her husband saw that Joseph's shirt was rent 12:28 from behind, he said to her: 'This is but one of your tricks.

12:29 Your cunning is great indeed! Joseph, say no more about this. Woman, ask pardon for your sin. You have assuredly done wrong.'

In the city, women were saying: 'The Prince's wife has sought to seduce her servant. She has conceived a passion for him. We can see that she has clearly gone astray.'

When she heard of their intrigues, she invited them to a banquet prepared at her house. To each she gave a knife, and ordered Joseph to present himself before them. When they saw him, they were amazed at him and cut their hands, exclaiming: 'God preserve us! This is no mortal, but a gracious angel.'

'This is he,' she said, 'on whose account you blamed me. I attempted to seduce him, but he was unyielding. If he declines to do my bidding, he shall be thrown into prison and shall be held in scorn.'

'Lord,' said Joseph, 'sooner would I go to prison than give in to their advances. Shield me from their cunning, or I shall yield to them and lapse into folly.'

12:34 His Lord answered his prayer and warded off their wiles from him. He hears all and knows all.

Yet, for all the evidence they had seen, they thought it right to jail him for a time.

Two young men entered the prison with him. One said: 'I dreamt that I was pressing grapes.' And the other: 'I dreamt I was carrying a loaf upon my head, and the birds came and ate of it. Tell us the meaning of these dreams, for we can see you are a man of virtue.'

Joseph replied: 'Whatever food you are provided with, I can divine for you its meaning, even before it reaches you. This knowledge my Lord has given me, for I have left the faith of those that disbelieve in God and deny the life to come. I follow the faith of my forefathers, Abraham, Isaac and Jacob. We will serve no idols besides God. Such is the grace which God has bestowed on us and on all mankind. Yet most do not give thanks.

'Fellow prisoners! Are sundry gods better than God, the
12:40 One who conquers all? Those you serve besides Him

are nothing but names which you and your fathers have devised and for which God has revealed no sanction. Judgement rests only with God. He has commanded you to worship none but Him. That is the true faith: yet most do not know it.

'Fellow prisoners, one of you will serve his lord with 12:41 wine. The other will be crucified, and the birds will peck at his head. That is the answer to your question.'

And Joseph said to the prisoner who he knew would survive: 'Remember me in the presence of your lord.'

But Satan made him forget to mention Joseph to his lord, so that he stayed in prison for several years.

The king said: 'I saw seven fatted cows which seven lean ones devoured; also seven green ears of corn and seven others dry. Tell me the meaning of this vision, my nobles, if you can interpret visions.'

They replied: 'They are but a medley of dreams; nor are we skilled in the interpretation of dreams.'

Thereupon the man who had been freed remembered after all that time. He said: 'I shall tell you what it means. Give me leave to go.'

'Joseph,' he said, 'man of truth, tell us of the seven 12:46 fatted cows which seven lean ones devoured; also of the seven green ears of corn and the other seven which were dry: so that I may go back to the people and inform them.'

He replied: 'You shall sow for seven consecutive years. Leave in the ear the corn you reap, except a little which you may eat. There shall follow seven hungry years which will consume all but a little of what you stored. Then will come a year of abundant rain, in which the people will press the grape.'

The king said: 'Bring this man before me.'

But when the envoy came to him, Joseph said: 'Go back to your master and ask him about the women who cut their hands. My master knows their cunning.'

The king questioned the women, saying: 'What made 12:51 you attempt to seduce Joseph?'

'God forbid!' they replied. 'We know no evil of him.'

'Now the truth must come to light,' said the Prince's wife.
'It was I who attempted to seduce him. He has told the truth.'

12:52 'From this,' said Joseph, 'my lord will know that I did
not betray him in his absence, and that God does not guide
the mischief of the treacherous. Not that I claim to be free
from sin: man's soul is prone to evil, except his to whom
my Lord has shown mercy. My Lord is forgiving and
merciful.'

The king said: 'Bring him before me. I will choose him
for my own.'

And when he had spoken with him, the king said: 'You
shall henceforth dwell with us, honoured and trusted.'

Joseph said: 'Give me charge of the granaries of the
land. I shall husband them wisely.'

Thus did We establish Joseph in the land, and he dwelt
there as he pleased. We bestow Our mercy on whom We
will, and shall never deny the righteous their reward. Surely
better is the recompense of the life to come for those who
believe in God and keep from evil.

12:58 Joseph's brothers arrived and presented themselves
before him. He recognized them, but they knew him not.
And when he had given them their provisions, he said:
'Bring me your other brother from your father. Do you not
see that I give just measure and am the best of hosts? If you
refuse to bring him, you shall have no measure, nor shall you
come near me again.'

They replied: 'We will endeavour to fetch him from his
father. This we will surely do.'

He said to his servants: 'Put their silver[1] into their
packs, so that they may discover it when they return to their
people. Perchance they will come back.'

When they returned to their father, they said: 'Father, corn
is henceforth denied us. Send our brother with us and we shall
have our measure. We will take good care of him.'

12:64 He replied: 'Am I to trust you with him as I once trusted
you with his brother? But God is the best of guardians: and
of all those that show mercy He is the most merciful.'

---

1. Literally, 'their merchandise'.

When they opened their packs, they discovered that their 12:65 money had been returned to them. 'Father,' they said, 'what more can we desire? Here is our money paid back to us. We will buy provisions for our people, and take good care of our brother. We should receive an extra camel-load; a camel-load should be easy enough.'

He replied: 'I will not send him with you until you promise in God's name to bring him back to me, unless the worst befall you.'

And when they had given him their pledge, he said: 'God is the witness of what we say. My sons, do not enter from one gate; enter from different gates. In no way can I shield you from the might of God; judgement is His alone. In Him I have put my trust. In Him let the faithful put their trust.'

And when they entered as their father bade them, he could in no way shield them from the might of God. It was but a wish in Jacob's soul which he had thus fulfilled. He was possessed of knowledge which We had given him. But most men have no knowledge.

When they went in to Joseph, he embraced his brother, 12:69 and said: 'I am your brother. Do not grieve at what they did.'

And when he had given them their provisions, he hid a drinking-cup in his brother's pack.

Then a crier called out after them: 'Travellers, you are surely thieves!'

They turned back, and asked: 'What have you lost?'

'We miss the king's drinking-cup,' they replied. 'He that brings it shall have a camel-load of corn. I pledge my word for it.'

'In God's name,' they cried, 'you know we did not come to do evil in the land. We are no thieves.'

The Egyptians said: 'What punishment shall be his who stole it, if you prove to be lying?'

They replied: 'He in whose pack the cup is found shall render himself your bondsman. Thus do we punish the wrongdoers.'

Joseph searched their bags before his brother's, and then 12:76 took out the cup from his brother's bag.

Thus We directed Joseph. By the king's law he had no right to seize his brother: but God willed otherwise. We exalt whom We will to a lofty station: and above those that have knowledge there is One who is all-knowing.

12:77 They said: 'If he has stolen – know then that a brother of his stole before him.'

But Joseph kept his secret and revealed nothing to them. He said: 'Your deed was worse. God best knows the things you speak of.'

They said: 'Noble prince, this boy has an aged father. Take one of us, instead of him. We can see you are a generous man.'

He replied: 'God forbid that we should take any but the man with whom our property was found: for then we should surely be unjust.'

When they despaired of him, they went aside to confer in private. The eldest said: 'Do you not know that your father took from you a pledge in God's name, and that long ago you did your worst with Joseph? I will not stir from the land until my father gives me leave or God makes known to 12:81 me His judgement: He is the best of judges. Return to your father and say to him: "Father, your son has stolen. We testify only to what we know. How could we guard against the unforeseen? Inquire at the city where we lodged, and from the caravan with which we travelled. We surely speak the truth."'

'No!' cried their father. 'Your souls have tempted you to evil. But I will have sweet patience. God may bring them all to me. He alone is all-knowing and wise.' And he turned away from them, crying: 'Alas for Joseph!' His eyes went white with grief, and he was oppressed with silent sorrow.

His sons exclaimed: 'In God's name, will you not cease to think of Joseph until you ruin your health and die?'

He replied: 'I complain to God of my sorrow and sadness. God has made known to me things that you know not. 12:87 Go, my sons, and seek news of Joseph and his brother. Do not despair of God's spirit; none but unbelievers despair of God's spirit.'

And when they went in to him, they said: 'Noble prince, 12:88
we and our people are scourged with famine. We have
brought but little money. Give us our full measure, and
be charitable to us: God rewards the charitable.'

'Do you know,' he replied, 'what you did to Joseph and
his brother? You are surely unaware.'

They cried: 'Can you indeed be Joseph?'

'I am Joseph,' he answered, 'and this is my brother. God
has been gracious to us. Those that keep from evil and
endure with fortitude, God will not deny them their
reward.'

'By the Lord,' they said, 'God has exalted you above us
all. We have indeed done wrong.'

He replied: 'None shall reproach you this day. May God
forgive you: of all those that show mercy He is the most
merciful. Take this shirt of mine and throw it over my
father's face: he will recover his sight. Then return to me
with all your people.'

When the caravan departed their father said: 'I feel the 12:94
breath of Joseph, though you will not believe me.'

'In God's name,' said those who heard him, 'it is but your
old illusion.'

And when the bearer of good news arrived, he threw
Joseph's shirt over the old man's face, and he regained his
sight. He said: 'Did I not tell you, God has made known to
me what you know not?'

His sons said: 'Father, implore forgiveness for our sins.
We have indeed done wrong.'

He replied: 'I shall implore my Lord to forgive you. He is
forgiving and merciful.'

And when they went in to Joseph, he embraced his
parents and said: 'Welcome to Egypt, safe, if God wills!'

He helped his parents to a couch, and they all fell on their 12:100
knees and prostrated themselves before him.

'This,' said Joseph to his father, 'is the meaning of my
old vision: my Lord has fulfilled it. He has been gracious to
me. He has released me from prison, and brought you out of
the desert after Satan had stirred up strife between me and

my brothers. My Lord is gracious to whom He will. He alone is all-knowing and wise.

12:101 'Lord, You have given me authority and taught me to interpret dreams. Creator of the heavens and the earth, my Guardian in this world and in the world to come! Allow me to die in submission, and admit me among the righteous.'

That which We have now revealed to you[1] is a tale of the unknown. You were not present when Joseph's brothers conceived their plans and schemed against him. Yet strive as you may, most men will not believe.

You shall demand of them no recompense for this. It[2] is but an admonition to all mankind.

Many are the marvels of the heavens and the earth; yet they pass them by and pay no heed to them. The greater part of them believe in God only if they can worship other gods besides Him.

Are they confident that God's scourge will not fall upon them, or that the Hour of Doom will not overtake them unawares, without warning?

12:108 Say: 'This is my path. With sure knowledge I call on you to have faith in God, I and all my followers. Glory be to God! I am no idolater.'

Nor were the apostles whom We sent before you other than mortals inspired by Our will and chosen from among their people.

Have they not travelled the land and seen what was the end of those who disbelieved before them? Surely better is the life to come for those that keep from evil. Can you not understand?

And when at length Our apostles despaired and thought they were denied, Our help came down to them, delivering whom We pleased. The evil-doers could not be saved from 12:111 Our scourge. Their annals point a moral to men of understanding.

This[2] is no invented tale, but a confirmation of previous scriptures, an explanation of all things, a guide and a blessing to true believers.

1. Muḥammad.       2. The Koran.

# THUNDER

*In the Name of God, the Compassionate, the Merciful*

ALIF *lām mīm rā'*. These are the verses of the Book. That which has been revealed to you from your Lord is the Truth, yet most men do not believe. 13:1

It was God who raised the heavens without visible pillars. He then ascended the throne and pressed the sun and the moon into His service, each pursuing an appointed course. He ordains all things. He makes plain His revelations so that you may firmly believe in meeting your Lord.

It was He who spread out the earth and placed upon it mountains and rivers. He gave all plants their male and female parts and drew the veil of night over the day. Surely in these there are signs for thinking men.

And in the land there are adjoining plots: vineyards and cornfields and groves of palm, the single and the clustered. Their fruits are nourished by the same water: yet We make the taste of some more favoured than the taste of others. Surely in this there are signs for men of understanding.

If anything could make you marvel, then you should surely marvel at those who say: 'When we are dust, shall we be restored in a new creation?' 13:5

Such are those who deny their Lord. Their necks shall be bound with chains. They are the heirs of the Fire, and shall abide therein for ever.

They bid you hasten evil rather than good. Yet many were those who were punished before them. Your Lord is merciful to men, despite their wrongdoing: yet stern is your Lord in retribution.

The unbelievers ask: 'Why has no sign been sent down to him by his Lord?' But you are only to give warning. Every nation has its mentor.

God knows what every female bears: He knows of every change within her womb. For everything He has a finite measure. 13:8

13:9 He knows the unknown and the manifest. He is the Supreme One, the Most High.

It is the same whether you converse in secret or aloud, whether you hide under the cloak of night or walk about in the light of day. Each has guardian angels before him and behind him, who watch him by God's command.

God does not change a people's lot unless they change what is in their hearts. If God seeks to afflict them with a misfortune, none can ward it off. Besides Him, they have no protector.

It is He who makes the lightning flash upon you, inspiring you with fear and hope, and gathers up the heavy clouds. The thunder sounds His praises, and the angels, too, in awe of Him. He hurls His thunderbolts at whom He pleases. Yet the unbelievers wrangle about God. Stern is His might.

13:14 To Him is the true prayer. The idols to which the pagans pray give them no answer. They are like a man who stretches out his hands to the water and bids it rise to his mouth: it cannot reach it. Vain are the prayers of the unbelievers.

All who dwell in the heavens and on the earth shall prostrate themselves before God: some willingly, some perforce; and their very shadows, morning and evening.

Say: 'Who is the Lord of the heavens and the earth?'

Say: 'God.'

Say: 'Why then have you chosen other gods besides Him, who, even to themselves, can do neither good nor harm?'

Say: 'Are the blind and the seeing equal? Is darkness equal to the light?'

Have their idols brought into being a creation like His, so that both creations appear to them alike?

Say: 'God is the Creator of all things. He is the One who conquers all.'

13:17 He sends down water from the sky which fills the riverbeds to overflowing, so that the torrent bears a swelling foam, akin to that which rises from smelted ore when men make ornaments and tools. Thus God depicts truth and falsehood. The scum is cast away, but that which is of use to man remains behind. Even thus God speaks in parables.

Rich is the recompense of those that obey God. But those 13:18 that disobey Him – if they possessed all that the earth contains, and as much besides, they would gladly offer it for their ransom. Theirs shall be an evil reckoning. Hell shall be their home, an evil resting-place.

Is then he who knows that the Truth has been revealed to you by your Lord like him who is blind?

Truly, none will take heed but the wise: those who keep faith with God and do not break their pledge; who join together what God has bidden to be united; who fear their Lord and dread the terrors of an evil reckoning; who for the sake of God endure with fortitude, attend to their prayers, and give alms in private and in public; and who ward off evil with good. These shall have the recompense of Paradise. They shall enter the gardens of Eden, together with the righteous among their fathers, their spouses, and their descendants. From every gate the angels will come in to them, saying: 'Peace be to you for all that you have steadfastly endured. Blessed is the recompense of Paradise.'

As for those who break God's covenant after confirming 13:25 it, who put asunder what God has bidden to be united and perpetrate corruption in the land, the curse shall be laid on them; the scourge of Hell awaits them.

God gives abundantly to whom He will and sparingly to whom He pleases. The unbelievers rejoice in the life of this world: yet the life of this world is but a brief diversion compared with the life to come.

The unbelievers ask: 'Why has no sign been sent down to him by his Lord?'

Say: 'God leaves in error whom He will, and guides to Himself those who repent and have faith; whose hearts find comfort in the remembrance of God. Surely in the remembrance of God all hearts are comforted. Blessed are those who have faith and do good works; blissful is their end.

Thus have We sent you forth to a community before 13:30 whom other communities had passed away, that you may recite to them Our revelations. Yet they deny the Lord of Mercy. Say: 'He is my Lord. There is no god but Him. In Him I have put my trust, and to Him I shall return.'

13:31 And even if there be a Koran whereby the mountains could be set in motion, the earth rent asunder, and the dead communed with, surely all things are subject to God's will. Are the faithful unaware that, had God pleased, He could have guided all mankind?

As for the unbelievers, because of their misdeeds disaster shall not cease to afflict them or to crouch at their very doorstep until God's promise be fulfilled. God will not fail His promise.

Other apostles were mocked before you: but, though I bore long with the unbelievers, My scourge at length overtook them. And how terrible was My scourge!

Who is it that watches every soul and all its actions? Yet they set up other gods besides God. Say: 'Name them. Would you tell Him of that which is unknown to Him on the earth? Or are they merely empty words?'

Indeed, their foul devices seem fair to the unbelievers, for they are debarred from the right path. None can guide those 13:34 whom God has led astray. Punishment awaits them in this nether life: but more grievous is the punishment of the life to come. From God they will have no protector.

Such is the Paradise which the righteous have been promised: it is watered by running streams: eternal is its fruit, and eternal is its shade. Such shall be the end of the righteous. But the Fire shall be the end of the unbelievers.

Those to whom We gave the Scriptures rejoice in what is revealed to you, while some factions deny a part of it. Say: 'I am only commanded to serve God and to associate none with Him. To Him I pray, and to Him I shall return.'

Thus have We revealed it, a code of judgements in the Arabic tongue. If you succumb to their desires after all the knowledge you have been given, from God you shall have no saviour or protector.

13:38 We sent forth other apostles before you and gave them wives and children. Yet none of them could work a miracle except by God's leave. Every age has a term decreed. God

abrogates and confirms what He pleases. His is the Decree 13:39
Eternal.

Whether We let you glimpse in some measure the
scourge We promise them, or call you back to Us before We
smite them, your mission is only to give warning: it is for
Us to do the reckoning.

Do they not see how We invade their land and diminish
its borders? If God decrees a thing, none can reverse it.
Swift is His reckoning.

Those who have gone before them also schemed, but
God is the master of all scheming: He knows what every
soul has done. The unbelievers will then learn for whom the
blissful end is destined.

And the unbelievers say: 'You are no true apostle.' Say: 13:43
'Sufficient is God as my witness, and your witness; and so
are those who know the Scriptures.'

# ABRAHAM

### In the Name of God, the Compassionate, the Merciful

ALIF *lām rā'*. We have revealed to you this Book so that, 14:1
by their Lord's leave, you may lead the people from darkness
to the light, to the path of the Mighty, the Praiseworthy One:
the path of God, to whom belongs all that the heavens and
the earth contain.

Woe betide the unbelievers, for they shall be sternly
punished! Woe betide those who love this life more than the
life to come; who debar others from the path of God and
seek to make it crooked. They have strayed far into error.

Each apostle We have sent has spoken only in the language
of his own people, so that he might make his precepts clear
to them. But God leaves in error whom He will and guides
whom He pleases. He is the Mighty, the Wise One.

We sent forth Moses with Our signs, saying: 'Lead your
people out of the darkness into the light, and remind them
of God's favours.' Surely in this are signs for every
steadfast, thankful man.

Moses said to his people: 'Remember God's goodness to 14:6

you when He delivered you from Pharaoh's nation, who had oppressed you cruelly, slaughtering your sons and sparing only your daughters. Surely that was a grievous 14:7 trial by your Lord. For He had declared: "If you give thanks, I will bestow abundance upon you: but if you deny My favours, My punishment is terrible indeed."'

And Moses said: 'If you and all who dwell on earth prove thankless, He does not need your thanks, though He deserves your praise.'

Have you not heard what befell those that have gone before you? The people of Noah, 'Ād, and Thamūd, and those who came after? God alone knows their number. Their apostles came to them with veritable signs, but they bit their hands with their mouths and said: 'We will not believe in your message. Indeed, we strongly doubt the faith to which you call us.'

Their apostles answered: 'Is God, the Creator of the heavens and the earth, to be doubted? He calls you to Him that He may forgive you your sins and reprieve you till your appointed hour.'

They said: 'You are but mortals like ourselves. You wish to turn us away from the gods our fathers worshipped. Bring us some clear authority.'

14:11 Their apostles replied: 'We are indeed but mortals like yourselves. Yet God bestows His grace on such of His servants as He chooses. We cannot give you proof, except by God's leave. In God let true believers put their trust. And why should we not trust in God, when He has already guided us to our paths? We will endure your persecution patiently. In God let all the trusting put their trust.'

'Return to our ways,' the unbelievers said to their apostles, 'or we will banish you from our land.'

But their Lord revealed His will to them, saying: 'We shall destroy the wrongdoers and give you the land to dwell in after they are gone. Let him take heed who dreads My eminence and fears My threats.'

14:15 And when they called for help, every hardened sinner came to grief.

Hell will stretch behind him, and putrid water shall he 14:16
drink: he will sip, but scarcely swallow. Death will assail
him from every side, yet he shall not die. Harrowing
torment awaits him.

The works of the unbelievers are like ashes which the
wind scatters on a stormy day: they shall gain nothing from
what they do. To act thus is to stray far into error.

Do you not see that God has created the heavens and the
earth with truth? He can remove you if He wills and bring
into being a new creation: that is no difficult thing for God.

All shall appear before God. The humble will say to those
who thought themselves mighty: 'We were your followers.
Can you protect us from God's punishment?'

They will reply: 'Had God given us guidance, we would
have guided you. Neither panic nor patience will help us
now. There is no escape for us.'

And when Our judgement has been passed, Satan will say to 14:22
them: 'True was the promise which God made you. I too made
you a promise, but did not keep it. Yet had I no power over
you. I only called you, and you answered me. Do not now
blame me, but blame yourselves. I cannot help you, nor can
you help me. I never believed, as you did, that I was God's
equal.'

The wrongdoers shall be sternly punished. As for those that
have faith and do good works, they shall be admitted to
gardens watered by running streams, in which, by their Lord's
leave, they shall abide for ever. Their greeting shall be:
'Peace!'

Do you not see how God compares a good word to a good
tree? Its root is firm and its branches are in the sky; it yields its
fruit in every season by its Lord's leave. God speaks in parables to people so that they may take heed. But an evil word is
like an evil tree torn out of the earth and shorn of all its roots.

God will strengthen the faithful with His steadfast Word,
both in this life and in the life to come. He leads the wrongdoers astray. God accomplishes what He pleases.

Have you not seen those who repay the grace of God
with unbelief and drive their people into the House of
Perdition? In Hell shall they burn; evil shall be their fate. . 14:29

14:30 They set up false gods as the equals of God to lead men away from His path. Say to them: 'Take your pleasure now: you are surely destined for the Fire.'

Tell My servants, those who are true believers, to be steadfast in prayer and to give alms in private and in public, before that day arrives when all trading shall cease and friendships be no more.

It was God who created the heavens and the earth. He has sent down water from the sky with which He brings forth fruits for your sustenance. He has subdued the ships which by His leave sail the ocean in your service. He has subdued the rivers for your benefit, and subdued for you the sun and the moon, which steadfastly pursue their courses. And He has subdued for you the night and the day. Of everything you have asked for He has given you some. If you reckoned up God's favours you could not count them. Truly, man is wicked and thankless.

Abraham said: 'Lord, make this[1] a secure land. Preserve
14:36 me and my descendants from serving idols. Lord, many have they led astray. He that follows me shall become my brother, but if anyone turns against me, You are surely forgiving and merciful.

'Lord, I have settled some of my offspring in a barren valley near Your Sacred House, so that they may observe true worship, Lord. Put in people's hearts kindness towards them, and provide them with the earth's fruits, so that they may give thanks.

'Lord, You have knowledge of all that we conceal and all that we reveal: nothing on earth or in heaven is hidden from God.

'Praise be to God who has given me Ishmael and Isaac in my old age! All prayers are heard by Him.

'Lord, make me and my descendants steadfast in prayer. Lord, accept my prayer.

'Forgive me, Lord, and forgive my parents and all the
14:42 faithful on the Day of Reckoning.'

Never think that God is unaware of the wrongdoers' actions. He only gives them respite till the day on which all

1. Mecca.

eyes will stare with consternation. They shall rush in terror  14:43
with heads uplifted and hearts utterly vacant. They shall
stare, but see nothing.

Forewarn people of the day when the scourge will overtake them; when the wrongdoers will say: 'Lord, grant us
respite for a while. We will obey Your call, and follow the
apostles.'

But a voice will say to them: 'Did you not once swear
that you would never disappear? You lived in the dwellings
of those who wronged their souls before you: yet you knew
full well how We had dealt with them, and We spoke to you
in parables about them.'

They plot, but their plots are known to God, even if their
plots could move mountains.

Never think that God will break the pledge He gave to
His apostles. Mighty is God, and capable of revenge.

On the day when the earth is changed into a different earth
and the heavens into new heavens, mankind shall stand
before God, the One, who conquers all. On that day you
shall see the guilty bound with chains, their garments pitch,
and their faces covered with flames.

God will recompense each soul according to its deeds.
Swift is God's reckoning.

This is an exhortation to the people. Let them be warned  14:52
thereby and know that He is but one God. Let the wise bear
this in mind.

# AL-ḤIJR

*In the Name of God, the Compassionate, the Merciful*

ALIF *lām rā'*. These are the verses of the Book, a Glorious  15:1
Koran:

The day will surely come when those who disbelieve
will wish that they were Muslims. Let them feast and
make merry; and let their hopes beguile them. They shall
learn.

Never have We destroyed a nation whose term of life was  15:5
not ordained beforehand. Men cannot forestall their doom,
nor can they retard it.

15:6    They say: 'You to whom the Admonition was revealed, you are surely possessed. Bring down the angels, if what you say be true.'

We shall send down the angels only with the truth. Then shall they never be reprieved.

It was We that revealed the Admonition, and shall Ourself preserve it. We have sent forth apostles before you to the older nations: but they scoffed at each apostle We sent them. Thus do We put doubt into the hearts of the guilty: they deny him, despite the example of the ancients.

If We opened for the unbelievers a gate in heaven and they ascended through it higher and higher, still they would say: 'Our eyes were dazzled: truly, we must have been bewitched.'

We have decked the sky with constellations and made them lovely to behold. We have guarded them from every cursèd devil. Eavesdroppers are pursued by fiery comets.

15:19    We have spread out the earth and set upon it immovable mountains. We have planted it with every seasonable fruit, providing sustenance for yourselves and for those whom you do not provide for. We hold the store of every blessing and send it down in appropriate measure. We let loose the fertilizing winds and bring down water from the sky for you to drink; its stores are beyond your reach.

It is surely We who ordain life and death. We are the Heir of all things.

We know those who have gone before you, and know those who will come hereafter. It is your Lord who will gather them all before Him. He is wise and all-knowing.

We created man from dry clay, from black moulded loam, and before him Satan from smokeless fire. Your Lord said to the angels: 'I am creating man from dry clay, from black moulded loam. When I have fashioned him and breathed of My spirit into him, kneel down and prostrate yourselves before him.'

The angels, one and all, prostrated themselves, except Satan. He refused to prostrate himself as the others did.

15:32    'Satan,' said God, 'why do you not prostrate yourself?'

He replied: 'I will not bow to a mortal whom You created 15:33
of dry clay, of black moulded loam.'

'Get you hence,' said God, 'you are accursed. The curse
shall be on you till Judgement-day.'

'Lord,' said Satan, 'reprieve me till the Day of Resurrection.'

He answered: 'You are reprieved till the Appointed Day.'

'Lord,' said Satan, 'since You have thus seduced me, I
will tempt mankind on earth: I will seduce them all, except
those of them who are your faithful servants.'

He replied: 'This is My straight path. You shall have no
power over My servants, only the sinners who follow you.
They are all destined for Hell. It has seven gates, and
through each gate they shall come in separate bands. But
the righteous shall dwell among gardens and fountains; in
peace and safety they shall enter them. We shall remove all
hatred from their hearts, and they shall take their ease on
couches face to face, a band of brothers. Toil shall not
weary them, nor shall they ever be driven out.'

Tell My servants that I alone am the Forgiving One, the
Merciful; and that only My scourge is the woeful scourge.

Tell them of Abraham's guests. They went in to him and 15:51
said: 'Peace,' but he replied: 'We fear your intent.'

'Have no fear,' they answered. 'We come to you with good
news. You shall have a son endowed with knowledge.'

He said: 'Do you bring me such news in my old age?
What news do you bring me?'

They replied: 'We have made known to you the truth.
Do not despair.'

He said: 'Who but a sinner would despair of God's
mercy? Messengers,' he said, 'what is your errand?'

They replied: 'We are sent forth to a guilty nation. The
house of Lot alone we shall deliver, except his wife.' We
had decreed that she should stay with those who were to
stay behind.

And when the envoys came to the house of Lot, he said
to them: 'I do not know you.'

'No,' they replied. 'We bring you news of that concerning 15:63

185

15:64 which they are disputing. We bring you the truth, for what we say is true. Depart with your kinsfolk in the dead of night. Walk in their rear and let none turn round. Go where you are commanded.'

Such were the instructions We gave him; for the wrong-doers were to be utterly destroyed next morning.

The townsfolk came to him rejoicing. He said: 'These are my guests; do not disgrace me. Have fear of God and do not shame me.'

They replied: 'Did we not forbid you to entertain strangers?'

He said: 'Here are my daughters: take them, if you are bent on evil.'

By your life, they were reeling in their frenzy! At sunrise the Cry took them. We razed their city to the ground and let loose a shower of clay-stones upon them.

Surely in this there are signs for prudent men. The road on which their city stood is trodden still. Surely in this there is a sign for true believers.

15:78 The dwellers of the Forest[1] were also guilty. On them, too, We took vengeance, and made of both a manifest example.

The people of Ḥijr[2] also denied Our apostles. We gave them Our signs, but they ignored them. They hewed their dwellings into the mountains and led their lives in safety. But one morning the Cry took them. Nothing did their gains avail them.

It was but to reveal the Truth that We created the heavens and the earth and all that lies between them. The Hour of Doom is sure to come: bear with them nobly. Your Lord is the all-knowing Creator.

We have given you the seven oft-repeated verses[3] and the
15:88 Glorious Koran. Do not regard with envy what We have given some among them to enjoy, nor grieve on their

1. The people of Midian.

2. Territory to the north of Medina, where the Thamūd are said to have dwelt.

3. The seven verses of the Fātiḥah, or Exordium.

account. Show kindness to the faithful, and say: 'I am he 15:89
that gives plain warning.'

We will surely punish the schismatics, who have broken
up the scriptures into separate parts, believing in some and
denying others. By the Lord, We will question them all
about their doings.

Proclaim, then, what you are bidden and let the idolaters be. We will Ourself sustain you against those that
mock you and serve other deities besides God. They shall
learn.

We know you are distressed by what they say. Give glory
to your Lord and prostrate yourself. Worship your Lord till 15:99
certain death overtakes you.

# THE BEE

*In the Name of God, the Compassionate, the Merciful*

THE JUDGEMENT of God will surely come to pass: do not 16:1
seek to hurry it on. Glory be to Him! Exalted be He above
their idols!

By His will He sends down the angels with the Spirit to
those among His servants whom He chooses, bidding
them proclaim: 'There is no god but Me: therefore fear
Me.'

He created the heavens and the earth to manifest the
Truth. Exalted be He above their idols!

He created man from a little germ: yet is he openly contentious.

He created the beasts which give you warmth and food
and other benefits. How pleasant they look when you bring
them home to rest and when you lead them out to pasture!

They carry your burdens to far-off lands, which you
could not otherwise reach except with painful toil. Compassionate is your Lord, and merciful.

He has given you horses, mules, and donkeys, which you 16:8
may ride or put on show; and He has created other things
beyond your knowledge.

16:9    God alone points to the right path. Some turn aside but, had He pleased, He would have given you guidance all.

It is He who sends down water from the sky, which provides you with your drink and brings forth the pasturage on which your cattle feed. And with it He brings forth corn and olives, dates and grapes and fruits of every kind. Surely in this there is a sign for thinking men.

He has pressed the night and the day, and the sun and the moon, into your service: the stars also serve you by His leave. Surely in this there are signs for men of understanding.

On the earth He has fashioned for you objects of various hues: surely in this there is a sign for prudent men.

It is He who has subdued the ocean, so that you may eat of its fresh fish and bring up from its depths ornaments to wear. Behold the ships ploughing their course through it. All this, that you may seek His bounty and render thanks.

He set firm mountains upon the earth lest it should move away with you; and rivers, roads, and landmarks, so 16:16 that you may be rightly guided. By the stars, too, are men directed.

Is He, then, who has created, like him who cannot create? Will you not take heed?

If you reckoned up God's blessings, you could not count them. God is forgiving and merciful.

God has knowledge of what you conceal and what you reveal. The gods which infidels invoke create nothing: they are themselves created. They are dead, not living; nor do they know when they will be raised to life.

Your God is one God. Those that deny the life to come have faithless hearts and are puffed up with pride. God surely knows what they conceal and what they reveal. He does not love the proud.

When they are asked: 'What has your Lord revealed?' 16:25 they say: 'Fables of the ancients!' They shall bear the full brunt of their burdens on the Day of Resurrection, together with the burdens of those who in their ignorance were misled by them. Evil is that which they shall bear.

Those who had gone before them also plotted. But God 16:26
smote their edifice at its foundations, and its roof collapsed
upon their heads. The scourge overtook them whence they
did not know.

He will hold them up to shame on the Day of Resurrection. He will say: 'Where are your idols now, the theme of
your disputes?' And those endowed with knowledge will
say: 'Shame and sorrow shall this day smite the unbelievers.'

Those whom the angels will claim back while steeped in
sin will offer their submission, saying: 'We have done no
wrong!' 'Indeed!' they will reply. 'God well knows what
you have done. Enter the gates of Hell: there you shall
abide for ever.' Evil is the abode of the arrogant.

But when the righteous are asked: 'What has your Lord
revealed?' they will reply: 'That which is best.' Good is the
reward of those that do good works in this present life: but
far better is the abode of the life to come. Blessed is the
abode of the righteous. They shall enter the gardens of 16:31
Eden, where rivers will roll at their feet; and there shall they
have all that they desire. Thus shall God recompense the
righteous, whom the angels will reclaim, in all their virtue,
saying: 'Peace be on you. Come in to Paradise, the reward
of your labours.'

Are they waiting for the angels to come down or for the
fulfilment of your Lord's will? Those who had gone before
them also waited. God did not wrong them, but they
wronged themselves: the evil which they did recoiled upon
them, and the scourge at which they scoffed encompassed
them.

The idolaters say: 'Had God pleased, neither we nor our
fathers would have served other gods besides Him; nor
would we have declared anything unlawful without His
sanction.' Such also was the pleas of those who had gone
before them. Yet what should apostles do but give plain
warning?

We raised an apostle in each community, saying: 'Serve 16:36
God and keep away from false gods.' Among them were
some to whom God gave guidance, and others destined to

go astray. Roam the world and see what was the end of the disbelievers!

16:37    Strive as you may to guide them, God will not guide those whom He confounds. There shall be none to help them.

They solemnly swear by God that He will never raise the dead to life. But God's promise shall be fulfilled, though most may not know it. He will resolve for them their differences, and the unbelievers will know that they were lying. When We decree a thing, We need only say: 'Be,' and it is.

As for those who after persecution fled their homes in the cause of God, bearing ills with patience and putting their trust in their Lord, We will provide them with a fine abode in this life: yet better still is the reward of the life to come, if they but knew it.

The apostles We sent before you were but men whom We inspired with revelations and with scriptures. Ask the People of the Book, if you know not. To you We have revealed the Admonition, so that you may proclaim to men what was sent down for them, and that they may take thought.

16:45    Are those who plot evil so certain that God will not cause the earth to cave in beneath them, or that the scourge will not descend on them whence they know not? Or smite them in the course of their journeys when they cannot escape, or give them over to slow destruction? Yet is your Lord benevolent and merciful.

Do they not see how every object God created casts its shadow right and left, prostrating itself before God in all humility? To God bow all the creatures of the heavens and the earth, and the angels too. They are not disdainful; they fear their Lord on high and do as they are bidden.

God has said: 'You shall not serve two gods, for He is but one God. Fear none but Me.'

His is what the heavens and the earth contain. His is the Faith everlasting. Would you then fear any but God?

There is no blessing you enjoy which does not come from God, and to Him you turn for help when misfortune
16:54  befalls you. Yet no sooner does He remove your ills than some among you set up other gods besides their Lord,

showing no gratitude for what We give them. Take your 16:55 pleasure now, and you shall learn.

To idols they know nothing of they assign a share of what We gave them. By the Lord, you shall be questioned about the lies you fabricated!

They foist daughters upon God (glory be to Him!), but for themselves they choose what they desire. When the birth of a girl is announced to any of them, his countenance darkens and he is filled with gloom. On account of the bad news he hides himself from men: should he put up with the shame or bury her in the earth? How ill they judge!

Evil are the ways of those who deny the life to come. But most sublime are the ways of God. He is the Mighty, the Wise One.

If God punished people for their sins, not one creature would be left alive. He reprieves them till a time ordained; when their time arrives, not for one hour shall they stay behind: nor can they go before it.

They foist upon God what they themselves abhor. They 16:62 falsely claim that a good reward awaits them. But let there be no doubt: the Fire awaits them, and they have strayed far into error.

By the Lord, We have sent apostles before you to other nations. But Satan made their foul deeds seem fair to them, and to this day he is their patron. A woeful scourge awaits them.

We have revealed to you the Book so that you may resolve their differences for them: a guide and a blessing to true believers.

God sends down water from the sky with which He quickens the earth after its death. Surely in this there is a sign for prudent men.

In cattle too you have a worthy lesson. We give you to drink of that which is in their bellies, between the bowels and the blood-streams: pure milk, pleasant for those who drink it.

And the fruits of the palm and the vine, from which you 16:67 derive intoxicants and wholesome food. Surely in this there is a sign for men of understanding.

16:68 Your Lord inspired the bee, saying: 'Make your homes in the mountains, in the trees, and in the hives which men shall build for you. Feed on every kind of fruit, and follow the trodden paths of your Lord.'

From its belly comes forth a syrup of different hues, a cure for men. Surely in this there is a sign for those who would take thought.

God created you, and He will then reclaim you. Some shall have their lives prolonged to abject old age, when all that they once knew they shall know no more. All-knowing is God, and mighty.

In what He has provided, God has favoured some among you above others. Those who are so favoured will not allow their slaves an equal share in what they have. Would they deny God's goodness?

God has given you wives from among yourselves and, through your wives, sons and grandchildren. He has provided you with good things: will they then believe in falsehood and deny God's favours?

16:73 They worship helpless idols which can confer on them no benefits from heaven or earth. Compare God with none: God has knowledge, but you have not.

God makes this comparison. On the one hand there is a helpless slave, the property of his master. On the other, a man on whom We have bestowed Our bounty, so that he gives of it both in private and in public. Are the two equal? God forbid! Most men have no knowledge.

God also makes this comparison. Take a dumb and helpless man, a burden on his master: wherever he sends him he returns with empty hands. Is he as good as he that enjoins justice and follows a straight path?

To God belong the secrets of the heavens and the earth. The business of the Final Hour shall be accomplished in the twinkling of an eye, or in a shorter time. God has power over all things.

16:78 God brought you out of your mothers' wombs devoid of all knowledge, and gave you ears and eyes and hearts, so that you may give thanks.

Do they not see the birds that wing their way in heaven's 16:79
vault? None but God sustains them. Surely in this there are
signs for true believers.

God has given you houses to dwell in, and animals' skins
for tents, so that you may find them light when you travel
and easy to pitch when you halt for shelter; while from their
wool, fur, and hair, He has for a space of time provided you
with comforts and domestic goods.

By means of that which He created, God has given you
shelter from the sun. He has given you refuge in the
mountains. He has furnished you with garments to protect
you from the heat, and with coats of armour to shield you in
your wars. Thus He perfects His favours to you, so that you
may submit to Him.

But if they[1] pay no heed, your[2] mission is only to give
clear warning.

They recognize God's favours, yet they deny them. Most
of them are ungrateful.

On the day We call a witness from each community, their 16:84
pleas shall not avail the unbelievers, nor shall they be
allowed to make amends. And when the guilty face the
scourge, it shall not be eased for them, nor shall they ever
be reprieved.

When the pagans behold their idols, they will say: 'Lord,
these are the idols to whom we prayed.' But their idols will
retort: 'You are surely lying!' They shall proffer submission
to God on that day, and the gods of their own invention
will forsake them.

As for those that disbelieve and debar others from the
path of God, We shall chastise them all the more for their
misdeeds.

The day will surely come when We shall call a witness 16:89
from each community to testify against it. We shall call *you*
to testify against your people: for to you We have revealed
the Book which manifests the truth about all things, a
guide, a blessing, and good news for those who submit.

1. The Meccans.        2. Muḥammad.

193

16:90 God enjoins justice, kindness and charity to one's kindred, and forbids lewdness, reprehensible conduct and oppression. He admonishes you so that you may take heed.

Keep faith with God when you make a pledge. You shall not break your oaths after you have sworn them: for by swearing in His name you make God your surety. God has knowledge of all your actions.

Do not, like the woman who unravels the thread she has firmly spun, take oaths with mutual deceit and break them on finding yourselves superior in numbers. In this, God puts you to the proof. On the Day of Resurrection He will resolve your differences for you.

Had God pleased, He would have united you in one community. But He confounds whom He will and gives guidance to whom He pleases. You shall be questioned about all your deeds.

You shall not take oaths to deceive each other, lest your foot should slip after being rightly guided, and lest evil should befall you for debarring others from the path of God: for then indeed you should incur a grievous punishment.

You shall not barter God's covenant for a trifling price.
16:95 God's reward is better for you, if you but knew it. Your worldly riches are transitory, but God's reward is everlasting.

We shall recompense the steadfast according to their noblest deeds. Be they men or women, to those that embrace the Faith and do what is right We will surely grant a happy life; We shall reward them according to their noblest deeds.

When you recite the Koran, seek refuge in God from accursèd Satan: no power has he over those who believe and who put their trust in their Lord. He has power only over those who befriend him and those who serve other deities besides God.

16:101 When We change one verse for another (God knows best what He reveals), they say: 'You[1] are an impostor.' Indeed most of them have no knowledge.

1. Muḥammad.

Say: 'The Holy Spirit brought it down from your Lord in 16:102
truth to reassure the faithful, and to give guidance and good
news to those that submit.

We know they say: 'A mortal taught him.' But the man[1]
to whom they allude speaks a foreign tongue, while this is
eloquent Arabic speech.

God will not guide those who disbelieve God's revelations. Woeful punishment awaits them.

None invents falsehoods save those who disbelieve God's
revelations: it is they that are the liars.

Those who are forced to recant while their hearts remain
loyal to the Faith shall be absolved; but those who deny God
after professing Islām and open their bosoms to unbelief
shall incur the wrath of God; grievous punishment awaits
them. For such men love the life of this world more than
the life to come. God does not guide the unbelievers.

Such are those whose hearts and ears and eyes are sealed
by God; such are the heedless. In the life to come they will
surely be the losers.

As for those who after persecution fled their homes and 16:110
fought and remained constant to the last, your Lord will be
forgiving and merciful to them on the day when every soul
will come pleading for itself; when every soul will be
requited for its deeds. None shall be wronged.

God has made an example of a city[2] which was once
safe and peaceful. Its provisions came to it abundantly from
every quarter: but it denied God's favours. Therefore God
afflicted it with famine and fear as punishment for what its
people did.

An apostle of their own was sent to them, but they
denied him. Therefore the scourge smote them in their sins.

Eat of the good and lawful things which God bestowed on 16:114
you, and give thanks for God's favours if you truly serve Him.

---

1. Scholars differ as to the identity of this 'foreigner'. Some
suppose him to be Salmān the Persian, others Ṣuhaib bin Sinān,
and yet others ʿAdas the Monk.

2. Mecca.

16:115 He has forbidden you carrion, blood and the flesh of swine; also any flesh consecrated other than in the name of God. But whoever is driven by necessity, intending neither to sin nor to transgress, will find that God is forgiving and merciful.

You shall not falsely declare: 'This is lawful, and that is forbidden,' in order to invent a falsehood about God. Those who invent falsehoods about God shall never prosper. Brief is their enjoyment of this life, and woeful punishment awaits them.

To those who follow the Jewish Faith We have pronounced unlawful what We recounted to you before. We never wronged them, but they wronged themselves.

To those who commit evil through ignorance, and then repent and mend their ways, your Lord is forgiving and merciful.

Abraham was a paragon of piety, an upright man obedient to God. He was no idolater. He rendered thanks for His favours, so that He chose him and guided him to a straight path. We bestowed on him a blessing in this world, and in the world to come he shall dwell among the righteous.

16:123 And now We have revealed to you Our will, saying: 'Follow the faith of saintly Abraham: he was no idolater.'

The Sabbath was ordained only for those who differed about it. On the Day of Resurrection your Lord will judge their disputes.

Call men to the path of your Lord with wisdom and kindly exhortation. Reason with them in the most courteous manner. Your Lord best knows those who stray from His path and those who are rightly guided.

If you punish, let your punishment be commensurate with the wrong that has been done you. But it shall be best for you to endure your wrongs with patience.

Be patient, then: God will grant you patience. Do not grieve for the unbelievers, nor distress yourself at their 16:128 intrigues. God is with those who keep from evil and do good works.

# THE NIGHT JOURNEY

*In the Name of God, the Compassionate, the Merciful*

GLORY BE to Him who made His servant go by night 17:1
from the Sacred Temple[1] to the farther Temple[2] whose
surroundings We have blessed, that We might show him
some of Our signs. He alone hears all and observes all.

We gave Moses the Book and made it a guide for the
Israelites, saying: 'Take no other guardian than Myself. You
are the descendants of those whom We carried in the ark
with Noah. He was a truly thankful servant.'

In the Book We solemnly declared to the Israelites: 'Twice
you shall do evil in the land. You shall become great
transgressors.'

And when the prophecy of your first transgression came
to be fulfilled, We sent against you a formidable army[3]
which ravaged your land and carried out the punishment
you had been promised.

Then We granted you victory over them and multiplied 17:6
your riches and your descendants, so that once again you
became more numerous than they. We said: 'If you do
good, it shall be to your advantage; but if you do evil, you
shall sin against your own souls.'

And when the prophecy of your next transgression came
to be fulfilled, We sent another army[4] to afflict you and to
enter the Temple as the former entered it before, utterly
destroying all that they laid their hands on.

We said: 'Your Lord may yet be merciful to you. If you
again transgress, you shall again be scourged. We have
made Hell a prison-house for the unbelievers.'

This Koran will give guidance to that which is most 17:9

1. Of Mecca.
2. Of Jerusalem (and thence to the Throne of God, accompanied
by the Angel Gabriel). Some Muslim commentators give a literal
interpretation to this passage, others regard it as a vision.
3. The Assyrians.
4. The Romans.

upright. It promises the faithful who do good works a rich
17:10 recompense, and those who deny the life to come a woeful
scourge. Yet man prays for evil as fervently as he prays for
good. Truly, man is ever impatient.

We made the night and the day twin marvels. We
enshrouded the night with darkness and gave light to the
day, so that you might seek the bounty of your Lord and
learn to count the seasons and the years. We have made all
things manifestly plain to you.

The fate of each man We have bound about his neck. On
the Day of Resurrection We shall confront him with a book
spread wide open, saying: 'Here is your book: read it.
Enough for you this day that your own soul should call you
to account.'

He that seeks guidance shall be guided to his advantage,
but he that errs shall err at his peril. No soul shall bear
another's burden. Nor do We punish until We have sent
forth a messenger.

17:16 When We resolve to raze a city, We first give warning
to those of its people who live in comfort. If they persist in sin,
judgement is irrevocably passed, and We destroy it utterly.

How many generations have We cut down since Noah's
time! Suffice it that your Lord is well aware of His
servants' sins and observes them all.

He that desires this fleeting life shall soon receive in it
whatever We will for whomever We please. But then We
have prepared Hell for him, where he will burn despised
and rejected.

As for him that desires the life to come and strives for it
as he ought to, being a true believer, his endeavours shall be
recompensed by God.

On all – on these and those – We bestow the bounty of
your Lord: none shall be denied the bounty of your Lord.

See how We have exalted some above others. Yet the life
to come has greater honours and is more exalted.

Serve no other deity besides God, lest you incur disgrace
17:23 and ruin. Your Lord has enjoined you to worship none but
Him, and to show kindness to your parents. If either or

both of them attain old age in your dwelling, show them no sign of impatience, nor rebuke them; but speak to them kind words. Treat them with humility and tenderness and 17:24 say: 'Lord, be merciful to them. They nursed me when I was an infant.'

Your Lord best knows what is in your hearts; He knows if you are good. He will surely forgive those that turn to Him.

Give to the near of kin their due, and also to the destitute and to the traveller in need. Do not squander your substance wastefully, for the wasteful are Satan's brothers; and Satan is ever ungrateful to his Lord. But if, while waiting for your Lord's bounty, you lack the means to assist them, then at least speak to them kindly.

Be neither miserly nor prodigal, for then you should either earn reproach or be reduced to penury.

Your Lord gives abundantly to whom He will and sparingly to whom He pleases. He knows and observes His servants.

You shall not kill your children for fear of want.[1] We will 17:31 provide for them and for you. To kill them is a grievous sin.

You shall not commit adultery, for it is lewd and evil.

You shall not kill any man whom God has forbidden you to kill, except for a just cause. If a man is slain unjustly, his heir shall be entitled to satisfaction. But let him not carry his vengeance to excess, for his victim is sure to be assisted and avenged.

Do not approach the property of orphans except with the best of motives, until they reach maturity. Keep your promises; you are accountable for all that you promise.

Give full measure, when you measure, and weigh with even scales. That is better and fairer in the end.

Do not follow what you know not. Man's eyes, ears, and heart – each of his senses shall be closely questioned.

Do not walk proudly on the earth. You cannot split the 17:37 earth, nor can you rival the mountains in stature.

1. An allusion to the pre-Islamic custom of burying alive unwanted newborn girls.

17:38     Evil is all this in the sight of your Lord, and odious.

These are but some of the wise precepts your Lord has inspired you[1] with. Serve no other deity besides God, lest you should be cast into Hell, condemned and rejected.

What! Has your Lord favoured *you*[2] with sons and Himself adopted daughters from among the angels? A monstrous blasphemy is that which you utter.

We have made plain Our revelations in this Koran so that the unbelievers may take warning. Yet it has only added to their aversion. Say: 'If, as they claim, there were other gods besides God, they would surely seek to dethrone Him.'

Glory be to Him! Exalted be He, high above their falsehoods!

The seven heavens, the earth, and all who dwell in them give glory to Him. All creatures celebrate His praises. Yet you cannot understand their praises. Benevolent is He and forgiving.

17:45     When you recite the Koran, We place between you and those who deny the life to come a hidden barrier. We have cast veils over their hearts lest they understand it, and made them hard of hearing. When you make mention of your Lord alone in the Koran, they turn their backs with much aversion.

We well know what they wish to hear when they listen to you, and what they say when they converse in private; when the wrongdoers declare: 'The man you follow is surely bewitched.'

Behold what epithets they bestow upon you. They have surely gone astray and cannot find the right path.

'What!' they say. 'When we are turned to bones and dust, shall we be restored in a new creation?'

17:51     Say: 'Whether you turn to stone or iron, or any other substance you may think unlikely to be given life.'

They will ask: 'Who will restore us?'

Say: 'He that created you at first.'

---

1. Muḥammad.      2. The unbelievers.

They will shake their heads at you and ask: 'When will this be?'

Say: 'It may well be near at hand. On that day He will summon you all, and you shall answer Him with praises. 17:52 You shall think that you have lingered but a little while.'

Tell My servants to be courteous in their speech. Satan would sow discord among them; Satan is surely the sworn enemy of man.

Your Lord knows you best. He will show you mercy if He will, and punish you if He pleases.

We have not sent you to be their guardian. Your Lord is best aware of all who dwell in the heavens and the earth.

We have exalted some prophets above others. To David We gave the Psalms.

Say: 'Pray if you will to those whom you deify besides Him.[1] They cannot relieve your distress, nor can they change it.'

Those to whom they pray, themselves seek to approach their Lord, vying with each other to be near Him. They crave His mercy and fear His punishment; for your Lord's punishment is to be feared indeed.

There is no community but We shall destroy or sternly 17:58 punish before the Day of Resurrection. That is decreed in the Eternal Book.

Nothing hinders us from giving signs except that the ancients disbelieved them. To Thamūd We gave the she-camel as a visible sign, yet they laid violent hands on her. We give signs only by way of warning.

We have told you that your Lord encompasses mankind. We have made the vision We showed you, as well as the tree[2] cursed in the Koran, but a test for people's faith. We seek to put fear in their hearts, but this only makes their wickedness all the more outrageous.

When We said to the angels: 'Prostrate yourselves before 17:61 Adam,' they all prostrated themselves, except Satan, who replied: 'Shall I bow to him whom You have made

---

1. The allusion is to saint-worship.    2. The Zaqqūm tree.

17:62 of clay? Do You see this being whom You have exalted above me? If You give me respite till the Day of Resurrection, I will exterminate all but a few of his descendants.'

'Go!' said He. 'Hell is your reward, and the reward of those that follow you. An ample recompense it shall be. Rouse with your voice whomever you are able. Muster against them your battalions of horse and foot. Be their partner in their riches and in their offspring. Promise them what you will. (Satan promises them only to deceive them.) But over My true servants you shall have no authority. Your Lord will be their all-sufficient Guardian.'

It is your Lord who drives for you the ships across the ocean, so that you may seek His bounty. Surely He is ever merciful towards you.

When at sea a misfortune befalls you, all but Him of those to whom you pray forsake you; yet when He brings you safe to dry land you turn your backs upon Him. Truly, man is ever thankless.

17:68 Are you confident He will not cause the earth to cave in beneath you, or let loose a deadly sand-storm upon you? Then you shall find none to protect you.

Are you confident that when again you put to sea He will not smite you with a violent tempest and drown you for your thanklessness? Then you shall find none to prosecute your case against Us.

We have bestowed blessings on Adam's children and guided them by land and sea. We have provided them with wholesome things and exalted them above many of Our creatures.

The day will surely come when We shall summon each community with its leader. Those who are given their books in their right hands will read their recorded doings, and shall not in the least be wronged. But those who have been blind in this life shall be blind in the life to come and more misguided.

They sought to entice you from Our revelations – they nearly did – hoping that you might invent some other
17:74 scripture in Our name, and thus become their trusted friend.

Indeed, had We not strengthened your faith, you might have made some compromise with them and thus incurred a 17:75 double punishment in this life and in the next. Then you should have found none to help you against Us.

They sought to provoke you – they nearly did – and thus drive you out of the land. Had they succeeded, they would have scarcely survived your departure.

Such was Our way with the apostles We sent before you. And you shall find no change in Our way.

Recite your prayers at sunset, at nightfall, and at dawn; the dawn prayer has its witnesses. Pray during the night as well; an additional duty, for the fulfilment of which your Lord may exalt you to an honourable station.

Say: 'Lord, grant me a goodly entrance and a goodly exit, and sustain me with Your own authority.'

Say: 'Truth has come and Falsehood has departed. Falsehood was bound to be routed.'

That which We reveal in the Koran is a balm and a blessing to true believers, although it only adds to the wrongdoers' prospects of damnation.

When We bestow favours on man, he turns his back and 17:83 holds aloof. But when evil befalls him, he grows despondent.

Say: 'Each man behaves after his own fashion. But your Lord best knows who is more rightly guided.'

They put questions to you about the Spirit. Say: 'The Spirit is at my Lord's command. Little indeed is the knowledge vouchsafed to you.'

If We pleased, We could take away that which We have revealed to you: then you should find none to plead with Us on your behalf, except through a favour from your Lord. His goodness to you has been great indeed.

Say: 'If men and jinn combined to produce a book akin to this Koran, they would surely fail to produce its like, though they helped one another as best they could.'

We have set forth for people in this Koran all manner of arguments, yet most of them persist in unbelief. They say: 17:90 'We will not believe in you until you make a spring gush

17:91   from the earth before our very eyes, or cause rivers to flow in a grove of palms and vines; until you cause the sky to fall upon us in pieces, as you have threatened to do, or bring down God and the angels in our midst; until you build a house of gold, or ascend to heaven: nor will we believe in your ascent until you have sent down for us a book which we can read.'

Say: 'Glory be to my Lord! Am I not but an emissary, made of flesh and blood?'

Nothing prevents people from having faith when guidance is revealed to them but the excuse: 'Can it be that God has sent a human being as an emissary?'

Say: 'Had the earth been safe enough for angels to walk on, We would have sent down to them an angel from heaven as an emissary.'

Say: 'Sufficient is God as my witness, and your witness. He knows and observes His servants.'

17:97   Those whom God guides are rightly guided; but those whom He confounds shall find no friend besides Him. We shall gather them all on the Day of Resurrection, prostrate upon their faces, blind, dumb, and deaf. Hell shall be their home: whenever its flames die down We will rekindle them into a greater fire.

Thus shall they be rewarded: because they disbelieved Our revelations and said: 'When we are turned to bones and dust, shall we be restored in a new creation?'

Do they not see that God, who has created the heavens and the earth, has power to create their like? Their term He pre-ordained beyond all doubt. Yet the wrongdoers persist in unbelief.

Say: 'Had you possessed the treasures of my Lord's mercy, you would have covetously hoarded them. How niggardly is man!'

To Moses We gave nine clear signs. Ask the Israelites how he first appeared among them.

Pharaoh said to him: 'Moses, I can see that you are bewitched.'

17:102   'You know full well,' he replied, 'that none but the Lord

of the heavens and the earth has revealed these visible signs.
Indeed, Pharaoh, I can see that you are doomed.'

He sought to scare them out of the land: but We 17:103
drowned him, together with all who were with him. Then
We said to the Israelites: 'Dwell in the land. When the
promise of the hereafter comes to be fulfilled, We shall
assemble you all together.'

We have revealed the Koran with the Truth, and with the
Truth it has come down. We have sent you forth only to
proclaim good news and to give warning.

We have divided the Koran into sections so that you may
recite it to the people with deliberation. We have imparted
it by gradual revelation.

Say: 'It is for you to believe in it or to deny it. Those who
were endowed with knowledge before its revelation prostrate themselves when it is recited and say: "Glorious is our
Lord. Our Lord's promise has surely been fulfilled." They
fall down upon their faces, weeping; and as they listen, their
humility increases.'

Say: 'You may call on God or you may call on the
Merciful: by whatever name you call on Him, His are the
most gracious names.'

Pray neither with too loud a voice nor in silence, but,
between these extremes, seek a middle course. Say: 'Praise 17:111
be to God who has never begotten a son; who has no
partner in His Kingdom; who needs none to defend Him
from humiliation.' Proclaim His greatness.

# THE CAVE

*In the Name of God, the Compassionate, the Merciful*

PRAISE BE to God who has revealed the Book to His 18:1
servant shorn of contradictions and unswerving from the
truth, so that he may give warning of a dire scourge from
Himself, proclaim to the faithful who do good works that a
rich and everlasting recompense awaits them, and admonish
those who say that God has begotten a son. Surely of this

18:5 they could have no knowledge, neither they nor their fathers: a monstrous blasphemy is that which they utter. They preach nothing but falsehood.

Yet, if they deny this revelation, you may destroy yourself with grief, sorrowing over them.

We have decked the earth with all manner of ornaments to test mankind and to see who would acquit himself best. But We will surely reduce all that is on it to barren dust.

Did you think the Sleepers of the Cave[1] and Al-Raqīm[2] a wonder among Our signs?

When the youths sought refuge in the Cave, they said: 'Lord, have mercy on us and guide us through our ordeal.'

We made them sleep in the cave for many years, and then awakened them to find out who could best tell the length of their stay.

We shall recount to you their story in all truth. They were young men who had faith in their Lord, and on whom 18:14 We had lavished Our guidance. We put courage in their hearts when they stood up and said: 'Our Lord is the Lord of the heavens and the earth. We call on no other god besides Him: for if we did we should be blaspheming. Our people serve other gods besides Him, though they have no convincing proof of their divinity. Who is more wicked than the man who invents a falsehood against God?

'When you depart from them and from their idols, go to the Cave for shelter. God will extend to you His mercy and prepare for you a means of safety.'

18:17 You might have seen the rising sun decline to the right of their cavern and, as it set, go past them on the left, while they stayed within. That was one of God's signs. He whom God guides is rightly guided; but he whom He confounds shall find no friend to guide him.

1. The allusion is to the story of the Seven Sleepers. Compare Gibbon's account in *Decline and Fall of the Roman Empire*.

2. This may be the name of their dog, the tablet on which their names were inscribed, or the mountain in which the cave was situated.

You might have thought them awake, though they were  18:18
sleeping. We turned them about to right and left, while
their dog lay at the cave's entrance with legs outstretched.
Had you looked upon them, you would have surely turned
your back and fled in terror.

We roused them that they might question one another.
'How long have you been here?' asked one. 'A day, or but a
few hours,' replied another; and yet another: 'Your Lord
knows best how long you have stayed here. Let one
of you go to the city with this silver coin and bring you
back whatever food he finds most wholesome there. Let
him conduct himself with caution and not disclose your
whereabouts to anyone. For if they find you out they will
stone you to death, or force you back into their faith. Then
you will surely never prosper ever.'

Thus did We reveal their secret, so that men might know  18:21
that God's promise was true and that the Hour of Doom
was sure to come.

The people argued among themselves concerning them.
Some said: 'Build a monument over their remains. Only
their Lord knows who they were.' Those who were to win
said: 'Let us build a place of worship over them.'

Some will say: 'The sleepers were three: their dog was the
fourth.' Others, guessing at the unknown, will say: 'They
were five: their dog was the sixth.' And yet others: 'Seven:
their dog was the eighth.'

Say: 'My Lord best knows their number. Few know
them.'

Therefore, when you dispute about them, adhere only to
that which is manifest and do not ask any of these
concerning them.

Do not say of anything: 'I will do it tomorrow,' without
adding: 'If God wills.' When you forget, remember your
Lord and say: 'May God guide me and bring me nearer to
the Truth.'

Some say they stayed in the cave three hundred years and
nine. Say: 'None but God knows how long they stayed in it.  18:26
His are the secrets of the heavens and the earth. Clear is His

sight, and keen His hearing. Man has no other guardian besides Him. He allows none to share His sovereignty.'

18:27 Proclaim what has been revealed to you from the Book of your Lord. None can change His words. You shall find no refuge besides Him.

Restrain yourself, together with those who pray to their Lord morning and evening, seeking His pleasure. Do not turn your eyes away from them in quest of the allurements of this life, nor obey him whose heart We have made heedless of Our remembrance; who follows his appetite and gives a loose rein to his desires.

Say: 'This is the truth from your Lord. Let him who will, believe in it, and him who will, deny it.'

For the wrongdoers We have prepared a fire which will encompass them like the walls of a pavilion. When they cry out for help they shall be showered with water as hot as molten brass, which will scald their faces. Evil shall be their drink, evil their resting-place.

18:30 As for those that have faith and do good works, We shall not deny them their reward. They shall dwell in the gardens of Eden, where rivers will roll at their feet. Reclining there upon soft couches, they shall be decked with bracelets of gold, and arrayed in garments of fine green silk and rich brocade: blissful their reward and happy their resting-place!

Give them this parable. Once there were two men, to one of whom We gave two vineyards set about with palm-trees and watered by a running stream, with a cornfield lying in between. Each of the vineyards yielded an abundant crop, and when their owner had gathered in the harvest, he said to his companion while conversing with him: 'I am richer than you, and my clan is mightier than yours.'

And when, having thus wronged his soul, he entered his vineyard, he said: 'Surely this will never perish! Nor do I believe that the Hour of Doom will ever come. Even if I returned to my Lord, I should surely find a better place than this.'

His companion replied, while still conversing with him: 'Have you no faith in Him who created you from dust, from 18:38 a little germ, and fashioned you into a man? As for myself,

God is my Lord. I will associate none with my Lord. When   18:39
you entered your garden, why did you not say: "What God
has ordained must surely come to pass: there is no strength
except in God"? Though you see me poorer than yourself
and blessed with fewer children, yet my Lord may give me a
garden better than yours, and send down thunderbolts from
heaven upon your vineyard, turning it into a barren waste,
or drain its water deep into the earth so that you will find
none of it.'

His fruits were destroyed, and he wrung his hands with
grief at all that he had spent on the garden: for the vines had
tumbled down upon their trellises. 'Would that I had
served no other gods besides my Lord!' he cried. He had
none to help him besides God, nor was he able to defend
himself.

In such ordeals protection comes only from God, the true
God. His is the best recompense, and His the best requital.

Coin for them a simile about the life of this world. It is
like the vegetation of the earth that thrives when watered
by the rain We send down from the sky, soon turning into
stubble which the wind scatters abroad. God has power
over all things.

Wealth and children are the ornament of this life. But   18:46
deeds of lasting merit are better rewarded by your Lord and
hold for you a greater hope of salvation.

Tell of the day when We shall blot out the mountains and
make the earth a barren waste; when We shall gather all
mankind together, leaving not a soul behind.

They shall be ranged before your Lord, and He will say
to them: 'You have returned to Us as We created you at
first. Yet you supposed We had not set for you a predestined
time.'

Their book will be laid down, and you shall see the
sinners dismayed at the content. They will say: 'Woe betide
us! What can this book mean? It omits nothing small or
great: all is noted down!' and they shall find their deeds
recorded there. Your Lord will wrong none.

When We said to the angels: 'Prostrate yourselves before   18:50
Adam,' all prostrated themselves except Satan, who was a

jinnee disobedient to his Lord. Would you then serve him and his offspring as your masters rather than Myself, despite their enmity towards you? A sad substitute the wrongdoers have chosen!

18:51 I did not call them to witness at the creation of the heavens and the earth, nor at their own creation; nor was I to seek the aid of those who were to lead mankind astray.

On that day God will say to them: 'Call on the idols which you supposed divine.' They will invoke them, but they will make no answer; for We shall place a deadly gulf between them. And when the sinners behold the Fire they will realize that there they shall be flung. Nor shall they ever escape from it.

In this Koran We have set forth for men all manner of parables. But man is exceedingly contentious.

Nothing can prevent men from having faith and seeking forgiveness of their Lord, now that guidance has been revealed to them: unless they are waiting for the fate of the ancients to overtake them or to behold the scourge with their own eyes.

18:56 We send Our apostles only to proclaim good news and to give warning. But with false arguments the unbelievers seek to confute the truth, deriding My revelations and My warnings.

Who is more wicked than the man who, when reminded of his Lord's revelations, turns away from them and forgets what his own hands have done? We have cast veils over their hearts lest they understand Our words, and made them hard of hearing. Call them as you may to the right path, they shall never be guided.

Your Lord is forgiving and merciful. Had it been His will to scourge them for their sins, He would have hurried on their punishment; but He has set for them a predestined time they cannot evade.

And all those nations! We destroyed them for the wrongs they did, and for their destruction We set a predestined time.

18:60 Moses said to his servant: 'I will journey on until I reach the land where the two seas meet, though I may march for ages.'

But when at last they came to the land where the two seas 18:61
met, they forgot their fish, which made its way into the
water, swimming at will.

And when they had journeyed farther on, Moses said to
his servant: 'Bring us some food; we are worn out with
travelling.'

'Know,' he replied, 'that I forgot the fish when we were
resting on the rock. It was Satan who made me forget to
mention this. The fish made its way miraculously into the
sea.'

'This is what we have been seeking,' said Moses. They
went back the way they came, and found one of Our
servants to whom We had vouchsafed Our mercy and
whom We had endowed with knowledge of Our own.
Moses said to him: 'May I follow you, so that you may guide
me by that which you have been taught?'

'You will not bear with me,' replied the other. 'For how
can you bear with that which is beyond your knowledge?'

Moses said: 'If God wills, you shall find me patient: I
shall in no way cross you.'

He said: 'If you are bent on following me, you must not 18:70
question me about anything until I mention it to you myself.'

The two set forth, but as soon as they embarked, Moses'
companion bored a hole in the bottom of the ship.

'Is it to drown her passengers that you have bored a hole
in her?' Moses asked. 'A strange thing you have done.'

'Did I not tell you,' he replied, 'that you would not bear
with me?'

'Pardon my forgetfulness,' said Moses. 'Do not be angry
with me on account of this.'

They journeyed on until they fell in with a certain youth.
Moses' companion slew him, and Moses said: 'You have
killed an innocent man who has slain no one. Surely you
have done a wicked thing.'

'Did I not tell you,' he replied, 'that you would not bear
with me?'

Moses said: 'If ever I question you again, abandon me; 18:76
for then I should deserve it.'

18:77    They travelled on until they came to a city. They asked its people for some food, but they declined to receive them as their guests. There they found a wall on the point of falling down. His companion restored it, and Moses said: 'Had you wished, you could have demanded payment for your labours.'

'Now has the time arrived when we must part,' said the other. 'But first I will explain to you those acts of mine which you could not bear to watch with patience.

'Know that the ship belonged to some poor fishermen. I damaged it because at their rear there was a king who was taking every ship by force.

'As for the youth, his parents both are true believers, and we feared lest he should plague them with wickedness and unbelief. It was our wish that their Lord should grant them another in his place, a son more righteous and more filial.

18:82    'As for the wall, it belonged to two orphan boys in the city whose father was an honest man. Beneath it their treasure is buried. Your Lord decreed, as a mercy from your Lord, that they should dig up their treasure when they grew to manhood. What I did was not done by my will.

'That is the meaning of what you could not bear to watch with patience.'

They will ask you about Dhūl-Qarnayn.[1] Say: 'I will give you an account of him.

'We made him mighty in the land and gave him means to achieve all things. He journeyed on a certain road until he reached the West and saw the sun setting in a pool of black mud. Hard by he found a certain people.

'"Dhūl-Qarnayn," We said, "you must either punish them or show them kindness."

'He replied: "The wicked we shall surely punish. Then shall they return to their Lord and be sternly punished by
18:88    Him. As for those that have faith and do good works, we shall bestow on them a rich reward and deal indulgently with them."

---

1. Alexander the Great.

'He then journeyed along another road until he reached 18:89
the East and saw the sun rising upon a people whom We
had exposed to its flaming rays. So he did; and We had full
knowledge of all the forces at his command.

'Then he followed yet another route until he came
between the Two Mountains and found a people who could
barely understand a word. "Dhūl-Qarnayn," they said,
"Gog and Magog are ravaging this land. Build a rampart
between us, and we will pay you tribute."

'He replied: "The power my Lord has given me is better
than any tribute. Lend me a force of men, and I will raise a
rampart between you and them. Come, bring me blocks of
iron."

'He dammed up the valley between the Two Mountains,
and said: "Ply your bellows." And when the iron blocks
were red with heat, he said: "Bring me molten brass to pour
on them."

'Gog and Magog could not scale it, nor could they dig
their way through it. He said: "This is a blessing from my
Lord. But when my Lord's promise has been fulfilled, He
will level it to dust. The promise of my Lord is ever true."'

On that day We will let them come in tumultuous 18:99
throngs. The Trumpet shall be sounded and We will gather
them all together.

On that day We shall lay Hell bare before the unbelievers,
who have turned a blind eye to My admonition and a deaf
ear to My warning.

Do the unbelievers think that they can make My servants
patrons besides Me? We have prepared Hell for the unbelievers to dwell in.

Say: 'Shall we tell you who will lose most through their
labours? Those whose endeavours in this world are misguided and who yet think that what they do is right; who
disbelieve the revelations of their Lord and deny that they
will ever meet Him.' Vain are the works of these. On the
Day of Resurrection We shall give them no consequence.

Hell is their reward: because they had no faith, and 18:106
because they mocked My apostles and My revelations. As

for those that have faith and do good works, they shall for ever dwell in the gardens of Paradise, desiring no change.

Say: 'If the waters of the sea were ink with which to write the words of my Lord, the sea would surely run dry before the words of my Lord were spent, though we found another sea to replenish it.'

18:110 Say: 'I am but a mortal like yourselves. It is revealed to me that your God is one God. Let him that hopes to meet his Lord do what is right and worship none besides his Lord.'

# MARY

*In the Name of God, the Compassionate, the Merciful*

19:1 K A F *bā' yā' 'ain ṣād.* An account of your Lord's goodness to his servant Zacharias:

He invoked his Lord in secret, saying: 'Lord, my bones are enfeebled, and my head glows silver with age. Yet never, Lord, have I prayed to You in vain. I now fear my kinsmen who will succeed me, for my wife is barren. Grant me, from Yourself, a son who will be my heir and an heir to the house of Jacob, and make him worthy, Lord, of Your pleasure.'

'Rejoice, Zacharias,' came the answer. 'You shall be given a son, and his name shall be John; a name no man has borne before him.'

19:8 'Lord,' said Zacharias, 'how shall I have a son when my wife is barren, and I am well-advanced in years?'

He replied: 'Thus did your Lord speak. That is easy for Me; even as I brought you into being when you were nothing before.'

'Lord,' said Zacharias, 'give me a sign.'

'Your sign is that for three days and nights,' He replied, 'you shall be bereft of speech, though otherwise sound in body.'

19:11 Then Zacharias came out from the Shrine and exhorted his people to give glory morning and evening.

To John We said: 'Observe the Scriptures with a firm 19:12
resolve.' We bestowed on him wisdom, grace, and purity
while yet a child, and he grew up a righteous man; honouring
his father and mother, and neither arrogant nor rebellious.
Blessed was he on the day he was born and the day of his
death; and peace be on him when he is raised to life.

And you shall recount in the Book the story of Mary:
how she left her people and betook herself to a solitary
place to the east.

We sent to her Our spirit in the semblance of a full-grown
man. And when she saw him she said: 'May the Merciful
defend me from you! If you fear the Lord, [leave me and go
your way].'

'I am but your Lord's emissary,' he replied, 'and have
come to give you a holy son.'

'How shall I bear a child,' she answered, 'when I have
neither been touched by any man nor ever been un-
chaste?'

'Thus did your Lord speak,' he replied. '"That is easy
enough for Me. He shall be a sign to mankind and a
blessing from Ourself. Our decree shall come to pass."'

Thereupon she conceived him, and retired to a far-off 19:22
place. And when she felt the throes of childbirth she lay
down by the trunk of a palm-tree, crying: 'Oh, would that I
had died before this and passed into oblivion!'

But a voice from below cried out to her: 'Do not despair.
Your Lord has provided a brook that runs at your feet, and
if you shake the trunk of the palm-tree it will drop fresh
ripe dates in your lap. Therefore eat and drink and rejoice;
and should you meet any mortal say to him: "I have vowed a
fast to the Merciful and will not speak with any man today."'

Carrying the child, she came to her people, who said to
her: 'Mary, this is indeed a strange thing! Sister of Aaron,[1] 19:28

1. Muslim commentators deny the charge that there is confusion
here between Miriam, Aaron's sister, and Maryam (Mary), mother
of Jesus. 'Sister of Aaron', they argue, simply means 'virtuous
woman' in this context.

your father was never a whore-monger, nor was your mother a harlot.'

19:29 She made a sign to them, pointing to the child. But they replied: 'How can we speak with a babe in the cradle?'

Whereupon he spoke and said: 'I am the servant of God. He has given me the Book and ordained me a prophet. His blessing is upon me wherever I go, and He has exhorted me to be steadfast in prayer and to give alms as long as I shall live. He has exhorted me to honour my mother and has purged me of vanity and wickedness. Blessed was I on the day I was born, and blessed I shall be on the day of my death and on the day I shall be raised to life.'

Such was Jesus son of Mary. That is the whole truth, which they still doubt. God forbid that He Himself should beget a son! When He decrees a thing He need only say: 'Be,' and it is.

God is my Lord and your Lord: therefore serve Him. That is a straight path.

Yet are the sects at odds among themselves. But when the fateful day arrives, woe betide the unbelievers! Their hearing and their sight will be sharpened on the day they appear before Us. Truly, the wrongdoers are today in evident error.

19:39 Forewarn them of that woeful day, when Our decree shall be fulfilled while they heedlessly persist in unbelief. We Ourself shall inherit the earth and all who dwell upon it. To Us they shall return.

You shall also recount in the Book the story of Abraham:

He was a saintly man and a prophet. He said to his father: 'Why do you serve a worthless idol, a thing that can neither hear nor see?

'Father, things you know nothing of have come to my knowledge: therefore follow me, that I may guide you along an even path.

'Father, do not worship Satan; for Satan has rebelled against the Lord of Mercy.

19:45 'Father, I fear that a scourge will fall upon you from the Merciful, and you will become one of Satan's minions.'

He replied: 'Do you dare renounce my gods, Abraham? 19:46 Desist, or I will stone you. Leave my house this instant!'

'Peace be with you,' said Abraham. 'I shall implore my Lord to forgive you: for to me He has ever been gracious. But I will not live with you or with your idols. I will pray to my Lord, and may my prayers to my Lord not be in vain.'

And when Abraham had cast off his people and the idols which they worshipped, We gave him Isaac and Jacob. Each of them We made a prophet, and We bestowed on them gracious gifts and high renown.

In the Book tell also of Moses, who was a chosen man, an apostle, and a prophet.

We called out to him from the right side of the Mountain, and when he came near We communed with him in secret. We gave him, of Our mercy, his brother Aaron, himself a prophet.

And in the Book you shall tell of Ishmael: he, too, was a 19:54 man of his word, an apostle, and a prophet.

He enjoined prayer and almsgiving on his people, and his Lord was pleased with him.

And of Idrīs:[1] he, too, was a saint and a prophet, whom We honoured and exalted.

These are the men to whom God has been gracious: the prophets from among the descendants of Adam and of those whom We carried in the ark with Noah; the descendants of Abraham, of Israel, and of those whom We have guided and chosen. For when the revelations of the Merciful were recited to them they fell down on their knees in tears and adoration.

But the generations who succeeded them neglected their prayers and succumbed to their desires. These shall assuredly be lost. But those that repent and embrace the Faith and do what is right shall enter Paradise and shall in no way be wronged: the gardens of Eden, which the Merciful has 19:61

1. Enoch.

promised on trust to His servants. His promise shall be fulfilled.

19:62     There they shall hear no idle talk, but only the voice of peace. And their sustenance shall be given them there morning and evening. Such is the Paradise which We shall give the righteous among our servants to inherit.

We descend only at the bidding of your Lord.[1] To Him belongs what is before us and behind us, and all that lies between.

Your Lord does not forget. He is the Lord of the heavens and the earth and all that is between them. Worship Him, then, and be patient in His service; for do you know any other worthy of His name?

'What!' says man, 'When I am once dead, shall I be raised to life?'

Does man forget that We created him when he was nothing before? By the Lord, We will call them to account in company with all the devils and set them on their knees around the fire of Hell: from every sect We will carry off its stoutest rebels against the Lord of Mercy. We surely know best who most deserve to be burnt in its flames.

19:71     There is not one among you who shall not pass through it: such is the absolute decree of your Lord. We will deliver those who fear Us, and leave the wrongdoers there, on their knees.

When Our clear revelations are recited to them the unbelievers say to the faithful: 'Which of us two will have a finer abode and better companions?'

How many generations have We destroyed before them, far greater in riches and in splendour!

19:75     Say: 'The Merciful will bear long with those in error until they see the fulfilment of His promise: be it a worldly scourge or the Hour of Doom. Then shall they learn whose is the worse plight and whose the smaller following.'

1. Commentators say that these are the words of the Angel Gabriel, in reply to Muḥammad's complaint of long intervals elapsing between periods of revelation.

God will increase His guidance to those that follow the 19:76
right guidance. Deeds of lasting merit shall earn you a
better recompense in the sight of your Lord and a more
auspicious end.

Mark the words of him who denies Our signs and
who yet boasts: 'I shall surely be given wealth and children!'

Has the future been revealed to him? Or has the Merciful
made him such a promise?

By no means! We will record his words and make his
punishment long and terrible. All he speaks of he shall leave
behind and come before us all alone.

They have chosen deities other than God to help them.
By no means! They will renounce their worship and turn
against them.

Know that We send down to the unbelievers devils who
incite them to evil. Therefore have patience: their days are
numbered. The day will surely come when We will gather
the righteous in multitudes before the Lord of Mercy, and
drive the guilty to Hell in thirsty hordes. None has power
to intercede for them save him who has received the
sanction of the Merciful.

Those who say: 'The Lord of Mercy has begotten a son,' 19:88
preach a monstrous falsehood, at which the very heavens
might crack, the earth split asunder, and the mountains
crumble to dust. That they should ascribe a son to the Merciful, when it does not become the Lord of Mercy to beget one!

There is none in the heavens or on earth but shall return
to the Merciful in utter submission. He has kept strict count
of all His creatures, and one by one they shall approach Him
on the Day of Resurrection. The Merciful will cherish those
who accepted the true faith and were charitable in their lifetime.

We have revealed to you the Koran in your own tongue
that you may thereby proclaim good tidings to the upright
and give warning to a contentious nation.

How many generations have We destroyed before them! 19:98
Can you find one of them still alive, or hear so much as a
whisper from them?

# ṬĀʼ HĀʼ

*In the Name of God, the Compassionate, the Merciful*

20:1 Ṭāʼ hāʼ.

It was not to distress you that We revealed the Koran, but to admonish the God-fearing. It is a revelation from Him who has created the earth and the lofty heavens, the Merciful who sits enthroned on high.

His is what the heavens and the earth contain, and all that lies between them and underneath the soil. You have no need to speak aloud; for He has knowledge of all that is secret, and all that is hidden.

He is God. There is no god but Him. His are the most gracious names.

Have you heard the story of Moses?

When he saw a fire, he said to his people: 'Stay here, for I can see a fire. Perchance I can bring you a lighted torch or find a guide hard by.'

When he came near, a voice called out to him: 'Moses, I am your Lord. Take off your sandals, for you are now in the sacred valley of Ṭuwā.

20:13 'Know that I have chosen you. Therefore listen to what shall be revealed.

'I am God. There is no god but Me. Serve Me, and recite your prayers in My remembrance.

'The Hour of Doom is sure to come. But I choose to keep it hidden, so that every soul shall be rewarded for its labours. Let those who disbelieve in it and yield to their desires not turn your thoughts from it, lest you perish. What is it you are carrying in your right hand, Moses?'

He replied: 'It is my staff; upon it I lean and with it I beat down the leaves for my flock. And I have other uses for it besides.'

He said: 'Moses, cast it down.'

Moses threw it down, and thereupon it turned into a slithering serpent.

20:21 'Take it up and have no fear,' He said. 'We will change it

back to its former state. Now put your hand under your  20:22
armpit. It shall come out white, although unharmed: another
sign.

'We shall show you the most wondrous of all Our signs.
Go to Pharaoh; he has transgressed all bounds.'

'Lord,' said Moses, 'put courage into my heart, and make
my task easy. Free my tongue from its impediment, that
men may understand my speech. Appoint for me a helper
from among my kinsmen, Aaron my brother. Grant me
strength through him and let him share my task, so that we
may give glory to You always and remember You always.
You are surely watching over us.'

He replied: 'Your request is granted, Moses. We had
already shown you favour when We revealed Our will to
your mother, saying: "Put your child in the ark and let him
be carried away by the river. The river will cast him on to
the bank, and he shall be taken up by an enemy of Mine and
his." I lavished My love on you, so that you might be reared
under My watchful eye.

'Your sister went to them and said: "Shall I direct you to  20:40
one who will nurse him?"

'Thus did We restore you to your mother, so that her mind
might be set at ease and that she might not grieve.

'And when you slew a man We delivered you from
distress and then proved you by other trials.

'You stayed among the people of Midian for many years,
and at length you came here, Moses, as was ordained. I have
chosen you for Myself. Go, you and your brother, with My
signs, and do not cease to remember Me. Go both of you to
Pharaoh, for he has transgressed all bounds. Speak to him
with gentle words; he may yet take heed and fear Our
punishment.'

'Lord,' they said, 'we dread his malevolence and tyranny.'

He replied: 'Have no fear. I shall be with you. I hear all
and see all. Go to him and say: "We are the emissaries of  20:47
your Lord. Let the Israelites depart with us, and oppress
them no more. We have come to you with a revelation from
your Lord: blessed is he that follows the right guidance. It

20:48 is revealed to us that the scourge will fall on those who deny His signs and pay no heed to them."'

Pharaoh said: 'And who is your Lord, Moses?'

'Our Lord,' he replied, 'is He that gave all creatures their distinctive form and then rightly guided them.'

'How was it, then, with the early generations?' asked Pharaoh.

He answered: 'My Lord alone has knowledge of that, recorded in a Book. He does not err, neither does He forget. It is He who has made the earth your cradle and traced on it paths for you to walk on. It is He who sends down water from the sky with which We bring forth every kind of plant, saying: "Eat and graze your cattle. Surely in this there are signs for men of understanding. From the earth We have created you, and to the earth We will restore you; and from it We will bring you back to life."'

20:56 We showed Pharaoh all Our signs, but he denied them and paid no heed. He said: 'Have you come to drive us from our land with your sorcery, Moses? Know that we will confront you with sorcery as powerful as yours. Appoint a day when both of us can meet, a tryst which neither we nor you shall fail to keep, and a place at an equal distance from us both.'

He said: 'Meet me on the day of the Feast, and let all the people come together before noon.'

Pharaoh withdrew; he gathered his sorcerers and returned. 'Woe betide you!' said Moses to them. 'Invent no falsehoods against God, or He will destroy you with a scourge. Impostors will surely come to grief.'

The sorcerers conferred among themselves, whispering to one another. They said to Pharaoh: 'These two are sorcerers who intend to drive you from your land by their sorcery and do away with your best traditions. Muster all your forces and array them in their ranks; those who win today will surely triumph.'

To Moses they said: 'Will you throw down, or shall we throw down first?'

20:66 'Throw you down,' he answered.

And by their sorcery their ropes and staffs appeared to Moses' eyes as though they were running.

Moses was much alarmed. But We said to him: 'Have no 20:67 fear; you shall surely win. Throw that which is in your right hand. It will swallow up their devices, for their devices are but the deceitful show of a sorcerer. Sorcerers shall not prosper, whatever they do.'

The sorcerers prostrated themselves, crying: 'We believe in the Lord of Aaron and Moses.'

'Do you dare believe in Him before I give leave?' said Pharaoh. 'This man must be your master, who taught you witchcraft. I will cut off your hands and feet on alternate sides and crucify you on the trunks of palm-trees. You shall learn whose punishment is more terrible, and more lasting.'

They replied: 'We cannot have greater faith in you than in the miracles which we have witnessed and in Him who has created us. Therefore do your worst; you can punish us only in this present life. We have put our faith in our Lord so that He may forgive us our sins and the sorcery you have imposed upon us. Better is God's recompense, and more lasting. He that comes before his Lord laden with sin shall 20:74 be consigned to Hell, where he shall neither die nor live. But he that comes before Him with true faith, having done good works, shall be exalted to the highest ranks. He shall abide for ever in the gardens of Eden, in gardens watered by running streams. Such shall be the recompense of those that keep themselves pure.'

Then We revealed Our will to Moses, saying: 'Set forth with My servants in the night and strike for them a dry path across the sea. Have no fear of being overtaken, nor let anything dismay you.'

Pharaoh pursued them with his legions, but the waters overwhelmed them. For Pharaoh misled his people: he did not guide them.

Children of Israel! We delivered you from your enemies and made a covenant with you on the right flank of the Mountain. We sent down manna and quails for you. 'Eat of 20:81

the wholesome things with which We have provided you and do not transgress, lest you should incur My wrath,' We said. 'He that incurs My wrath shall assuredly be lost, but he

20:82 that repents and believes in Me, does good works and follows the right path shall be forgiven. But, Moses, why have you come with such haste from your people?'

Moses replied: 'They are close behind me. I hastened to You, Lord, so that I might earn Your pleasure.'

God said: 'We proved your people in your absence, but the Sāmirī¹ has led them astray.'

Angry and sorrowful, Moses went back to them. 'My people,' he said, 'did your Lord not make you a gracious promise? Did my absence seem too long to you, or was it to incur your Lord's anger that you failed me?'

They replied: 'We did not fail you of our own free will. We were made to carry the people's trinkets and throw them into the fire. The Sāmirī threw likewise, and forged a calf for them, an image with a hollow sound. "This," they said, "is your god and the god of Moses whom he has forgotten."'

20:89 Did they not see that it returned no answer, and that it could neither harm nor help them?

Aaron had said to them: 'My people, this is but a test for you. Your Lord is the Merciful. Follow me and do as I bid you.' But they had replied: 'We will worship it until Moses returns.'

Moses said to Aaron: 'Why did you not seek me out when you saw them go astray? Why did you disobey me?'

'Son of my mother,' he replied, 'let go, I pray you, of my beard and my head. I was afraid that you might say: "You have sown discord among the Israelites and did not wait for my orders."'

'Sāmirī,' cried Moses, 'what had come over you?'

20:96 He replied: 'I saw what they did not see. I took a handful of dust from the trail of the Messenger and flung it away: thus did my soul prompt me.'

---

1. It is not clear who the Sāmirī is.

'Go!' cried Moses. 'An outcast shall you be in this 20:97
life, nor shall you escape your appointed doom. Behold this
idol which you have served with such devotion: we will
burn it to cinders and scatter its ashes far and wide over the
sea.'

Your Lord is God, other than whom there is no god. His
knowledge encompasses all things.

Thus do We recount to you the history of past events. A
Scripture of Our own have We given you: those that reject
it shall bear a heavy burden on the Day of Resurrection.
Forever shall they bear it: an evil burden on the Day of
Resurrection, the day when the Trumpet shall be blown.

On that day We shall assemble all the sinners. Their eyes
will turn blue with terror and they shall murmur among
themselves: 'You lingered on the earth but ten days.'

We know full well what they will say. The most upright
among them will declare: 'You lingered on the earth but one
day.'

They ask you about the mountains. Say: 'My Lord will 20:105
crush them to fine dust and reduce them to a desolate waste,
with no hollows nor jutting mounds to be seen.'

On that day men will follow their truthful summoner,
their voices hushed before the Lord of Mercy; and you shall
hear only the sound of marching feet. On that day no
intercession will avail except from him that has received the
sanction of the Merciful and whose word is pleasing to
Him. He knows what is before them and behind them, but
of Him they have no knowledge.

They will hang their heads with awe before the Living
One, the Ever-existent. Those who are burdened with sin
shall come to grief: but those who have believed and done
good works shall fear no tyranny or injustice.

Thus have We sent it down: a Koran in the Arabic
tongue, and proclaimed in it warnings and threats so that
they may take heed and be admonished. Exalted be God, the 20:114
True King!

Do not be quick to recite the Koran before its revelation
is completed, but rather say: 'Lord, increase my knowledge.'

20:115   We made a covenant with Adam, but he forgot, and We found him lacking in steadfastness. And when We said to the angels: 'Prostrate yourselves before Adam,' they all prostrated themselves except Satan, who refused.

'Adam,' We said, 'Satan is an enemy to you and to your wife. Let him not turn you both out of Paradise and plunge you into affliction. Here you shall not hunger or be naked; you shall not thirst, or feel the scorching heat.'

But Satan whispered to him, saying: 'Adam, shall I show you the Tree of Immortality and an imperishable kingdom?'

They both ate of its fruit, so that they saw their shameful parts and began to cover themselves with the leaves of the Garden. Thus did Adam disobey his Lord and stray from the right path.

Then his Lord had mercy on him; He relented towards him and rightly guided him.

'Get you down hence, both,' He said, 'and may your offspring be enemies to each other. When My guidance is revealed to you, he that follows it shall neither err nor grieve; but he that rejects My warning shall live in woe and come 20:125 before Us blind on the Day of Resurrection. "Lord," he will say, "why have You brought me blind before You when I had once been clear-sighted?"'

He will answer: 'Just as Our revelations were declared to you and you forgot them, so on this day you are yourself forgotten.'

Thus shall We reward the transgressor who denies the revelations of his Lord. But the scourge of the life to come is more terrible and more lasting.

Do they not see how many generations We have destroyed before them? They walk amidst the very ruins where once they dwelt. Surely in this there are signs for men of judgement.

But for a Word from your Lord, long since decreed, their destruction in this life would have been certain. Therefore 20:130 bear with what they say. Give glory to your Lord before sunrise and before sunset. Praise Him night and day, so that you may find comfort.

Do not regard with envy what We have given some 20:131
among them to enjoy – the flower of the present life – for
with this We seek only to try them. Better is your Lord's
provision, and more lasting.

Enjoin prayer on your people and be diligent in its ob- 20:132
servance. We demand of you no provision: We shall Ourself provide for you. Blessed shall be the end of the devout.

They say: 'Why does he not bring us a sign from his Lord?'
Have they not been given sufficient proof in previous
scriptures?

Had We destroyed them with a scourge before his[1]
coming they would have said: 'Lord, if only You had sent
us an apostle! We would have followed Your revelations
before we were humbled and disgraced.'

Say: 'All are waiting: so wait if you will. You shall learn
who has followed the even path and who has been rightly 20:135
guided.'

# THE PROPHETS

*In the Name of God, the Compassionate, the Merciful*

THE DAY of Reckoning for mankind is drawing near, yet 21:1
they blithely persist in unbelief. They listen with ridicule to
each fresh warning that their Lord gives them: their hearts
are set on pleasure.

In private the wrongdoers say to each other: 'Is this man
not a mortal like yourselves? Would you follow witchcraft
with your eyes open?'

Say: 'My Lord has knowledge of whatever is said in
heaven and earth. He hears all and knows all.'

Some say: 'It[2] is but a medley of dreams.' Others: 'He has
invented it himself.' And yet others: 'He is a poet: let him
show us some sign, as did the apostles in days gone by.'

[Yet though We showed them signs,] the communities 21:6
whom We destroyed before them did not believe either.
Will *they* believe?

1. Muḥammad.     2. The Koran.

227

21:7    The apostles We sent before you were but men whom We inspired. Ask the People of the Book if you do not know this. The bodies We gave them could not dispense with food, nor were they immortal. Then We fulfilled Our promise: We delivered them and those We willed, and utterly destroyed the transgressors.

And now We have revealed a Book for your admonishment. Will you not understand?

We have destroyed many a sinful nation and replaced them by other men. And when they felt Our might they took to their heels and fled. They were told: 'Do not run away. Return to your comforts and to your dwellings. You shall be questioned all.'

'Woe betide us, we have done wrong!' was their reply. And this they kept repeating until We mowed them down and put out their light.

It was not in sport that We created the heaven and the earth and all that lies between them. Had it been Our will to find a diversion, We could have found one near at hand.

21:18    Indeed, We will hurl Truth at Falsehood, until Truth shall triumph and Falsehood be no more. Woe betide you, for all the falsehoods you have uttered.

His are all who dwell in the heavens and on earth. Those who stand in His presence do not disdain to worship Him, nor are they ever wearied. They praise Him night and day, tirelessly.

Have they chosen earthly deities? And can these deities restore the dead to life? Were there other gods in heaven or earth besides God, both heaven and earth would be ruined. Exalted be God, Lord of the Throne, above their falsehoods!

None shall question Him about His works, but they shall be questioned. Have they chosen other gods besides Him?

Say: 'Show us your proof. Here are the Scriptures of today and those of long ago.' But most of them know not the Truth, and this is why they pay no heed.

21:25    We inspired all the apostles We sent before you, saying: 'There is no god but Me. Therefore serve Me.'

They say: 'The Merciful has begotten children.' God 21:26
forbid! They are but His honoured servants. They do not
speak till He has spoken: they act by His command. He
knows what is before them and behind them. They intercede
for none save those whom He accepts, and tremble in awe
of Him. Whoever of them declares: 'I am a god besides
Him,' We shall requite with Hell. Thus shall We reward the
wrongdoers.

Are the disbelievers unaware that the heavens and the
earth were but one solid mass which We tore asunder, and
that We made every living thing from water? Will they not
have faith?

We set firm mountains upon the earth lest it should move
away with them, and hewed out highways in the rock so
that they might be rightly guided.

We spread the heaven like a canopy and provided it with
strong support: yet of its signs they are heedless.

It was He who created the night and the day, and the
sun and the moon: each moves swiftly in an orbit of its
own.

No man before you[1] have We made immortal. If you 21:34
yourself are doomed to die, will they live on for ever?

Every soul shall taste death. We will prove you all with
evil and good. To Us shall you return.

When the unbelievers see you, they only mock you,
saying: 'Is this the man who fulminates against your gods?'
And they deny all mention of the Merciful.

Impatience is the very stuff man is made of. I shall
show you My signs: do not ask Me to hurry them
on.

They say: 'When will this promise be fulfilled, if what
you say be true?'

If only the unbelievers knew the day when they shall
strive in vain to shield their faces and their backs from the
fire of Hell; the day when none shall help them! Indeed, it 21:40
will overtake them unawares and stupefy them. They shall

1. Muḥammad.

have no power to ward it off, nor shall they be reprieved.

21:41 Other apostles have been mocked before you; but those who derided them were felled by the very scourge they mocked.

Say: 'Who will protect you, by night and by day, from the Lord of Mercy?' Yet are they unmindful of their Lord's remembrance.

Have they other gods to defend them? Their idols shall be powerless over their own salvation, nor shall they be protected from Our scourge.

Yet have We indulged them and their fathers, so that they have lived too long. Can they not see how We invade their land and diminish its borders? Is it they who will triumph?

Say: 'I warn you only by inspiration.' But the deaf can hear no plea when they are warned.

Yet if the lightest whiff from the vengeance of your Lord touched them, they would say: 'Woe betide us: we have done wrong!'

21:47 We shall set up just scales on the Day of Resurrection, so that no man shall in the least be wronged. Actions as small as a grain of mustard seed shall be weighed out. Our reckoning shall suffice.

We showed Moses and Aaron the distinction between right and wrong, and gave them a light and an admonition for righteous men: those who truly fear their Lord, although unseen, and dread the terrors of the final hour.

And this¹ is a blessed admonition We have sent down. Will you then reject it?

We formerly bestowed guidance on Abraham, for We knew him well. He said to his father and to his people: 'What are these images to which you are so devoted?'

They replied: 'They are the gods our fathers worshipped.'

21:54 He said: 'Then you and your fathers have surely been in evident error.'

1. The Koran.

'Is it the truth that you are preaching,' they asked, 'or is 21:55
this but a jest?'

'Indeed,' he answered, 'your Lord is the Lord of the
heavens and the earth. It was He that made them: to this I
bear witness. By the Lord, I will overthrow your idols as
soon as you have turned your backs.'

He broke them all in pieces, except their supreme god, so
that they might return to him.

'Who has done this to our deities?' asked some. 'He must
surely be a wicked man.'

Others replied: 'We have heard a youth called Abraham
speak of them.'

They said: 'Then bring him here in sight of all the people,
that they may act as witnesses.'

'Abraham,' they said, 'was it you who did this to our
deities?'

'No,' he replied. 'It was their chief who smote them. Ask
*them*, if they can speak.'

Thereupon they turned their thoughts upon themselves
and said to each other: 'Surely you are the ones who have
done wrong.'

Crest-fallen as they were, [they said to Abraham:] 'You 21:65
know they cannot speak.'

He answered: 'Would you then worship that, instead of
God, which can neither help nor harm you? Shame on you
and on your idols! Have you no sense?'

They cried: 'Burn him and avenge your gods, if you must
punish him!'

'Fire,' We said, 'be cool to Abraham and keep him safe.'

They sought to lay a snare for him, but it was they whom
We ruined. We delivered him and Lot, and brought them to
the land which We had blessed for all mankind.

We gave him Isaac, and then Jacob for a grandson; and
We made each a righteous man. We ordained them leaders
to give guidance at Our behest, and enjoined on them
charity, prayer and almsgiving. They served none but Ourself.

To Lot We gave wisdom and knowledge and delivered 21:74

him from the city that had committed deeds of abomina-
21:75 tion; surely they were men of iniquity and evil. We admitted him to Our mercy: he was a righteous man.

Before him Noah invoked Us, and We answered his prayer. We saved him and all his kinsfolk from the great calamity, and delivered him from those who had denied Our revelations. Evil were they; We drowned them all.

And tell of David and Solomon: how they passed judgement regarding the cornfield in which strayed lambs had grazed by night. We gave Solomon insight into the case and bore witness to their judgement.

We bestowed on both of them wisdom and knowledge, and caused the mountains and the birds to join with David in Our praise. All this We did.

We taught him the armourer's craft, so that you might have protection in your wars. Will you then give thanks?

To Solomon We subjected the raging wind: it sped at his bidding to the land which We had blessed. We had knowledge of all things.

21:82 We assigned him devils who dived for him into the sea and who performed other tasks besides. Over them We kept a watchful eye.

And tell of Job: how he called on his Lord, saying: 'I am sorely afflicted: but of all those that show mercy You are the most merciful.'

We answered his prayer and relieved his affliction. We restored to him his family and as many more with them: a blessing from Ourself and an admonition to the devout.

And you shall also tell of Ishmael, Idrīs,[1] and Dhūl-Kifl,[2] who all endured with patience. To Our mercy We admitted them, for they were upright men.

21:87 And of Dhūl-Nūn:[3] how he went away in anger, thinking We had no power over him. But in the darkness he cried: 'There is no god but You. Glory be to You! I have done wrong.'

---

1. Enoch.    2. Probably Ezekiel.    3. Jonah.

We answered his prayer and delivered him from distress. 21:88
Thus shall We save the true believers.

And of Zacharias, who invoked his Lord, saying: 'Lord,
let me not remain childless, though of all heirs You are the
best.'

We answered his prayer and gave him John, curing his
wife of sterility. They vied with each other in good works
and called on Us with piety, fear, and submission.

And of the woman who kept her chastity. We breathed
into her of Our spirit, and made her and her son a sign to all
mankind.

Your community is but one community, and I am Your
only Lord. Therefore serve Me. Men have divided themselves into factions, but to Us shall they all return. He that
does good works in the fullness of his faith, his endeavours
shall not be lost: We record them all.

It is ordained that no community We have destroyed
shall ever rise again. But when Gog and Magog are let loose 21:96
and rush headlong down every hill; when the true promise
nears its fulfilment; the unbelievers shall stare in amazement,
crying: 'Woe betide us! Of this we have been heedless. We
have assuredly done wrong.'

You and your idols shall be the fuel of Hell; therein
shall you all go down. Were they true gods, your idols
would not go there: but there shall they abide for ever. They
shall groan with anguish and be bereft of hearing.

But those to whom We have long since shown Our
favour shall be far removed from Hell. They shall not hear
its roar, but shall delight for ever in what their souls desire.

The Supreme Terror shall not grieve them, and the
angels will receive them, saying: 'This is the day you have
been promised.'

On that day We shall roll up the heaven like a scroll of
parchment. Just as We brought the First Creation into
being, so will We restore it. This is a promise We shall
assuredly fulfil.

We wrote in the Psalms[1] after the Torah was revealed: 21:105

---

1. Psalm XXXVII, 29.

'The righteous among My servants shall inherit the earth.'
21:106 That is an admonition to those who serve Us.

We have sent you forth but as a blessing to mankind. Say: 'It is revealed to me that your God is one God. Will you submit to Him?'

If they pay no heed, say: 'I have warned you all alike, though I cannot tell whether the scourge you are promised is imminent or far off. He knows your spoken words and hidden thoughts. For all I know, this may be a test for you and a short reprieve.'

21:112 Say: 'Lord, judge with fairness. Our Lord is the Merciful, whose help We seek against your blasphemies.'

# PILGRIMAGE

*In the Name of God, the Compassionate, the Merciful*

22:1 YOU PEOPLE, have fear of your Lord. The catastrophe of the Hour of Doom shall be terrible indeed.

When that day comes, every suckling mother shall forsake her infant, every pregnant female shall cast her burden, and you shall see people reeling like drunkards although not drunk: such shall be the horror of God's chastisement.

Yet there are some who in their ignorance dispute about God and follow every rebellious devil, though these are doomed to seduce their followers and lead them to the scourge of the Fire.

22:5 You people! If you doubt the Resurrection remember that We first created you from dust, then from a living germ, then from a clot of blood, and then from a half-formed lump of flesh, so that We might manifest to you Our power.

We cause to remain in the wombs whatever We please for an appointed term, and then We bring you forth as infants, that you may grow up and reach your prime. Some die young, and some live on to abject old age when all that they once knew they know no more.

You sometimes see the earth dry and barren: but no sooner do We send the water down upon it than it begins to stir and swell, putting forth every kind of radiant bloom. That is because God is Truth: He resurrects the dead and has power over all things. 22:6

The Hour of Doom is sure to come – of this there is no doubt. Those who are in their graves God will raise to life.

Some wrangle about God, though they have neither knowledge nor guidance nor divine revelation. They turn away in scorn, leading others astray from God's path. Such men shall incur disgrace in this life, and on the Day of Resurrection taste the torment of the Conflagration. 'This,' We shall say, 'is the reward of your misdeeds. God is not unjust to His servants.'

Some profess to serve God and yet stand on the very fringe of the true faith. When blessed with good fortune they are content, but when an ordeal befalls them they turn upon their heels, forfeiting this life and the hereafter. That way true perdition lies.

They call on idols which can neither harm nor help them. That is the extreme error.

They call on that which would sooner harm than help them: an evil master and an evil friend.

As for those that have faith and do good works, God will admit them to gardens watered by running streams. God's will is ever done. 22:14

If anyone thinks that God will not give victory to His apostle in this world and in the world to come, let him tie a rope to the ceiling of his house and hang himself. Then let him ponder if his cunning has done away with that which has enraged him.

We have revealed the Koran in clear verses. God gives guidance to whom He will.

As for the true believers, those who follow the Jewish Faith, the Sabaeans, the Christians, the Magians, and the pagans, God will judge them on the Day of Resurrection. God is witness of all things.

Do you not see that those in the heavens and the earth, the sun and the moon and the stars, the mountains and the trees, the beasts, and countless men – all do homage to God? Yet many have deserved the scourge. He who is humbled 22:18

by God has none to honour him. God's will is ever done.

22:19 Here are two antagonists who contend about their Lord. Garments of fire have been prepared for the unbelievers. Scalding water shall be poured upon their heads, melting their skins and that which is in their bellies. They shall be lashed with rods of iron.

Whenever, in their anguish, they try to escape from Hell, back they shall be dragged, and will be told: 'Taste the torment of the Conflagration!'

As for those that have faith and do good works, God will admit them to gardens watered by running streams. They shall be decked with bracelets of gold and of pearls, and arrayed in garments of silk. For they have been guided to the noblest of words; they have been guided to the path of the Glorious Lord.

The unbelievers who debar others from the path of God and from the Sacred Mosque which We provided for the people, natives and strangers alike, and those who seek to do evil within its walls – We shall let them taste a grievous torment.

22:26 When We prepared for Abraham the site of the Sacred Mosque We said: 'Worship none besides Me. Keep My House clean for those who walk around it, and those who stand upright or kneel in worship.'

Exhort all people to make the pilgrimage. They will come to you on foot and on the backs of swift camels from every distant quarter; they will come to avail themselves of many a benefit, and to pronounce on the appointed days the name of God over the cattle which He has given them for food. Eat of their flesh, and feed the poor and the unfortunate.

Then let the pilgrims tidy themselves, make their vows, and circle the Ancient House. Such is God's commandment. He that reveres the sacred rites of God shall fare better in the sight of his Lord.

The flesh of cattle is lawful for you, except for that which has been specified before. Guard yourselves against the filth of idols; and avoid the utterance of falsehoods.

22:31 Dedicate yourselves to God, and serve none besides Him.

The man who serves other deities besides God is like him who falls from heaven and is snatched by the birds or carried away by the wind to some far-off region. Even such is he.

He that reveres the offerings made to God shows the 22:32 piety of his heart. Your cattle are useful to you in many ways until the time of their slaughter. Then they are offered for sacrifice at the Ancient House.

For every community We have ordained a ritual, that they may pronounce the name of God over the cattle which He has given them for food. Your God is one God; to Him surrender yourselves. Give good news to the humble, whose hearts are filled with awe at the mention of God; who endure adversity with fortitude, attend to their prayers, and give in alms from what We gave them.

We have made the camels a part of God's rites. They are of much use to you. Pronounce over them the name of God as you draw them up in line and slaughter them; and when they have fallen to the ground eat of their flesh and feed the uncomplaining beggar and the demanding suppliant. Thus have We subjected them to your service, so that you may give thanks.

Their flesh and blood does not reach God; it is your piety 22:37 that reaches Him. Thus has He subjected them to your service, so that you may give glory to God for guiding you.

Give good news to the righteous. God will ward off evil from true believers. God does not love the treacherous and the thankless.

Permission to take up arms is hereby given to those who are attacked, because they have been wronged. God has power to grant them victory: those who have been unjustly driven from their homes, only because they said: 'Our Lord is God.' Had God not defended some by the might of others, monasteries and churches, synagogues and mosques in which His praise is daily celebrated, would have been utterly destroyed. But whoever helps God shall be helped by Him. God is powerful and mighty: He will as- 22:41 suredly help those who, once made masters in the land, will

237

attend to their prayers and render the alms levy, enjoin justice and forbid evil. God governs the destiny of all things.

22:42 If they deny you, remember that before them the people of Noah, 'Ād and Thamūd, the people of Abraham and of Lot, and the dwellers of Midian had also denied their apostles: Moses was likewise rejected. I bore long with the unbelievers, and then I smote them. How awesome was the way I rejected them!

How many cities, teeming with sin, have We laid waste! They lie in desolate ruin, their wells abandoned and their proud palaces empty.

Have they never journeyed through the land? Have they no hearts to reason with, or ears to hear with? It is their hearts, and not their eyes, that are blind.

They bid you hasten the scourge. God will not fail His promise. Each day of your Lord's is like a thousand years in your reckoning.[1]

I bore long with many nations, teeming though they were with sin, and in the end I smote them. To Me shall all return.

22:49 Say: 'You people! I have been sent to warn you plainly. Those that accept the true faith and do good works shall be forgiven and richly recompensed; but those that seek to confute Our revelations shall be the tenants of Hell.'

Never have We sent a single prophet or apostle before you with whose wishes Satan did not tamper. But God abrogates the interjections of Satan and confirms His own revelations. God is all-knowing and wise. He makes Satan's interjections a temptation for those whose hearts are tainted, whose hearts are hardened – this is why the wrongdoers are in open schism – so that those who are endowed with knowledge may realize that this[2] is the truth from your Lord and thus believe in it and humble their hearts towards Him. God will surely guide the faithful to a straight path.

Yet will the unbelievers never cease to doubt it, until the Hour of Doom overtakes them unawares, or the scourge of 22:56 a baleful day descends upon them. On that day God will

1. Cf. Psalm xc, 4    2. The Koran.

reign supreme. He will judge them all. Those that have embraced the true Faith and done good works shall enter the gardens of delight; but the unbelievers who have denied Our 22:57 revelations shall receive an ignominious punishment.

As for those that have fled their homes in the cause of God and afterwards died or were slain, God will surely make a generous provision for them. God is the most munificent Provider. He will surely admit them with a welcome that will please them. All-knowing is God, and gracious.

Thus shall it be. He that repays an injury in kind and then is wronged again shall be helped by God. God is merciful and forgiving.

Thus shall it be. God causes the night to pass into day, and the day to pass into night. God hears all and observes all.

Thus shall it be. God is Truth, and Falsehood all that they invoke besides Him. God alone is the Most High, the Supreme One.

Do you not see how God sends down water from the sky and forthwith the earth turns green? Gracious is God and all-knowing.

His is all that the heavens and the earth contain. Surely 22:64 God is the Self-sufficient, the Glorious One.

Do you not see how God has subdued for you all that is in the earth? And the ships which sail the sea at His bidding? He holds the sky from falling down upon the earth: this it shall not do except by His own leave. Compassionate is God, and merciful to mankind.

It is He who has given you life, and He who will cause you to die and make you live again. Surely man is ungrateful.

For every community We have ordained a ritual which they observe. Let them not dispute with you concerning this. Call them to the path of your Lord: you are rightly guided. If they argue with you, say: 'God knows best all that you do. On the Day of Resurrection God will judge your differences.'

Are you not aware that God has knowledge of what 22:70 heaven and earth contain? All is recorded in a Book. That is easy enough for God.

22:71    Yet they worship besides God that for which no sanction is revealed and of which they know nothing. The wrongdoers shall have none to help them.

When Our revelations are recited to them in all their clarity, you will note denial in the faces of the unbelievers. Barely can they restrain themselves from assaulting those who recite Our revelations.

Say: 'Shall I tell you what is worse than that? The Fire which God has promised those who deny Him. An evil fate.'

You people! Listen to this aphorism. Those whom you invoke besides God could never create a single fly though they combined their forces. And if a fly carried away a speck of dust from them, they could never retrieve it. Powerless is the supplicant, and powerless he whom he supplicates.

They do not render to God the homage due to Him. Yet God is powerful and mighty.

22:75    God chooses messengers from the angels and from men. God hears all and observes all. He knows what is before them and behind them. To God shall all things return.

You that are true believers, kneel and prostrate yourselves. Worship your Lord and do good works, so that you may triumph.

22:78    Fight for the cause of God with the devotion due to Him. *He* has chosen you, and laid on you no burdens in the observance of your faith, the faith of Abraham your father. In this, as in former scriptures, He has given you the name of Muslims, so that the Apostle may testify against you, and that you may yourselves testify against people.

Therefore attend to your prayers, render the alms levy, and hold fast to God; for He is your Guardian. A gracious guardian and a gracious helper!

# THE BELIEVERS

*In the Name of God, the Compassionate, the Merciful*

23:1    BLESSED ARE the believers, who are humble in their prayers; who avoid profane talk, and give alms to the destitute;

who restrain their carnal desires (except with their wives 23:5
and slave-girls, for these are lawful to them: transgressors are
those who lust after other than these); who are true to
their trusts and promises, and diligent in their prayers. These
are the heirs of Paradise; they shall abide in it for ever.

We first created man from an essence of clay: then placed
him, a living germ, in a secure enclosure.[1] The germ We
made a clot of blood, and the clot a lump of flesh. This We
fashioned into bones, then clothed the bones with flesh,
thus bringing forth another creation. Blessed be God, the
noblest of creators.

You shall surely die hereafter, and be restored to life on
the Day of Resurrection. We have created seven heavens[2]
above you; of Our creation We are never heedless.

We sent down water from the sky in due measure, and lodged it in the earth. But if We please, We can take it all away.

With it We caused palm-groves and vineyards to spring up,
yielding abundant fruit for your sustenance. The tree[3] which
grows on Mount Sinai gives oil and a condiment for all to eat.

In the cattle, too, you have but an example of Our power. 23:21
We give you to drink of that which is in their bellies, you
eat their flesh, and gain other benefits from them besides.
By them, as by the ships that sail the sea, you are carried.

We sent forth Noah to his people. 'Serve God, my
people,' he said, 'for you have no god but Him. Will you
not take heed?'

The unbelieving elders of his people said: 'This man is
but a mortal like yourselves, feigning to be your superior.
Had God willed, He could have sent down angels. Nor did
we hear that such a thing ever happened to our forefathers.
He is surely possessed. Keep an eye on him awhile.'

Noah said: 'Help me, Lord. They will not believe me.'

We revealed Our will to him, saying: 'Build the ark under 23:27
Our watchful eye, according to Our instructions. When
Our judgement comes to pass and water wells out from the

---

1. The womb.    2. Literally, 'highways' (Al-Jalālayn).
3. The olive.

Oven, take aboard a pair from every species and the members of your household, except those of them already doomed. Do not plead with Me for those who have done wrong: they shall

23:28 be drowned. And when you and all your followers have gone aboard, say: "Praise be to God who has delivered us from a sinful nation. Lord, let my landing from the ark be blessed. You alone can make me land in safety."'

Surely in that there were veritable signs. Thus did We put mankind to the proof.

Then We raised a new generation, and sent forth to them an apostle of their own. 'Serve God,' he said, 'for you have no god but Him. Will you not take heed?'

But the unbelieving elders of his people, who denied the life to come and on whom We had bestowed the good things of this life, said: 'This man is but a mortal like yourselves, nourished by the same food and drink. If you obey a mortal like yourselves, you shall indeed be lost. Does he promise you, when you are dead and turned to dust and bones,

23:37 you will be raised to life? A foolish promise, indeed. There is no other life but this, our earthly life: we die and live, never to be restored to life. This man is but an impostor who tells of God what is untrue. Never will We believe in him.'

He said: 'Help me, Lord, they have rejected me.'

He replied: 'Before long they shall rue it.' The Cry took them in all justice, and We swept them away like withered leaves. Gone are those wicked men.

After them We raised other generations – no people can delay their doom or go before it – and sent forth Our apostles in succession. Yet time after time they disbelieved their apostles, so that We destroyed them one by one and held them up as an example. Gone are the unbelievers.

Then We sent Moses and his brother Aaron, with Our signs and with clear authority, to Pharaoh and his nobles. But they received them with contempt, for they were arrogant men. 'What!' said they. 'Are we to believe in two men like ourselves, whose people are our bondsmen?' They denied them, and thus incurred destruction. And

23:49 We gave Moses the Book, so that they might be rightly guided.

We made the son of Mary and his mother a sign to 23:50 mankind, and gave them a shelter on a peaceful hill-side watered by a fresh spring.

Apostles! Eat of that which is wholesome, and do good works: I have knowledge of all your actions. Your community is but one community, and I am your only Lord: therefore fear Me.

Yet men have divided themselves into factions, each rejoicing in its own doctrines. Leave them in their error till a time appointed.

Do they think that, in giving them wealth and children, We are solicitous for their welfare? By no means! They cannot see.

Those who walk in fear of their Lord; who believe in the revelations of their Lord; who worship none besides their Lord; who give alms with hearts filled with awe, knowing that they will return to their Lord: these vie with each other for salvation and shall be the first to attain it.

We charge no soul with more than it can bear. Our Book records the truth: none shall be wronged.

But the unbelievers' hearts are blind to all this; their deeds 23:63 are of a different sort, and they are bent on doing them. But when We visit Our scourge upon those of them that live in comfort, they will cry out for help. We shall say: 'Do not howl this day, for from Us you shall receive no help. My revelations were recited to you many a time, but you turned your backs in scorn, and passed the nights reviling them.'

Should they not heed the Word?

Was anything revealed to them that had not been revealed to their forefathers?

Or is it because they do not know their apostle that they deny him?

Do they say he is possessed?

Surely he has proclaimed to them the truth. But most of them abhor the truth. Had the truth followed their appetites, the heavens, the earth, and all who dwell in them, would have surely been corrupted. We have given them their scriptures: yet to their scriptures they pay no heed.

Are you seeking a reward from them? Far better is your 23:72 Lord's recompense. He is the most munificent Giver.

23:73    You have called them to a straight path, but those who deny the life to come will ever stray from the right path.

If We showed them mercy and relieved their misfortunes, they would persist in sin, ever straying from the right path. We punished them, but they neither entreated their Lord nor humbled themselves before Him. And when We smote them with a dreadful scourge, they yielded to utter despair.

It was He who gave you ears, eyes, and hearts: yet you are seldom thankful.

It was He who placed you on the earth, and before Him shall you be assembled.

It is He who ordains life and death, and He who alternates the night with the day. Can you not understand?

They say what the ancients said before them. 'After our death, when we are dust and bones,' they say, 'shall we be raised to life? This we have been promised before, we and our fathers. It is but a fable of the ancients.'

Say: 'Whose is the earth and all that it contains? Tell me, if you know the truth.'

'God's,' they will reply.

Say: 'Then will you not take heed?'

23:86    Say: 'Who is the Lord of the seven heavens, and of the Glorious Throne?'

'God,' they will reply.

Say: 'Will you fear Him, then?'

Say: 'In whose hands is the sovereignty of all things, protecting all, while against Him there is no protection? Tell me, if you know the truth.'

'In God's,' they will reply.

Say: 'How then can you be so bewitched?'

We have revealed to them the truth; but they are surely lying.

Never has God begotten a son, nor is there any other god besides Him. Were this otherwise, each god would govern his own creation, each holding himself above the other. Exalted be God above their falsehoods!

23:92    He knows alike the unknown and the manifest. Exalted be He above the gods they serve besides Him!

Say: 'Lord, if You will indeed let me see the scourge 23:93
they are promised, do not abandon me, Lord, among these
wicked people.' Indeed, We do have power enough to let
you see the scourge We promise them.

Requite evil with good. We know their slanders well. And
say: 'Lord, I seek refuge in You from the promptings of the
devils. Lord, I seek refuge in You from their presence.'

When death comes to a wrongdoer, he will say: 'Lord, let
me go back, that I may do good works in the world I have
left behind.'

Never! These are the very words which he will speak.
Behind them there shall stand a barrier till the Day of
Resurrection. And when the Trumpet is sounded, on that
day their ties of kindred shall be broken, nor shall they ask
help of one another.

Those whose good deeds weigh heavy in the scales shall
triumph, but those whose deeds are light shall forfeit their
souls and abide in Hell for ever. The fire will scorch their
faces and they will writhe in anguish.

We shall say: 'Were My revelations not recited to you,
and did you not deny them?'

'Lord,' they will reply, 'fortune betrayed us and we went 23:106
astray. Lord, deliver us from Hell. If we relapse, then
we shall indeed be evil-doers.'

He will say: 'Stay here in shame and do not plead with
Me. Among My servants there were those who said: "Lord,
we believe in You. Forgive us and have mercy on us: You
are the best of those that show mercy." But you derided
them until they caused you to forget My warning; and you
laughed at them. Today I shall reward them for their
fortitude, for it is they who have triumphed.'

And He will ask: 'How many years did you linger on the
earth?'

They will reply: 'A day, or possibly less. Ask those who
have kept count.'

He will say: 'Brief indeed was your sojourn, if you but
knew it! Did you think that We created you in vain and 23:115
that to Us you would never be recalled?'

Exalted be God, the True King. There is no god but Him, the Lord of the Glorious Throne.

He that invokes another god besides God – a god of whose divinity he has no proof – his Lord will bring him to account. The unbelievers shall never prosper.

23:118 Say: 'Lord, forgive and have mercy. You are the best of those that show mercy.'

# LIGHT

*In the Name of God, the Compassionate, the Merciful*

24:1 A CHAPTER which We have revealed and sanctioned, proclaiming in it clear revelations, so that you may take heed.

The adulterer and the adulteress shall each be given a hundred lashes. Let no pity for them cause you to disobey God, if you truly believe in God and the Last Day; and let their punishment be witnessed by a number of believers.

The adulterer may marry only an adulteress or an idolatress; and the adulteress may marry only an adulterer or an idolater. True believers are forbidden such marriages.

Those that defame honourable women and cannot produce four witnesses shall be given eighty lashes. Do not accept their testimony ever after, for they are great transgressors – except those among them that afterwards repent and mend their ways. God is forgiving and merciful.

24:6 If a man accuses his wife but has no witnesses except himself, he shall swear four times by God that his charge is true, calling down upon himself the curse of God if he is lying. But if his wife swears four times by God that his charge is false and calls down His curse upon herself if it be true, she shall receive no punishment.[1]

But for God's grace and mercy, His forgiveness and His wisdom, [this would never have been revealed to you].

24:11 Those who concocted that slander[2] were a band of

1. Cf. Numbers v, 11–31.

2. The reference is to the scandal instigated by the Prophet's opponents involving Muḥammad's wife 'Ā'ishah with Ṣafwān b. al-Muʿaṭṭal.

your own people. Do not regard it as a misfortune, for it has proved an advantage. Each one of them shall be punished according to his crime. As for him who had the greater share in it, his punishment shall be terrible indeed.

When you heard it, why did the faithful, men and 24:12 women, not think well of their own people, and say: 'This is an evident falsehood'? Why did they not produce four witnesses? If they could not produce any witnesses, then they were surely lying in the sight of God.

But for God's grace and mercy towards you in this life and in the life to come, you would have been sternly punished for what you did. You carried with your tongues and uttered with your mouths what you did not know. You may have thought it a trifle, but in the sight of God it was a grave offence.

When you heard it, why did you not say: 'It is not right for us to speak of this. God forbid! This is a monstrous slander'?

God bids you never to repeat the like, if you are true believers. God makes plain to you His revelations. God is all-knowing and wise.

Those who delight in spreading salacious slander against 24:19 the faithful shall be sternly punished in this life and in the life to come. God knows, but you know not.

But for God's grace and mercy, His compassion and forgiveness, [you would have long since been punished].

You that are true believers, do not walk in Satan's footsteps. He that walks in Satan's footsteps is incited by him to lewdness and evil. But for God's grace and mercy, none of you would ever have kept himself pure. But God purifies whom He will; God hears all and knows all.

Let not the rich and honourable among you swear to withhold their gifts from their kindred, the destitute, and those who have fled their homes in the cause of God. Rather let them pardon and forgive. Do you not wish God to forgive you? God is forgiving and merciful.

Those who defame honourable but careless believing 24:23

women shall be cursed in this world and in the world to
24:24 come. Grievous punishment awaits them on the day when
their own tongues, hands, and feet will testify to what they
did. On that day God will justly requite them. They shall
know that God is the Glorious Truth.

Unclean women are for unclean men, and unclean men
for unclean women. But good women are for good men,
and good men for good women. These shall be cleared
of calumny; forgiveness, and a generous provision, await
them.

Believers, do not enter the dwellings of other men until
you have asked their owners' permission and wished them
peace. That will be best for you. Perchance you will take heed.

If you find no one in them, do not go in till you are given
leave. If you are refused admission, it is but more proper that
you should go away. God has knowledge of all your actions.

It shall be no offence for you to seek shelter in empty
dwellings. God knows what you reveal and what you hide.
24:30 Enjoin believing men to turn their eyes away from
temptation and to restrain their carnal desires. This will make
their lives purer. God has knowledge of all their actions.

Enjoin believing women to turn their eyes away from
temptation and to preserve their chastity; not to display their
adornments (except such as are normally revealed); to
draw their veils over their bosoms and not to display their
finery except to their husbands, their fathers, their husbands'
fathers, their sons, their step-sons, their brothers, their
brothers' sons, their sisters' sons, their women-servants,
and their slave-girls; male attendants lacking in natural
vigour, and children who have no carnal knowledge of
women. And let them not stamp their feet[1] when walking so
as to reveal their hidden trinkets.

Believers, turn to God in penitence, that you may
prosper.
24:32 Take in marriage those among you who are single and
those of your male and female slaves who are honest. If they

---

1. Cf. Isaiah iii, 16, 18.

are poor, God will enrich them from His own bounty. God is munificent and all-knowing.

Let those who cannot afford to marry live in continence 24:33 until God shall enrich them from His own bounty. As for those of your slaves who wish to buy their liberty, free them if you find in them any promise and bestow on them a part of the riches which God has given you.

You shall not force your slave-girls into prostitution in order that you may enrich yourselves, if they wish to preserve their chastity. If anyone compels them, God will be forgiving and merciful to them.

We have sent down to you revelations showing you the right path. We have given you an account of those who have gone before you, and an admonition to righteous men.

God is the light of the heavens and the earth. His light 24:35 may be compared to a niche that enshrines a lamp, the lamp within a crystal of star-like brilliance. It is lit from a blessed olive tree neither eastern nor western. Its very oil would almost shine forth, though no fire touched it. Light upon light; God guides to His light whom He will.

God speaks in parables to mankind. God has knowledge of all things.

His light is found in temples which God has sanctioned to be built for the remembrance of His name. In them, morning and evening, His praise is sung by men whom neither trade nor profit can divert from remembering God, from offering prayers, or from giving alms; who dread the day when men's hearts and eyes shall writhe with anguish; who hope that God will requite them for their noblest deeds and lavish His grace upon them. God gives without reckoning to whom He will.

As for the unbelievers, their works are like a mirage in a desert. The thirsty traveller thinks it is water, but when he comes near he finds that it is nothing. He finds God there, who pays him back in full. Swift is God's reckoning.

Or like darkness on a bottomless ocean spread with 24:40 clashing billows and overcast with clouds: darkness upon darkness. If he stretches out his hand he can scarcely see it. Indeed the man from whom God withholds His light shall find no light at all.

24:41    Do you not see how God is praised by those in the heavens and those on earth? The very birds praise Him as they wing their way. He notes the prayers and praises of all His creatures; God has knowledge of all their actions.

It is God who has sovereignty over the heavens and the earth. To God shall all return.

Do you not see how God drives the clouds, then gathers and piles them up in masses which pour down torrents of rain? From heaven's mountains He sends down the hail, pelting with it whom He will and turning it away from whom He pleases. The flash of His lightning almost snatches out men's eyes.

God makes the night succeed the day: surely in this there is a lesson for clear-sighted men.

God created every beast from water. Some creep upon their bellies, others walk on two legs, and others yet on four. God creates what He pleases. God has power over all things.

24:46    We have sent down revelations demonstrating the Truth. God guides whom He will to a straight path.

They declare: 'We believe in God and the Apostle and obey.' But no sooner do they utter these words than some among them turn their backs. Surely these are no believers.

And when they are called to God and His apostle that he may judge between them, some turn away. Had justice been on their side they would have come to him in all obedience.

Is there a sickness in their hearts, or are they full of doubt? Do they fear that God and His apostle may deny them justice? Surely they are themselves the wrongdoers.

But when true believers are called to God and His apostle that he may pass judgement upon them, their only reply is: 'We hear and obey.' Such men will surely prosper.

Those that obey God and His apostle, those that revere God and fear Him, will surely triumph.

24:53    They solemnly swear by God that if you order them, they will march forth. Say: 'Do not swear: your obedience, not your oaths, will count. God is cognizant of all your actions.'

Say: 'Obey God and obey the Apostle. If you do not, he 24:54 is still bound to fulfil his duty, as you yourselves are bound to fulfil yours. If you obey him, you shall be rightly guided. An apostle's duty is but to give plain warning.'

God has promised those of you who believe and do good works to make them masters in the land as He made those who went before them, to strengthen the Faith He chose for them, and to change their fears to safety. Let them worship Me and serve none besides Me. Wicked indeed are they who after this deny Me.

Attend to your prayers, render the alms levy, and obey the Apostle, so that you may be shown mercy.

Never think that the unbelievers can escape their fate in this world. The Fire shall be their home: an evil end.

Believers, let your slaves and those who are under age 24:58 ask your leave on three occasions when they come in to see you: before the dawn prayer, when you have put off your garments in the heat of noon, and after the evening prayer. These are the three occasions when none may intrude upon your privacy. At other times, it shall be no offence for you, or them, to go around visiting one another. Thus God makes plain to you His revelations: God is all-knowing and wise.

And when they have reached the age of puberty, let your children still ask your leave as their elders do. Thus God makes plain to you His revelations: God is all-knowing and wise.

It shall be no offence for old spinsters who have no hope of marriage to discard their cloaks without revealing their adornments. Better if they do not discard them. God hears all and knows all.

It shall be no offence for the blind, the lame, and the sick, 24:61 to eat at your table. Nor shall it be an offence for you to eat in the houses of your own children, your fathers, your mothers, your brothers, your sisters, your paternal uncles, your paternal aunts, your maternal uncles, your maternal aunts, or your friends; or in houses with the keys of which you are entrusted. It shall be equally lawful whether you eat together or apart.

When you enter a house, salute one another in the name of God, and let your greeting be devout and kindly. Thus God makes clear to you His revelations, so that you may grow in wisdom.

24:62 They only are true believers who have faith in God and His apostle, and who, when gathered with him upon a grave occasion, do not depart till they have begged his leave. The men who ask your leave are those who truly believe in God and His apostle. When they ask your leave to go away on any business of their own, grant it to whomever you please and implore God to forgive them; God is forgiving and merciful.

Do not address the Apostle in the manner you address one another. God knows those of you who steal away, concealing themselves behind others. Let those who disobey his orders beware, lest some affliction or some woeful scourge be visited upon them.

24:64 Surely to God belongs what the heavens and the earth contain. He has knowledge of all your thoughts and actions. On the day when they return to Him, He will declare to them all that they have done. God has knowledge of all things.

# AL-FURQĀN[1]

*In the Name of God, the Compassionate, the Merciful*

25:1 BLESSED BE He who has revealed Al-Furqān to His servant, that he may warn the nations; Sovereign of the heavens and the earth, who has begotten no children and

1. 'The distinction between right and wrong; also one of the names of the Koran.' The word has puzzled Muslim commentators. It is probably identical with the Aramaic *porqan* (salvation).

has no partner in His sovereignty; who has created all things and ordained them in due proportion.

Yet the unbelievers serve, besides Him, other gods which 25:3 can create nothing and were themselves created: which can neither harm nor help themselves, and which have no power over death or life, or the raising of the dead.

The unbelievers say: 'This[1] is but a forgery of his own invention, in which others have helped him.' Unjust is what they say and false.

And they say: 'Fables of the ancients he has written: they are dictated to him morning and evening.'

Say: 'It is revealed by Him who knows the secrets of the heavens and the earth. He is surely forgiving and merciful.'

They also say: 'How is it that this apostle eats and walks about the market-squares? Why has no angel been sent down with him to give warning? Why has no treasure been given him, no garden to provide his sustenance?'

And the wrongdoers say: 'The man you follow is surely bewitched.'

See what epithets they bestow upon you![2] Surely they 25:9 have gone astray and cannot return to the true path.

Blessed be He who, if He wills, can give you better things than these; gardens watered by running streams, and palaces too.

Indeed, they deny the Hour of Doom. For those who deny that hour We have prepared a blazing fire. From far away they shall hear it raging and roaring. And when, chained together, they are flung into some narrow space, they will fervently call for death. But they will be told: 'Do not call today for one death; call for many deaths!'

Say: 'Which is better, this or the Paradise of Immortality which the righteous have been promised? It is their recompense and their retreat. Abiding there for ever, they shall find in it all that they desire. That is a promise which your Lord must needs fulfil.'

On the day He gathers them with all their idols, He 25:17

1. The Koran.      2. Muḥammad.

253

will say: 'Was it you who misled these My servants, or did they choose to go astray?'

25:18 They will answer: 'Glory be to You! We should never have chosen other guardians besides You. But You gave them and their fathers the comforts of this life, so that they forgot Your warning and thus incurred destruction.'

[Then to the idolaters God will say:] 'Your idols have denied your charges. You cannot avert your doom, nor can you be helped. Those of you who have done wrong We will sternly punish.'

We have sent no apostles before you who did not eat or walk about the market-squares. We test you by means of one another. Will you not have patience? Surely your Lord observes all.

Those who entertain no hope of meeting Us ask: 'Why have no angels been sent down to us? Why can we not see our Lord?' How arrogant they are, and how gross is their iniquity!

25:22 On the day when they behold the angels, the evil-doers will not rejoice that day. The angels will say to them: 'You shall never cross that barrier.' Then We shall turn to that which they have done and render it as vain as scattered dust.

As for the heirs of Paradise, they shall lodge in a more auspicious dwelling on that day, and in a cooler resting-place.

On that day the sky with all its clouds shall be rent asunder and the angels sent down in their ranks. On that day the Merciful will truly reign supreme. A day of woe it shall be to the unbelievers.

On that day the wrongdoer will bite his hands and say: 'Would that I had walked in the Apostle's path! Oh, would that I had never chosen so-and-so for my companion! It was he that made me disbelieve in God's warning after it had reached me. Satan is ever treacherous to man.'

The Apostle says: 'Lord, my people have forsaken this 25:31 Koran.' Thus to every prophet We have assigned adversaries among the wrongdoers: but you need none besides your Lord to guide and help you.

The unbelievers ask: 'Why was the Koran not revealed to 25:32 him entire in a single revelation?'

We have revealed it thus so that We may sustain your heart. We have imparted it to you by gradual revelation. No sooner will they come to you with an argument than We shall reveal to you the truth, better expounded. Those who are dragged upon their faces into Hell shall have a viler place to dwell in, having strayed farther from the right path.

We gave the Book to Moses and assigned to him his brother Aaron as a helper. We sent them to those who had denied Our signs, and utterly destroyed them.

As for Noah's people, We drowned them when they denied their apostles and made of them an example to mankind. For the wrongdoers We have prepared a woeful scourge.

The tribes of 'Ād and Thamūd were also destroyed, and so were those who dwelt at Rass, and many generations in between. To each of them We gave examples, and each of them We exterminated.

They must surely have passed by the city which was 25:40 destroyed by the fatal rain: have they never seen its ruins? Yet have they no faith in the Resurrection.

Whenever they see you they deride you, saying: 'Is this the man whom God has sent as His emissary? Had we not stood firm, he would have turned us away from our gods.' But when they face the scourge they shall realize who has strayed farther from the right path.

Have you considered the man who has made a god of his own appetite? Would you be a guardian over him?

Do you think most of them can hear or understand? They are but like cattle; indeed, even more misguided.

Do you not see how your Lord lengthens the shadows? Had it been His will He could have made them constant. But We make the sun their guide; little by little We shorten them.

It is He who has made the night a mantle for you, and 25:47 sleep a rest. He makes each day a resurrection.

25:48 It is He who drives the winds as harbingers of His mercy; and We send down pure water from the sky, so that We may give life to a dead land and quench the thirst of countless beasts and men We have created.

We have made it flow freely among them, so that they may remember. Yet most decline to render thanks.

Had it been Our will, We could have sent to every city someone to give warning. Do not yield to the unbelievers, but fight them vigorously with this.

It was He who sent the Two Seas rolling, the one sweet and fresh, the other salt and bitter, and set a rampart between them, an insurmountable barrier.

It was He who created man from water, and gave him kindred of blood and of marriage. All-powerful is your Lord.

Yet they worship idols which can neither help nor harm them. Surely the unbeliever is an enemy to his Lord.

We have sent you only to proclaim good news and to give warning. Say: 'I demand of you no recompense for this. Let him who will, take the right path to his Lord.'

25:58 Put your trust in the Ever-living who never dies. Celebrate His praise: He well knows all His servants' sins. In six days He created the heavens and the earth and all that lies between them, and then ascended the throne. He is the Lord of Mercy. Ask those who know, concerning Him.

When they are told: 'Bow down before the Merciful,' they ask: 'Who is the Merciful? Would you have us bow down to whatever you will?' And they grow more rebellious.

Blessed be He who decked the sky with constellations and set in it a lamp and a shining moon. He makes the night succeed the day: a sign for those who would take heed and render thanks.

True servants of the Merciful are those who walk humbly on the earth and say: 'Peace!' to the ignorant who accost them; who pass the night standing and on their knees in adoration of their Lord; who say: 'Lord, ward off from us the punishment of Hell, for its punishment is everlasting: an 25:66 evil dwelling and an evil resting-place'; who are neither

extravagant nor niggardly, but keep the golden mean; who 25:67
invoke no other deity besides God, and do not kill except
for a just cause (manslaughter is forbidden by Him); who
do not commit adultery (he that does shall meet with
evil: his punishment shall be doubled on the Day of
Resurrection and in disgrace he shall abide for ever – unless
he repent and believe and do good works, for then God will
change his sins to good actions: God is forgiving and
merciful: he that repents and does good works shall truly
return to God); who do not bear false witness, and who 25:72
maintain their dignity when listening to profane abuse; who
do not turn a deaf ear and a blind eye to the revelations of
their Lord when they are reminded of them; who say:
'Lord, give us joy in our spouses and our children, and
make us examples to those who fear You.' These shall be
rewarded for their fortitude with the loftiest abode in
Paradise. There shall they find a greeting and a welcome,
and there shall they abide for ever: a pleasant dwelling and a
pleasant resting-place.

Say: 'Little cares my Lord if you do not invoke Him. 25:77
Now that you have denied His revelations, His punishment
is bound to overtake you.'

# THE POETS

*In the Name of God, the Compassionate, the Merciful*

*Ṭā' sīn mīm.* These are the revelations of the Glorious Book: 26:1
You will perhaps fret yourself to death on account of their
unbelief. If We will, We can reveal to them a sign from heaven
before which they will bow their necks in utter humility.

They deny and turn their backs on each fresh warning they
receive from the Merciful: but the truth of that which they
have laughed to scorn will before long dawn upon them.

Do they not see the earth, how We have brought forth
from it all kinds of beneficial plants? Surely in this there is a
sign; yet most of them do not believe.

Surely your Lord is the Mighty One, the Merciful. Your 26:10

Lord called out to Moses, saying: 'Go to those wicked
26:11 people, the people of Pharaoh. Will they not take heed?'

'Lord,' he replied, 'I fear they will reject me. I may
become impatient and stammer in my speech. Send for
Aaron. They accuse me of a crime,[1] and I fear that they may
put me to death.'

'Have no fear,' said He. 'Go both of you with Our signs;
We shall be with you and shall hear all. Go to Pharaoh and
say to him: "We are messengers from the Lord of the Universe. Let the Israelites depart with us."'

Pharaoh said to Moses: 'Did we not bring you up when
you were an infant? And did you not stay in our midst
several years of your life? Yet you have done what you have
done; surely you are ungrateful.'

Moses replied: 'I did that when I was a misguided youth.
I fled from you because I feared you. But my Lord has
given me wisdom and made me an apostle. And this is the
favour with which you taunt me: you have made the
Israelites your bondsmen.'

26:23 'Who is the Lord of the Universe?' asked Pharaoh.

He replied: 'The Lord of the heavens and the earth and
all that lies between them. If only you had faith!'

'Do you hear?' said Pharaoh to those around him.

'He is your Lord,' went on Moses, 'and the Lord of your
forefathers.'

Pharaoh said: 'The apostle who has been sent to you is
surely possessed!'

'The Lord of the East and the West,' said Moses, 'and all
that lies between them. If only you could understand!'

'If you serve any other god but myself,' replied Pharaoh,
'I shall have you thrown into prison.'

'Even if I showed you a convincing sign?' said Moses.

He replied: 'Show us your sign, if what you say be true.'

Moses threw down his staff and thereupon it changed to
26:33 a veritable serpent. Then he drew out his hand, and it
was white to all who saw it.

---

1. Moses had killed an Egyptian.

'This man,' he said to the nobles around him, 'is a skilful 26:34
sorcerer who seeks to drive you from your land by his
sorcery. What is your counsel?'

They replied: 'Put them off awhile, him and his brother,
and send forth heralds to the cities to summon every skilled
enchanter to your presence.'

The sorcerers were gathered on an appointed day, and
the people were asked if they had all assembled. They
declared: 'We will follow the sorcerers if they win the
day.'

And when the sorcerers came they said to Pharaoh:
'Shall we be rewarded if we win?'

'Yes,' he answered, 'and you shall become my favoured
friends.'

Moses said to them: 'Throw down all that you wish to
throw.'

They cast down their ropes and staffs, saying: 'By
Pharaoh's glory, we shall surely win!'

Then Moses threw down his staff, and it swallowed their
false devices. The sorcerers prostrated themselves in adoration, saying: 'We now believe in the Lord of the Universe,
the Lord of Moses and Aaron.'

Pharaoh said: 'Do you dare believe in him before I give 26:49
you leave? He must surely be your master, who has taught
you witchcraft. But you shall see. I will cut off your hands
and feet on alternate sides and crucify you all.'

'That cannot harm us,' they replied, 'for to our Lord we
shall return. We trust that our Lord will forgive us our sins,
since we are the first who have believed.'

Then We revealed Our will to Moses, saying: 'Set forth
with My servants in the night, for you will be pursued.'

Pharaoh sent forth heralds to all the cities. 'These,' they
said, 'are but a puny band, who have provoked us much.
But we are a numerous army, well-prepared.'

Thus did We make them leave their gardens and their
fountains, their treasures and their sumptuous dwellings.
Even thus; and to the Israelites We gave those.

At sunrise the Egyptians followed them. And when the 26:60

26:61 two multitudes came within sight of each other, Moses'
companions said: 'We are surely undone!'

'No,' Moses replied, 'my Lord is with me, and He will
guide me.'

We bade Moses strike the sea with his staff, and the sea
was cleft asunder, each part as high as a massive mountain.
In between We made the others follow. We delivered Moses
and all who were with him, and drowned the rest.

Surely in that there was a sign; yet most of them did not
believe.

Surely, your Lord is the Mighty One, the Merciful. Recount
to them the story of Abraham. He said to his father and to his
people: 'What is that which you worship?'

They replied: 'We worship idols and pray to them with all
fervour.'

'Do they hear you when you call on them?' he asked.
'Can they help you or do you harm?'

They replied: 'This was what our fathers did before us.'

He said: 'Do you see those which you have worshipped,
you and your forefathers? They are my enemies. Not so the
26:78 Lord of the Universe, who has created me; who gives me
guidance, food and drink; who, when I am sick, restores
me; who will cause me to die and bring me back to life
hereafter; who, I hope, will forgive me my sins on the Day
of Judgement.

'Lord, bestow wisdom upon me, and admit me among
the righteous. Make me deserving of praise among
posterity and count me among the heirs of the Blissful
Garden. Forgive my father, for he has gone astray. Do not
hold me up to shame on the Day of Resurrection; the day when
wealth and offspring will be of no avail, and when none shall
be saved but him who comes before his Lord with a pure
heart; when Paradise shall be brought within sight of the
righteous and Hell be revealed to the erring. They will be
asked: "Where are your idols now? Can they help you or
even help themselves?" And into Hell they shall be hurled,
they and those who misled them, and Satan's legions all.
26:96 "By the Lord," they will say to their idols, as they contend

with them, "we erred indeed when we made you equals 26:97
with the Lord of the Universe. It was but the evil-doers
who led us astray. We have no intercessors now, no loving
friend. Could we but live our lives again we would be true
believers."'

Surely in that there was a sign, yet most of them did not
believe.

Surely your Lord is the Mighty One, the Merciful. The
people of Noah, too, disbelieved the apostles. 'Will you not
fear God?' said Noah, their kinsman, to them. 'I am indeed
your true apostle. Fear God, then, and follow me. For this I
demand of you no recompense, for none can reward me
except the Lord of the Universe. Have fear of God and
follow me.'

They replied: 'Are we to believe in you when your
followers are but the lowest of the low?'

'I have no knowledge of what they may have done,' said
Noah. 'My Lord alone can bring them to account. Would
that you understood! I will not drive away the true believers. I am sent only to give plain warning.'

'Noah,' they replied, 'desist, or you shall be stoned to 26:116
death.'

He said: 'Lord, my people have rejected me. Judge
rightly between us. Save me and the believers who are with
me.'

We delivered him and those who were with him in the
laden ark, and overwhelmed the others with the Flood.

Surely in that there was a sign; yet most of them did not
believe.

Your Lord is the Mighty One, the Merciful. 'Ād, too,
disbelieved the apostles. Their kinsman Hūd had said to
them: 'Will you not fear God? I am indeed your true
apostle. Fear God, then, and follow me. For this I demand of
you no recompense; none can reward me except the Lord of
the Universe. Will you erect a monument on every hill?
Vain is your work. You build strong fortresses, hoping that
you may last for ever. When you exercise your power, you
act like cruel tyrants. Have fear of God, and follow me. Fear 26:131

26:132 Him who has given you all the things you know. He has given you flocks and children, gardens and fountains. Beware the torment of a fateful day.' ·

They replied: 'We care nothing whether or not you preach to us. That with which you threaten us is but an ancient myth. Surely we shall not be punished.'

They rejected him, and thus We utterly destroyed them. Surely in that there was a sign; yet most of them did not believe.

Your Lord is the Mighty One, the Merciful. Thamūd, too, disbelieved the apostles. Their kinsman Ṣāliḥ had said to them: 'Will you not fear God? I am indeed your true apostle. Fear God and follow me. For this I demand of you no recompense; none can reward me except the Lord of the Universe. Are you to be left secure in this land, amidst gardens and fountains, cornfields and palm-trees laden with fine fruit, hewing your dwellings in the mountains and leading a wanton life? Have fear of God and follow me. Do not obey the bidding of transgressors who perpetrate corruption in the land and do no good at all.'

26:153 They replied: 'Surely you are bewitched. You are but a mortal like ourselves. Show us a sign, if what you say be true.'

'Here,' he said, 'is this she-camel. She shall have her share of water as you have yours, each drinking on an appointed day. Do not molest her, or the scourge of a fateful day shall take you.'

Yet they slew her, and then repented of their deed. The scourge took them.

Surely in that there was a sign. Yet most of them did not believe.

Your Lord is the Mighty One, the Merciful. Lot's people, too, disbelieved the apostles. Their kinsman Lot had said to them: 'Will you not fear God? I am indeed your true apostle. Fear God and follow me. For this I demand of you no recompense; none can reward me except the Lord of the 26:166 Universe. Will you fornicate with males and eschew the wives whom God has created for you? Surely you are great transgressors.'

'Lot,' they replied, 'desist or you shall be banished.'   26:167

He said: 'I abhor your ways. Lord, deliver me and my household from their evil doings.'

We delivered Lot and all his household, save for one old woman who stayed behind, and the rest We utterly destroyed. We pelted them with rain, and evil was the rain which fell on those who were forewarned.

Surely in that there was a sign. Yet most of them did not believe.

Your Lord is the Mighty One, the Merciful. The dwellers of the Forest,[1] too, disbelieved the apostles. Shu'aib had said to them: 'Will you not fear God? I am indeed your true apostle. Fear God and follow me. For this I demand of you no recompense: none can reward me except the Lord of the Universe. Give just measure and defraud none. Weigh with even scales and do not cheat your fellow men of what is rightly theirs; nor shall you corrupt the land with evil. Fear Him who created you and those who have gone before you.'

They replied: 'You are surely bewitched. You are but a   26:185 mortal like ourselves. Indeed, we believe that you are lying. Bring down upon us a part of heaven if what you say be true.'

He said: 'My Lord has full knowledge of all your actions.' They disbelieved him, and thus the scourge of the Day of Darkness smote them; it was surely the scourge of a fateful day.

Surely in that there was a sign; yet most of them did not believe.

Your Lord is the Mighty One, the Merciful. This is surely revealed by the Lord of the Universe. The faithful Spirit has brought it down into your heart, that you may give warning in eloquent Arabic speech. It was surely foretold in the scriptures of the ancients. Is it not sufficient proof for them that the doctors of the Israelites recognize it? If We had revealed it to a foreign man, and he had recited it to them, they still would not have believed. Thus do We put   26:200

1. The people of Midian.

26:201 unbelief in the hearts of the guilty: they shall not believe in it until they see the woeful scourge, which will suddenly smite them when they are heedless. And then they will say: 'Shall we ever be reprieved?'

Is it their wish to hurry on Our scourge? Think! If We let them live in ease for many years, and then the promised scourge does fall upon them, of what avail will their past enjoyments be to them?

Never have We destroyed a nation whom We did not warn and admonish beforehand. We are never unjust.

It was not the devils who brought this down: it is neither in their interest nor in their power. Indeed, they are too far away to overhear it.

26:213 Call on no other god besides God, lest you incur His punishment. Admonish your nearest kinsfolk and show kindness to those of the believers who follow you. If they disobey you, say: 'I am not accountable for what you do.'

Put your trust in the Mighty One, the Merciful, who observes you when you stand upright and when you walk among the worshippers. He alone hears all and knows all.

Shall I tell you on whom the devils descend? They descend on every lying sinner. They eagerly listen, but most of them are liars.

Poets are followed by erring men. Behold how aimlessly they rove in every valley, preaching what they never
26:227 practise. Not so the true believers, who do good works and remember God with fervour and defend themselves only when wronged. The wrongdoers will then learn what a welcome awaits them.

# THE ANT

*In the Name of God, the Compassionate, the Merciful*

27:1 *Ṭā' sīn.* These are the revelations of the Koran, a Glorious Book; a guide and joyful tidings to true believers, who attend to their prayers and render the alms levy and firmly believe in the life to come.

As for those that deny the life to come, We make their 27:4 foul deeds seem fair to them, so that they stray from the right path. Such are those who shall be sternly punished and in the life to come lose most.

You have received the Koran from Him who is wise and all-knowing. Tell of Moses, who said to his people: 'I can descry a fire. I will go and bring you news and a lighted torch to warm yourselves with.'

And when he came near, a voice called out to him: 'Blessed be He who is in the fire and all around it! Glory to God, Lord of the Universe! Moses, I am God, the Mighty, the Wise One. Throw down your staff.'

And when he saw it slithering like a serpent, he turned and fled, without a backward glance.

'Moses, do not be alarmed,' said He. 'My apostles are never afraid in My presence. As for those who sin and then do good after evil, I am forgiving and merciful to them.

'Put your hand into your pocket. It will come out 27:12 white, although unharmed. This is but one of the nine signs for Pharaoh and his people; surely they are wicked men.'

But when Our visible signs were shown to them, they said: 'This is plain sorcery.' Their souls knew them to be true, yet they denied them in their wickedness and their pride. Consider the fate of the evil-doers.

We bestowed knowledge on David and Solomon. The two said: 'Praise be to God who has exalted us above many of His believing servants.'

Solomon succeeded David. He said: 'Know, you people, we have been taught the tongue of birds and endowed with all good things. Surely this is the signal favour.'

His forces of jinn and men and birds were called to Solomon's presence, and ranged in battle array. When they came to the Valley of the Ants, an ant said: 'Go into your dwellings, ants, lest Solomon and his warriors should unwittingly crush you.'

He smiled at her words, and said: 'Inspire me, Lord, to 27:19

render thanks for the favours You have bestowed on me and on my parents, and to do good works that will please You. Admit me, through Your mercy, among Your righteous servants.'

27:20 He inspected the birds and said: 'Why is it that I do not see the lapwing? Is he not here? If he does not offer me a good excuse, I shall sternly punish him or even slay him.'

The bird, who was not long in coming, said: 'I have just seen things unknown to you. With truthful news I come to you from Sheba, where I found a woman reigning over the people. She is possessed of every virtue and has a splendid throne. I found that she and her subjects worship the sun instead of God. Satan has seduced them and debarred them from the right path, so that they might not be guided to the worship of God, who brings to light all that is hidden in the heavens and the earth and knows what you conceal and what you reveal. God; there is no god but Him, the Lord of the Glorious Throne.'

He replied: 'We shall soon see if what you say is true or false. Go and deliver to them this message of mine. Then turn aside and wait their answer.'

27:29 The Queen of Sheba said: 'Know, my nobles, that I have received a gracious message. It is from Solomon: "In the Name of God, the Compassionate, the Merciful. Do not exalt yourselves above me, but come to me in all submission." Nobles, let me hear your counsel, for I make no decision without your consent.'

They replied: 'We are a valiant and mighty people. It is for you to decide; so consider what you should ordain.'

She said: 'When kings invade a city they ravage it and abase the mightiest of its people. These men will do the same. But I shall send them a present and see with what reply the envoys will return.'

And when her envoy came to him, Solomon said: 'Is it gold that you would give me? That which God has bestowed on me is better than all the riches He has given 27:37 you. Yet you glory in your gift. Go back to your people: we will march against them with forces they cannot oppose, and drive them from their land humbled and contemned.'

And to his nobles he said: 'Which of you will bring to me 27:38
her throne, before they sue for peace?'

A demon from among the jinn replied: 'I will bring it to
you before you rise from your seat. I am strong enough and
faithful.'

But he who was deeply versed in the Book,[1] said: 'I will
bring it to you in a twinkling.'

And when he saw it set before him, Solomon said:
'This is a favour from my Lord with which He would
test my gratitude. He that gives thanks has much to gain;
but he who is ungrateful ... My Lord is all-sufficient and
gracious!'

Then he said: 'Let her throne be altered, so that we may
see whether or not she will recognize it.'

And when she came to Solomon, she was asked: 'Is your
throne like this?' And she replied, 'It looks as though it
were the same.'

He said: 'Before her we were endowed with knowledge,
and before her we submitted to the Lord. Her false gods
have led her astray, for she comes from an unbelieving
nation.'

She was bidden to enter the palace; and when she saw it 27:44
she thought it was a pool of water, and bared her legs. But
Solomon said: 'It is a palace paved with glass.'

'Lord,' she said, 'I have sinned against my own soul.
Now I submit with Solomon to God, Lord of the Universe.'

To Thamūd We sent their kinsman Ṣāliḥ. He said:
'Serve none but God.' But they divided themselves into two
discordant factions.

'My people,' he said, 'why do you wish to hasten evil
rather than good? If you seek forgiveness of God, you may
be shown mercy.'

They said: 'We presage evil from you and from your fol- 27:47
lowers.'

---

1. Assaf ben Berachia, according to the commentators.

He replied: 'The evil you presage can come only from God; you are a people put to the proof.'

27:48 In the town there was a band of nine men, who did evil in the land and nothing that was good. They said: 'Let us swear in the name of God to kill him in the night, together with all his household. We will say to his next of kin: "We were not even present when they were slain. It is the truth we are telling."'

Thus they plotted: but We too plotted, without their knowledge. And behold the consequences of their plots! We destroyed them utterly, together with all their people. Because they sinned, their dwellings are desolate ruins. Surely in this there is a sign for prudent men. Yet We delivered the true believers and those who kept from evil.

And tell of Lot. He said to his people: 'Do you commit lewdness with your eyes open, lustfully seeking men instead of women? Surely you are an ignorant people.'

Yet this was his people's only reply: 'Banish the house of Lot from your city. They are men who would keep chaste.'

27:57 So We delivered him and all his household, except his wife, whom We caused to stay behind, and pelted the others with pouring rain; and evil was the rain which fell on those who were forewarned.

Say: 'Praise be to God, and peace upon His servants whom He has chosen! Who is more worthy, God or the idols they serve besides Him? [Surely worthier is] He who created the heavens and the earth and sent down water from the sky for you, bringing forth gardens of delight. Try as you may, you cannot cause such trees to grow.' Another god besides God? Yet they make others His equals.

[Surely worthier is] He who has established the earth and watered it with running rivers; who has set mountains upon it and placed a barrier between the Two Seas. Another god besides God? Indeed, most of them have no knowledge.

27:62 [Surely worthier is] He who answers the oppressed when they cry out to Him, and relieves their affliction. It is He who has given you the earth to inherit. Another god besides God? How little you reflect!

[Surely worthier is] He who guides you in the darkness 27:63 of land and sea, and sends the winds as harbingers of His mercy. Another god besides God? Exalted be He above their idols!

[Surely worthier is] He who has brought the Creation into being and will then restore it; who gives you sustenance from heaven and earth. Another god besides God? Say: 'Show us your proof, if what you say be true!'

Say: 'No one in the heavens or on earth has knowledge of what is hidden except God. Nor shall men ever know when they will be raised to life.'

Have they attained a knowledge of the life to come? By no means! They are in doubt about it and their eyes are sealed.

The unbelievers say: 'When we and our fathers are turned to dust, shall we be raised to life? We were promised this once before, and so were our fathers. It is but a fable of the ancients.'

Say: 'Roam the earth and see what was the end of the 27:69 guilty.' Do not grieve for them, nor be distressed at their intrigues.

And they ask: 'When will this promise be fulfilled, if what you say be true?'

Say: 'A part of what you challenge may well be near at hand.'

Surely your Lord is bountiful to men: yet most of them do not give thanks.

Your Lord surely knows what their bosoms hide and what they say in public. There is no secret in heaven or earth but is recorded in a glorious book.

This Koran expounds to the Israelites most of the matters over which they disagree. It is surely a guide and a blessing to true believers. Your Lord will rightly judge them. He is the Mighty One, the All-knowing. Therefore 27:79 put your trust in God; yours is surely the path to the glorious truth.

27:80   You cannot make the dead hear you, nor can you make the deaf hear your call if they turn their backs and pay no heed; nor can you guide the blind out of their error. None shall give ear to you save those who believe in Our revelations and are submissive to Our will.

On the day when the Doom overtakes them, We will bring out from the earth a monster that shall speak to them. Truly, men have no faith in Our revelations.

On that day We shall gather from each community a multitude of those who disbelieved Our revelations. They shall be led in separate bands, and, when they come, He will say: 'You denied My revelations although you knew nothing of them. What was it you were doing?' The Doom will smite them in their sins, and they shall be dumbfounded.

Do they not see how We have made the night for them to rest in, and the day to give them light? Surely there are signs in this for true believers.

On that day the Trumpet shall be sounded and all who dwell in the heavens and on earth be seized with fear, except for those whom God will choose to spare. All shall come to Him in utter humility.

27:88   The mountains, firm though you may think them, will pass away like clouds. Such is the might of God, who has perfected all things. He has knowledge of all your actions.

Those that have done good shall be rewarded with what is better, and shall be secure from the terrors of that day.

But those that have done evil shall be hurled headlong into the Fire. Shall you not be rewarded according only to your deeds?

[Say:] 'I am bidden to serve the Lord of this City, which He has made sacred. All things are His.

27:92   'I am commanded to submit to Him, and to proclaim the Koran. He that takes the right path shall take it for his own good.'

To him who strays from the right path, say: 'I am only to give warning.'

Then say: 'Praise be to God! He will show you His signs 27:93
and you will recognize them. Your Lord is never heedless
of what you do.'

# THE STORY

*In the Name of God, the Compassionate, the Merciful*

*Ṭā' sīn mīm.* These are the verses of the Glorious Book. In 28:1
all truth We shall recount to you the tale of Moses and
Pharaoh for the instruction of the faithful.

Now Pharaoh made himself a tyrant in the land. He
divided his people into castes, one group of which he
persecuted, putting their sons to death and sparing only
their daughters. Truly, he was an evil-doer.

But it was Our will to favour those who were oppressed
in the land and to make them leaders among men, to bestow
on them a noble heritage and to give them power in the
land; and to inflict on Pharaoh, Haman, and their warriors
the very scourge they dreaded.

We revealed Our will to Moses' mother, saying: 'Give
him suck, but if you are concerned about his safety, then
put him down onto the river. Have no fear, nor be
dismayed; for We shall restore him to you and shall invest
him with a mission.'

Pharaoh's household picked him up, though he was to 28:8
become their adversary and their scourge. For Pharaoh,
Haman, and their warriors were sinners all.

His wife said to Pharaoh: 'This child may bring joy to us
both. Do not slay him. He may show promise, and we may
adopt him as our son.' But they little knew what they were
doing.

Moses' mother's heart was sorely troubled. She would
have revealed who he was, had We not given her strength
so that she might become a true believer. She said to his
sister: 'Go, and follow him.'

She watched him from a distance, unseen by others. Now
We had caused him to refuse his nurses' breasts. His 28:12

sister said to them: 'Shall I direct you to a family who will bring him up for you and take good care of him?'

28:13 Thus did We restore him to his mother, so that she might rejoice in him and grieve no more, and that she might learn that God's promise was true. Yet most men are not aware of this.

And when he had reached maturity and grown to manhood We bestowed on him wisdom and knowledge. Thus do We reward the righteous.

He entered the town unnoticed by its people, and found two men at each other's throats, the one of his own race, the other an enemy. The Israelite appealed for Moses' help against his enemy, so that Moses struck him with his fist and slew him. 'This is the work of Satan,' said Moses. 'He is the sworn enemy of man and seeks to lead him astray. Forgive me, Lord,' he said, 'for I have sinned against my soul.'

And God forgave him; for He is the Forgiving One, the Merciful. He said: 'By the favour You have shown me, Lord, I vow that I will never lend a helping hand to wrongdoers.'

28:18 Next morning, as he was walking in the town in fear and caution, the man who sought his help the day before cried out to him again for help. 'Clearly,' said Moses, 'you are a quarrelsome man.'

And when Moses was about to lay his hands on their enemy, the Egyptian said: 'Moses, would you slay me as you slew that man yesterday? You are surely seeking to be a tyrant in the land, not an upright man.'

A man came running from the farthest quarter of the city. 'Moses,' he cried, 'the elders are plotting to kill you. Fly for your life, if you will heed my counsel!'

He went away in fear and caution, saying: 'Lord, deliver me from the wicked people.' And as he made his way towards Midian, he said: 'May the Lord guide me to the even path.'

28:23 When he came to the well of Midian he found around it a multitude of people watering their flocks, and beside them two women who were keeping back their sheep. 'What is it that troubles you?' he asked.

They replied: 'We cannot water them until the shepherds have driven away their flocks. Our father is an aged man.'

Moses watered their sheep for them and then retired to the shade, saying: 'Lord, I surely stand in need of the blessing which You have sent me.' 28:24

One of the two girls came bashfully towards him and said: 'My father calls you. He wishes to reward you for watering our flock.'

And when Moses went and recounted to him his story, the old man said: 'Fear nothing. You are now safe from the wicked people.'

One of the girls said: 'Father, take this man into your service. A man who is strong and honest is the best that you can hire.'

The old man said: 'I will give you one of these two daughters of mine in marriage if you stay eight years in my service; but if you wish it, you may stay ten. I shall not deal harshly with you; God willing, you shall find me an upright man.'

'So be it between us,' said Moses. 'Whichever term I shall fulfil, I trust I shall not be wronged. God is the witness of what we say.'

And when he had fulfilled his term and was journeying with his folk, Moses descried a fire on the mountain-side. He said to his people: 'Stay here, for I can see a fire. Perhaps I can bring you news, or a lighted torch to warm yourselves with.' 28:29

When he came near, a voice called out to him from a bush in a blessed spot on the right side of the valley, saying: 'Moses, I am God, Lord of the Universe. Throw down your staff.'

And when he saw it slithering like a serpent, he turned and fled, without a backward glance.

'Moses,' said the voice, 'approach and have no fear. You are safe. Put your hand in your pocket: it will come out white, although unharmed. Now draw back your arm, and do not stretch it out in terror. These are two signs from your Lord for Pharaoh and his people. Surely, they are sinful men.' 28:32

28:33     'Lord,' said Moses, 'I have killed one of their number and fear that they will slay me. Aaron my brother is more fluent of tongue than I; send him with me that he may help me and confirm my words, for I fear they will reject me.'

He replied: 'We will strengthen your arm with your brother, and will bestow such power on you both, that none shall harm you. Set forth, with Our signs. You, and those who follow you, shall surely triumph.'

And when Moses came to them with Our undoubted signs, they said: 'This is nothing but baseless sorcery; nor have we heard of the like among our forefathers.'

Moses replied: 'My Lord knows best the man who brings guidance from His presence and gains the recompense of the life to come. The wrongdoers shall never prosper.'

'Nobles,' said Pharaoh, 'you have no other god that I know of except myself. Make me, Haman, bricks of clay, and build for me a tower that I may climb to the god of Moses. I am convinced that he is lying.'

28:39     Pharaoh and his warriors conducted themselves with arrogance and injustice in the land, thinking they would never be recalled to Us. But We took him and his warriors, and We cast them into the sea. Consider the fate of the evildoers.

We made them leaders who called men to the Fire, but on the Day of Resurrection none shall help them. In this world We laid a curse on them, and on the Day of Resurrection they shall be among the damned.

After We had destroyed the first generations We gave the Book to Moses as a clear sign, a guide and a blessing for mankind, so that they might take thought.

You[1] were not present on the western side of the Mountain when We charged Moses with his commission, 28:45 nor did you witness the event. We raised many generations after him whose lives were prolonged. You did not dwell among the people of Midian, nor did you recite to them Our revelations; but it was We who sent you forth.

1. Muḥammad.

You were not present on the mountain-side when We 28:46 called out. Yet have We sent you forth, as a blessing from your Lord, to forewarn a nation to whom no one has been sent before, so that they may take heed and may not say, when evil befalls them on account of their misdeeds: 'Lord, had You sent us an apostle, we should have obeyed Your revelations and believed in them.'

And now that they have received the truth from Us, they ask: 'Why is he not given the like of what was given to Moses?' But do they not deny what was formerly given to Moses? They say: 'Two works[1] of sorcery complementing one another!' And they declare: 'We will believe in neither of them.'

Say: 'Bring down from God a scripture that is a better guide than these and I will follow it, if what you say be true!'

If they make you no answer, know that they are led by their desires. And who is in greater error than the man who is led by his desire, without guidance from God? God does not guide the evil-doers.

We have caused the Word to reach them so that they 28:51 may take thought. Those to whom We gave the Scriptures before this believe in it. When it is recited to them they say: 'We believe in it; it is the truth from our Lord. We submitted to Him long before it came.'

Twice shall their reward be given them, because they have endured with fortitude, requiting evil with good and giving in alms from what We gave them; and because they pay no heed to idle talk, but say: 'We have our actions and you have yours. We wish you peace. We will have nothing to do with ignorant men.'

You cannot guide whomever you please: it is God who guides whom He will. He best knows those who yield to guidance.

They say: 'If we accept your guidance, we shall be driven 28:57 from our land.' But have We not given them a sanctuary of safety to which fruits of every kind are brought as a

1. The Torah and the Koran.

provision from Ourself? Indeed, most of them have no knowledge.

28:58   How many nations have We destroyed who once flourished in wanton ease! The dwellings they left behind are but scarcely inhabited; We Ourself were the only heirs.

Nor did your Lord destroy the nations until He had sent apostles to their capital cities proclaiming to them Our revelations. We destroyed those cities only because their inhabitants were wrongdoers.

What you have been given is but the pleasure and the gaudy show of this present life. Better is God's recompense and more lasting. Have you no sense to reason with?

Can he who has received Our gracious promise, and will see it fulfilled, be compared with him to whom We have given the enjoyment of this life and who will be summoned on the Day of Resurrection?

On that day He will call to them, saying: 'Where are the gods whom you alleged to be My partners?'

Those who have justly earned Our doom will say: 'Lord, these are the men whom we misled. We led them astray as we ourselves were led astray. We disown them before You; it was not us that they worshipped.'

28:64   Then they will be told: 'Call on your idols!' And they will call on them, but they shall get no answer. They shall behold the scourge and wish that they were rightly guided.

On that day God will call to them, saying: 'What answer did you give Our apostles?' And on that day such will be their confusion that they will ask no questions. But those that repent and embrace the Faith and do what is right may hope for salvation.

Your Lord creates what He will and chooses freely, but their idols have no power to choose. Glorified and exalted be He above their false gods!

Your Lord knows what their bosoms hide and what they say in public. He is God: there is no god but Him. Praise is His in the first world and in the last. His is the Judgement, and to Him shall you be recalled.

28:71   Say: 'Think! If God should enshroud you in perpetual night till the Day of Resurrection, what other god could give you light? Will you not hear?'

Say: 'Think! If God should give you perpetual day until 28:72 the Day of Resurrection, what other god could bring you the night to rest in? Will you not see?'

Of His mercy He has given you the night that you may rest in it, and the day that you may seek His bounty and give thanks.

On that day He will call out to them, saying: 'Where are the gods whom you alleged to be My partners?' From each community We will seize a witness, and We shall say to them: 'Show Us your proof.' Then shall they learn that the Truth is God's, and the deities of their own invention will forsake them.

Korah was one of Moses' people, but he treated them unjustly. We had given him such treasures that their very keys would have weighed down a band of sturdy men. His people said to him: 'Do not exult in your riches; God does not love the exultant. But seek, by means of that which God has given you, to attain the abode of the hereafter. Do not forget your share in this world. Be good to others as God has been good to you, and do not strive for evil in the land, for God does not love the evil-doers.'

But he replied: 'These riches were given me on account 28:78 of the knowledge I possess.'

Did he not know that, from the generations gone before him, God destroyed some who were mightier and more avaricious than he? The wrongdoers shall not be questioned about their sins.

And when he went out in all his finery among his people, those who loved this nether life said: 'Would that we had the like of what Korah has been given! He is indeed a man of great good fortune.'

But those who were endowed with knowledge said: 'Alas for you! Better is God's recompense for him that has faith and does good works; but none shall attain it save those who have endured with fortitude.'

We caused the earth to swallow him, together with his 28:81 dwelling, so that he found none besides God to protect him;

28:82 nor was he able to defend himself. And those who on the day before had coveted his lot next morning said: 'Behold! God gives abundantly to whom He will and sparingly to whom He pleases. But for the grace of God, He could have caused the earth to swallow us. Behold! The ungrateful shall never prosper.'

28:83 As for the abode of the hereafter, We shall assign it to those who seek neither grandeur on the earth nor evil-doing. The righteous shall have a blessed end.

He that does good shall be rewarded with what is better. But he that does evil shall be requited according only to his deeds.

He who has committed the Koran to your keeping will surely bring you home[1] again. Say: 'My Lord best knows him who brings guidance and him who is in evident error.'

Never did you expect the Book to be revealed to you. Yet through your Lord's mercy you have received it. Therefore give no help to the unbelievers. Let no one turn you away from God's revelations, now that they have been revealed to you. Call men to your Lord, and serve none besides Him.

28:88 Invoke no other god together with God. There is no god but Him. All things shall perish except Himself. His is the Judgement, and to Him shall you be recalled.

# THE SPIDER

*In the Name of God, the Compassionate, the Merciful*

29:1 ALIF *lām mīm*. Do people think that once they say: 'We are believers', they will be left alone and not be tested?

We tested those who have gone before them. God surely knows the truthful, and He surely knows the liars.

Or do the evil-doers think they will escape Our reach? How ill they judge!

29:5 He that hopes to meet God must know that God's

---

1. To Mecca.

appointed hour is sure to come. He alone hears all and knows all.

He that fights for God's cause fights for himself. God 29:6 needs no man's help. As for those that have faith and do good works, We shall cleanse them of their sins and reward them according to their noblest deeds.

We have enjoined man to show kindness to his parents. But if they bid you serve besides Me deities you know nothing of, do not obey them. To Me you will all return, and I shall declare to you all that you have done. Those that accept the true Faith and do good works We shall assuredly admit among the righteous.

Some profess to believe in God, yet when they suffer in His cause they confuse the persecution of man with the punishment of God. But if your Lord gives you victory, they say: 'We were on your side.'

Does not God know best the thoughts of men? God well knows the true believers, and He well knows the hypocrites.

The unbelievers say to the faithful: 'Follow us, and we will bear the burden of your sins.' But they will bear none of their sins. They are surely lying.

They shall bear their own burdens, and other burdens 29:13 besides their burdens. On the Day of Resurrection they shall be questioned about the lies they told.

We sent forth Noah to his people, and he dwelt among them for a thousand years less fifty. Then in their sinfulness the Flood overwhelmed them. But We delivered him and all who were in the ark, and made the event a sign for mankind.

And tell of Abraham. He said to his people: 'Serve God and fear Him. That would be best for you, if you but knew it. You worship idols besides God and fabricate falsehoods. Those whom you serve besides God cannot give you your daily bread. Therefore seek your daily bread from God, and worship Him. Give thanks to Him, for to Him you shall return.

'If you disbelieve, other communities before you likewise disbelieved. Yet an apostle's duty is but to give plain warning.'

Do they not see how God conceives Creation, and then 29:19 renews it? That is easy enough for God.

29:20     Say: 'Roam the earth and see how God has brought the Creation into being. Then will God initiate the Latter Creation. God has power over all things; He punishes whom He will and shows mercy to whom He pleases. To Him shall you be recalled.'

Neither on earth nor in heaven shall you escape His reach: nor have you any besides God to protect or help you.

Those that disbelieve God's revelations and deny that they will ever meet Him shall despair of My mercy. Woeful punishment awaits them.

His people's only reply was: 'Kill him!' or 'Burn him!'

But from the fire God delivered him. Surely in this there are signs for true believers.

Abraham said: 'You have chosen idols instead of God, but your love of them will last only in this nether life. On the Day of Resurrection you shall disown one another, and you shall curse one another. The Fire shall be your home and none shall help you.'

Lot believed in him. He said: 'I will fly this land whither my Lord bids me.[1] He is the Mighty One, the Wise One.'

29:27     We gave him Isaac and Jacob and bestowed on his descendants prophethood and the Book. We gave him his reward in this life, and in the life to come he shall dwell among the righteous.

And We sent forth Lot to his people. He said to them: 'You commit lewd acts which no other nation has committed before you. You lust after men and assault them on your highways. At your gatherings you perpetrate abominations.'

But his people's only answer was: 'Bring down the scourge of God upon us, if what you say be true.'

'Lord,' said he, 'deliver me from these degenerate men.'

And when Our messengers brought Abraham the good news[2] they said: 'We are to destroy the people of this town, for its people have done wrong.'

29:32     Abraham said: 'Lot dwells in it.'

'We well know who dwells in it,' they replied. 'We shall

---

    1. Thus Al-Jalālayn.     2. The birth of a son in his old age.

deliver him and all his household, except his wife, who shall remain behind.'

And when Our messengers came to Lot, he was troubled 29:33 and distressed on their account. They said: 'Have no fear, and do not grieve. We shall deliver you and all your household, except your wife, who shall remain behind. We shall bring down a scourge from heaven upon the people of this town to punish them for their sins.'

Surely the ruins We left of that city are a veritable sign for men of understanding.

And to the people of Midian We sent their kinsman Shu'aib. He said: 'Serve God, my people. Look forward to the Last Day. Do not corrupt the earth with wickedness.'

But they denied him. The earthquake took them, and when morning came they were crouching lifeless in their dwellings.

'Ād and Thamūd We also destroyed. This is vouched for by their ruins. Satan had made their foul deeds seem fair to them and debarred them from the right path, keen-sighted though they were.

And Korah, Pharaoh, and Haman! Moses came to them 29:39 with veritable signs, but they behaved arrogantly in the land, powerless though they were to escape Us: and in their sinfulness, one and all, We smote them. On some We sent down a violent whirlwind; others the Cry overtook; some We caused to be swallowed up by the earth, and yet others We overwhelmed by the Flood. God did not wrong them, but they wronged themselves.

Those who serve other masters besides God may be compared to the spider which builds a cobweb for itself. Surely the spider's is the frailest of all dwellings, if they but knew it. God knows whatever they invoke besides Him; He is the Mighty, the Wise One.

Such are the comparisons we make for the instruction of mankind; but none will grasp their meaning save those that have knowledge.

God created the heavens and the earth to establish the truth. Surely in this there is a sign for true believers.

Proclaim the portions of the Book that have been revealed 29:45 to you and be steadfast in prayer. Prayer fends off all that is foul and reprehensible. But your foremost duty is to remember God. God has knowledge of all your actions.

29:46    Be courteous when you argue with the People of the Book, except with those among them who do evil. Say: 'We believe in that which has been revealed to us and which was revealed to you. Our God and your God is one. To Him we submit.'

Thus have We revealed the Book to you.[1] Those to whom We gave the Scriptures believe in it, and so do some of your own people. Only the unbelievers deny Our signs.

Never have you[1] read a book before this, nor have you ever transcribed one with your right hand. Had you done either, the unbelievers might have doubted. But to those who are endowed with knowledge it is an undoubted sign. Only the wrongdoers deny Our signs.

They ask: 'Why have no signs been sent down to him by his Lord?' Say: 'Signs are in the hands of God. My mission is only to give plain warning.'

Is it not enough for them that We have revealed to you the Book for their instruction? Surely in this there is a blessing and an admonition for true believers.

29:52    Say: 'Sufficient is God as my witness, and your witness. He knows all that the heavens and the earth contain. Those who believe in falsehood and deny God will surely be the losers.'

They challenge you to hasten on the scourge. Had there not been a time appointed for it, the scourge would have long since taken them. Indeed, it will come down upon them suddenly, and catch them unawares.

They challenge you to hasten on the scourge. But Hell will encompass the unbelievers, when the scourge will assail them from above and from beneath their feet, and God will say: 'Taste the reward of your own deeds.'

You that are true believers among My servants, My earth 29:57  is vast. Therefore serve Me. Every soul shall taste death, and then to Us shall you be recalled.

1. Muḥammad.

Those that embrace the true Faith and do good works 29:58
We shall lodge for ever in the mansions of Paradise,
where rivers will roll at their feet. Blessed is the reward
of those who labour patiently and put their trust in
their Lord.

Countless are the beasts that cannot fend for themselves.
God provides for them, as He provides for you. He alone
hears all and knows all.

If you ask them who it is that has created the heavens and
the earth, and subdued the sun and the moon, they will
surely reply: 'God.' How then can they turn away from
Him?

God gives abundantly to whom He will and sparingly to
whom He pleases. God has knowledge of all things.

If you ask them who it is that sends down water from the
sky and thus resurrects the earth after its death, they will
surely reply: 'God.' Say: 'Praise, then, be to God!' But most
of them are senseless.

The life of this world is but a sport and a diversion. It is 29:64
the life to come that is the true life: if they but knew it.

When they embark they pray to God with all fervour; but
when He brings them safe to land, they serve other gods
besides Him, showing ingratitude for Our favours and
revelling in wanton ease. But they shall learn.

Do they not see how We have given them a sanctuary
of safety,[1] while all around them people are carried off by
force? Would they believe in falsehood and deny God's
goodness?

And who is more wicked than the man who invents a
falsehood about God and denies the truth when it is
declared to him? Is there not a home in Hell for the unbelievers?

Those that fight for Our cause We will surely guide to 29:69
Our own paths. Surely God is with the righteous.

---

1. At the Ka'bah.

# THE GREEKS

*In the Name of God, the Compassionate, the Merciful*

30:1 ALIF *lām mīm*. The Greeks have been defeated[1] in a neighbouring land. But in a few years they shall themselves gain victory: such being the will of God before and after.

On that day the believers will rejoice in God's help. He gives victory to whom He will. He is the Mighty One, the Merciful.

That is God's promise; God will never break His promise. Yet most men do not know it.

They know the outward show of this nether life, but of the life to come they are heedless. Have they not pondered within their own minds that God created the heavens and the earth and all that lies between them only for a worthy end, and for an appointed term? Yet many deny they will ever meet their Lord.

Have they never journeyed through the land and seen what was the fate of their forebears? Far mightier were they; they tilled the land and built upon it more than these have ever built. And to them, too, their apostles came with undoubted signs. God did not wrong them but they wronged themselves. Evil was the end of those who did evil, because they had disbelieved God's revelations and derided them.

30:11 God brings the Creation into being and will then restore it. To Him shall you be recalled.

On the day the Hour strikes, the wrongdoers will be speechless with despair. None of their idols will intercede for them: indeed, they will deny their idols.

On the day the Hour strikes, mankind will divide. Those who have embraced the Faith and done good works will 30:16 rejoice in a fair garden; but those who have disbelieved and denied Our revelations and the life to come, shall be delivered up for punishment.

1. By the Persians, in Syria – A.D. 615. Muḥammad's sympathies were with the Christians, not with the idolatrous Persians.

Therefore give glory to God evening and morning. 30:17
Praise be to Him in the heavens and the earth, at twilight
and at noon.

He brings forth the living from the dead, and the dead
from the living: He resurrects the earth after its death.
Likewise shall you be raised to life.

By one of His signs He created you from dust; and,
behold, you became humans and multiplied throughout the
earth. By another sign He created for you spouses from
among yourselves, that you might live in peace with them,
and planted love and kindness in your hearts. Surely there
are signs in this for thinking men.

Among His other signs are the creation of the heavens
and the earth and the diversity of your tongues and colours.
Surely there are signs in this for all mankind.

By another sign of His you sleep at night and seek by day
His bounty. Surely there are signs in this for those who hear.

Lightning is yet another of His signs, inspiring you with
fear and hope. He sends down water from the sky, and with
it He quickens the earth after its death. Surely in this there
are signs for men of understanding.

By another sign heaven and earth stand firm at His 30:25
bidding. And when with one shout He summons you out of
the earth, you shall go forth to Him.

To Him belongs whosoever is in the heavens and the
earth. All are obedient to Him.

It is He who brings the Creation into being, and will then
restore it: that is easier for Him.

His is the most exalted attribute in the heavens and the
earth. He is the Mighty, the Wise One.

He makes you this comparison, drawn from your own
lives. Do your slaves share with you on equal terms the
riches which We have given you? Do you fear them as you
fear one another? Thus do We make plain Our revelations to
men of understanding.

Indeed, the wrongdoers are led unwittingly by their own 30:29
appetites. And who can guide those whom God has led
astray? There shall be none to help them.

30:30 Therefore, stand firm in your devotion to the true Faith, the upright Faith which God created for mankind to embrace. God's Creation cannot be changed. This is surely the right faith, although most men may not know it.

Turn to Him and fear Him. Be steadfast in prayer and serve no other god besides Him. Do not divide your religion into sects, each exulting in its own doctrines.

When evil befalls people, they turn in prayer to their Lord. But no sooner does He let them taste a blessing from Himself than some among them take up other gods besides their Lord, showing no gratitude for what We gave them. Take your pleasure now, and you shall learn.

Have We revealed to them a sanction enjoining them to serve idols?

When We give people the taste of a good thing they rejoice in it, but when evil befalls them through their own fault, they grow despondent. Do they not see that God gives abundantly to whom He will and sparingly to whom He pleases? Surely there are signs in this for true believers.

30:38 Therefore give their due to the next of kin, to the destitute, and to the traveller in need. That is best for those that strive to please God; such men will surely prosper.

That which you seek to increase by usury will not be blessed by God; but the alms you give for His sake shall be repaid to you many times over.

It is God who has created you and given you your daily bread. He will cause you to die hereafter and will then bring you back to life. Can any of your idols do the least of these? God forbid! Exalted be He above their false gods!

Corruption has become rife on land and sea in consequence of mankind's misdeeds. [He has ordained it thus] so that they may taste the fruit of their own works and mend their ways.

30:42 Say: 'Roam the earth and see what was the end of those who came before you. Most of them worshipped false gods.'

Therefore stand firm in your devotion to the true Faith 30:43
before that day arrives which none may put off against the
will of God. On that day mankind will be parted in two.
The unbelievers will answer for their unbelief, while the
righteous will make ready for their blissful home: for then
He will of His bounty recompense those who have embraced
the Faith and done good works. He does not love the
unbelievers.

By another sign He sends the winds as bearers of good
tidings, so that you may rejoice in His mercy and your ships
may sail at His bidding; so that you may seek His bounty
and render thanks.

We sent before you apostles to their peoples, and they
showed them veritable signs. We took vengeance on the
guilty, and rightly succoured the true believers.

It is God who drives the winds that stir the clouds. He
spreads them as He will in the heavens and breaks them
up, so that you can see the rain falling from their midst.
When He sends it down upon those of His servants whom
he chooses they are filled with joy, though before its
coming they may have lost all hope.

Behold then the tokens of God's mercy; how He resur- 30:50
rects the earth after its death. It is He who will resurrect the
dead. He has power over all things.

Yet if We let loose on them a searing wind they would
return to unbelief.

You cannot make the dead hear you, nor can you make
the deaf hear your call if they turn their backs and pay no
heed; nor can you guide the blind out of their error. None
shall give ear to you save those who believe in Our
revelations, and are submissive to Our will.

God creates you weak: after weakness He gives you
strength, and after strength infirmity and grey hairs. He
creates whatever He will. He is the All-knowing, the
Almighty.

On the day the Hour strikes, the wrongdoers will swear 30:55
that they had lingered but one hour. Thus are they ever
deceived.

30:56　　But those to whom knowledge and faith have been given will say: 'You lingered there, as God ordained, till the Day of Resurrection. This is the Day of Resurrection: yet you did not know it.'

On that day their pleas shall not avail the wrongdoers, nor shall they be asked to make amends.

In this Koran we have set forth for men all manner of arguments. Yet if you recite to them a single verse, the unbelievers will surely say: 'You preach nothing but falsehoods.' Thus God seals the hearts of ignorant men.

30:60　　Therefore have patience. God's promise is true. Let not those who disbelieve drive you to despair.

# LUQMĀN

*In the Name of God, the Compassionate, the Merciful*

31:1　　ALIF *lām mīm.* These are the revelations of the Wise Book, a guide and a blessing to the righteous, who attend to their prayers, render the alms levy, and firmly believe in the life to come. These are rightly guided by their Lord, and will surely prosper.

Some there are who would indulge in frivolous talk, so that they may without knowledge lead men away from the path of God and hold it up to ridicule. For these there shall be shameful punishment.

When Our revelations are recited to them, they turn their backs in scorn, as though they never heard them: as though their ears were sealed. To these proclaim a woeful punishment.

But those that have faith and do good works shall enter the gardens of delight, where they shall dwell for ever. God's promise shall be fulfilled: He is the Mighty, the Wise One.

He raised the heavens without visible pillars, and set firm mountains on the earth lest it should shake with you. He dispersed upon it all manner of beasts; and We sent down water from the sky with which We caused all kinds of goodly plants to grow.

31:11　　Such is God's Creation: now show Me what your other

gods created. Surely the unbelievers are in evident error.

We bestowed wisdom on Luqmān,[1] saying: 'Give thanks 31:12
to God. He that gives thanks has much to gain, but if anyone denies His favours, God is self-sufficient and glorious.'

Luqmān admonished his son, saying: 'Serve no other
deity besides God, for idolatry is an abominable sin.'

(We enjoined man to show kindness to his parents, for
with much pain his mother bears him, and he is not weaned
before he is two years of age. We said: 'Give thanks to
Me and to your parents. To Me shall all return. But if
they press you to serve besides Me deities you know
nothing of, do not obey them. Be kind to them in this
world, and follow the path of those who turn to Me. To Me
shall you return, and I will declare to you all that you have
done.')

'My son, God will bring all things to light, be they as small
as a grain of mustard seed, be they hidden inside a rock or in
the heavens or the earth. Gracious is God and all-knowing.

'My son, be steadfast in prayer, enjoin justice, and forbid
evil. Endure with fortitude whatever befalls you. That is a
duty incumbent on all.

'Do not treat people with scorn, nor walk proudly on the 31:18
earth: God does not love the arrogant and the vainglorious.
Rather let your stride be modest and your voice low: the
most hideous of voices is the braying of the ass.'

Do you not see how God has subjected to you all that the
heavens and the earth contain, and lavished on you both His
visible and unseen favours? Yet some still argue about God,
without knowledge or guidance or illuminating scriptures.

When they are told: 'Follow what God has revealed,'
they reply: 'We will follow the faith of our fathers.' Yes,
even though Satan invites them to the scourge of the Fire.

He that surrenders himself to God and leads a righteous
life stands on the firmest ground.[2] To God shall all things 31:22

---

1. A sage who, we are told, was a grandson of a sister or an aunt
of Job.

2. Literally, grasps the firmest handle.

31:23 return. As for those that disbelieve, let not their unbelief grieve you. To Us shall they return and We will declare to them all that they have done. God has knowledge of their innermost thoughts.

We suffer them to take their ease awhile, and will then subject them to a grievous scourge.

If you ask them: 'Who has created the heavens and the earth?' they will surely reply: 'God.' Say: 'Praise, then, be to God!' But most of them have no knowledge.

His is what the heavens and the earth contain. God alone is self-sufficient and worthy of praise.

If all the trees of the earth were pens, and the sea, replenished by seven more seas, were ink, the words of God could not be finished still. Mighty is God, and wise.

You were created but as one soul, and as one soul you shall be raised to life. God hears all and observes all.

Do you not see how God causes the night to pass into the day and the day to pass into the night? He has pressed the sun and the moon into His service, each running for an appointed term. God is cognizant of all your actions. Because God is the Truth, and false are the idols they invoke besides Him. Surely God is the Most High, the Supreme One.

31:31 Do you not see how the ships speed upon the ocean by God's grace, so that He may reveal to you His wonders? Surely there are signs in this for every steadfast, thankful man.

When the waves, like giant shadows, envelop them, they pray to God with all devotion. But no sooner does He bring them safe to land than some of them falter between faith and unbelief. None will deny Our revelations except the treacherous and the ungrateful.

You people! Fear your Lord, and fear the day when no parent shall avail his child nor any child his parent. God's promise is surely true. Let the life of this world never deceive you, nor let the Dissembler trick you about God.

31:34 God alone has knowledge of the Hour of Doom. He sends down the abundant rain and knows what every womb contains.

No mortal knows what he will earn tomorrow; no mortal knows where he will breathe his last. God alone is omniscient and takes cognizance of all things.

# ADORATION

*In the Name of God, the Compassionate, the Merciful*

ALIF *lām mīm*. This Book is beyond all doubt revealed by 32:1 the Lord of the Universe.

Do they say: 'He[1] has invented it himself'?

Surely it is the truth from your Lord, so that you may forewarn a nation whom none has warned before you, and that they may be rightly guided.

It was God who in six days created the heavens and the earth and all that lies between them, and then ascended the throne. You have no guardian or intercessor besides Him. Will you not take heed?

He governs all, from heaven to earth. And all will ascend to Him in a single day, a day whose space is a thousand years by your reckoning.

He knows the unknown and the manifest. He is the 32:6 Mighty One, the Merciful, who excelled in the creation of all things. He first created man from clay, then made his offspring from a drop of humble fluid. He moulded him and breathed His spirit into him. He gave you ears and eyes and hearts: yet you are seldom thankful.

They say: 'Once lost into the earth, shall we be created afresh?' Indeed, they deny they will ever meet their Lord.

Say: 'The angel of death in charge of you will reclaim your souls. Then to your Lord shall you be recalled.'

Would that you could see the wrongdoers when they hang their heads before their Lord! They will say: 'Lord, we now see and hear. Send us back and we will do good works. Now we are firm believers.'

Had it been Our will, We could have given every soul its 32:13

1. Muḥammad.

guidance. But My word shall be fulfilled: 'I will surely fill Hell with jinn and humans all.'

32:14 We shall say to them: 'Taste this, for you forgot you would ever meet this day. We, too, will forget you. Taste the eternal scourge, which you have earned by your misdeeds.'

None believes in Our revelations save those who, when reminded of them, prostrate themselves in adoration and give glory to their Lord in all humility; who forsake their beds to pray to their Lord in fear and hope; who give in alms from what We gave them. No mortal knows what bliss will be in store for these as a reward for their labours.

Can he, then, who is a true believer, be compared to him who is an evil-doer? Surely they are not equal.

Those that have faith and do good works shall be lodged in the gardens of Paradise in recompense for their labours. But those that do evil, the Fire shall be their home. Whenever they desire to emerge from it they shall be driven back, and shall be told: 'Taste the torment of the Fire, which you have persistently denied.'

32:21 We will inflict on them the lighter torment of this world before the greater torment of the world to come, so that they may perchance return to the right path. And who is more wicked than the man who pays no heed to the revelations of his Lord when he is reminded of them? We will surely take vengeance on the guilty.

We gave the Book to Moses (never doubt that you[1] will meet him) and made it a guide for the Israelites. And when they grew steadfast and firmly believed in Our revelations, We appointed leaders from among them who gave guidance at Our bidding. On the Day of Resurrection your Lord will resolve their differences for them.

Do they not know how many generations We have destroyed before them? They walk among their ruined dwellings. Surely in this there are conspicuous signs. Have they no ears to hear with?

32:27 Do they not see how We drive the water to the parched

---

1. Muḥammad.

land and bring forth crops which they and their cattle eat? Have they no eyes to see with?

They ask: 'When will this judgement come, if what you say be true?'

Say: 'On the Day of Judgement their faith shall not avail the unbelievers, nor shall they be reprieved.'

Therefore pay no heed to them, and wait as they are 32:30 waiting.

# THE CONFEDERATE TRIBES

*In the Name of God, the Compassionate, the Merciful*

PROPHET, HAVE fear of God and do not yield to the 33:1 unbelievers and the hypocrites. God is all-knowing and wise.

Obey what is revealed to you from your Lord, for God is cognizant of all your actions, and put your trust in God; God is your all-sufficient guardian.

God has never put two hearts within one man's body. He does not regard the wives whom you divorce as your mothers,[1] nor your adopted sons as your own sons. These are mere words which you utter with your mouths: but God declares the truth and gives guidance to the right path.

Name your adopted sons after their fathers; that is more just in the sight of God. If you do not know their fathers, regard them as your brothers in the Faith and as your cousins. Your unintentional mistakes shall be forgiven, but not your deliberate errors. God is forgiving and merciful.

The Prophet has a greater claim on the faithful than they 33:6 have on each other. His wives are their mothers.

God ordains that blood relations are closer to one another than to other believers or *muhājirīn*,[2] although you are permitted to do your friends a kindness.[3] That is in the Book decreed.

---

1. An allusion to the formula: 'Be to me as my mother's back', accepted among pagan Arabs as a declaration of divorce.

2. Muḥammad's early followers who fled with him to Medina.

3. By leaving them bequests.

33:7    We made a covenant with you, as We did with the other prophets; with Noah and Abraham, with Moses and Jesus son of Mary. A solemn covenant We made with them, so that He might question the truthful about their truthfulness. But for the unbelievers He has prepared a woeful punishment.

Believers, remember God's goodness to you when you were attacked by your enemy's army. We unleashed against them a violent wind and invisible warriors: God saw all that you were doing.

They attacked you from above and from below, so that your eyes were blurred, your hearts leapt up to your throats, and your faith in God was shaken. There the faithful were put to the proof; there they were severely afflicted. The hypocrites and the faint-hearted said: 'God and His apostle made us promises only to deceive us.' Others said: 'People of Yathrib,[1] you cannot stand much longer. Go back to your city.' And yet others sought the Prophet's leave, saying: 'Our homes are defenceless,' while defenceless they were not. They only wished to flee.

33:14    Had the city been entered from every quarter, and had they been roused to rebellion, they would have surely rebelled. But they would have occupied it only for a little while.

Before that they swore to God never to turn their backs in flight. And an oath to God must needs be answered for.

Say: 'Nothing will your flight avail you. If you escaped from death or slaughter you would enjoy this world only for a little while.'

Say: 'Who can protect you from God if it is His will to scourge you? And who can prevent Him from showing you mercy?' They shall find none besides God to protect or help them.

33:18    God well knows those of you who hold the others back; who say to their comrades: 'Join our side,' and seldom take

---

1. The old name of Medina.

part in the fighting, being ever reluctant to assist you. 33:19
When fear overtakes them they look to you[1] for help, their
eyes rolling as though they were on the point of death. But
once they are out of danger they assail you with their sharp
tongues, covetously demanding the richest part of the
booty. Such men have no faith. God will bring their deeds
to nothing. That is easy enough for God.

They thought the confederate tribes would never withdraw. Indeed, if the confederates should come again, they
would sooner be in the desert among the wandering Arabs.
There they would ask news of you, but were they with you
they would take but little part in the fighting.

There is a good example in God's apostle for those of you
who look to God and the Last Day and remember God always.

When the true believers saw the confederates, they said:
'This is what God and His apostle have promised us; surely
the promise of God and His apostle has come true.' And
this only increased their faith and submission.

Among the believers there are men who have been true 33:23
to God. Some have died, and others await their end,
yielding to no change. God will surely recompense the faithful for their faith and sternly punish the hypocrites – or show
them mercy if He will: God is forgiving and merciful.

God turned back the unbelievers in their rage, and they
went away empty-handed. God helped the faithful in the
stress of war: mighty is God, and all-powerful.

He brought down from their strongholds those who had
supported them from among the People of the Book[2] and
cast terror into their hearts, so that some you slew and
others you took captive.

He made you masters of their land, their houses, and
their goods, and of yet another land[3] on which you had
never set foot before. Truly, God has power over all things.

Prophet, say to your wives: 'If you seek this nether life and 33:28
all its finery, come, I will make provision for you and release

---

1. Muḥammad.        2. The Jews of Banī Qurayẓah.
3. Khaybar.

33:29 you honourably. But if you seek God and His apostle and the abode of the hereafter, know that God has prepared a rich recompense for those of you who do good works.'

Wives of the Prophet! Those of you who clearly commit a lewd act shall be doubly punished. That is easy enough for God. But those of you who obey God and His apostle and do good works shall be doubly recompensed; for them We have made a rich provision.

Wives of the Prophet, you are not like other women. If you fear God, do not be too complaisant in your speech, lest the lecherous-hearted should lust after you. Show discretion in what you say. Stay in your homes and do not display your finery as women used to do in the days of ignorance.[1] Attend to your prayers, give alms and obey God and His apostle.

Women of the Household, God seeks only to remove uncleanness from you and to purify you. Commit to memory the revelations of God and the wise sayings that are recited in your dwellings. Gracious is God and all-knowing.

33:35 Those who submit to God and accept the true Faith; who are devout, sincere, patient, humble, charitable, and chaste; who fast and are ever mindful of God – on these, both men and women, God will bestow forgiveness and a rich recompense.

It is not for true believers – men or women – to order their own affairs if God and His apostle decree otherwise. He that disobeys God and His apostle strays far indeed.

33:37 You[2] said to the man[3] whom God and yourself have favoured: 'Keep your wife and have fear of God.' You sought to hide in your heart what God was to reveal.[4] You were afraid of man, although it would have been more proper to fear God. And when Zayd divorced his wife, We gave her to you in marriage, so that it should become legitimate for true believers to wed the wives of their

---

1. Pre-Islamic days.    2. Muḥammad.
3. Zayd, Muḥammad's adopted son.
4. Your intention to marry Zayd's wife.

adopted sons if they divorced them. God's will must needs be done.

No blame shall be attached to the Prophet for doing what 33:38 is sanctioned for him by God. Such was the way of God with those who went before him (God's decrees are pre-ordained); who fulfilled the mission with which God had charged them, fearing God and fearing none besides Him. Sufficient is God's reckoning.

Muḥammad is the father of no man among you.[1] He is the Apostle of God and the Seal of the Prophets. Surely God has knowledge of all things.

Believers, be ever mindful of God: praise Him morning and evening. He and His angels bless you, so that He may lead you from darkness to the light. He is ever merciful to true believers.

On the day they meet Him their greeting shall be: 'Peace!' A rich reward He has prepared for them.

Prophet, We have sent you forth as a witness, a bearer of 33:45 good tidings, and a warner; one who shall call men to God by His leave and guide them like a shining light.

Tell the faithful that God has bounteous blessings in store for them. Do not yield to the unbelievers and the hypocrites: disregard their insolence. Put your trust in God; God is your all-sufficient guardian.

Believers, if you marry believing women and divorce them before the marriage is consummated, you are not required to observe a waiting period. Provide well for them and release them honourably.

Prophet, We have made lawful for you the wives to whom 33:50 you have granted dowries and the slave-girls whom God has given you as booty; the daughters of your paternal and maternal uncles and of your paternal and maternal aunts who fled with you; and any believing woman who gives herself to the Prophet and whom the Prophet wishes to take in marriage. This privilege is yours alone, being granted to no other believer.

1. Muḥammad left no male heirs.

We well know the duties We have imposed on the faithful concerning their wives and slave-girls. [We grant you this privilege] so that none may blame you. God is ever forgiving and merciful.

33:51 You may put off any of your wives you please and take to your bed any of them you please. Nor is it unlawful for you to receive any of those whom you have temporarily set aside. That is more proper, so that they may be contented and not vexed, and may all be pleased with what you give them.

God knows what is in your[1] hearts. Surely God is all-knowing and gracious.

It shall be unlawful for you[2] to take more wives or to change your present wives for other women, though their beauty please you, unless they are slave-girls whom you own. God takes cognizance of all things.

33:53 Believers, do not enter the houses of the Prophet for a meal without waiting for the proper time, unless you are given leave. But if you are invited, enter; and when you have eaten, disperse. Do not engage in familiar talk, for this would annoy the Prophet and he would be ashamed to bid you go; but of the truth God is not ashamed. If you ask his wives for anything, speak to them from behind a curtain. This is more chaste for your hearts and their hearts.

You must not speak ill of God's apostle, nor shall you ever wed his wives after him; this would surely be a grave offence in the sight of God. Whether you reveal or conceal them, God has knowledge of all things.

It shall be no offence for the Prophet's wives to be seen unveiled by their fathers, their sons, their brothers, their brothers' sons, their sisters' sons, their women, or their slave-girls. Women, have fear of God; surely God observes all things.

33:56 The Prophet is blessed by God and His angels. Bless him,

1. The believers.
2. Muḥammad.

then, you that are true believers, and greet him with a worthy salutation.

Those who speak ill of God and His apostle shall be 33:57 cursed by God in this life and in the life to come. He has prepared for them a shameful punishment.

Those who traduce believing men and believing women undeservedly shall bear the guilt of slander and grievous sin.

Prophet, enjoin your wives, your daughters, and the wives of true believers to draw their veils close round them. That is more proper, so that they may be recognized and not be molested. God is ever forgiving and merciful.

If the hypocrites and those who have tainted hearts and the scandal mongers of Madīnah do not desist, We will rouse you against them, and their days in that city will be numbered. Cursed wherever they are found, they shall be seized and put to death without mercy.

Such has been the way of God with those who have gone before them. And you shall find no change in the ways of God.

People ask you about the Hour of Doom. Say: 'God 33:63 alone has knowledge of it. Who knows? The Hour may well be near at hand.'

God has laid His curse upon the unbelievers and prepared for them a blazing Fire. Abiding there for ever, they shall find none to protect or help them.

On the day when their heads roll about in the Fire, they shall say: 'Would that we had obeyed God and obeyed the Apostle!' And they shall say: 'Lord, we obeyed our masters and our great ones, but they led us away from the right path. Lord, mete out to them a double scourge; lay on them a mighty curse.'

Believers, do not behave like those who slandered Moses. God cleared him of their calumny, and he was exalted by God. Believers, fear God and speak the truth. He will bless your works and forgive you your sins. Those who obey God and His apostle shall win a signal victory.

We offered Our trust to the heavens, to the earth, and to 33:72 the mountains, but they refused the burden and were afraid to receive it. Man undertook to bear it, but he has proved a sinner and a fool.

33:73   God will surely punish the hypocrites and the idolaters, both men and women; but to believing men and to believing women He shall show mercy. God is forgiving and merciful.

# SHEBA

*In the Name of God, the Compassionate, the Merciful*

34:1   PRAISE BE to God, to whom belongs all that the heavens and the earth contain! Praise be to Him in the world to come. He is the Wise One, the All-knowing.

He has knowledge of all that goes into the earth and all that springs up from it; all that comes down from heaven and all that ascends to it. He is the Forgiving One, the Merciful.

The unbelievers declare: 'The Hour of Doom will never come.' Say: 'Yes, by the Lord, it is surely coming! He knows all that is hidden. Not an atom's weight in the heavens or the earth escapes Him; nor is there anything smaller or greater but is recorded in a glorious book. He will surely recompense those who have faith and do good works; they shall be forgiven and a rich provision shall be made for them. But those who strive to confute Our revelations shall suffer the torment of a harrowing scourge.'

34:6   Those endowed with knowledge can see that what has been revealed to you from your Lord is the Truth, leading to the path of the Almighty, the Glorious One.

The unbelievers say: 'Shall we show you a man¹ who claims that when you have been mangled into dust you will be raised in a new creation? Has he invented a lie about God, or is he mad?' Truly, those who deny the life to come are doomed, for they have strayed far into error.

34:9   Do they not see what is before them and behind them in heaven and earth? If We will, We can cause the earth to cave in beneath their feet or let fragments of the sky fall upon them. Surely there is a sign in this for every penitent man.

1. Muḥammad.

On David We bestowed Our bounty. We said: 'Moun- 34:10
tains, and you birds, echo his songs of praise.' We made
hard iron pliant to him, saying: 'Make coats of mail and
measure their links with care. Do what is right: I am
watching over all your actions.'

To Solomon We subjected the wind, travelling a month's
journey morning and evening. We gave him a spring
flowing with molten brass, and jinn who served him by
leave of his Lord. Those of them who did not do Our
bidding We shall chasten with the torment of the Fire. They
made for him whatever he pleased: shrines and statues,
basins as large as watering-troughs, and built-in cauldrons.
We said: 'Give thanks, House of David.' Yet few of My
servants are truly thankful.

And when We had decreed his death, they did not know
that he was dead until they saw a worm eating away his
staff. And when his corpse fell down, the jinn realized that
had they had knowledge of the unknown, they would
not have remained in shameful bondage.

For the natives of Sheba there was indeed a sign in their 34:15
dwelling-place: a garden on their right and a garden on their
left. We said to them: 'Eat of what your Lord has given you
and render thanks to Him. Pleasant is your land and
forgiving is your Lord.'

But they paid no heed. So We let loose upon them the
waters of the dam and replaced their gardens by two others
bearing bitter fruit, tamarisks, and a few nettles. Thus did
We punish them for their ingratitude: do We punish any
but the ungrateful?

Between them and the cities that We have blessed, We
placed roadside hamlets so that they could journey to and
fro in measured stages. We said: 'Travel through them by
night and day in safety.'

But they said: 'Lord, make our journeys longer.' They
sinned against their souls; so We held them up as an
example and scattered them throughout the land. Surely
there is a sign in this for every steadfast, thankful man.

Satan had judged them rightly; they followed him all, 34:20

34:21 except for a band of true believers. Yet had he no power over them: Our only aim was to recognize those who believed in the life to come and those who were in doubt. Your Lord takes cognizance of all things.

Say: 'Call on those whom you deify besides God. They do not control an atom's weight in the heavens or the earth, nor have they any share in either. Nor has He any helpers among them.'

None can intercede with God save him who has received His sanction. When fear is banished from their hearts, they shall ask each other: 'What has your Lord ordained?' 'The Truth,' they shall answer. 'He is the Most High, the Supreme One.'

Say: 'Who provides for you from the heavens and the earth?'

Say: 'God. Either we or you are right, or clearly in the wrong.'

Say: 'You are not accountable for our sins, nor are we accountable for your actions.'

34:26 Say: 'Our Lord will bring us all together, then He will rightly judge between us. He is the All-knowing Judge.'

Say: 'Show me those whom you have named with Him as partners. Never. God alone is the Mighty One, the Wise One.'

We have sent you forth to all mankind, so that you may give them good news and forewarn them. But most men have no knowledge. They ask: 'When will this promise be fulfilled, if what you say be true?'

Say: 'Your day is already appointed. Not for one hour can you hold it back, nor can you hurry it on.'

The unbelievers say: 'We will never believe in this Koran, nor in the scriptures which came before it.'

If only you could see the wrongdoers when they are brought before their Lord! Bandying charges with one another, those who were despised will say to those who deemed themselves mighty: 'But for you, we would have been believers.'

34:32 Then those who deemed themselves mighty will say to those who were despised: 'Was it we who debarred you from God's guidance when it was given you? No. You yourselves were wrongdoers.'

'By no means,' the others will rejoin. 'You have plotted, 34:33
night and day, bidding us disbelieve in God and set up
rivals to Him.'

And they will repent in secret when they see the scourge.
We will put chains round the necks of the unbelievers. Shall
they not be rewarded but according to their deeds?

We have sent no apostle to any nation whose message was
not denied by those of them that lived in comfort. The
unbelievers say: 'We have been given greater wealth and
more children than the faithful. Surely we shall not be
punished.'

Say: 'My Lord gives abundantly to whom He will and
sparingly to whom He pleases. But most men do not
know it.'

Neither your riches nor your children shall bring you one
jot nearer to Us. Those that have faith and do what is right
shall be doubly rewarded for their deeds: in the High
Pavilions they shall dwell in peace. But those that strive to
confute Our revelations shall be summoned up for punishment.

Say: 'My Lord gives abundantly to whom He will and 34:39
sparingly to whom He pleases. Whatever you give in alms
He will recompense you for it. He is the most munificent
Provider.'

On the day He gathers them all together, He will say to
the angels: 'Was it you that these men worshipped?'

'Glory be to You!' they will answer. 'Defend us from
them! They worshipped jinn, and it was in jinn that most of
them believed.'

On that day you shall be powerless to help or harm one
another. To the wrongdoers We shall say: 'Taste the torment of the Fire, which you persistently denied.'

When Our clear revelations are recited to them, they say: 34:43
'This is but a man who would turn you away from the gods
your fathers worshipped.' And they say: 'This¹ is nothing
but an invented falsehood.' While those who denied the
truth when it was first made known to them declare: 'This
is but plain sorcery.'

1. The Koran.

34:44 ․ Yet have We given them no scriptures to study, nor have We sent before you any apostle to warn them.

Those who have gone before them likewise denied Our revelations. They were ten times as prosperous and mighty: yet they rejected My apostles. And then how terrible was the way I rejected them!

Say: 'One thing I would ask you: stand up before God in pairs or singly and ponder whether your compatriot[1] is truly mad. He is sent forth only to forewarn you of a grievous scourge.'

Say: 'I demand no recompense of you: keep it for yourselves. None but God can reward me. He is the witness of all things.'

34:48 Say: 'My Lord hurls forth the truth. He has knowledge of all that is hidden.

Say: 'Truth has come. Falsehood has vanished and shall return no more.'

Say: 'If I am in error, the loss is surely mine; but if I am in the right, it is thanks to that which my Lord has revealed to me. He hears all and is near at hand.'

If you could only see the unbelievers when they are seized with terror! There shall be no escape; they shall be taken from their graves.[2] They will say: 'We believe in Him.' But how will they attain the Faith when they are far away, since they at first denied it, and sneered at the unseen when they were far away?

34:54 They shall be barred from their desires, as were those before them; they, too, were perplexed with doubt.

# THE CREATOR

*In the Name of God, the Compassionate, the Merciful*

35:1 PRAISE BE to God, Creator of the heavens and the earth! He sends forth the angels as His messengers, with two, three or four pairs of wings. He multiplies His creatures according to His will. God has power over all things.

1. Muḥammad.
2. Literally, 'from a place near at hand' (Al-Jalālayn).

The blessings God bestows on people none can withhold; 35:2
and what He withholds none can bestow, apart from Him.
He is the Mighty, the Wise One.

You people! Bear in mind God's goodness to you. Is there
any other creator who provides for you from heaven and
earth? There is no god but Him. How then can you turn away?

If they deny you, other apostles have been denied before
you. To God shall all things return.

You people! The promise of God is true. Let not the life
of this world deceive you, nor let the Dissembler deceive
you about God. Satan is your enemy: therefore treat him as
an enemy. He tempts his followers so that they may become
the heirs of Hell.

The unbelievers shall be sternly punished, but those that
accept the true Faith and do good works shall be forgiven
and richly recompensed.

Is he whose foul deeds seem fair to him [like the man
who is rightly guided]? God leaves in error whom He will
and guides whom He pleases. Do not destroy yourself[1]
with grief on their account: God has knowledge of all their
actions.

God sends forth the winds which set the clouds in 35:9
motion. We drive them on to some dead land and give fresh
life to the earth after it has died. Such is the Resurrection.

If anyone seeks glory, let him know that glory is God's
alone. The good word is heard by Him and the good deed
exalted. But those that plot evil shall be sternly punished;
their plots will be brought to nothing.

God created you from dust, then from a little germ. Into
two sexes He divided you. No female conceives or gives
birth without His knowledge. No man grows old or has his
life cut short but in accordance with His decree. All this is
easy enough for God.

The Two Seas are not alike. The one is fresh, sweet, and 35:12
pleasant to drink from, while the other is salt and bitter.
From both you eat fresh fish, and from both you bring out
ornaments to wear. See how the ships plough their course

1. Muḥammad.

through them as you sail away to seek His bounty.
Perchance you will give thanks.

35:13    He causes the night to pass into the day, and the day to
pass into the night. He has pressed the sun and the moon
into His service, each running for an appointed term. Such
is God, your Lord. His is the sovereignty. The idols whom
you invoke besides Him have power over nothing. If you
pray to them they cannot hear your prayer, and even if they
hear you they cannot answer you. On the Day of Resurrection they will deny that you ever served them. None can
make known to you the Truth like the One who is all-
knowing.

You people, it is you who stand in need of God. God is
all-sufficient and glorious. He can destroy you if He will
and replace you with a new creation; this is no impossible
thing for God.

No soul shall bear another's burden. If a laden soul cries
out for help, not even a near relation shall share its burden.

You shall admonish none but those who fear their Lord
though they cannot see Him, and are steadfast in prayer. He
that keeps himself pure has much to gain. To God shall all
return.

35:19    The blind and the seeing are not equal, nor are the
darkness and the light. The shade and the heat are not equal,
nor are the living and the dead. God can cause whom He
will to hear Him, but you cannot make those who are in
their graves hear you.

Your only duty is to give warning. We have sent you
with the Truth to proclaim good news and to give warning;
for there is no community that has not had a warner. If they
disbelieve you, know that those who have gone before them
also disbelieved. Their apostles came to them with veritable
signs, with scriptures, and with the light-giving Book. But
in the end I smote the unbelievers: and how terrible was the
way I disowned them!

35:27    Did you not see how God sent down water from the sky
with which We brought forth fruits of different hues? In the
mountains there are streaks of various shades of white and

red, and jet-black rocks. Humans, beasts, and cattle have 35:28
their different colours, too.

From among His servants, only those fear God who
know that God is mighty and forgiving.

Those who recite the Book of God and attend to their
prayers and give from what We gave them, in private and in
public, may hope for imperishable gain. He will give them
their rewards and enrich them from His own abundance. He
is forgiving and bountiful in His rewards.

What We have revealed to you in the Book is the truth
confirming previous scriptures. God knows and observes
His servants.

We have bestowed the Book on those of Our servants
whom We have chosen. Some sin against their souls, some
follow a middle course, and some, by God's leave, vie with
each other in charitable works: this is the supreme virtue.

They shall enter the gardens of Eden, where they shall be
decked with bracelets of gold and pearls, and arrayed in
robes of silk. They will say: 'Praise be to God who has
taken away all sorrow from us. Our Lord is forgiving and
bountiful in His rewards. Through His grace He has
admitted us to the Eternal Mansion, where we shall endure
no toil, no weariness.'

As for the unbelievers, the fire of Hell awaits them. 35:36
Death shall not deliver them, nor shall its torment ever be
eased for them. Thus shall We reward the thankless.

There they will cry out: 'Lord, remove us hence! We will
live a good life and will not do as we have done.' But He
will answer: 'Did We not make your lives long enough for
anyone who would be warned to take warning? Besides,
someone *did* come to warn you: have a taste of it then. None
shall help the wrongdoers.'

God knows the mysteries of the heavens and the earth.
He knows the innermost thoughts of men.

It is He who has given you the earth to inherit. He that 35:39
denies Him shall bear the burden of his unbelief. In denying
Him the unbelievers earn nothing but odium in the sight of
God; their unbelief earns them nothing but perdition.

35:40 Say: 'Behold your other gods on whom you call besides God. Show me what part of the earth they have created! Have they a share in the heavens?'

Or have We given them a scripture affording them evident proof? Truly, vain are the promises the wrongdoers give each other.

It is God who keeps the heavens and the earth from falling. Should they fall, none could hold them back but Him. Gracious is God, and forgiving.

They solemnly swore by God that if a prophet should come to warn them, they would accept his guidance more readily than did the other nations. Yet when someone did come to warn them, they turned away from him with
35:43 greater aversion, behaving arrogantly in the land and plotting evil. But evil shall recoil on those that plot evil.

What end are they awaiting, except the end which overtook the ancients? You will find no change in the ways of God; nor will you find in the ways of God any alteration.

Have they never journeyed through the land and seen the fate of those who went before them, nations far mightier than they?

There is nothing in the heavens or the earth beyond the power of God. All-knowing is He, and mighty.
35:45 If it were God's will to punish people for their misdeeds, not one creature would be left alive on the earth's surface. He respites them till an appointed time. And when their time comes, they shall learn that God has been watching all His servants.

# YĀ' SĪN

*In the Name of God, the Compassionate, the Merciful*

36:1 *Yā' sīn.* I swear by the Wise Koran that you are sent upon a straight path.

This is revealed by the Mighty One, the Merciful, so that you may forewarn a nation who, because their fathers were not warned before them, live in heedlessness. On most of them judgement has been passed, yet still they disbelieve. 36:7

We have bound their necks with chains of iron reaching up to their chins, so that they cannot bow their heads. We have put a barrier before them and a barrier behind them and covered them over, so that they cannot see.

It is the same whether or not you forewarn them: they will never have faith.

You shall forewarn none but those who observe Our precepts and fear the Merciful, though they cannot see Him. To these give news of pardon and a rich reward.

It is We who will resurrect the dead. We record the deeds of men and the marks they leave behind: We note all things in a glorious book.

You shall cite, as a case in point, the people of the city[1] to which Our messengers made their way. At first We sent to them two messengers, but when they rejected both We strengthened them with a third. They said: 'We have been sent to you as apostles.' But the people replied: 'You are but mortals like ourselves. The Merciful has revealed nothing: you are surely lying.'

They said: 'Our Lord knows that we are true apostles. 36:16 Our only duty is to give plain warning.'

The people answered: 'Your presence bodes but evil for us. Desist, or we will stone you or inflict on you a painful scourge.'

They said: 'The evil you forebode can come only from yourselves. Will you not take heed? Surely you are great transgressors.'

Thereupon a man came running from the far quarter of the city. 'My people,' he said, 'follow those who have been sent to you. Follow those who ask no recompense of you and are rightly guided. Why should I not serve Him who has created me and to whom you shall all be recalled? Should I serve other gods than Him? If it is the will of the Merciful 36:23 to afflict me, their intercession will avail me nothing, nor

1. Probably Antioch, to which, we are told, Jesus sent two disciples, and then a third.

36:24  will they save me. Indeed, I should then be in evident error. I believe in your Lord; so hear me.'

We said to him: 'Enter Paradise,' and he exclaimed: 'Would that my people knew how gracious my Lord has been to me, how highly He has exalted me!'

After him, We sent down no host from heaven against his people: this We never do. There was but one shout – and they fell down lifeless.

Alas for My bondsmen! They laugh to scorn every apostle that comes to them. Do they not see how many generations We have destroyed before them? Never shall they return to them: all shall be brought before Us.

Let the once-dead earth be a sign for them. We gave it life, and from it produced grain for their sustenance. We planted it with the palm and the vine, and watered it with gushing springs, so that men might feed on its fruit. It was not their hands that made all this. Should they not give thanks?

Glory be to Him who made all things in pairs: the plants of the earth, mankind themselves, and the living things which they know not.

36:37  The night is another sign for men. From the night We lift the day – and they are plunged in darkness.

The sun hastens to its resting-place: its course is laid for it by the Mighty One, the All-knowing.

We have ordained phases for the moon, which daily wanes and in the end appears like a bent old twig.

The sun is not allowed to overtake the moon, nor does the night outpace the day. Each in its own orbit swims.

We gave them yet another sign when We carried their offspring in the laden ark. And similar vessels We have made for them to voyage in. We drown them if We will: none can help or rescue them, except through Our mercy and unless We please to prolong their lives awhile.

When they are told: 'Have fear of that which is before you and behind you, so that you may be shown mercy,' [they pay no heed.] Indeed, they turn away from every sign that comes to them from their Lord.

36:47  And when they are told: 'Give alms from that which

God has given you,' the unbelievers say to the faithful: 'Are we to feed those whom God can feed if He chooses? Surely you are in glaring error.' They also say: 'When will this 36:48 promise be fulfilled, if what you say be true?'

They must be waiting but for a single blast, which will take them while they are still disputing. They will have no time to make a will, nor shall they return to their kinsfolk.

The Trumpet will be blown and, behold, they will rise up from their graves and hasten to their Lord. 'Woe betide us!' they will say. 'Who has roused us from our resting-place? This is what the Lord of Mercy promised: the apostles have told the truth!' And with but one blast they shall be gathered all before Us.

On that day no soul shall suffer the least injustice. You shall be rewarded according only to your deeds.

On that day the heirs of Paradise will be busy with their joys. Together with their spouses, they shall recline in shady groves upon soft couches. They shall have fruits therein, and all that they desire.

'Peace!' shall be the word spoken by a merciful God. But 36:58 to the guilty He will say: 'Away with you this day! Sons of Adam, did I not charge you never to worship Satan, your acknowledged foe, but to worship Me? Surely that is a straight path. Yet he has led a multitude of you astray. Had you no sense? This is the Hell you have been promised. Burn in it this day on account of your unbelief.'

On that day We shall seal their mouths. Their hands will speak to Us, and their very feet will testify to their misdeeds. Had it been Our will, We could have put out their eyes: yet even then they would have rushed headlong upon their wonted path. For how could they have seen their error?

Had it been Our will, We could have transformed them where they stood, so that they could neither go forward nor retrace their steps.

We reverse the growth of those to whom We give long life. Can they not understand?

· We have taught him[1] no poetry, nor does it become him 36:69

---

1. Muḥammad.

to be a poet. This is but an admonition: an eloquent Koran to
36:70 exhort the living and to pass judgement on the unbelievers.

Do they not see how, among the things Our hands have
made, We have created for them the beasts of which they are
masters? We have subjected these to them, that they may
ride on some and eat the flesh of others; they drink their milk
and put them to other uses. Will they not give thanks?

They have set up other gods besides God, hoping that
they may help them. They cannot help them: yet their
worshippers stand like warriors ready to defend them.

Let not their words grieve you. We have knowledge of
all that they conceal and all that they reveal.

36:77 Is man not aware that We created him from a little germ?
Yet is he flagrantly contentious. He answers back with
arguments, and forgets his own creation. He asks: 'Who
will give life to rotten bones?'

Say: 'He who first brought them into being will give
them life again: He has knowledge of every creature; He
who gives you from the green tree a flame, and lo! you light
a fire.'

Has He who created the heavens and the earth no power
to create others like them? That He surely has. He is the all-
knowing Creator. When He decrees a thing He need only
say: 'Be,' and it is.

36:83 Glory be to Him who has control of all things. To Him
shall you all be recalled.

# THE RANKS

*In the Name of God, the Compassionate, the Merciful*

37:1 I SWEAR by those who range themselves in ranks, by those
who cast out demons, and by those who recite the Word,
that your God is One: the Lord of the heavens and the earth
and all that lies between them: the Lord of the Eastern
Regions.

We have decked the lower heaven with constellations.
37:8 They guard it against rebellious devils, so that they may not

listen in to those on high. Meteors are hurled at them from
every side; then, driven away, they are consigned to an  37:9
eternal scourge. Eavesdroppers are pursued by fiery comets.

Ask the unbelievers if they deem themselves of a nobler
make than the rest of Our creation. Of coarse clay We
created them.

You marvel, while they scoff. When they are warned they
heed no warning. When they are shown a sign they mock at
it and say: 'This is but plain sorcery. What! When we are
dead and turned to dust and bones, shall we be raised to life,
we and our forefathers?'

Say: 'Yes. And you shall be utterly humbled.'

One blast will sound, and they shall see it all. 'Woe betide
us!' they will exclaim. 'This is the Day of Reckoning. This is
the Judgement-day which you denied.'

But We shall say: 'Call the sinners, their spouses, and the
idols which they worshipped besides God, and lead them to
the path of Hell. Hold them there for questioning. But what
has come over you that you cannot help each other?'

Indeed, on that day they will all submit. They will  37:26
reproach each other, saying: 'You have imposed upon us!' –
'No! It was you who would not be believers. We had no
power over you: you were sinners all. Just is the verdict
which Our Lord has passed upon us; we shall surely taste
the scourge. We misled you, but we ourselves have been
misled.'

On that day they will all share in the scourge. Thus
shall We deal with the evil-doers, for when they were told:
'There is no deity but God,' they replied with scorn:
'Are we to renounce our gods for the sake of a mad poet?'

Surely he has brought the truth, confirming those who
were sent before. You shall all taste the grievous scourge:
you shall be rewarded according only to your deeds.

But the true servants of God shall be well provided for,
feasting on fruit, and honoured in the gardens of delight.
Reclining face to face upon soft couches, they shall be
served with a goblet filled at a gushing fountain, white, and
delicious to those who drink it. It will neither dull their  37:47

37:48 senses nor befuddle them. They shall sit with bashful, dark-eyed virgins, as chaste as the sheltered eggs of ostriches.

They will put questions to each other. One will say: 'I had a friend who used to ask: "Do you really believe? When we are dead and turned to dust and bones, shall we ever be brought to judgement?"' And he will say: 'Come, let us look down.' He will look down and see his friend in the very midst of Hell. 'By the Lord,' he will say to him, 'you almost ruined me! But for the grace of God I should have surely been summoned myself. Shall we never die again, having died once, and shall we never be scourged at all?'

Surely that is the supreme triumph. To this end let every good man labour.

Is this not a better welcome than the Zaqqūm tree? We have made this tree a scourge for the unjust. It grows in the nethermost part of Hell, bearing fruit like devils' heads: on it they shall feed, and with it they shall cram their bellies, together with draughts of scalding water. Then to Hell shall they return.

37:69 They found their fathers erring, yet they eagerly followed in their footsteps. Most of the ancients went astray before them, though We had sent apostles to give them warning. Consider the fate of those whom We have warned: they perished all, except God's true servants.

Noah prayed to Us, and his prayers were graciously answered. We delivered him, and his household, from the mighty scourge, and made his descendants the sole survivors. We bestowed on him the praise of later generations: 'Peace be on Noah among all men!'

Thus do We reward the righteous: he was one of Our believing servants. The others We peremptorily drowned.

Abraham was of the self-same faith and came to his Lord with a pure heart. He said to his father and to his people: 'What are these that you worship? Would you serve false deities instead of God? What think you of the Lord of the Universe?'

37:90 He lifted up his eyes to the stars and said: 'I am sick!' And his people turned their backs and went off.

He stole away to their idols and said to them: 'Will you 37:91
not eat your offerings? Why do you not speak?' With that
he fell upon them, striking them down with his right hand.

The people came running to the scene. 'Would you
worship that which you have carved with your own hands,'
he said, 'when it was God who created you and all that you
have made?'

They replied: 'Build up a pyre and cast him into the
blazing flames.' Thus did they scheme against him: but We
abased them all.

He said: 'I will take refuge with my Lord; He will give
me guidance. Lord, grant me a righteous son.'

We gave him news of a gentle son. And when he reached
the age when he could work with him, his father said to him:
'My son, I dreamt that I was sacrificing you. Tell me what
you think.'

He replied: 'Father, do as you are bidden. God willing,
you shall find me steadfast.'

And when they had both submitted to God, and Abraham
had laid down his son prostrate upon his face, We called out
to him, saying: 'Abraham, you have fulfilled your vision.' 37:105
Thus do We reward the righteous. That was indeed a bitter
test. We ransomed his son with a noble sacrifice and
bestowed on him the praise of later generations. 'Peace be
on Abraham!'

Thus do We reward the righteous. He was one of Our
believing servants.

We gave him Isaac, a saintly prophet, and blessed them
both. Among their offspring were some who did good
works and others who clearly sinned against their souls.

We showed favour to Moses and to Aaron and delivered
them, with all their people, from the mighty scourge. We
succoured them, and they became victorious. We gave them
the Glorious Book and guided them to the straight path. We
bestowed on them the praise of later generations: 'Peace be
on Moses and Aaron!'

Thus do We reward the righteous. They were two of Our 37:122
believing servants.

37:123     We also sent forth Elias,[1] who said to his people: 'Have you no fear? Would you invoke Baal and forsake the Most Gracious Creator? God is your Lord and the Lord of your forefathers.'

But they rejected him, and will thus be called to account. Not so God's true servants. We bestowed on him the praise of later generations: 'Peace on Elias!'

Thus do We reward the righteous. He was one of Our believing servants.

Lot was also sent with a message. We delivered him and all his kinsfolk, except for an old woman who stayed behind, and utterly destroyed the others. You pass by their ruins morning and evening: will you not take heed?

Jonah was also sent with a message. He fled to the laden ship, cast lots, and was condemned. The whale swallowed him, for he had sinned; and had he not devoutly praised the Lord he would have stayed in its belly till the Day of Resurrection. We threw him, gravely ill, upon a desolate shore and caused a gourd-tree to grow over him. Thus did We send him to a nation a hundred thousand strong or more. They believed in him, and We let them live in ease awhile.

37:149     Ask the unbelievers if it be true that God has daughters, while they themselves choose sons. Did We create the angels females? And were they present at their creation? Surely they lie when they declare: 'God has begotten children.'

Would He choose daughters rather than sons? What has come over you that you should judge so ill?

Will you not take heed? Have you a positive proof? Show us your scriptures, if what you say be true!

They assert kinship between Him and the jinn. But the jinn well know that they will all be called to account. Exalted be God above their imputations! Not so God's true servants.

Neither you nor your idols shall deceive any about God save him who is destined for Hell. We[2] each have our
37:166     appointed place. We range ourselves in adoration and give glory to Him.

---

    1. Elijah. Cf. I Kings xviii, 17–21.     2. The angels.

They say: 'Had we received an admonition from the 37:167
ancients, we would have become God's true servants.'
Yet they disbelieve in the Koran. But they shall learn.

Long ago We promised the apostles who served Us that
they would receive Our help and that Our armies would be
victorious. So pay no heed to them awhile: you will surely
see their downfall as they shall see your triumph.

Do they wish to hurry on Our scourge? Evil shall be
that morning when it smites them in their courtyards,
forewarned though they have been.

So pay no heed to them awhile. You will surely see their
downfall as they shall see your triumph. Exalted be your
Lord, the Lord of Glory, above their imputations!

Peace be on the apostles, and praise to God, Lord of the 37:182
Universe!

# ṢĀD

*In the Name of God, the Compassionate, the Merciful*

*Ṣād.* BY the Koran, with all its precepts! Surely the 38:1
unbelievers are imbued with arrogance and perverseness.

How many generations have We destroyed before
them! They all cried out for mercy, when it was too late
to escape.

They marvel that a prophet of their own should arise
among them. 'This is a sorcerer, a teller of lies,' say the
unbelievers. 'Does he claim that all the gods are one god?
This is indeed a strange thing.'

Their leaders go about saying: 'Pay no heed and stand
firm in the worship of your gods: it is a binding duty. We
have not heard of this¹ in the Christian faith.² It is nothing
but a false invention. Was the Word revealed to him alone
among us?'

Yes, they are in doubt about My warning, for they have
not yet tasted My scourge.

Do they possess the treasures of the mercy of your Lord, 38:9

---

1. Monotheism.        2. Lit., the last faith.

38:10 the Mighty, the Munificent One? Is theirs the sovereignty over the heavens and the earth and all that lies between them? Then let them climb up to the sky by ropes!

Their faction is no more than a beaten army. The people of Noah, 'Ād, and Pharaoh, who impaled his victims upon the stake; Thamūd, the compatriots of Lot, and the dwellers of the Forest[1] – all denied their Lord and divided themselves into factions: all charged their apostles with imposture. My punishment justly smote them.

Yet these are waiting but for a single blast – the blast which none may retard. They say: 'Lord, hasten our doom before the Day of Reckoning comes!'

Bear with what they say, and remember Our servant David, who was both a mighty and a penitent man. We made the mountains[2] join with him in praise evening and morning, and the birds, too, in all their flocks; all were obedient to him. We made his kingdom strong, and gave him wisdom and discriminating judgement.

38:21 Have you heard the story of the two litigants who entered his chamber by climbing over the wall? When they went in to David and saw that he was alarmed, they said: 'Have no fear. We are two litigants, one of whom has wronged the other. Judge rightly between us and do not be unjust; guide us to the right path.

'My brother here has ninety-nine ewes, but I have only one ewe.[3] He demanded that I should entrust it to him, and got the better of me in the dispute.'

David replied: 'He has certainly wronged you in seeking to add your ewe to his flock. Many partners are unjust to one another; but not so those that have faith and do good works, and they are few indeed.'

David realized that We were only testing him. He sought forgiveness of his Lord and fell down penitently on his 38:25 knees. We forgave him his sin, and in the world to come he shall be honoured and well received.

---

1. The people of Midian.      2. Cf. Psalm CXLVIII, 9–10.

3. The allusion is to Uriah's wife.

We said: 'David, We have made you master in the land. 38:26
Rule with justice among the people and do not yield to lust,
lest it turn you away from God's path. Because they forget
the Day of Reckoning, those that stray from God's path shall
be sternly punished.'

It was not in vain that We created the heavens and the
earth and all that lies between them. That is what the
unbelievers think. But woe betide the unbelievers when
they are cast into the Fire!

Are We to equate those that have faith and do good
works with those that perpetrate corruption in the land?
Are We to equate the righteous with the ungodly?

We have revealed to you this Book with Our blessing, so
that the wise might ponder its revelations and take warning.

We gave Solomon to David; and he was a good and
faithful servant. When, one evening, his prancing steeds
were ranged before him, he said: 'My love for good things
has distracted me from the remembrance of my Lord; for
now the sun has vanished behind the veil of darkness. Bring
me back my chargers!' And with this he fell to hacking their
legs and necks.

We put Solomon to the proof and placed a body upon his 38:34
throne, so that he at length repented. He said: 'Forgive me,
Lord, and bestow upon me such power as shall belong to
none after me. You are the Bountiful Giver.'

We subjected the wind to him, so that it blew softly at his
bidding wherever he directed it; and the devils, too, among
whom were builders and divers and others bound with
chains. 'All this We give you,' We said. 'It is for you to
bestow or to withhold, without reckoning.' In the world to
come he shall be honoured and well received.

And tell of Our servant Job. He called out to his Lord,
saying: 'Satan has afflicted me with sorrow and misfortune.'

We said: 'Stamp your feet upon the earth, and a cool
spring will gush forth. Wash and refresh yourself.'

We restored to him his people and as many more with
them: a blessing from Ourself and an admonition to 38:43
prudent men.

38:44 We said to him: 'Take a bunch of twigs and beat with it; do not break your oath.'[1] We found him full of patience. He was a good and faithful man.

And tell of Our servants Abraham, Isaac, and Jacob: men of might and vision whom We made pure with the thought of the hereafter. They shall dwell with Us among the righteous whom We have chosen.

And of Ishmael, Elisha, and Dhūl-Kifl,[2] who were all just men.

This is but an admonition. The righteous shall return to a blessed retreat: the gardens of Eden, whose gates shall open wide to receive them. Reclining there with bashful virgins for companions, they will call for abundant fruit and drink.

All this shall be yours on the Day of Reckoning; Our gifts can have no end.

But doleful shall be the return of the transgressors. They shall burn in Hell, an evil resting-place. There let them taste 38:58 their drink: scalding water, festering blood, and other putrid things.

[We shall say to their leaders:] 'This band shall be thrown in headlong with you. No welcome shall await them; they shall be promptly cast into the Fire.'

And the damned will say to their leaders: 'No welcome for you either! It was you who prepared this for us, an evil plight.'

Then they will say: 'Lord, inflict on those who brought this fate upon us a twofold punishment in the Fire. But why do we not see those whom we deemed wicked and whom we laughed to scorn? Or have our eyes missed them?'

All this shall come to pass. The heirs of the Fire will wrangle among themselves.

38:65 Say: 'My mission is only to give warning. There is no

1. Job had sworn to give his wife a hundred blows. The oath was kept by his giving her one blow with a bunch of a hundred twigs. Commentators quote this passage as permitting any similar release from an oath rashly taken.

2. Probably Ezekiel.

divinity but God, the One who conquers all. He is the 38:66
Lord of the heavens and the earth and all that lies between
them: the Illustrious, the Forgiving One.'

Say: 'This is a fateful message: yet you pay no heed to it.
I had no knowledge of the disputes of those on high. It was
revealed to me, only that I might warn you plainly.'

Your Lord said to the angels: 'I am creating man from
clay. When I have fashioned him and breathed My spirit
into him, kneel down and prostrate yourselves before him.'

The angels all prostrated themselves except Satan, who
was too proud, for he was an unbeliever.

'Satan,' said He, 'why do you not bow to him whom My
own hands have made? Are you too proud, or do you deem
yourself superior?'

Satan replied: 'I am nobler than he. You created me from 38:76
fire, but him from clay.'

'Begone, you are accursed!' said He. 'My curse shall
remain on you until the Day of Reckoning.'

He replied: 'Reprieve me, Lord, till the Day of Resurrection.'

He said: 'Reprieved you shall be till the Appointed Day.'

'I swear by Your glory,' said Satan, 'that I will seduce
them all except your faithful servants.'

He replied: 'Learn the truth, then (and I speak nothing
but the truth): I will surely fill Hell with your offspring and
with your followers all.'

Say: 'For this I demand of you no recompense. Nor do I
pretend to be what I am not. This is an admonition to
mankind; in a while you shall learn its truth.'                    38:88


# THE THRONGS

*In the Name of God, the Compassionate, the Merciful*

THIS BOOK is revealed by God, the Mighty, the Wise 39:1
One. We have revealed to you the Book with the Truth:
therefore serve God and worship none but Him.

To God alone is true worship due. As for those who

39:3 choose other guardians[1] besides Him, saying: 'We serve them only that they may bring us nearer to God,' God Himself will resolve their differences for them. God does not guide the untruthful disbeliever.

Had it been God's will to adopt a son, He would have chosen whom He pleased out of His own Creation. But God forbid! He is God, the One, the Almighty.

It was to reveal the Truth that He created the heavens and the earth. He caused the night to succeed the day and the day to overtake the night. He made the sun and the moon obedient to Him, each running for an appointed term. He is surely the Mighty, the Forgiving One.

He created you from a single soul, then from that soul He created its spouse. He has given you four different pairs of cattle.[2] He moulds you in your mothers' wombs by stages in threefold darkness.

Such is God, your Lord. His is the sovereignty. There is no god but Him. How, then, can you turn away from Him?

39:7 If you render Him no thanks, know that God does not need you. Yet the ingratitude of His servants does not please Him. If you are thankful, your thanks will please Him.

No soul shall bear another's burden. To your Lord shall you return and He will declare to you what you have done. He knows your innermost thoughts.

When evil befalls man, he prays to his Lord and turns to Him in penitence; yet no sooner does He bestow on him His favour than he forgets what he has prayed for and makes other deities God's equals, in order to lead men away from His path.

Say: 'Enjoy your unbelief awhile; but the Fire shall be

39:9 your home. Can he who passes the night in adoration, standing or on his knees, who dreads the terrors of the life to come and hopes to earn the mercy of his Lord [be compared to the unbeliever]?' Say: 'Are those who have

---

1. The allusion is to the worship of saints.
2. Camels, cows, sheep, and goats.

knowledge the equal of those who have none?' Truly, none
will take heed but men of understanding.

Say: 'Fear your Lord, you that serve God and are true 39:10
believers. Those who do good works in this life shall
receive a good reward. God's earth is vast. Those that
endure with fortitude shall be recompensed unstintingly.'

Say: 'I am commanded to serve God and to worship none
besides Him. I am commanded to be the first of those who
shall submit to Him.'

Say: 'I fear, if I disobey my Lord, the torment of a fateful
day.'

Say: 'God I serve, and Him alone I worship. As for
yourselves, serve what you will besides Him.'

Say: 'They shall lose much, those who will forfeit their
souls and all their kinsfolk on the Day of Resurrection.
That shall be the ultimate loss. Above them there shall be
sheets of fire, and sheets of fire shall be beneath them. By
this, God puts fear into His servants' hearts.' Fear Me, then,
My servants.

But let those rejoice who keep from idol-worship and 39:17
turn to God in penitence. Give good news to My servants,
who listen to My precepts and follow what is best in them.
It is these whom God has guided. It is these who are
endowed with understanding.

Can you rescue from the Fire those who have rightly
earned the scourge? As for those who truly fear their Lord,
they shall be lodged in towering mansions set about with
running streams. Such is God's promise: God will not fail
His promise.

Do you not see how God sends down water from the sky
which penetrates the earth and gathers in springs beneath?
With it He brings forth plants of various hues. They wither,
they turn yellow, and then He turns them into dust. Surely
in this there is an admonition for men of understanding.

He whose heart God has opened to Islām shall receive 39:22
light from his Lord. But woe betide those whose hearts are
hardened against the remembrance of God! Truly, they are
in evident error.

39:23     God has now revealed the best of scriptures, a Book uniform in style proclaiming promises and warnings. Those who fear their Lord tremble with awe at its revelations, and their skins and hearts melt at the remembrance of God. Such is God's guidance: He bestows it on whom He will. But he whom God confounds shall have none to guide him.

Can he who shall face the terrors of the Resurrection [be compared to the true believer]? The wrongdoers will be told: 'Taste the punishment which you have earned.'

Those who have gone before them also disbelieved, so that the scourge overtook them unawares. God made them taste dishonour in this life, but the punishment of the life to come shall be more terrible, if they but knew it.

We have given mankind in this Koran all manner of parables, so that they may take heed: a Koran in the Arabic tongue, free from any flaw, that they may guard themselves against evil.

39:29     God makes this comparison. There are two men: the one has many masters who are ever at odds among themselves; the other has one master, to whom he is devoted. Are these two to be held alike? God be praised! But most of them have no knowledge.

You,[1] as well as they, are doomed to die. Then, on the Day of Resurrection, you[2] shall dispute in your Lord's presence with one another.

Who is more wicked than the man who invents a falsehood about God and denies the truth when it is declared to him? Is there not a home in Hell for the unbelievers?

Those who proclaim the truth, and those who give credence to it – they surely are the God-fearing. Their Lord will give them all that they desire. Thus shall the righteous be rewarded.

God will expunge their foulest deeds and reward them according to their noblest actions.

39:36     Is God not all-sufficient for His servant? Yet they threaten you with those they serve besides Him. He whom

---

1. Muḥammad.      2. The unbelievers.

God confounds has none to guide him. But he whom God 39:37
guides none can lead astray. Is God not mighty and capable
of revenge?

If you ask them who created the heavens and the earth,
they will surely reply: 'God.' Say: 'Do you think then that,
if God be pleased to afflict me, your idols could relieve my
affliction; or that if He be pleased to show me mercy, they
could withhold His mercy?'

Say: 'God is my all-sufficient patron. In Him let the
faithful put their trust.'

Say: 'My people, do as best you can and so will I. You
shall learn who will be seized by a scourge that will
disgrace him, and be smitten by a scourge everlasting.'

We have revealed to you the Book with the Truth, for the
instruction of the people. He that follows the right path shall
follow it for his own good; and he that goes astray shall do
so at his own peril. You are not accountable for them.

God takes away men's souls upon their death, and the 39:42
souls of the living during their sleep. Those that are
doomed He keeps with Him, and restores the others for a
time ordained. Surely there are signs in this for thinking
men.

Have they chosen others besides God to intercede for them?
Say: 'Even though they have no power nor understanding?'

Say: 'Intercession is wholly in the hands of God. He has
sovereignty over the heavens and the earth. To Him shall
you be recalled.'

When God alone is named, the hearts of those who deny
the hereafter shrink with aversion; but when their other
gods are named, they are filled with joy.

Say: 'Lord, Creator of the heavens and the earth, who
have knowledge of the unknown and the manifest, You
alone can judge the disputes of Your servants.'

If the wrongdoers possessed all the treasures of the earth
and as much besides, they would gladly offer it to redeem
themselves from the harrowing scourge on the Day of
Resurrection. For God will show them what they have
never reckoned with. The evil of their deeds will manifest 39:48

itself to them, and that which they derided will encompass them.

39:49     When evil befalls man he calls out to Us; but when We vouchsafe him a favour from Ourself, he says: 'It is my due.' By no means! It is but a test: yet most of them do not know it.

The same was said by those before them: but they gained nothing from what they did, and the very evil of their deeds recoiled upon them.

The wrongdoers among these[1] shall also have the evil of their deeds recoil upon them: nor shall they ever be immune.

Do they not know that God gives abundantly to whom He will and sparingly to whom He pleases? Surely there are signs in this for true believers.

Say: 'Servants of God, you that have sinned against your souls, do not despair of God's mercy, for God forgives all sins. It is He who is the Forgiving One, the Merciful. Turn in penitence to your Lord, and submit to Him before His scourge overtakes you; for then there will be none to help

39:55     you. Follow the best of what is revealed to you by your Lord before the scourge suddenly takes you when you are heedless; lest any man should say: "Alas! I have disobeyed God and scoffed at His revelations." Or: "If God had guided me I would have been a righteous man." Or, when he sees the scourge: "Could I but live again, I would lead a righteous life." For God will say to him: "Yes, indeed. My revelations did come to you; but you denied them. You were arrogant and had no faith at all."'

On the Day of Resurrection you shall see their faces blackened, those who uttered falsehoods about God. Is there not in Hell a home for the haughty?

But God will deliver those who fear Him, for they have earned salvation. Harm shall not touch them, nor shall they ever grieve.

God is the Creator of all things, and of all things He is
39:63     the Guardian. His are the keys of the heavens and the earth.

---

1. The Meccans.

Those that deny God's revelations will surely be the losers.

Say: 'Ignorant men! Would you bid me serve a deity 39:64 other than God?'

You have been warned, you and those who have gone before you, that if you worship other deities besides God, your works will come to nothing and you will surely be among the losers. Therefore serve God and render thanks to Him.

They underrate the might of God. But on the Day of Resurrection He will hold the entire earth in His grasp and fold up the heavens in His right hand. Glory be to Him! Exalted be He above their idols!

The Trumpet shall be blown, and all who are in the heavens and on earth shall fall down fainting, except those that shall be spared by God. Then the Trumpet will be blown again and they shall rise and gaze around them. The earth will shine with the light of her Lord, and the Book will be laid open. The prophets and the witnesses shall be brought in, and all shall be judged with fairness: none shall be wronged. Every soul shall be recompensed according to its deeds, for He best knows all that they did.

In throngs the unbelievers shall be led to Hell. When they 39:71 draw near, its gates will be opened, and its keepers will say to them: 'Did there not come to you apostles of your own who proclaimed to you the revelations of your Lord and forewarned you of this day?'

'Yes,' they will answer. And thus the promised scourge will smite the unbelievers. They will be told: 'Enter the gates of Hell and stay therein for ever.' Evil shall be the dwelling-place of the haughty.

But those who fear their Lord shall be led in throngs to Paradise. When they draw near, its gates will be opened, and its keepers will say to them: 'Peace be to you; you have led good lives. Enter Paradise and dwell in it for ever.'

They will say: 'Praise be to God who has made good to us His promise and given us the earth to inherit, that we may dwell in Paradise wherever we please.' Blessed is the 39:74 reward of the righteous.

39:75    You shall see the angels circling about the Throne, giving glory to their Lord. They shall be judged with fairness, and all shall say: 'Praise be to God, Lord of the Universe!'

# THE BELIEVER[1]

*In the Name of God, the Compassionate, the Merciful*

40:1    *Ḥā' mīm.* This Book is revealed by God, the Mighty One, the All-knowing, who forgives sin and accepts repentance.

His punishment is stern, and His bounty infinite. There is no god but Him. All shall return to Him.

None but the unbelievers dispute the revelations of God. Do not be deceived by their prosperous dealings in the land. Before them the people of Noah also disbelieved, and so did the factions after them. Each community strove to lay hands on their apostle, seeking with false arguments to refute the truth; but I smote them, and how stern was My punishment! Thus shall the word of your Lord be fulfilled concerning the unbelievers: they are the heirs of the Fire.

40:7    Those who bear the Throne and those who stand around it give glory to their Lord and believe in Him. They implore forgiveness for the faithful, saying: 'Lord, You embrace all things with Your mercy and Your knowledge. Forgive those that repent and follow Your path. Shield them from the scourge of Hell. Admit them, Lord, to the gardens of Eden which You have promised them, together with all the righteous among their fathers, their spouses, and their descendants. You are the Almighty, the Wise One. Shield them from all evil. He whom You will shield from evil on that day will surely earn Your mercy. That is the supreme triumph.'

But to the unbelievers a voice will cry: 'God's abhorrence of you is greater than your hatred of yourselves. You were called to the Faith, but you denied it.'

40:11    They shall say: 'Lord, twice have You made us die, and

1. This *sūrah* is also known by another title: 'The Forgiving One'.

twice have You given us life. We now confess our sins. Is there no way out?'

They shall be answered: 'This is because when God was 40:12 invoked alone, you disbelieved; but when you were bidden to serve other gods besides Him you believed in them. Today judgement rests with God, the Most High, the Supreme One.'

It is He who reveals His signs to you, and sends down sustenance from the sky for you. Yet none takes heed except the repentant. Pray, then, to God and worship none but Him, however much the unbelievers may dislike it.

Exalted and throned on high, He lets the Spirit descend at His behest on those of His servants whom He chooses, that He may warn them of the day when they shall meet Him; the day when they shall rise up from their graves with nothing hidden from God. And who shall reign supreme on that day? God, the One, the Almighty.

On that day every soul shall be recompensed according to what it did. On that day none shall be wronged. Swift is God's reckoning.

Forewarn them of the approaching day, when men's 40:18 hearts will leap up to their throats and choke them; when the wrongdoers will have neither friend nor intercessor to be heard. He knows the furtive look and the secret thought. God will judge with fairness, but the idols to which they pray besides Him can judge nothing. God alone hears all and observes all.

Have they never journeyed through the land and seen what was the end of those who have gone before them, nations far greater in prowess and in splendour? God scourged them for their sins, and from God they had no protector. That was because their apostles had come to them with veritable signs and they denied them. So God smote them. Mighty is God, and stern His retribution.

We sent forth Moses with Our signs and with clear authority to Pharaoh, Haman, and Korah. But they said: 'A sorcerer, a teller of lies.'

And when he brought them the Truth from Ourself, they 40:25

said: 'Put to death the sons of those who share his faith, and spare only their daughters.' Futile were the schemes of the unbelievers.

40:26 Pharaoh said: 'Let me slay Moses, and then let him invoke his god! I fear that he will change your religion and spread disorder in the land.'

Moses said: 'I take refuge in my Lord and in your Lord from every tyrant who denies the Day of Reckoning.'

But one of Pharaoh's kinsmen, who in secret was a true believer, said: 'Would you slay a man merely because he says: "My Lord is God"? He has brought you evident signs from your Lord. If he is lying, may his lie be on his head; but if he is speaking the truth, a part at least of what he threatens will smite you. God does not guide the lying transgressor. Today you are the masters, my people, illustrious throughout the earth. But who will save us from the might of God when it bears down upon us?'

Pharaoh said: 'I have told you what I think. I will surely guide you to the right path.'

40:30 He who was a true believer said: 'I warn you, my people, against the fate which overtook the factions: the people of Noah, 'Ād, and Thamūd, and those that came after them. God does not seek to wrong His servants.

'I warn you, my people, against the day when men will cry out to one another, when you will turn and flee, with none to defend you against God. He whom God confounds shall have none to guide him. Long before this, Joseph came to you with veritable signs, but you never ceased to doubt them; and when he died you said: "After him God will never send another apostle." Thus God confounds the doubting transgressor. Those who dispute God's revelations, with no authority vouchsafed to them, are held in deep abhorrence by God and by the faithful. Thus God seals up the heart of every scornful tyrant.'

Pharaoh said to Haman: 'Build me a tower that I may
40:37 reach the highways – the very highways – of the heavens, and look upon the god of Moses. I am convinced that he is lying.'

Thus was Pharaoh seduced by his foul deeds and was turned away from the right path. Pharaoh's cunning led only to perdition.

He who was a true believer said: 'Follow me, my people, 40:38 that I may guide you to the right path. My people, the life of this world is but a fleeting pleasure; the life to come is the everlasting mansion. Those that do evil shall be rewarded with evil; but those that have faith and do good works, both men and women, shall enter Paradise and therein receive blessings without number.

'My people, how is it that I call you to salvation, while you call me to the Fire? You bid me deny God and serve other gods I know nothing of; while I call you to the Almighty, the Forgiving One. Indeed, the gods to whom you call me can be invoked neither in this world nor in the world to come. To God we shall return. The transgressors shall be the inmates of the Fire.

'Bear in mind what I have told you. To God I commend myself. God is cognizant of all His servants.'

God delivered him from the evils which they planned, 40:45 and a grievous scourge encompassed Pharaoh's people. Before the Fire they shall be brought morning and evening, and on the day the Hour strikes, a voice will cry: 'Mete out the sternest punishment to Pharaoh's people!'

And when they argue in the Fire, the humble will say to those who deemed themselves mighty: 'We have been your followers: will you now ward off from us some of the flames?' But those who deemed themselves mighty will reply: 'Here are all of us now. God has judged His servants.'

And those in the Fire will say to the keepers of Hell: 'Implore your Lord to relieve our torment for a single day!'

'But did your apostles not come to you with undoubted signs?' they will ask.

'Yes,' they will answer. And their keepers will say: 'Then offer your prayers.' But vain shall be the prayers of the unbelievers.

We will surely help Our apostles and the true believers 40:51

both in this world and on the day when the witnesses rise to
40:52 testify. On that day no excuse will avail the guilty. The
Curse shall be their lot, and the scourge of the hereafter.

We gave Moses Our guidance and the Israelites the Book
to inherit: a guide and an admonition to men of understanding.
Therefore have patience; God's promise is surely true.
Implore forgiveness for your sins, and celebrate the praise
of your Lord evening and morning.

As for those who dispute the revelations of God, with no
authority vouchsafed to them, they nurture in their hearts
ambitions they shall never attain. Therefore seek refuge in
God; it is He that hears all and observes all.

Surely, the creation of the heavens and the earth is
greater than the creation of man; yet most have no knowledge.

The blind and the seeing are not equal, nor are the
wicked the equals of those that have faith and do good
works. Yet do you seldom take thought.

40:59 The Hour of Doom is sure to come: of this there is no
doubt; yet most do not believe.

Your Lord has said: 'Call on me and I will answer you.
Those that disdain My service shall enter Hell with all
humility.'

It was God who made for you the night to rest in and the
day to give you light. God is bountiful to people, yet most
do not give thanks.

Such is God your Lord, the Creator of all things. There is
no god but Him. How then can you turn away from Him?
Yet, even thus, those who deny God's revelations turn
away from Him.

It is God who has made the earth a dwelling-place for
you, and the sky a ceiling. He has moulded your bodies into
a comely shape and provided you with wholesome things.

Such is God, your Lord. Blessed be God, Lord of the
Universe.

40:65 He is the Living One; there is no god but Him. Pray to
Him, then, and worship none besides Him. Praise be to
God, Lord of the Universe!

Say: 'I am forbidden to serve your idols, now that clear 40:66
proofs have been given me from my Lord. I am commanded
to submit to the Lord of the Universe.'

It was He who created you from dust, then from a little
germ, and then from a clot of blood. He brings you as
infants into the world; you reach manhood, then decline
into old age (though some of you die young), so that you
may serve your appointed term and grow in wisdom.

It is He who ordains life and death. If He decrees a thing,
He need only say: 'Be,' and it is.

Do you not see how those who dispute the revelations of
God are turned away from the right path? Those who have
denied the Book and the message We sent through Our
apostles will learn hereafter: when, with chains and shackles
round their necks, they shall be dragged through scalding
water and burnt in the fire of Hell.

They will be asked: 'Where are the gods whom you have 40:72
served besides God?'

'They have forsaken us,' they will reply. 'Indeed, they
were nothing, those gods to whom we prayed.' Thus God
confounds the unbelievers.

And they will be told: 'That is because on earth you took
delight in falsehoods, and led a wanton life. Enter the gates
of Hell and stay therein for ever. Evil is the home of the
arrogant.'

Therefore have patience: God's promise is surely true.
Whether We let you[1] glimpse in some measure the scourge
We promise them, or claim you back before We smite them,
to Us shall they be recalled.

We sent forth other apostles before your time; of some
We have already told you, of others We have not yet told
you. None of those apostles could bring a sign except by
God's leave. And when God's will was done, justice
prevailed and there and then the disbelievers lost out.

It is God who has provided you with beasts, that you
may ride on some and eat the flesh of others. You put them 40:80

---

1. Muḥammad.

to many uses; they take you where you wish to go, carrying you by land as ships carry you by sea.

40:81    He reveals to you His signs. Which of God's signs do you deny?

Have they never journeyed through the land and seen what was the end of those who have gone before them? More numerous were they in the land, and far greater in prowess and in splendour; yet all their labours proved of no avail to them.

When their apostles brought them veritable signs they proudly boasted of their own knowledge; but soon the scourge they mocked encompassed them. And when they beheld Our might they said: 'We now believe in God alone. We deny the idols which We served besides Him.'

40:85    But their new faith was of no avail to them, when they beheld Our might: such being the way of God with His creatures; and there and then the unbelievers lost out.

# REVELATIONS WELL EXPOUNDED

*In the Name of God, the Compassionate, the Merciful*

41:1    *Ḥā' mīm.* Revealed by the Compassionate, the Merciful: a Book of revelations well expounded, an Arabic Koran for men of knowledge.

It proclaims good news and a warning: yet most men turn their backs and pay no heed. They say: 'Our hearts are proof against the faith to which you call us. Our ears are stopped, and a thick veil stands between us. Do as you think fit, and so will we.'

Say: 'I am but a mortal like yourselves. It is revealed to me that your God is one God. Therefore take the straight path to Him and implore His forgiveness. Woe betide those who

41:7    serve other gods besides Him; who give no alms and

disbelieve in the life to come. As for those who have faith 41:8
and do good works, an endless recompense awaits them.'

Say: 'Do you indeed disbelieve in Him who created the
earth in two days? And do you make other gods His equals?
The Lord of the Universe is He.'

He set upon the earth mountains towering high above it.
He pronounced His blessing upon it, and in four days
provided it with sustenance for all alike. Then, turning to
the sky, which was but a cloud of vapour, He said to it and
to the earth: 'Come forward both, willingly or perforce.'

'We will come willingly,' they answered. In two days He
formed the sky into seven heavens, and to each heaven He
assigned its task. We decked the lowest heaven with
brilliant stars and guardian comets. Such is the design of the
Mighty One, the All-knowing.

If they pay no heed, say: 'I have given you warning of a
thunderbolt, like the thunderbolt which struck ʿĀd and
Thamūd. When their apostles came to them from before
them and from behind them, saying: "Serve none but
God," they answered: "Had it been our Lord's will He
would have sent down angels. We will never believe in your
message."'

As for ʿĀd, they conducted themselves with arrogance 41:15
and injustice in the land. 'Who is mightier than we?' they
used to say. Could they not see that God, who had created
them, was mightier than they? Yet they denied Our revelations.

So, over a few ill-omened days We let loose on them a
howling gale, to make them taste a shameful scourge in this
nether life; but more shameful still will be the scourge of the
life to come. They shall have none to help them.

As for Thamūd, We offered them Our guidance, but they
preferred blindness to guidance. Therefore the thunderbolt
of a humiliating scourge struck them for their misdeeds;
and We delivered those who believed and those who feared
God.

Forewarn them of the day when the enemies of God will 41:19
be brought together and led into the Fire, so that when they

41:20 enter it, their ears, their eyes, and their very skins will testify to their misdeeds. 'Why did you speak against us?' they will say to their skins, and their skins will reply: 'God, who gives speech to all things, has made us speak. It was He who in the beginning created you, and to Him shall you be recalled. You did not hide yourselves, so that your ears and eyes and skins could not be made to testify against you. Yet you thought that God did not know much of what you did. It was the thoughts you entertained about your Lord that ruined you, so that you are now among the lost.'

If they resign themselves, the Fire shall be their home: and if they sue for pardon, their suit shall not be granted.

We have assigned to them companions who make their past and present seem fair and right to them. Well have they deserved the fate of bygone nations of jinn and men. They shall assuredly be lost.

41:26 The unbelievers say: 'Pay no heed to this Koran. Cut short its recital with booing and laughter, so that you may gain the upper hand.'

We will sternly punish the unbelievers, and pay them back for the worst of their misdeeds. Thus shall the enemies of God be recompensed. The Fire shall for ever be their home, because they have denied Our revelations.

The unbelievers will say: 'Lord, show us the jinn and men who led us astray. We will trample them under our feet and bring them low.'

As for those who say: 'Our Lord is God,' and take the straight path to Him, the angels will descend to them, saying: 'Have no fear, and do not grieve. Rejoice in the Paradise you have been promised. We are your guardians in this world and in the world to come. There you shall find all that your souls desire and all that you can ask for: a rich provision from a forgiving and a merciful God.'

And who speaks better than he who calls men to the service of God, does what is right, and says: 'I am a Muslim'?

41:34 Good deeds and evil deeds are not equal. Requite evil with good, and he who is your enemy will become your dearest friend. But none will attain this attribute save those who 41:35 patiently endure; none will attain it save those who are truly fortunate.

If Satan tempts you, seek refuge in God. It is God who hears all and knows all.

Among His signs are the night and the day, and the sun and the moon. But do not prostrate yourselves before the sun or the moon; rather prostrate yourselves before God, who created them both, if you would truly serve Him.

If they[1] disdain His service, let them remember that those who dwell with God give glory to Him night and day and are never wearied.

And among His signs is the resurrection of the earth. You see it dry and barren: but when We send down the rain upon it, it stirs and swells. He that gives it life will surely raise the dead to life. He has power over all things.

Those that deny Our revelations are not hidden from 41:40 Our view. Is he who is cast into the Fire better off than he who emerges safe on the Day of Resurrection? Do as you will, He is watching all your actions.

Those who deny the Admonition when it is preached to them [shall be sternly punished]. It is a mighty scripture. Falsehood cannot reach it from before or from behind. It is a revelation from a wise and glorious God.

Nothing is said to you that has not been said to other apostles before you. Your Lord is forgiving, but stern in retribution.

Had We revealed the Koran in a foreign tongue they would have said: 'If only its verses were expounded! Why in a foreign tongue, and he an Arabian?'

Say: 'To true believers it is a guide and a healing balm. But those who deny it are deaf and blind. They are like men who are called to from a far-off place.'

We gave the Torah to Moses, but contentions arose 41:45 about it. And but for a word from your Lord, long since

---

1. The pagans.

decreed, their differences would have been justly settled, grave though their doubts were about it.

41:46 He that does good does it for his own soul; and he that commits evil does so at his own peril. Your Lord is never unjust to His servants.

He alone has knowledge of the Hour of Doom. No fruit is borne, no female conceives or gives birth, but with His knowledge.

On a certain day He will call mankind to Him and say: 'Where are those fellow-gods of Mine?'

'We confess,' they will reply, 'that none of us can vouch for them.' The idols to which they once prayed will vanish from them, and they shall learn there is no escape.

Man never wearies of praying for good things. But when evil befalls him he loses hope and grows despondent. And if 41:50 after affliction We vouchsafe him a favour from Ourself, he is sure to say: 'This is my own. I do not think the Hour of Doom will ever come. And even if I do return to my Lord, He will surely reward me well.' We shall tell the unbelievers what they did, and We will surely visit upon them a grievous scourge.

When We show favour to man, he turns his back and holds aloof; but when evil befalls him he is loud in prayer.

Say: 'Do but consider: if this Koran is indeed from God and you deny it, who can err more than the man who openly defies Him?'

We will show them Our signs in all the regions of the earth and in their own souls, until they clearly see that this is the truth. Does it not suffice that your Lord is the witness of all things?

41:54 Yet they still doubt that they will ever meet their Lord. Surely He encompasses all things.

# COUNSEL

*In the Name of God, the Compassionate, the Merciful*

42:1 Ḥā' mīm: 'ain sīn qāf. Thus God, the Mighty One, the Wise

One, inspires you as He inspired others before you.

His is what the heavens and the earth contain. He is the 42:4
Most High, the Supreme One.

The heavens above well-nigh split asunder as the angels
give glory to their Lord and beg forgiveness for those on
earth. Surely God is the Forgiving One, the Merciful.

As for those that serve other masters besides Him, God
Himself is watching them. You are not accountable for
what they do.

Thus have We revealed to you an Arabic Koran, that you
may warn the mother-city[1] and those who dwell around it;
that you may forewarn them of the day which is sure to
come: when all are brought together, some in Paradise and
some in the blazing Fire.

Had it been God's will, He could have united them in
one community. But God brings whom He will into His
mercy; the wrongdoers have none to befriend or help them.

Have they set up other guardians besides Him? Surely 42:9
God alone is the Guardian. He resurrects the dead and has
power over all things.

Whatever the subject of your disputes, the final word
belongs to God. Such is God, my Lord. In Him I have put
my trust, and to Him I turn in penitence.

Creator of the heavens and the earth, He has given you
spouses from among yourselves, and cattle male and female;
by this means He multiplies His creatures. Nothing can be
compared with Him. He alone hears all and sees all.

His are the keys of the heavens and the earth. He gives
abundantly to whom He will and sparingly to whom He
pleases. He has knowledge of all things.

He has ordained for you the faith which He enjoined on
Noah, and which We have revealed to you; which We 42:13
enjoined on Abraham, Moses, and Jesus, saying: 'Observe
the Faith and do not divide yourselves into factions.' But
hard for the pagans is that to which you call them. God
chooses for it whom He will, and guides to it those that repent.

---

1. Mecca.

42:14     Yet men did not divide themselves, through their own wickedness, until knowledge was given them. And but for a word that had already gone forth from your Lord reprieving them for an appointed term, their fate would have been justly settled. Those who inherited the Scriptures after them have their grave doubts too.

42:15     Therefore call men to the true Faith, and follow the straight path as you are commanded. Do not be led by their desires, but say: 'I believe in all the scriptures that God has revealed. I am commanded to exercise justice among you. God is our Lord and your Lord. We have our own works and you have yours; let there be no argument between us. God will bring us all together, for to Him we shall return.'

As for those who argue about God after pledging obedience to Him, their arguments will have no weight with their Lord, and His wrath will fall upon them. Grievous punishment awaits them.

It is God who has revealed the Book with truth and justice. And how can you tell? The Hour of Doom may be fast approaching.

42:18     Those who deny it seek to hurry it on; but the true believers dread its coming, and know it is the truth. Indeed, those who doubt the Hour have strayed far into error.

Benign is God towards His servants. He is bountiful to whom He will. He is the Invincible One, the Almighty.

Whoever seeks the harvest of the world to come, to him We will give in great abundance; and whoever desires the harvest of this world, a share of it shall be his: but in the world to come he shall have no share at all.

Have they idols which in the practice of their faith have made lawful to them what God has not allowed? Had the decisive word not been pronounced already, their fate would have long been sealed. Woeful punishment awaits the wrongdoers.

42:22     You shall behold the wrongdoers aghast at their own deeds, for then Our scourge will surely smite them. But those that have faith and do good works shall dwell in the fair gardens of Paradise, and shall receive from their Lord all that they desire. Surely that will be the supreme boon.

Such is God's promise to His servants who believe and do 42:23 good works. Say: 'For this I demand of you no recompense. I ask you only to love your kindred. He that does a good deed shall be repaid many times over. God is forgiving and bountiful in His rewards.'

Do they say: 'He has framed a falsehood about God?' But if God pleased, He could seal your heart. God will bring falsehood to nothing and vindicate the truth by His words. He surely knows the innermost thoughts of men.

He accepts the repentance of His servants, and pardons their sins. He has knowledge of all your actions.

He answers those who have faith and do good works, and enriches them through His bounty. But grievous punishment awaits the unbelievers.

Had God bestowed abundance upon His servants, they 42:27 would have committed much injustice in the land. But He gives them what He will in due measure; He knows and observes His servants.

It is He who sends down the rain when they have lost all hope, and spreads abroad His mercy. He is the Guardian worthy of praise.

Among His signs is the creation of the heavens and the earth and the living things He has dispersed over them. If He will, He can gather them all together.

Whatever misfortune befalls you, it is the fruit of your own labours. He forgives much.

On the earth you cannot escape, nor have you any besides God to protect or help you.

And among His signs are the ships which sail like mountains upon the ocean. If He will, He calms the wind, so that they lie motionless upon its bosom[1] (surely there are signs in this for steadfast men who render thanks); or causes them to founder as punishment for their misdeeds.[2] Yet 42:34 many are the sins that He forgives.

---

1. Literally, back.    2. The misdeeds of those who sail in them.

42:35    Those who dispute Our revelations shall learn they have no escape.

That which you have been given is but the fleeting pleasure of this life. Better and more enduring is God's recompense to those who believe and put their trust in Him; who avoid grievous sins and lewd acts and, when angered, are willing to forgive; who obey their Lord, attend to their prayers, and conduct their affairs by mutual consent; who give in alms from what We gave them and, when oppressed, seek to redress their wrongs.

Let evil be rewarded with evil. But he that forgives and seeks reconcilement shall be recompensed by God. He does not love the wrongdoers.

Those who seek to redress their wrongs incur no guilt. But great is the guilt of those who oppress their fellow men and conduct themselves with wickedness and injustice in the land. Woeful punishment awaits them.

42:43    To endure with fortitude and to forgive is a duty incumbent on all. He whom God confounds has none to protect him.

When they face the scourge, you shall see the wrongdoers exclaim: 'Is there no way back?' You shall see them ranged before the Fire. Awed and humiliated, they shall look upon it with furtive glances. The true believers will say: 'The losers are those who forfeited their souls and all their kindred on the Day of Resurrection.'

The wrongdoers shall surely suffer everlasting torment. They shall have no friends besides God to help them. He whom God confounds shall be lost indeed.

Obey your Lord before that day arrives which none can put off against the will of God. There shall be no refuge for you on that day, nor shall you deny your sins.

42:48    If they pay no heed, know that We have not sent you[1] to be their keeper. Your only duty is to give warning.

When We give man a taste of Our mercy, he rejoices in it;

---

1. Muḥammad.

but when through his own fault evil befalls him, man is ungrateful.

God has sovereignty over the heavens and the earth. He 42:49 creates what He will. He gives daughters to whom He will and sons to whom He pleases. To some He gives both sons and daughters, and He makes sterile whom He will. Omniscient is God, and mighty.

It is not vouchsafed to any mortal that God should speak to him except by revelation, or from behind a veil, or through a messenger sent and authorized by Him to make known His will. Exalted is He, and wise.

Thus have We inspired you[1] with a spirit of Our will when you knew nothing of faith or scripture, and made it a light whereby We guide those of Our servants whom We please. You will surely guide them to a straight path: the path of God, to whom belongs all that the heavens and the 42:53 earth contain. Surely to God all things shall in the end return.


# ORNAMENTS OF GOLD

*In the Name of God, the Compassionate, the Merciful*

Ḥā' mīm. By the Glorious Book! 43:1

We have revealed the Koran in the Arabic tongue that you may understand its meaning. It is a transcript of the eternal book in Our keeping, sublime, and full of wisdom.

Should We ignore you because you are a sinful nation? Many a prophet did We send forth to the ancients: but they mocked each prophet that arose among them. We utterly destroyed them, though they were mightier than these.[2]

Such then, is the example of the ancients. Yet, if you ask them[2] who created the heavens and the earth, they are bound to answer: 'The Almighty, the All-knowing, created them.'

It is He who has made the earth a resting-place for you 43:10

1. Muḥammad.    2. The Meccans.

343

and traced out routes upon it that you may find your way;
43:11 who sends down water from the sky in due measure and
thereby resurrects a dead land (even thus shall you be raised
to life); who has created all living things in pairs and made
for you the ships and beasts on which you ride, so that, as
you mount upon their backs, you may recall the goodness
of your Lord and say: 'Glory to Him who has subjected
these to us. But for Him we could not be their masters. To
our Lord we shall surely return.'

Yet they[1] assign to Him offspring from among His
servants. Surely man is monstrously ungrateful. Would
God choose daughters for Himself and sons for you alone?[2]

Yet when the birth of a girl is announced to any of them
his countenance darkens and he is filled with gloom. Would
they ascribe to God females who adorn themselves with
trinkets and are powerless in disputation?

They regard as females the angels who are God's servants.
Did they witness their creation? Their testimony shall be
noted down. They shall be closely questioned.

43:20 They say: 'Had it been the will of the Merciful, we should
never have worshipped them.' Surely of this they have no
knowledge: they are only lying.

Or have We given them a scripture before this, so that
they should hold fast to it?

Indeed, they say: 'This was the faith our fathers practised.
We are merely walking in their footsteps.'

Thus, whenever, before you, We sent an apostle to
forewarn a nation, those who lived in comfort said: 'This
was the faith our fathers practised; we are merely following
in their footsteps.'

Each apostle said: 'What if I bring you a faith more
enlightened than your fathers'?' But they replied: 'We reject
43:25 the message you have been sent with.' So We took vengeance on them. Consider the fate of those who disbelieved.

1. The Meccans.

2. The pagan Arabs believed that the angels, and their own
goddesses, were daughters of Allāh.

Tell of Abraham, who said to his father and to his people: 43:26
'I renounce the gods you worship, except Him who created
me, for He will rightly guide me.' He made this an abiding
precept among his descendants, so that they might for ever
turn to Him.

Indeed, I made things pleasant for these and for their
fathers until there came to them the truth and an undoubted
apostle. But now that the truth has come to them, they say:
'This is sorcery. We utterly reject it.' They also say: 'Why
has this Koran not been revealed to some important man
from the two towns?' [1]

Is it they who apportion your Lord's blessings? It is We
who deal out to them their livelihood in this world, exalting
some in rank above others, so that the one may take the
other into his service. Better is your Lord's mercy than all
their hoarded treasures.

But for the fear that all mankind might have become one 43:33
race of unbelievers, We would have given those who denied
the Lord of Mercy dwellings with silver roofs, and gates
and stairs of silver; silver couches to recline upon and ornaments of gold: for all these are but the fleeting baubles of
this life. It is the life to come that your Lord reserves for
those who fear Him.

He that does not heed the warning of the Merciful shall
have a devil for his companion (devils turn men away from
the right path, though they may think themselves rightly
guided). And when he comes before Us, he shall say: [2]
'Would that we were as far apart as the East is from the
West.' Evil indeed is that companion.

But on that day, because you have done wrong, the
thought that you will share the scourge with others will not
console you.

Can you make the deaf hear, or guide the blind or those
in grievous error? Whether We take you hence or let you
live to see Our promises fulfilled, We shall surely be
avenged; for We have power over them.                    43:42

1. Mecca and Medina.    2. To his companion.

345

43:43   Therefore hold fast to that which was revealed to you: you are on a straight path. It is an admonition to you and to your people. You shall be questioned all.

Ask those of Our apostles whom We sent before you if We ever appointed gods besides the Merciful to be worshipped.

We sent forth Moses with Our signs to Pharaoh and his nobles. He said: 'I am the apostle of the Lord of the Universe.' But when he showed them Our signs they laughed at them; yet each fresh sign We revealed to them was more powerful than the one that came before. We therefore smote them with the scourge, so that they might return to the right path.

'Sorcerer,' they said, 'pray for us to your Lord and invoke the promise He has made you. We will accept your guidance.'

But when We removed the scourge from them, they broke their pledge.

43:51   Pharaoh made a proclamation to his people. 'My people,' said he, 'is the kingdom of Egypt not mine, and are these rivers which flow at my feet not mine also? Can you not see? Am I not better than this despicable wretch, who can scarcely make his meaning plain? Why have no bracelets of gold been given him, or angels sent down to accompany him?'

Thus did he incite his people. They obeyed him, for they were degenerate men. And when they provoked Us, We took vengeance on them and drowned them all, as a lesson and an example to those who succeeded them.

When Mary's son is cited as an example, your people laugh and say: 'Who is better, he or our gods?' They cite him to you merely to provoke you. They are indeed a contentious nation.

He was but a mortal whom We favoured and made an example to the Israelites. Had it been Our will, We could have turned you into angels, your successors on the earth.

He is a portent of the Hour of Doom. Have no doubt
43:62 about its coming and follow Me. This is a straight path: let not Satan debar you, for he is your inveterate foe.

And when Jesus came with evident signs, he said: 'I have  43:63
come to give you wisdom, and to make plain to you some
of the things you differ about. Fear God and follow me.
God is my Lord and your Lord: therefore serve Him. That
is a straight path.'

Yet the factions disagreed among themselves. But woe
betide the wrongdoers, for they shall suffer the anguish of a
woeful day.

Are they waiting for the Hour of Doom to take them
unawares, without warning? Friends shall on that day
become enemies to one another, except the God-fearing.

But you, My servants, who have believed in Our revelations and submitted to Our will, shall on that day have
nothing to fear or to regret. Enter Paradise, you and your
spouses, in all delight. You shall be served with golden
dishes and golden cups. Abiding there for ever, you shall
find all that your souls desire and all that your eyes rejoice in.

Such is the Paradise you shall inherit by virtue of your  43:72
good deeds. Your sustenance shall be abundant fruit.

But the evil-doers shall endure for ever the torment of
Hell, which will not be assuaged for them; they shall be
speechless with despair. We did not wrong them, but they
themselves did wrong.

'Mālik,'[1] they will call out, 'let your Lord make an end of
us!' But he will answer: 'Here you shall remain!'

We have made known to you the truth, but most of you
abhor the truth.

If they are resolved to ruin you,[2] We are resolved to ruin
them. Do they think We cannot hear their secret talk and
private converse? Yes! Our angels, who are at their side,
record it all.

Say:[3] 'If the Lord of Mercy had a son, I would be the first
to worship him.'

Exalted be the Lord of the heavens and the earth, the
Lord of the Throne, above their falsehoods! Let them  43:83

---

1. One of the keepers of Hell.    2. Muḥammad.
3. To the Christians.

paddle, let them play, until they face the day they are promised.

43:84 It is He who is God in heaven and God on earth; He is the Wise One, the All-knowing. Blessed be He who has sovereignty over the heavens and the earth and all that lies between them! He alone has knowledge of the Hour of Doom, and to Him shall you be recalled.

The gods to whom they pray besides Him have not the power to intercede for them. None can intercede for them save him who knows the truth and testifies to it.

Yet if you ask them who created them, they will surely say, 'God.' How then can they turn away from Him?

The Apostle says: 'Lord, these men are unbelievers.'

43:89 Bear with them and wish them peace. They shall learn.

# SMOKE

*In the Name of God, the Compassionate, the Merciful*

44:1 *Ḥā' mīm.* By the Glorious Book, We revealed it[1] on a blessed night to give warning; on a night when every precept was made plain as a commandment from Ourself. We sent it down as a blessing from your Lord. He hears all and knows all.

He is the Lord of the heavens and the earth and all that lies between them. (Mark this, if you are true believers.) There is no god but Him. He ordains life and death. He is your God and the God of your forefathers. Yet they divert themselves with doubts.

Wait for the day when the sky will pour down palpable smoke, enveloping mankind: a woeful scourge. Then will they say: 'Lord, lift the scourge from us. We are now believers.' But how will their new faith help them, when an undoubted apostle did come to them and they denied him, saying: 'A madman, taught by others!'

44:15 Yet if We but slightly ease your torment, you will return

---

1. The Koran.

to unbelief. On the day We bring down the supreme 44:16
scourge We will surely be avenged.

We tested Pharaoh's people long before them. A gracious
apostle came to them, saying: 'Hand over to me God's
servants. I am a truthful messenger. Do not hold yourselves
above God. I bring you clear authority. I adjure you by
Him who is my Lord and your Lord not to stone me. If you
have no faith in me, leave me to myself.'

Then he cried out to his Lord, saying: 'These are sinful
men.'

He answered: 'Set forth with My servants in the night,
for you will be pursued. Leave the sea at rest behind you.
They are warriors doomed to drown.'

How many gardens, how many fountains, they left
behind them! Cornfields, and noble palaces, and good
things in which they took delight. All this they left; and
what was once theirs We gave to other men. Neither heaven
nor earth shed tears for them; nor were they reprieved. We 44:30
saved the Israelites from the degrading scourge, from
Pharaoh, who was a tyrant and a transgressor, and chose
them knowingly above the nations. We showed them
miracles which tested them beyond all doubt.

Yet the unbelievers say: 'We shall die but one death, nor
shall we ever be raised to life. Bring back to us our fathers,
if what you say be true.'

Are they better than the people of Tubba'[1] and those
who thrived before them? We destroyed them all, for they
too were wicked men.

It was not in jest that We created the heavens and the
earth and all that lies between them. We created them
to reveal the truth. But of this most men have no
knowledge.

The Day of Judgement is the appointed time for all. On
that day no friend shall help a friend; none shall be helped
save those to whom God shows mercy. He is the Mighty 44:42
One, the Merciful.

1. The people of Himyar, in Arabia.

44:43    The fruit of the Zaqqūm tree shall be the sinner's food. Like dregs of oil, like scalding water, it shall simmer in his belly. A voice will cry: 'Seize him and drag him into the depths of Hell. Then pour out scalding water over his head, saying: "Taste this, illustrious and honourable man! This is the punishment which you have doubted."'

As for the righteous, they shall be lodged in peace together amid gardens and fountains, arrayed in rich silks and fine brocade. Even thus: and We shall wed them to dark-eyed houris. Secure against all ills, they shall call for every kind of fruit; and, having died once, they shall die no more. Your Lord will in His mercy shield them from the scourge of Hell. That will be the supreme triumph.

We have revealed this to you in your own tongue so that
44:59 they may take heed. Wait, then; they too are waiting.

# KNEELING

*In the Name of God, the Compassionate, the Merciful*

45:1    Ḥā' mīm. This Book is revealed by God, the Mighty One, the Wise One.

Surely in the heavens and the earth there are signs for the faithful; in your own creation, and in the beasts He scatters far and near, signs for true believers; in the alternation of night and day, in the sustenance God sends down from heaven with which He resurrects the earth after its death, and in the marshalling of the winds, signs for men of understanding.

Such are God's revelations. We recite them to you in all truth. But in what scripture will they believe, if they deny God Himself and all His signs?

Woe betide the lying sinner! He hears God's revelations recited to Him and then, as though he never heard them, persists in scorn. Forewarn him of a woeful scourge. Those that deride Our revelations when they know little of them shall suffer degrading torment.

45:10    Hell is behind them. Their gains shall not avail them, nor shall the masters they have served besides God. Grievous punishment awaits them.

Such is Our guidance. Those that deny their Lord's 45:11 revelations shall suffer the anguish of a woeful scourge.

It is God who has subdued the ocean for you, so that ships may sail upon it at His bidding; so that you may seek His bounty and render thanks.

He has subjected to you what the heavens and the earth contain; all is from Him. Surely there are signs in this for thinking men.

Tell the believers to pardon those who dread the days of victory,[1] when God will reward men according to their deeds. He that does what is right does it for his own good; and he that commits evil does so at his own peril. Then to your Lord shall you be recalled.

We gave the Book to the Israelites and bestowed on them wisdom and prophethood. We provided them with wholesome things and exalted them above the nations. We gave them clear commandments: yet it was not till knowledge had been vouchsafed them that they disagreed maliciously among themselves. Your Lord will on the Day of Resurrection judge their differences.

And now We have set you on the right path. Follow it, 45:18 and do not yield to the desires of ignorant men; for they can in no way protect you from the wrath of God. The wrongdoers are patrons to each other; but the righteous have God Himself for their patron.

This is an admonition to mankind; a guide and a blessing to true believers.

Do the evil-doers think that they are equal in Our sight to those who believe and do good works, so that their lives and deaths shall be alike? How ill they judge!

God created the heavens and the earth to manifest the truth, and to recompense each soul according to its deeds. None shall be wronged.

Think! Who, besides God, can guide the man who makes 45:23

1. Literally, the days of God.

his lust his god, the man whom God deliberately confounds, setting a seal upon his ears and heart and drawing a veil over his eyes? Will you not take heed?

45:24  They say: 'There is this life and no other. We die and live; nothing but Time destroys us.' Surely of this they have no knowledge. They are merely guessing.

And when Our revelations are recited to them in all their clarity, their only argument is: 'Bring back to us our fathers, if what you say be true!'

Say: 'It is God who gives you life and then He causes you to die. It is He who will gather you all on the Day of Resurrection. Of this there is no doubt; yet most do not know it.'

It is God who has sovereignty over the heavens and the earth. On the day when the Hour strikes, those who have denied His revelations will assuredly lose all.

You shall see each community on its knees. Each community shall be summoned to its book, and a voice will say: 'You shall this day be rewarded for your deeds. This book of Ours speaks with truth against you. We have recorded all your actions.'

45:30  As for those who have faith and do good works, their Lord will admit them into His mercy. That shall be the glorious triumph.

To the unbelievers a voice will say: 'Were My revelations not declared to you? Did you not scorn them and commit evil? When you were told: "God's promise is true: the Hour of Doom is sure to come," you replied: "We know nothing of the Hour of Doom. It is but a vain conjecture, nor are we convinced."'

The evil of their deeds will manifest itself to them, and the scourge at which they scoffed will encompass them. We shall say: 'We will today forget you, as you yourselves forgot that you would meet this day. The Fire shall be your

45:35  home and none will help you. That is because you scoffed at God's revelations and were seduced by your earthly life.'

On that day there shall be no way out for them; nor shall they be asked to make amends.

Praise, then, be to God, Lord of the heavens and Lord of the earth, Lord of the Universe. Supremacy be His in the 45:37 heavens and on earth. He is the Mighty One, the Wise One.

# THE SAND DUNES

*In the Name of God, the Compassionate, the Merciful*

*Ḥā' mīm.* This Book is revealed by God, the Mighty One, 46:1 the Wise One.

It was but to manifest the Truth that We created the heavens and the earth and all that lies between them; We created them to last for an appointed term. Yet the unbelievers pay no heed to Our warning.

Say: 'Have you pondered on those whom you invoke besides God? Show me what part of the earth they have created! Have they a share in the heavens? Bring me a scripture revealed before this, or some other vestige of divine knowledge, if what you say be true.'

Who is in greater error than the man who prays to idols which will never hear him till the Day of Resurrection – which are, indeed, unconscious of his prayers; which, when all mankind are called together, will declare themselves their enemies and will disown their worship.

When Our revelations are recited to them, clear as they 46:7 are, the unbelievers say: 'This is plain sorcery.' Such is their description of the truth when it is declared to them.

Do they say: 'He has invented it[1] himself'?

Say: 'If I have indeed invented it, then there is nothing you can do to shield me from the wrath of God. He well knows what you say about it. Sufficient is He as my witness, and your witness. He is the Forgiving One, the Merciful.'

Say: 'I am no prodigy among the apostles; nor do I know 46:9 what will be done with me or you. I follow only what is revealed to me, and my only duty is to give plain warning.'

1. The Koran.

46:10 Say: 'Think if this Koran is indeed from God and you reject it; if an Israelite[1] has vouched for it and accepted Islām, while you yourselves deny it with disdain. Surely, God does not guide the wrongdoers.'

The unbelievers say of the faithful: 'Had there been any good in it[2] they would not have believed in it before us.' And since they reject its guidance, they say: 'This is an ancient falsehood.'

Yet before it the Book of Moses was revealed: a guide and a blessing. This Book confirms it. It is revealed in the Arabic tongue, to forewarn the wrongdoers and to give good tidings to the righteous.

Those that say: 'Our Lord is God,' and follow the straight path shall have nothing to fear or to regret. They are the heirs of Paradise, there to dwell for ever as a reward for their labours.

46:15 We have enjoined man to show kindness to his parents. With much pain his mother bears him, and with much pain she brings him into the world. He is born and weaned in thirty months. When he grows to manhood and attains his fortieth year, let him say: 'Inspire me, Lord, to give thanks for the favours You have bestowed on me and on my parents, and to do good works that will please You. Grant me good descendants. To You I turn and to You I submit.

Such are those from whom We will accept their noblest works and whose misdeeds We shall overlook. We shall admit them among the heirs of Paradise: true is the promise that has been given them.

But he that rebukes his parents and says to them: 'For shame! Do you threaten me with a resurrection, when generations have passed away before me?' – he that, when they pray for God's help and say: 'Woe betide you! Have faith. The promise of God is true,' replies: 'This is but a fable of the ancients' – shall justly deserve the fate of

46:18 bygone nations of jinn and men: he shall assuredly be lost.

1. 'Abdullāh b. Salām, according to the commentators.
2. The Koran.

354

There are rewards for all, according to their deeds, so 46:19
that He may duly requite them for their works. They shall
not be wronged.

The day the unbelievers are exposed before the Fire, We
shall say to them: 'You squandered away your precious gifts
in your earthly life, and took your fill of pleasure. Today
your reward will be degrading torment, because you acted
with pride and injustice in the land and committed evil.'

Tell of 'Ād's kinsman who warned his people in the
Valley of the Sand Dunes (and there have been other
apostles before and since his time), saying: 'Serve none but
God. Beware the torment of a fateful day.'

They replied: 'Have you come to turn us away from our
gods? Bring down the scourge you threaten us with, if what
you say be true!'

He said: 'God alone knows when it will come. I am here
to convey to you the message. But I can see that you are
ignorant men.'

And when they saw a cloud heading for their valleys, 46:24
they said: 'Here is a passing cloud that will bring us
rain.'

'By no means!' he replied. 'It is what you have sought to
hasten: a hurricane bringing a woeful scourge. It will lay
everything waste at the bidding of its Lord.'

And when morning came there was nothing to be seen
besides their ruined dwellings. Thus do We reward the
wrongdoers.

We had made them as powerful as yourselves,[1] and given
them ears and eyes and hearts. Yet nothing did their ears,
their eyes, or their hearts avail them since they denied the
revelations of God. The scourge they mocked encompassed
them.

We destroyed the cities which once flourished around
you, and made plain Our revelations to their people, so that
they might return to the right path. Why did their gods not 46:28
help them, the gods they had set up besides God to bring

1. The Meccans.

them close to Him? Indeed, they utterly forsook them. Such were their lies, and such their false inventions.

46:29 Tell how We sent to you a band of jinn who, when they came and listened to the Koran, said to each other: 'Hush! Hush!' As soon as it was ended they betook themselves to their people to give them warning. 'Our people,' they said, 'we have just been listening to a scripture revealed since the time of Moses, confirming previous scriptures and pointing to the truth and to a straight path. Our people, answer the call of God's summoner and believe in Him! He will forgive you your sins and deliver you from a woeful scourge. Those

46:32 that pay no heed to God's summoner shall not go unpunished on the earth. There shall be none to protect them besides Him. Surely they are in evident error.'

Do they not see that God, who created the heavens and the earth and was not wearied by their creation, has power to raise the dead to life? Yes. He has power over all things.

The day the unbelievers are arrayed before the Fire they shall be asked: 'Is this not real?' 'Yes, by the Lord,' they will answer. 'Then taste the scourge,' He will reply, 'for you were unbelievers.'

46:35 Bear up then with patience, as did the steadfast apostles before you, and do not seek to hurry on their doom. The day they behold the scourge they are promised, their life on earth will seem to them no longer than an hour.

That is a warning. Shall any be destroyed except the evildoers?

# MUḤAMMAD

*In the Name of God, the Compassionate, the Merciful*

47:1 GOD WILL bring to nothing the deeds of those who disbelieve and debar others from His path. As for the faithful who do good works and believe in what has been revealed to Muḥammad – which is the Truth from their Lord – He will forgive them their sins and ennoble their state.

This, because the unbelievers follow falsehood, while the 47:3 faithful follow the truth from their Lord. Thus God lays down for mankind their rules of conduct.

When you meet the unbelievers in the battlefield strike off their heads and, when you have laid them low, bind your captives firmly. Then grant them their freedom or take a ransom from them, until War shall lay down her burdens.

Thus shall you do. Had God willed, He could Himself have punished them; [but He has ordained it thus] that He may test you, the one by the other.

As for those who are slain in the cause of God, He will not allow their works to perish. He will vouchsafe them guidance and ennoble their state; He will admit them to the Paradise He has made known to them.

Believers, if you help God, God will help you and make you strong. But the unbelievers shall be consigned to perdition. He will bring their deeds to nothing. Because they have abhorred His revelations, He will frustrate their works.

Have they never journeyed through the land and seen 47:10 what was the end of those who have gone before them? God destroyed them utterly. A similar fate awaits the unbelievers, because God is the protector of the faithful: because the unbelievers have no protector.

God will admit those who embrace the true Faith and do good works to gardens watered by running streams. The unbelievers take their fill of pleasure and eat as cattle eat: but the Fire shall be their home.

How many cities were mightier than your own city, which has cast you[1] out! We destroyed them all, and there was none to help them.

Can he who follows the guidance of his Lord be compared to him who is led by his desires and whose foul deeds seem fair to him?

Such is the Paradise which the righteous have been 47:15 promised: Therein shall flow rivers of water undefiled, and rivers of milk for ever fresh; rivers of wine delectable to

1. Muhammad.

those that drink it, and rivers of clarified honey. There shall they eat of every fruit, and receive forgiveness from their Lord. Are they to be compared to those who shall abide in Hell for ever, and drink scalding water which will tear their bowels?

47:16 Some of them indeed listen to you, but no sooner do they leave your presence than they ask those endowed with knowledge: 'What did he say just now?' Such are the men whose hearts are sealed by God, and who follow their base desires.

As for those who follow the right path, He will increase their guidance and show them the way to righteousness.

Are they waiting for the Hour of Doom to overtake them unawares? Its portents have already come. How else will they be warned when it does overtake them?

Know that there is no deity but God. Implore Him to forgive your sins and to forgive the true believers, men and women. God knows your busy haunts and resting-places.

The faithful say: 'If only a Chapter were revealed!' But when a forthright Chapter is revealed and war is mentioned in it, you see the infirm of heart staring at you as though they are 47:21 fainting away for fear of death. Yet obedience and courteous speech would become them more. Indeed, should war be decided upon, it would be better for them to be true to God.

If you[1] renounced the Faith, you would surely do evil in the land and violate the ties of blood. Such are those on whom God has laid His curse, leaving them deaf and sightless.

Will they not ponder on the Koran? Are there locks upon their hearts?

Those who return to unbelief after God's guidance has been revealed to them are seduced by Satan and inspired by him. That is because they say to those who abhor the Word of God: 'We shall obey you in *some* matters.' God knows their secret talk.

What will they do when the angels carry off their souls, striking their faces and their backs?

47:28 That is because they follow what has incurred the wrath

---

1. The hypocrites.

of God and abhor what pleases Him. He will surely bring their works to nothing.

Or do the feeble-hearted think that God will not reveal their malice? If We pleased, We could point them out to you and you would recognize them promptly by their looks. But you will surely know them from the tenor of their words. God has knowledge of all your actions. 47:29

We shall put you to the proof until We know the valiant and the resolute among you, and test all that is said about you.

The unbelievers who debar others from the path of God and disobey the Apostle after they have seen the light shall in no way harm God. He will bring their works to nothing.

Believers, obey God and obey the Apostle, and let not your labours come to nothing.

Those that disbelieve and debar others from God's path and in the end die unbelievers shall not be shown forgiveness by God. Therefore do not falter or sue for peace when you have gained the upper hand. God is on your side and will not grudge you the recompense of your labours. 47:34

The life of this world is but a sport and a diversion. He will reward you if you believe in Him and guard yourselves against evil. He does not ask for all your wealth. If He demanded all and strongly pressed you, you would grow tight-fisted, and this would show your malice.

You are called upon to give in the cause of God. Some among you are ungenerous; yet whoever is ungenerous to this cause is ungenerous to himself. Indeed, God does not need you, but you need Him. If you pay no heed, He will replace you by others who shall bear no resemblance to yourselves. 47:38

# VICTORY

*In the Name of God, the Compassionate, the Merciful*

WE HAVE given you[1] a glorious victory,[2] so that God may 48:1

1. Muḥammad.
2. The taking of Mecca, A.D. 630, or of Khaybar a year earlier.

48:2 forgive you your past and future sins, and perfect His goodness to you; that He may guide you to a straight path and bestow on you His mighty help.

It was He who sent down tranquillity into the hearts of the faithful, so that their faith might grow stronger (God's are the legions of the heavens and the earth: God is all-knowing and wise); that He may bring the believers, both men and women, into gardens watered by running streams, there to abide for ever; that He may forgive them their sins (this, in God's sight, is a glorious triumph); and that He may punish the hypocrites and the idolaters, men and women, who think evil thoughts about God. A turn of evil shall befall them, for God is angry with them. He has laid on them His curse and prepared for them the fire of Hell: an evil fate.

God's are the legions of the heavens and the earth. God is mighty and wise.

48:8 We have sent you[1] forth as a witness and as a bearer of good news and warnings, so that you[2] may have faith in God and His apostle and that you may assist Him, honour Him, and praise Him morning and evening.

Those that swear fealty to you, swear fealty to God Himself. The Hand of God is above their hands. He that breaks his oath breaks it at his own peril, but he that keeps his pledge to God shall be richly recompensed by Him.

The desert Arabs who stayed behind[3] will say to you: 'We were occupied with our goods and families. Implore God to pardon us.' They will say with their tongues what they do not mean in their hearts.

Say: 'Who can intervene on your behalf with God if it be His will to do you harm or good? Indeed, God is cognizant of all your actions.'

48:12 No. You[4] thought the Apostle and the believers would

---

1. Muḥammad.        2. The Meccans.
3. Away from the war.    4. The desert Arabs.

never return to their people; and with this fancy your hearts were delighted. You harboured evil thoughts and thus incurred damnation.

As for those that disbelieve in God and His apostle, We 48:13 have prepared a blazing Fire for the unbelievers. God has sovereignty over the heavens and the earth. He pardons whom He will and punishes whom He pleases. God is forgiving and merciful.

When you set forth to take the spoils, those that stayed behind will say: 'Let us come with you.'

They seek to change the Word of God. Say: 'You shall not come with us. So God has said beforehand.'

They will reply: 'You are surely jealous of us.' But how little they understand!

Say to the desert Arabs who stayed behind: 'You shall be called upon to fight a mighty nation, unless they embrace Islām. If you prove obedient, God will reward you well. But if you run away, as you have done before this, He will inflict on you a stern chastisement.'

It shall be no offence for the blind, the lame, and the sick 48:17 to stay behind. He that obeys God and His apostle shall be admitted to gardens watered by running streams; but he that turns and flees shall be sternly punished by Him.

God was well pleased with the faithful when they swore allegiance to you under the tree. He knew what was in their hearts. Therefore He sent down tranquillity upon them, and rewarded them with a speedy victory and with the many spoils which they have taken. Mighty is God and wise.

God has promised you rich booty, and has given you this[1] with all promptness. He has stayed your enemies' hands, so that He may make your victory a sign to true believers and guide you along a straight path.

And God knows of other spoils which you have not yet taken. God has power over all things.

If the unbelievers join battle with you, they shall be put 48:22 to flight. They shall find none to protect or help them.

---

1. The spoils taken at Khaybar.

48:23　　Such were the ways of God in days gone by: and you shall find no change in the ways of God.

It was He who ended hostilities between you in the Valley of Mecca[1] after He had given you victory over them. God was watching all your actions.

Those were the unbelievers who debarred you from the Sacred Mosque and prevented your offerings from reaching their destination. But for the fear that you might have trampled underfoot believing men and women unknown to you and thus incurred unwitting guilt on their account, [God would have commanded you to fight it out with them; but He ordained it thus] that He might bring whom He will into His mercy. Had the faithful stood apart from them, We would have sternly punished the unbelievers.

And while bigotry – the bigotry of ignorance – was holding its sway in the hearts of the unbelievers, God sent down His tranquillity on His apostle and on the faithful and made the word of piety binding on them, for they were most worthy and deserving of it. God has knowledge of all things.

48:27　　God has in all truth fulfilled His apostle's vision, in which He had said: 'If God wills, you shall enter the Sacred Mosque secure and fearless, with hair cropped or shaven.' He knew what you knew not; and what is more, He granted you a speedy victory.

It is He that has sent forth His apostle with guidance and the true Faith, so that he may exalt it above all religions. Sufficient is God as a witness.

48:29　　Muḥammad is God's apostle. Those who follow him are ruthless to the unbelievers but merciful to one another. You see them worshipping on their knees, seeking the grace of God and His good will. Their marks[2] are on their faces, the traces of their prostrations. Thus are they described in the Torah and in the Gospel:[3] they are like the seed which puts forth its shoot and strengthens it, so that it rises stout and firm upon its stalk, delighting the sowers. Through them

1. The allusion is probably to the Peace of Ḥudaybīyya, A.D. 628.
2. Dust.　　3. Cf. Mark iv, 26–9.

He seeks to enrage the unbelievers. Yet to those of them who will embrace the Faith and do good works God has promised forgiveness and a rich recompense.

# THE CHAMBERS

*In the Name of God, the Compassionate, the Merciful*

BELIEVERS, DO not behave presumptuously in the presence of God and His apostle. Have fear of God: God hears all and knows all. 49:1

Believers, do not raise your voices above the voice of the Prophet, nor shout aloud when speaking to him as you do to one another, lest your labours should come to nothing without your knowledge. Those who speak softly in the presence of God's apostle are the men whose hearts God has tested for piety. Forgiveness and a rich reward await them.

Those who call out to you[1] while you are in your chambers are for the most part foolish men. If they waited until you went out to them, it would be better for them. But God is forgiving and merciful.

Believers, if an evil-doer brings you a piece of news, inquire first into its truth, lest you should wrong others unwittingly and then regret your action. 49:6

Know that God's apostle is among you. If he obeyed you in many matters, you would surely come to grief. But God has endeared the Faith to you and beautified it in your hearts, making unbelief, wrongdoing, and disobedience abhorrent to you. Such are those who are rightly guided through God's grace and bounty. God is all-knowing and wise.

If two parties of believers take up arms the one against the other, make peace between them. If either of them unjustly attacks the other, fight against the aggressors till they submit to God's judgement. When they submit, make 49:9

1. Muḥammad.

peace between them in equity and justice; God loves those who exercise justice.

49:10 The believers are a band of brothers. Make peace among your brothers and fear God, so that you may be shown mercy.

Believers, let no man mock another man, who may perhaps be better than himself. Let no woman mock another woman, who may perhaps be better than herself. Do not defame one another, nor call one another by nicknames. It is an evil thing to be called by a bad name after embracing the true Faith. Those that do not repent are wrongdoers.

Believers, avoid immoderate suspicion, for in some cases suspicion is a crime. Do not spy on one another, nor backbite one another. Would any of you like to eat the flesh of his dead brother? Surely you would loathe it. Have fear of God. God is forgiving and merciful.

You people! We have created you from a male and a female, and made you into nations and tribes, that you might get to know one another. The noblest of you in God's sight is he who is most righteous. God is all-knowing and wise.

49:14 The Arabs of the desert declare: 'We are true believers.' Say: 'Believers you are not. Rather say: "We profess Islām," for faith has not yet found its way into your hearts. If you obey God and His apostle, He will not deny you the reward of your labours. God is forgiving and merciful.'

The true believers are those that have faith in God and His apostle, and never doubt; and who fight with their wealth and with their persons in the cause of God. Such are those whose faith is true.

Say: 'Would you tell God of your religion, when God knows what the heavens and the earth contain? God has knowledge of all things.'

They think they have conferred on you a favour by embracing Islām. Say: 'In accepting Islām you have conferred on me no favour. It was God who bestowed a favour on you in guiding you to the true Faith. Admit this, if you are 49:18 men of truth. God knows all that is hidden in the heavens and the earth. God is cognizant of all your actions.'

# QĀF

*In the Name of God, the Compassionate, the Merciful*

*Qāf.* BY the Glorious Koran! 50:1

They marvel that a prophet of their own has arisen amongst them. The unbelievers say: 'This is indeed a strange thing. When we are dead and turned to dust . . .?[1] Such a return is most improbable!'

We know how the earth consumes them. We hold a book which records all things.

Yes. They denied the Truth when it was preached to them, and now they are perplexed. Have they never observed the sky above them, and marked how We built it up and furnished it with ornaments, leaving no crack in its expanse?

We spread out the earth and set upon it immovable mountains. We brought forth from it all kinds of delectable plants. A lesson and an admonition to penitent men.

We send down blessed water from the sky with which 50:9 We bring forth gardens and the harvest grain, and tall palm-trees laden with clusters of dates, a sustenance for men; thereby giving new life to a dead land. Such shall be the Resurrection.

Long before these the people of Noah and the dwellers of Al-Rass[2] denied the truth; and so did Thamūd and 'Ād, Pharaoh and the kinsmen of Lot, the dwellers of the 50:14 Forest[3] and the people of Tubba';[4] all disbelieved their apostles and thus brought down upon themselves My threatened scourge.

1. '. . . shall we be raised to life?'
2. Commentators are disagreed as to the identity of this place-name. Some say it is a town in Yamāmah, others a well in Midian.
3. The people of Midian.
4. The people of Himyar, whose kings bore the title of Tubba'.

50:15     Were We worn out by the First Creation? Yet they are in doubt about a new creation.[1]

*We* created man. We know the promptings of his soul, and are closer to him than his jugular vein.

When the twin keepers receive him, the one seated on his right, the other on his left, each word he utters shall be noted down by a vigilant guardian.

And when the agony of death justly takes him, they will say: 'This is the fate you endeavoured to avoid.' And the Trumpet shall be sounded. Such is the promised day.

Each soul shall come attended by one who will drive it on, and another to testify against it. One will say: 'Of this you have been heedless. But now we have removed your veil. Today your sight is keen.' And his companion will say: 'My testimony is ready to hand.'

Then a voice will cry: 'Cast into Hell every hardened unbeliever, every opponent of good, and every doubting transgressor who has set up another deity besides God. Hurl him into the harrowing scourge!'

50:27     His companion[2] will say: 'Lord, I did not mislead him. He had already strayed far into error.'

God will say: 'Do not dispute in My presence. I did forewarn you. My word cannot be changed, nor am I unjust to My servants.'

On that day, We shall ask Hell: 'Are you now full?' And Hell will answer: 'Are there any more?'

And, not far thence, Paradise shall be brought close to the righteous. We shall say to them: 'Here is all that you were promised. It is for every penitent and faithful man, who fears the Merciful, though He is unseen, and comes before Him with a contrite heart. Enter it in peace. This is the day of immortality.'

There they shall have all that they desire, and We shall have yet more to give.

50:36     How many generations, far greater in prowess, have We destroyed before them! They searched the entire land: but

---

1. The Resurrection.     2. The devil who is chained to him.

could they find a refuge? Surely in this there is a lesson for 50:37
every man who has a heart, and can hear and see.

In six days We created the heavens and the earth and all
that lies between them; nor were We ever wearied.

Bear then with what they¹ say. Give glory to your Lord
before sunrise and before sunset. Praise Him in the night,
and make the additional prostrations.

Listen on the day when the Crier will call from near; the
day when men will hear the fateful cry. On that day they
will rise up from their graves.

It is We who ordain life and death. To Us shall all return.

On that day the earth will be rent asunder over them, and
from it they shall emerge in haste. To assemble them all is
easy enough for Us.

We well know what they say. You shall not use coercion 50:45
with them. Admonish with the Koran whoever fears My
warning.²

## THE WINDS

*In the Name of God, the Compassionate, the Merciful*

BY THE dust-scattering winds and the heavily-laden clouds; 51:1
by the swiftly-gliding ships, and by the angels who deal out
blessings to mankind; that which you are promised shall be
fulfilled, and the Last Judgement shall surely come to pass!

By the heaven with its starry highways, you contradict
yourselves! None but the perverse turn away from the true
faith. Perish the liars, who dwell in darkness and are heedless
of the life to come!

'When will the Day of Judgement be?' they ask. On that
day they shall be scourged in the Fire, and a voice will say
to them: 'Taste this, the punishment which you have sought
to hasten!'

The righteous shall dwell amidst gardens and fountains,
and shall receive what their Lord will give them. For they
have done good works, sleeping but little in the night-time, 51:17

1. The unbelievers.    2. Literally, 'threat'.

51:18 praying at dawn for God's pardon, and sharing their goods with the beggar and the dispossessed.

On earth, and in yourselves, there are signs for firm believers. Can you not see?

Heaven holds your sustenance and all that you are promised. I swear by the Lord of heaven and earth that this is true, as true as you are speaking now!

Have you heard the story of Abraham's honoured guests?

They went in to him and said: 'Peace!' 'Peace!' he answered and, seeing that they were strangers, betook himself to his household and returned with a fatted calf. He placed it before them, saying: 'Will you not eat?'

He grew afraid of them, but they said, 'Have no fear,' and told him he was to have a son endowed with knowledge.

His wife came crying and beating her face. 'Surely I am a barren old woman,' she said.

'Such is the will of your Lord,' they replied. 'He is the Wise One, the All-knowing.'

51:31 'Messengers,' said Abraham, 'what is your errand?'

They replied: 'We are sent forth to a wicked people, so that we may bring down on them a shower of clay-stones marked by your Lord for the destruction of the sinful.'

We saved all the faithful in the town – We found but one household of true believers – and left therein a sign for those who fear the woeful scourge.

In Moses, too, there was a sign. We sent him forth to Pharaoh with clear authority, but he turned his back, he and his nobles, saying: 'A sorcerer, or a madman.' So We seized him and his warriors, and cast them into the sea. Indeed, he deserved much blame.

In the fate of 'Ād there was another sign. We let loose on them a blighting wind, which pounded into dust all that it swept before it.

And in Thamūd. They were allowed to take their ease awhile; but they disobeyed the commandments of their
51:45 Lord. The thunderbolt struck them as they looked on; they could not rise up from their fall, nor did they gain their end.

And the people of Noah before them. They too were 51:46 impious men.

We built the heaven with Our might, giving it a vast expanse, and stretched the earth beneath it. Gracious is He who spread it out. And all things We have made in pairs, so that you may take thought.

Therefore seek God. I come from Him to warn you plainly. Set up no other deity besides God. I come from Him to warn you plainly.

Thus whenever an apostle came to those that flourished before them[1] they cried: 'Sorcerer!' or 'Madman!' Have they handed down this cry from one generation to the next? Surely they are transgressors all.

Pay no heed to them; you shall incur no blame. Exhort them; exhortation helps the true believers.

I created the jinn and mankind only that they might worship Me. I demand no livelihood of them, nor do I ask that they should feed Me.

God alone is the Munificent Giver, the Mighty One, the Invincible. Those that now do wrong shall meet their predecessors' doom. Let them not challenge Me to hurry it on. Woe then betide the unbelievers when their promised day 51:60 arrives!

# THE MOUNTAIN

*In the Name of God, the Compassionate, the Merciful*

BY THE Mountain,[2] and by the Scripture penned on 52:1 unrolled parchment; by the Visited House,[3] the Lofty Vault,[4] and the swelling sea, your Lord's punishment shall surely come to pass! No power shall ward it off.

On that day the heaven will shake and reel, and the mountains move and pass away. On that day woe betide the unbelievers, who now divert themselves with vain disputes. 52:12

1. The Meccans.    2. Mount Sinai.
3. The Ka'bah.    4. The sky.

52:13    On that day they shall be sternly thrown into the fire of Hell, and a voice will say to them: 'This is the Fire which you denied. Is this sorcery, or do you not see? Burn in its flames. It is the same whether or not you show forbearance. You shall be recompensed according only to your deeds.'

But in fair gardens the righteous shall dwell in bliss, rejoicing in what their Lord will give them. Their Lord will shield them from the scourge of Hell. He will say: 'Eat and drink to your hearts' content. This is the reward of your labours.'

They shall recline on couches ranged in rows. To dark-eyed houris We shall wed them.

(We shall unite the true believers with those of their descendants who follow them in their faith, and shall not deny them the reward of their good works; each man is the hostage of his own deeds.)

Fruits We shall give them, and such meats as they desire. They will pass from hand to hand a cup inspiring no idle talk, no sinful urge; and there shall wait on them young boys of their own, as fair as virgin pearls.

52:25    They will converse with one another. 'When we were living among our kinsfolk,' they will say, 'we were troubled by many fears. But God has been gracious to us; He has preserved us from the fiery scourge, for we have prayed to Him. He is the Beneficent One, the Merciful.'

Therefore give warning. By the grace of God, you are neither soothsayer nor madman.

Do they say: 'He is but a poet: we are waiting for some misfortune to befall him'? Say: 'Wait if you will; I too am waiting.'

Does their reason prompt them to say this? Or is it merely that they are wicked men?

Do they say: 'He has invented it[1] himself'? Indeed, they have no faith. Let them produce a scripture like it, if what they say be true!

52:35    Were they created out of the void? Or were they their own creators?

1. The Koran.

Did *they* create the heavens and the earth? Surely they  52:36
have no faith!

Do they hold the treasures of your Lord, or have control
over them?

Have they a ladder by means of which they overhear
Him? Let their eavesdropper bring a positive proof!

Is He to have daughters and you[1] sons?

Are you[2] demanding payment of them, that they should
fear to be weighed down with debts?

Have they knowledge of what is hidden? Can they write
it down?

Are they seeking to ruin you? It is the unbelievers who  52:42
shall be ruined.

Have they a god other than God? Exalted be He above
their idols!

If they saw a part of heaven falling down, they would still
say: 'It is but a mass of clouds!'

Let them be, until they face the day when they shall stand
dumbfounded; the day when their designs will avail them
nothing and none will help them.

And besides this a scourge awaits the wrongdoers, though
most of them do not know it.

Therefore wait the judgement of your Lord: We are watching over you. Give glory to your Lord when you awaken,
in the night-time praise Him, and at the setting of the stars.  52:49

# THE STAR

*In the Name of God, the Compassionate, the Merciful*

BY THE declining star, your compatriot[3] is not in error, nor  53:1
is he deceived!

He does not speak out of his own fancy. This is an
inspired revelation. He is taught by one who is powerful  53:6
and mighty.[4]

---

    1. The unbelievers.    2. Muḥammad.
    3. Muḥammad.    4. Gabriel.

53:7    He stood on the uppermost horizon; then, drawing near, he came down within two bows' length or even closer, and revealed to his servant that which he revealed.

His[1] own heart did not deny his vision. How can you,[2] then, question what he sees?

He beheld him once again at the sidra tree, beyond which no one may pass. (Near it is the Garden of Repose.)

When that tree was covered with what covered it, his eyes did not wander, nor did they turn aside: for he saw some of his Lord's greatest signs.

Have you thought on Al-Lāt and Al-'Uzzā, and on Manāt, the third other?[3] Are you to have the sons, and He the daughters? This is indeed an unfair distinction!

They are but names which you and your fathers have invented: God has vested no authority in them. The unbelievers follow but vain conjectures and the whims of their own souls, although the guidance of their Lord has long since come to them.

53:24    Is man to attain all that he desires? To God belongs the life to come, and this present life.

Numerous are the angels in the heavens; yet their intercession shall avail nothing until God gives leave to whom He accepts and chooses.

Those that disbelieve in the hereafter call the angels by the names of females. Yet of this they have no knowledge: they follow mere conjecture, and conjecture is no substitute for truth.

Pay no heed, then, to those who ignore Our warning and seek only the life of this world. This is the sum of their knowledge. Your Lord best knows who has strayed from His path, and He best knows who has followed the right guidance.

53:31    His is what the heavens and the earth contain. He will requite the evil-doers according to their deeds, and richly recompense those who do good works.

1. Muḥammad's.          2. The unbelievers.
3. Names of Arabian idols, claimed by the pagans of Mecca to be daughters of God.

To those who avoid the grossest sins and indecencies and 53:32
commit only small offences, your Lord will show abundant
mercy. He knew you well when He created you from earth
and when you were still in your mothers' wombs. Do not
pretend to purity; He knows best those who guard themselves against evil.

Have you considered him who turns his back upon the
Faith, giving little at first and then nothing at all? Does he
know, and can he see, what is hidden? Has he not heard of
what is preached in the scriptures of Moses and Abraham,
who fulfilled his duty: that no soul shall bear another's
burden, and that man shall be judged only by his labours; that
his labours shall be scrutinized, and that he shall be justly
requited for them; that all things shall in the end return to
your Lord; that it is He who moves men to laughter and to 53:43
tears, and He who ordains death and life; that God created
the sexes, the male and the female, from a drop of ejaculated
semen, and will create all things anew; that it is He who
bestows and enriches, He who is the Lord of Sirius;[1] that it
was He who destroyed 'Ād first and then Thamūd, sparing
no one, and before them the people of Noah, who were
more wicked and more rebellious. The Mu'tafikah[2] He also
ruined, so that they were smitten by the scourge that smote
them.

Which then of your Lord's blessings would you deny? He
that now warns you is just like those who warned the others
before you. That which is coming is near at hand; none but
God can disclose the hour.

Do you marvel then at this revelation, and laugh and
rejoice instead of weeping? Rather prostrate yourselves 53:62
before God, and worship.

1. The Dog Star, worshipped by the pagan Arabs.
2. The Ruined Cities, where Lot's people lived.

# THE MOON

*In the Name of God, the Compassionate, the Merciful*

54:1 THE HOUR of Doom is drawing near, and the moon is cleft in two. Yet, when they see a sign, the unbelievers turn their backs and say: 'Ingenious sorcery!'

They deny the truth, and follow their own fancies. But in the end all issues shall be laid to rest.

Cautionary tales, profound in wisdom, have been narrated to them: but warnings are unavailing.

Let them be. The day the Crier summons them to the dread account, they shall come out from their graves with downcast eyes, and rush towards him like swarming locusts. The unbelievers will cry: 'This is indeed a woeful day!'

Long before them, the people of Noah disbelieved. They disbelieved Our servant, and called him a madman. Rejected and contemned, he cried out, saying: 'Help me, Lord, I am overcome!'

54:11 We opened the gates of heaven with pouring rain and caused the earth to burst with gushing springs, so that the waters met for a predestined end. We carried him in a vessel built with planks and nails, which drifted on under Our eyes: a recompense for him who had been disbelieved.

This We have left as a sign: but will any take heed? How grievous was My scourge, and how clear My warning!

We have made the Koran easy to remember: but will any take heed?

'Ād, too, did not believe. How grievous was My scourge, and how clear My warning! On a day of unremitting woe, We let loose on them a howling wind which snapped people off like trunks of uprooted palm-trees. How grievous was My scourge, and how clear My warning!

We have made the Koran easy to remember: but will any take heed?

Thamūd, too, disbelieved Our warnings. They said: 'Are
54:24 we to follow a mortal who stands alone among us? That

374

would surely be error and madness. Did he alone among us  54:25
receive the admonition? He is indeed a foolish liar.'

To him We said: 'Tomorrow they shall learn who the foolish liar is. We are sending to them the she-camel, that We
may put them to the proof. Observe them closely and have
patience. Tell them that they must share their drink with
her, and that for every draught they must attend in person.'

They called their friend, who took a knife and slew her.
How grievous was My scourge, and how clear My warning!
A single cry was heard, and they became like the dry twigs
of the sheep-fold builder.

We have made the Koran easy to remember: but will any
take heed?

The people of Lot disbelieved Our warnings. We let
loose on them a stone-charged whirlwind which destroyed
them all, except the house of Lot, whom We saved at dawn
through Our mercy. Thus do We reward the thankful.

Lot had warned them of Our punishment, but they
doubted his warnings. They demanded his guests of him.  54:37
We put out their eyes, and said: 'Taste My punishment,
now that you have scorned My warning.' And at daybreak a
heavy scourge took them. 'Taste My punishment, now that
you have scorned My warning!'

We have made the Koran easy to remember: but will any
take heed?

To Pharaoh's people also came the warnings. But they
disbelieved all Our signs, and We smote them with the
scourge of the Mighty One, the All-powerful.

Are your unbelievers better men than these? Or are you
given immunity in the Scriptures?

Do they say: 'We are a victorious army'? Their army shall
be routed and put to flight.

The Hour of Doom is their appointed time. More
calamitous, and more doleful, shall that Hour be than all
their worldly trials.

Yet the wrongdoers persist in error and madness. On the  54:48
day when they are dragged into the Fire with faces
down, We shall say to them: 'Feel the touch of Hell!'

54:49   We have surely made all things according to a fixed decree. We command but once: Our will is done in the twinkling of an eye.

We have destroyed many a nation like yourselves. Will you not take warning?

All their deeds are in their books: every action, small or great, is noted down. The righteous shall dwell in gardens watered by running brooks, honourably seated in the
54:55  presence of a Mighty King.

## THE MERCIFUL[1]

*In the Name of God, the Compassionate, the Merciful*

IT IS the Merciful who has taught the Koran.

55:1   He created man and taught him articulate speech. The sun and the moon pursue their ordered course. The plants and the trees bow down in adoration.

He raised the heaven on high and set the balance of all things, that you might not transgress that balance. Give just weight and full measure.

He laid the earth for His creatures, with all its fruits and blossom-bearing palm, chaff-covered grain and scented herbs. Which of your Lord's blessings would you[2] deny?

He created man from potter's clay, and the jinn from smokeless fire. Which of your Lord's blessings would you deny?

The Lord of the two easts[3] is He, and the Lord of the two wests. Which of your Lord's blessings would you deny?

55:19  He has let loose the two oceans:[4] they meet one another.

1. Compare this chapter with Psalm CXXXVI of the Old Testament.
2. The pronoun is in the dual number, the words being addressed to mankind and the jinn. This refrain is repeated no fewer than 31 times.
3. The points at which the sun rises in summer and in winter.
4. Salt water and fresh water.

Yet between them stands a barrier which they cannot 55:20
overrun. Which of your Lord's blessings would you deny?

Pearls and corals come from both. Which of your Lord's
blessings would you deny?

His are the ships that sail like mountains upon the ocean.
Which of your Lord's blessings would you deny?

All that lives on earth is doomed to die. But the face of
your Lord will abide for ever, in all its majesty and glory.
Which of your Lord's blessings would you deny?

All who dwell in heaven and earth entreat Him. Each day
some mighty task engages Him. Which of your Lord's
blessings would you deny?

Mankind and jinn, We shall surely find the time to judge
you! Which of your Lord's blessings would you deny?

Mankind and jinn, if you have power to penetrate the
confines of heaven and earth, then penetrate them! But this
you shall not do except with Our own authority. Which of
your Lord's blessings would you deny?

Flames of fire shall be lashed at you, and molten brass. 55:35
There shall be none to help you. Which of your Lord's
blessings would you deny?

When the sky splits asunder, and reddens like a rose or
stainèd leather (which of your Lord's blessings would you
deny?), on that day neither man nor jinnee will be asked
about his sins. Which of your Lord's blessings would you
deny?

The wrongdoers will be known by their looks; they shall
be seized by their forelocks and their feet. Which of your
Lord's blessings would you deny?

That is the Hell which the sinners deny. They shall
wander between fire and water fiercely seething. Which of
your Lord's blessings would you deny?

But for those that fear the majesty of their Lord there are
two gardens (which of your Lord's blessings would you
deny?) planted with shady trees. Which of your Lord's
blessings would you deny?

Each is watered by a flowing spring. Which of your 55:51
Lord's blessings would you deny?

55:52    Each bears every kind of fruit in pairs. Which of your Lord's blessings would you deny?

They shall recline on couches lined with thick brocade, and within reach will hang the fruits of both gardens. Which of your Lord's blessings would you deny?

Therein are bashful virgins whom neither man nor jinnee will have touched before. Which of your Lord's blessings would you deny?

Virgins as fair as corals and rubies. Which of your Lord's blessings would you deny?

Shall the reward of goodness be anything but good? Which of your Lord's blessings would you deny?

And beside these there shall be two other gardens (which of your Lord's blessings would you deny?) of darkest green. Which of your Lord's blessings would you deny?

55:66    A gushing fountain shall flow in each. Which of your Lord's blessings would you deny?

Each planted with fruit-trees, the palm and the pomegranate. Which of your Lord's blessings would you deny?

In each there shall be virgins chaste and fair. Which of your Lord's blessings would you deny?

Dark-eyed virgins, sheltered in their tents (which of your Lord's blessings would you deny?), whom neither man nor jinnee will have touched before. Which of your Lord's blessings would you deny?

They shall recline on green cushions and fine carpets. Which of your Lord's blessings would you deny?

55:78  Blessed be the name of your Lord, the Lord of majesty and glory!

# THAT WHICH IS COMING

*In the Name of God, the Compassionate, the Merciful*

WHEN THAT which is coming comes – and no soul shall
56:1 then deny its coming – some shall be abased and others exalted.

When the earth shakes and quivers, and the mountains

crumble away and scatter abroad into fine dust, you shall be  56:6
divided into three multitudes: those on the right (blessed
shall be those on the right); those on the left (damned shall
be those on the left); and those to the fore (foremost shall
be those). Such are they that shall be brought near to their
Lord in the gardens of delight: a whole multitude from the
men of old, but only a few from the latter generations.

They shall recline on jewelled couches face to face, and
there shall wait on them immortal youths with bowls and
ewers and a cup of purest wine (that will neither pain their
heads nor take away their reason); with fruits of their own
choice and flesh of fowls that they relish. And theirs shall be
the dark-eyed houris, chaste as virgin pearls: a guerdon for
their deeds.

There they shall hear no idle talk, no sinful speech, but
only the greeting, 'Peace! Peace!'

Those on the right hand – happy shall be those on the  56:27
right hand! They shall recline on couches raised on high in
the shade of thornless sidrs and clusters of ṭalḥ;[1] amidst
gushing waters and abundant fruits, unforbidden, never-
ending.

We created the houris and made them virgins, loving
companions for those on the right hand: a multitude from
the men of old, and a multitude from the latter generations.

As for those on the left hand (wretched shall be those on
the left hand!) they shall dwell amidst scorching winds and
seething water: in the shade of pitch-black smoke, neither
cool nor refreshing. For they have lived in comfort and
persisted in the heinous sin,[2] saying: 'When we are once
dead and turned to dust and bones, shall we be raised to
life? And our forefathers, too?'

Say: 'Those of old, and those of the present age, shall be
brought together on an appointed day. As for you sinners
who deny the truth, you shall eat the fruit of the Zaqqūm
tree and fill your bellies with it. You shall drink scalding
water: yet you shall drink it as the thirsty camel drinks.'  56:55

---

1. Probably the banana fruit.          2. Idolatry.

56:56　Such shall be their fare on the Day of Reckoning.

*We* created you: will you not believe then in Our power?

Behold the semen you discharge: did you create it, or We?

It was We that ordained death among you. Nothing can hinder Us from replacing you by others like yourselves or transforming you into beings you know nothing of.

You surely know of the First Creation. Why, then, do you not reflect? Consider the seeds you grow. Is it you that give them growth, or We? If We pleased, We could turn your harvest into chaff, so that, filled with wonder, you would exclaim: 'We are laden with debts! Surely we have been robbed!'

Consider the water which you drink. Was it you that poured it from the cloud, or We? If We pleased, We could turn it bitter. Why, then, do you not give thanks?

Observe the fire which you light. Is it you that create its wood, or We? A reminder for man We made it, and for the traveller a comfort.

56:74　Praise, then, the name of your Lord, the Supreme One.

I swear by the shelter of the stars (a mighty oath, if you but knew it) that this is a glorious Koran, safeguarded in a book which none may touch except the purified; a revelation from the Lord of the Universe.

Would you scorn a scripture such as this, and earn your daily bread denying it?

When under your very eyes a man's soul is about to leave him (We are nearer to him than you, although you cannot see Us), why do you not restore it, if you will not be judged hereafter? Answer this, if what you say be true!

Thus, if he is favoured, his lot will be repose and plenty, and a garden of delight. If he is one of those on the right hand, he will be greeted with, 'Peace be with you!' by those on the right hand.

But if he is an erring disbeliever, his welcome will be scalding water, and he will burn in Hell.

56:96　This is surely the indubitable truth. Praise, then, the name of your Lord, the Supreme One.

# IRON

ALL THAT is in the heavens and the earth gives glory to 57:1
God. He is the Mighty, the Wise One.

It is He that has sovereignty over the heavens and the
earth. He ordains life and death, and has power over all things.

He is the First and the Last, the Visible and the Unseen.
He has knowledge of all things.

It was He who created the heavens and the earth in six
days, and then mounted the throne. He knows all that goes
into the earth and all that emerges from it, all that comes
down from heaven and all that ascends to it. He is with you
wherever you are. God is cognizant of all your actions.

He has sovereignty over the heavens and the earth. To
God shall all things return. He causes the night to pass into
the day, and causes the day to pass into the night. He has
knowledge of the innermost thoughts of men.

Have faith in God and His apostle and give in alms of 57:7
that which He has made your inheritance; for whichever of
you believes and gives in alms shall be richly recompensed.

And what cause have you not to believe in God, when
the Apostle calls on you to have faith in your Lord, who has
made a covenant with you, if you are true believers?

It is He who brings down clear revelations to His
servant, so that he may lead you out of darkness into the
light. Surely God is compassionate to you and merciful.

And why should you not give to the cause of God, when
God alone will inherit the heavens and the earth? Those of
you that gave of their wealth before the victory, and took
part in the fighting, shall receive greater honour than the
others who gave and fought thereafter. Yet God has
promised you all a good reward; God has knowledge of all
your actions.

Who will give a generous loan to God? He will pay him
back twofold and he shall receive a noble recompense.

The day will surely come when you shall see the true 57:12

believers, men and women, with their light shining before them and on their right hands, and a voice saying to them: 'Rejoice this day. You shall enter gardens watered by running streams in which you shall abide for ever.' That is the supreme triumph.

57:13 On that day the hypocrites, both men and women, will say to the true believers: 'Wait for us, that we may borrow some of your light.' But they will be told: 'Go back, and seek some other light!'

A wall with a gate shall be set before them. Inside there shall be mercy, and without, to the fore, the scourge of Hell. They will call out to them, saying: 'Were we not on your side?' 'Yes,' they will reply, 'but you tempted yourselves, you wavered, you doubted, and were deceived by vain desires until God's will was done and the Dissembler misled you about God. Today no ransom shall be accepted from you, or from the unbelievers. The Fire shall be your home: you have justly earned it, an evil end!'

Is it not time for true believers to submit with fervent hearts to God's warning and to the truth He has revealed, so that they may not be like those who were given the scriptures before this, whose days were prolonged but whose hearts were hardened? Many of them were evildoers.

57:17 Know that God restores the earth to life after its death. We have made plain Our revelations to you, that you may grow in wisdom.

Those that give alms, be they men or women, and those that give a generous loan to God, shall be repaid twofold. They shall receive a noble recompense.

Those that believe in God and His apostles are the truthful men who shall testify in their Lord's presence. They shall have their guerdon and their light. But those that disbelieve Our revelations and deny them are the heirs of Hell.

57:20 Know that the life of this world is but a sport and a diversion, a show and an empty boast among you, a quest for greater riches and more children. It is like the plants that flourish after rain: the husbandman rejoices to see them grow; but then they wither and turn yellow, soon becoming worthless stubble. In the life to come a grievous scourge awaits you – or the forgiveness of God and His pleasure. The life of this world is but a vain provision.

Therefore strive for the pardon of your Lord, and for a 57:21 Paradise as vast as heaven and earth, prepared for those who believe in God and His apostles. Such is the grace of God: He bestows it on whom He will. God's grace is infinite.

Every misfortune that befalls the earth, or your own persons, is ordained before We bring it into being. That is easy enough for God; so that you may not grieve for the good things you miss, or be overjoyed at what you gain. God does not love the haughty, the vainglorious; nor those who, being tight-fisted themselves, enjoin others to be tight-fisted. He that pays no heed should know that God alone is self-sufficient and worthy of praise.

We have sent Our apostles with veritable signs, and 57:25 through them have brought down scriptures and the scales of justice, so that people might conduct themselves with fairness. We have sent down iron, with its mighty strength and diverse uses for mankind, so that God may recognize those who aid Him, though unseen, and help His apostles. Powerful is God, and mighty.

We sent forth Noah and Abraham, and bestowed on their offspring prophethood and the Scriptures. Some were rightly guided, but many were evil-doers. After them We sent other apostles, and after those Jesus son of Mary. We gave him the Gospel, and put compassion and mercy in the hearts of his followers. As for monasticism, they instituted it themselves (for We had not enjoined it on them), seeking thereby to please God; but they did not observe it faithfully. We rewarded only those who were true believers; for many of them were evil-doers.

Believers, have fear of God and put your trust in His 57:28 apostle. He will grant you a double share of His mercy, He will bestow on you a light to walk in, and He will forgive you: God is forgiving and merciful.

57:29  Let the People of the Book recognize that they have no control over the grace of God; that grace is in His hands alone, and that He vouchsafes it to whom He will. God's grace is infinite.

## SHE WHO PLEADED

*In the Name of God, the Compassionate, the Merciful*

58:1  GOD HAS heard the words of her[1] who pleaded with you against her husband and made her plaint to God. God has heard what you two said to each other. God hears all and observes all.

Those of you who divorce their wives by declaring them to be their mothers should know that they are *not* their mothers. Their mothers are those only who gave birth to them. The words they utter are unjust and false: but God pardons and forgives.

Those that divorce their wives by so saying, and afterwards retract their words, shall free a slave[2] before they touch each other again. This you are enjoined to do: God is

58:4  cognizant of all your actions. He that has no slave shall fast two successive months before they touch one another. If he cannot, he shall feed sixty of the destitute. This is enjoined on you so that you may have faith in God and His apostle. Such are the bounds set by God. Woeful punishment awaits the unbelievers.

Those that oppose God and His apostle shall be brought low, as have been those before them. We have sent down clear revelations. Shameful punishment awaits the unbelievers.

58:6  On the day when God restores them all to life He will inform them of their actions. God has counted these, although they have forgotten them. God is witness of all things.

1. Khawlah, daughter of Tha'labah, who had been divorced by the formula: 'Be to me as my mother's back', which was accepted as a declaration of divorce among pagan Arabs.
2. As a penalty.

Are you not aware that God knows what the heavens 58:7
and the earth contain? If three men converse in secret, He is
their fourth; if five, He is their sixth; whether fewer or
more, wherever they be, He is with them. Then, on the Day
of Resurrection, He will inform them of their doings. God
has knowledge of all things.

Have you not seen those who, though forbidden to
intrigue in secret, defiantly plot together in wickedness and
enmity and in disobedience to the Apostle? When they
come to you, they salute you in words which God does not
greet you with, and ask themselves: 'Why does God not
punish us for what we say?' Hell is scourge enough for
them: they shall burn in its flames, a wretched fate!

Believers, when you converse in private do not speak
with wickedness and enmity and in disobedience to the
Apostle, but with justice and with piety. Have fear of God,
before whom you shall be brought together.

Intrigue is the work of Satan, who means to vex the 58:10
faithful. Yet he can harm them not at all, except by the will
of God. In God let the faithful put their trust.

Believers, make room[1] in your assemblies when you are
bidden so to do: God will make room for you hereafter.
Again, rise up when you are told to rise: God will elevate
to high ranks those that have faith and knowledge among
you. God is cognizant of all your actions.

Believers, when you confer with the Apostle, give alms
before such conference. That is best and most righteous for
you. But if you lack the means, God is forgiving and
merciful.

Do you hesitate to offer alms before you speak with him?
If you do not (and God will pardon your offence), then at
least recite your prayers and render the alms levy and show
obedience to God and His apostle. God is cognizant of all
your actions.

Do you see those that have befriended a people with 58:14
whom God is angry? They belong neither to you nor to

---

1. For the Prophet, or for your fellow-Muslims.

58:15 them. They knowingly swear to falsehood. God has prepared for them a grievous scourge. Evil indeed is that which they have done.

They use their faith as a disguise, and debar others from the path of God. Shameful punishment awaits them.

Their wealth and children shall in no way protect them from God. They are the inmates of the Fire, and there they shall abide for ever.

On the day when God restores them all to life, they will swear to Him as they now swear to you, imagining that their oaths will help them. Surely they are lying.

58:19 Satan has gained possession of them, and caused them to forget God's warning. They are the confederates of Satan; Satan's confederates will surely be the losers.

Those that oppose God and His apostle shall be brought low. God has decreed: 'I will surely triumph, Myself and My apostles.' Powerful is God, and mighty.

58:22 You shall find no believers in God and in the Last Day on friendly terms with those who oppose God and His apostle, even though they be their fathers, their sons, their brothers, or their nearest kindred. God has inscribed the Faith in their very hearts, and strengthened them with a spirit of His own. He will admit them to gardens watered by running streams, where they shall dwell for ever. God is well pleased with them, and they are well pleased with Him. They are the confederates of God: and God's confederates will surely triumph.

# EXILE

*In the Name of God, the Compassionate, the Merciful*

59:1 ALL THAT is in the heavens and the earth gives glory to God. He is the Mighty, the Wise One.

It was He that drove the unbelievers among the People of the Book out of their dwellings into the first exile.[1] You did

1. An allusion to Muḥammad's expedition against the Jews of Banu al-Naḍīr in Arabia.

not think that they would go; and they, for their part, fancied that their strongholds would protect them from God. But God's scourge fell upon them whence they did not expect it, casting such terror into their hearts that their dwellings were destroyed by their own hands as well as by the faithful. Learn from their example, you that have eyes.

Had God not decreed exile for them, He would have surely 59:3 punished them in this world. But in the world to come the Fire shall be their scourge because they have set themselves against God and His apostle; and he that sets himself against God should know that God is stern in retribution.

It was God who gave you leave to cut down or spare their palm-trees, so that He might humiliate the evil-doers. As for those spoils of theirs which God has assigned to His apostle, you spurred neither horse nor camel to capture them: but God gives His apostles authority over whom He will. God has power over all things.

The spoils taken from the town-dwellers and assigned by 59:7 God to His apostle shall belong to God, to the Apostle and his kinsfolk, to orphans, to the destitute and to the traveller in need; they shall not become the property of the rich among you. Whatever the Apostle gives you, accept it; and whatever he forbids you, abstain from it. Have fear of God; God is stern in retribution.

A share of the spoils shall also fall to the poor among the *muhājirīn*[1] who have been driven from their homes and their possessions, who seek God's grace and bounty and who help God and His apostle. These are the true believers.

The men who stayed in their own city[2] and embraced the 59:9 Faith before them love those who have sought refuge with them; they do not covet what they are given, but rather prize them above themselves, though they are in want. Those that preserve themselves from their own greed shall surely prosper.

1. Those who fled with Muḥammad to Medina.
2. Medina.

59:10    Those that came after them say: 'Forgive us, Lord, and forgive our brothers who embraced the Faith before us. Do not put in our hearts any malice towards the faithful. Lord, You are compassionate and merciful.'

Have you not considered the hypocrites? They say to their fellow-unbelievers among the People of the Book: 'If they drive you out, we will go with you. We will never obey any one who seeks to harm you. If you are attacked, we will certainly help you.'

God bears witness that they are lying. If they are driven out, they will not go with them, nor, if they are attacked, will they help them. Indeed, if they do go to their help, they will turn their backs in flight and leave them in the lurch.

Their dread of you is more intense in their hearts than their fear of God: so devoid are they of understanding.

They will never fight against you in a body except in fortified cities and from behind walls. Great is their valour among themselves; you think of them as one band, yet their hearts are divided. They are surely lacking in judgement.

59:15    Like those who were but recently punished before them, they tasted the fruit of their own deeds. Woeful punishment awaits them.

The hypocrites may be compared to Satan, who, when he ordered man to disbelieve and man did his bidding, said to him: 'I here and now disown you. I fear God, Lord of the Universe.'

They shall both end in the Fire and remain therein for ever. Thus shall the wrongdoers be rewarded.

Believers, have fear of God. Let every soul look to what it offers for the morrow. Fear God; God is cognizant of all your actions.

Do not act like those who have forgotten God, so that He has caused them to forget themselves. Such men are evil-doers.

The heirs of the Fire and the heirs of Paradise shall not be held equal. The heirs of Paradise alone shall be triumphant.

59:21    Had We brought down this Koran upon a mountain, you would have seen it humble itself and break asunder for fear of God.

In such parables We speak to people, so that they may take thought.

He is God, besides whom there is no other deity. He 59:22 knows the unknown and the manifest. He is the Compassionate, the Merciful.

He is God, besides whom there is no other deity. He is the Sovereign Lord, the Holy One, the Giver of Peace, the Keeper of Faith; the Guardian, the Mighty One, the All-powerful, the Most High! Exalted be God above their idols!

He is God, the Creator, the Originator, the Modeller. His 59:24 are the most gracious names. All that is in the heavens and the earth gives glory to Him. He is the Mighty, the Wise One.

# SHE WHO IS TESTED

*In the Name of God, the Compassionate, the Merciful*

BELIEVERS, DO not make friends with those who are 60:1 enemies of Mine and yours. Would you show them kindness, when they have denied the truth that has been revealed to you and driven out the Apostle and yourselves, because you believe in God, your Lord?

If it was indeed to fight for My cause, and out of a desire to please Me, that you left your city, how can you be friendly to them in secret? I well know all that you conceal, and all that you reveal. Whoever of you does this will stray from the right path.

If they gain ascendancy over you, they will plainly show themselves your enemies, and stretch out their hands and tongues to you with evil. They long to see you unbelievers.

On the Day of Resurrection neither your kinsfolk nor your children shall avail you. God will separate you. He is cognizant of all your actions.

You have a good example in Abraham and those who 60:4 followed him. They said to their people: 'We disown you and the idols which you worship besides God. We renounce you: enmity and hate shall reign between us until you believe in God only.' (But do not emulate the words of Abraham to his father: 'I shall implore forgiveness for you, although I can in no way protect you from God.') 'Lord, in You we have put our trust; to You we turn and to You we shall 60:5 come at last. Lord, do not expose us to the designs of the unbelievers. Forgive us, Lord; You are the Mighty, the Wise One.'

Surely in those there is a good example for everyone who puts his hopes in God and in the Last Day. He that pays no heed shall learn that God alone is self-sufficient and worthy of praise.

It may well be that God will put good will between you and those with whom you have hitherto been at odds. God is mighty. God is forgiving and merciful.

God does not forbid you to be kind and equitable to those who have neither made war on your religion nor driven you from your homes. God loves the equitable. But He forbids you to make friends with those who have fought against you on account of your religion and driven you from your homes or abetted others to drive you out. Those that make friends with them are wrongdoers.

60:10 Believers, when believing women seek refuge with you, test them. God best knows their faith. If you find them true believers, do not return them to the infidels; they are not lawful for the infidels, nor are the infidels lawful for them. But hand back to the unbelievers the dowries they gave them. Nor is it an offence for you to marry such women, provided you give them their dowries. Do not maintain your marriages with unbelieving women: demand the dowries you gave them and let the infidels do the same. Such is the law which God lays down among you. God is all-knowing and wise.

If any of your wives go over to the unbelievers and you subsequently gain victory over them, pay those whose wives have fled the equivalent of the dowries they gave them. Fear God, in whom you believe.

60:12 Prophet, if believing women come to you and pledge

themselves to serve no other deity besides God, to commit neither theft, nor adultery, nor child-murder, to utter no monstrous falsehoods of their own invention, and to disobey you in nothing reasonable, accept their allegiance and implore God to forgive them. God is forgiving and merciful.

Believers, do not make friends with those who have 60:13 incurred the wrath of God. Such men despair of the life to come, just as the unbelievers despair of the buried dead.

# BATTLE ARRAY

*In the Name of God, the Compassionate, the Merciful*

ALL THAT is in the heavens and the earth gives glory to 61:1 God. He is the Mighty, the Wise One.

Believers, why do you profess what you never do? It is most odious in God's sight that you should say one thing and do another.

God loves those who fight for His cause in ranks as firm as a mighty edifice.

Tell of Moses, who said to his people: 'Why do you seek to harm me, my people, when you know that I am sent to you by God?' And when they went astray, God led their very hearts astray. God does not guide the evil-doers.

And of Jesus son of Mary, who said to the Israelites: 'I am sent forth to you from God to confirm the Torah already revealed, and to give news of an apostle that will come after me whose name is Aḥmad.'[1] Yet when he brought them conspicuous signs, they said: 'This is plain sorcery.'

And who is more wicked than the man who invents a falsehood about God when called upon to submit to Him? God does not guide the wrongdoers.

They seek to extinguish the light of God with their 61:8 mouths; but God will perfect His light, much as the unbelievers may dislike it.

---

1. Another name of Muḥammad's, meaning 'The Praised One'.

61:9    It is He who has sent forth His apostle with guidance and the True Faith, so that he may exalt it above all religions, much as the idolators may dislike it.

Believers! Shall I point out to you a profitable course that will save you from a woeful scourge? Have faith in God and His apostle, and fight for God's cause with your wealth and with your persons. That would be best for you, if you but knew it.

He will forgive you your sins and admit you to gardens watered by running streams; He will lodge you in pleasant mansions in the gardens of Eden. That is the supreme triumph.

And He will bestow upon you other blessings which you desire: help from God and a speedy victory. Proclaim the good tidings to the faithful.

61:14    Believers, be God's helpers. When Jesus son of Mary said to the disciples: 'Who will come with me to the help of God?' the disciples replied: '*We* are God's helpers.'

Some of the Israelites believed in him while others did not. We aided the believers against their enemies, and they triumphed over them.

# FRIDAY, OR THE
# DAY OF CONGREGATION

*In the Name of God, the Compassionate, the Merciful*

62:1    ALL THAT is in the heavens and the earth gives glory to God, the Sovereign Lord, the Holy One, the Almighty, the Wise One.

It is He that has sent forth among the Gentiles an apostle of their own to recite to them His revelations, to purify them, and to instruct them in the Book and in wisdom, though they have hitherto been in evident error, together with others of their own kin who have not yet followed them. He is the Mighty, the Wise One.

62:4    Such is the grace of God: He bestows it on whom He will. His grace is infinite.

Those to whom the burden of the Torah was entrusted 62:5 and yet refused to bear it are like a donkey laden with books. Wretched is the example of those who deny God's revelations. God does not guide the wrongdoers.

Say: 'You that follow the Jewish Faith, if you claim that of all people you alone are God's friends, then you should wish for death, if what you say be true!' But, because of what their hands have done, they will never wish for death. God knows the wrongdoers.

Say: 'The death from which you shrink is sure to 62:8 overtake you. Then you shall be sent back to Him who knows the unknown and the manifest, and He will declare to you all that you have done.'

Believers, when you are summoned to Friday prayers hasten to the remembrance of God and cease your trading. That would be best for you, if you but knew it. Then, when the prayers are ended, disperse and go your ways in quest of God's bounty. Remember God always, so that you may prosper.

Yet no sooner do they see some commerce or merriment 62:11 afoot than they flock eagerly to it, leaving you[1] standing all alone.

Say: 'That which God has in store is far better than any merriment or any commerce. God is the Most Munificent Giver.'

# THE HYPOCRITES

*In the Name of God, the Compassionate, the Merciful*

WHEN THE hypocrites come to you they say: 'We bear 63:1 witness that you are God's apostle.' God knows that you are indeed His apostle; and God bears witness that the hypocrites are surely lying.

They use their faith as a disguise, and debar others from 63:2 the path of God. Evil is what they do.

1. Muhammad.

63:3    They believed and then renounced their faith: their hearts are sealed, so that they are devoid of understanding.

When you see them, their good looks please you; and when they speak, you listen to what they say. Yet they are like propped-up beams of timber. Every shout they hear they take to be against them. *They* are the enemy. Guard yourself against them. God confound them! How perverse they are!

When they are told: 'Come, God's apostle will beg forgiveness for you,' they turn their heads and you see them go away in scorn.

It is the same whether or not you ask forgiveness for them: God will not forgive them. God does not guide the evil-doers.

It is they who say: 'Give nothing to those that follow God's apostle until they have deserted him.' God's are the treasures of the heavens and the earth: but the hypocrites cannot understand.

63:8    They say: 'If we return to Madīnah,[1] the strong will soon drive out the weak.' But strength belongs to God and to His apostle and to the faithful: yet the hypocrites do not know it.

Believers, let neither your riches nor your children divert you from remembering God. Those that are so diverted will surely be the losers.

Give, then, of that which We have given you before death befalls any of you and you say: 'Reprieve me, Lord, awhile, that I may give in charity and be among the righteous.'

63:11   But God reprieves no soul when its term expires. God has knowledge of all your actions.

# CHEATING

*In the Name of God, the Compassionate, the Merciful*

64:1    ALL THAT is in the heavens and the earth gives glory to God. His is the sovereignty, and His all praise. He has power over all things.

---

1. To which the Prophet and his followers had fled from Mecca.

It was He that created you: yet some of you are 64:2
unbelievers, while others have faith. God is cognizant of all
your actions.

He created the heavens and the earth to manifest the
Truth, and fashioned you into a comely shape. To Him
shall you return.

He knows what the heavens and the earth contain. He
knows all that you conceal and all that you reveal. God
knows your innermost thoughts.

Have you not heard of those who disbelieved before you?
They tasted the fruit of their unbelief, and grievous punishment is yet in store for them. That is because, when their
apostles brought them veritable signs, they said: 'Shall
mortals be our guides?' They disbelieved and paid no heed.
But God was in no need of them: God is self-sufficient and
glorious.

The unbelievers claim they shall not be raised to life. Say:
'Yes, by the Lord, you shall assuredly be raised to life! Then
you shall be told of all that you have done. That is easy
enough for God.'

Believe then in God and in His apostle, and in the light 64:8
which We have revealed. God has knowledge of all your
actions.

The day on which He will gather you, the day on which
you shall all be gathered – that shall be a day of cheating.[1]
Those that believe in God and do what is right shall be
forgiven their sins and admitted to gardens watered by
running streams, where they shall dwell for ever. That is the
supreme triumph. But those that disbelieve and deny Our
revelations shall be the inmates of the Fire, and shall abide
therein for ever: an evil fate.

No misfortune strikes except by God's leave. He guides 64:11
the hearts of those who believe in Him. God has knowledge
of all things.

1. i.e. when the blessed will 'cheat' the damned of their places
in Paradise which would have been theirs had they been true
believers (Al-Baiḍāwī).

64:12     Obey God and obey the Apostle. If you pay no heed, Our apostle's duty is but to give clear warning.

God – there is no god but Him. In God let the faithful put their trust.

Believers, you have an enemy in your spouses and in your children: beware of them. But if you overlook their offences and forgive and pardon them, then know that God is forgiving and merciful.

Your wealth and your children are but a temptation. God's recompense is great. Therefore fear God with all your hearts, and be attentive, obedient, and charitable. That will be best for you.

Those that preserve themselves from their own greed will surely prosper. If you give a generous loan to God, He will pay you back twofold and will forgive you. Gracious is God, and benignant.

64:18     He has knowledge of the unknown and the manifest. He is the Mighty, the Wise One.

# DIVORCE

*In the Name of God, the Compassionate, the Merciful*

65:1     PROPHET (and you believers), if you divorce your wives, divorce them at the end of their waiting period. Compute their waiting period and have fear of God, your Lord. You shall not expel them from their homes, nor shall they go away, unless they have committed a proven lewd act. Such are the bounds set by God; he that transgresses God's bounds wrongs his own soul. You never know; after that, God may bring about some new event.

When their waiting term is ended, either keep them honourably or part with them in honour. Call to witness two honest men among you and give your testimony before God. Whoever believes in God and the Last Day is exhorted to do this. He that fears God, God will give him a

65:3     means of salvation and will provide for him whence he does not reckon: God is all-sufficient for the man who puts his trust in Him. God will surely bring about what He decrees. God has set a measure for all things.

If you are in doubt concerning those of your wives who 65:4 have ceased menstruating, know that their waiting period shall be three months. The same shall apply to those who have not yet menstruated.[1] As for pregnant women, their term shall end with their confinement. God will ease the hardship of the man who fears Him.

Such is the commandment which God has revealed to you. He that fears God shall be forgiven his sins and richly recompensed.

Lodge them in your own homes, according to your means. You shall not harass them so as to make life intolerable for them. If they are with child, maintain them until the end of their confinement; and if, after that, they give suck to the infants they bore you, give them their pay and consult together in all reasonableness. But if you cannot tolerate each other, let other women suckle for you.

Let the rich man spend according to his wealth, and the 65:7 poor man according to what God has given him. God does not charge a man with more than He has given him; God, after hardship, will bring ease.

How many nations have rebelled against the commandments of their Lord and His apostles! Stern was Our reckoning with them, and harrowing was Our scourge. They tasted the fruit of their misdeeds: and the fruit of their misdeeds was ruin. God has prepared a grievous scourge for them. Have fear of God, you that have sense and faith.

God has now sent down to you an exhortation; an apostle proclaiming to you God's revelations in all plainness, so that he may lead the faithful who do good works from darkness to the light. He that believes in God and does good works shall be admitted to gardens watered by running streams, where he shall dwell for ever. A rich provision God has made for him.

It is God who has created seven heavens, and earths as 65:12

1. On account of their young age. Child marriages were common.

many. His commandment descends through them, so that you may learn that God has power over all things, and that God encompasses all things with His knowledge.

# PROHIBITION

*In the Name of God, the Compassionate, the Merciful*

66:1 PROPHET, WHY do you prohibit that which God has made lawful for you, in seeking to please your wives?[1] God is forgiving and merciful.

God has given you absolution from such oaths. God is your Master. He is the Omniscient One, the Wise One.

When the Prophet confided a secret to one of his wives; and when she disclosed it and God informed him of this, he made known one part of it and said nothing about the other. And when he had acquainted her with it she said: 'Who told you this?' He replied: 'The Wise One, the All-knowing, told me.'

66:4 If you two[2] turn to God in penitence (for your hearts have sinned) you shall be pardoned; but if you conspire against him, know that God is his protector, and Gabriel, and the righteous among the faithful. The angels too are his helpers.

It may well be that, if he divorce you, his Lord will give him in your place better wives than yourselves, submissive to God and full of faith, obedient, penitent, devout, and given to fasting; both formerly-wedded and virgins.

66:6 Believers, guard yourselves and guard your kindred against a Fire fuelled with men and stones, in the charge of stern and mighty angels who never disobey God's command

---

1. Muḥammad, we are told, was once found by his wife Ḥafṣah with a Coptic slave from whom he had promised her to separate. Of this Ḥafṣah secretly informed 'Ā'ishah, another wife of his. To free Muḥammad from his promise to Ḥafṣah was the object of this chapter. Some of the references are obscure.

2. Ḥafṣah and 'Ā'ishah.

and who promptly do His bidding. They will say to the un- 66:7
believers: 'Make no excuses for yourselves this day. You
shall be rewarded according only to your deeds.'

Believers, turn to God in true repentance. Your Lord
may forgive you your sins and admit you to gardens
watered by running streams, on a day when the Prophet
and those who believe with him will suffer no disgrace
at the hands of God. Their light will shine in front of
them and on their right, and they will say: 'Lord, perfect
our light for us and forgive us. You have power over all
things.'

Prophet, make war on the unbelievers and the hypocrites,
and deal sternly with them. Hell shall be their home, evil
their fate.

God gave an example to the unbelievers in the wife 66:10
of Noah and the wife of Lot. They were married to two
of Our righteous servants and deceived them. Their
husbands could in no way protect them from God. They
were told: 'Enter the Fire with those that shall enter it.'

But to the faithful God gave an example in Pharaoh's
wife, who said: 'Lord, build me a house with You in
Paradise and deliver me from Pharaoh and his misdeeds.
Deliver me from a wicked nation.'

And in Mary, 'Imrān's daughter, who preserved her 66:12
chastity and into whose womb We breathed Our spirit; who
put her trust in the words of her Lord and His scriptures,
and was truly devout.

# SOVEREIGNTY

*In the Name of God, the Compassionate, the Merciful*

BLESSED BE He who in His hand holds all sovereignty: 67:1
He has power over all things.

He created death and life that He might put you to the
proof and find out which of you acquitted himself best. He
is the Mighty, the Forgiving One.

He created seven heavens, one above the other. You will 67:3

not see a flaw in the Merciful's creation. Turn up your eyes: can you detect a single crack?

67:4 Then look once more and yet again: your eyes will in the end grow dim and weary.

We have adorned the lowest heaven with lamps, missiles to pelt the devils with. We have prepared the scourge of the Fire for these, and the scourge of Hell for those who deny their Lord: an evil fate!

When they are flung into its flames, they shall hear it roaring and seething, as though bursting with rage. And every time a multitude is thrown therein, its keepers will say to them: 'Did no one come to warn you?' 'Yes,' they will reply, 'he did come, but we rejected him and said: "God has revealed nothing: you are in grievous error."' And they will say: 'If only we listened and understood, we should not now be among the inmates of the Fire.' Thus shall they confess their sin. Far from God's mercy are the inmates of the Fire.

But those that fear their Lord although they cannot see Him shall be forgiven and richly recompensed.

67:13 Whether you speak in private or aloud, He knows your innermost thoughts. Shall He who has created all things not know them all? Gracious is He and all-knowing.

It is He who has made the earth subservient to you. Walk about its regions and eat of His provisions. To Him shall all return at the Resurrection.

Are you confident that He who is in heaven will not cause the earth to cave in beneath you, so that it will shake to pieces and overwhelm you?

Are you confident that He who is in heaven will not let loose on you a sandy whirlwind? You will surely learn the truth of My warning.

Those who have gone before them likewise disbelieved: but how grievous was the way I rejected them!

Do they not see the birds above their heads, spreading their wings and folding them? None save the Merciful sustains them. He observes all things.

67:20 Who is it that will defend you like an army, if not the Merciful? Truly, the unbelievers are in error.

Who will provide for you if *He* withholds His sustenance? 67:21
Yet they persist in arrogance and in rebellion.

Who is more rightly guided, he that goes grovelling on
his face, or he that walks upright upon a straight path?

Say: 'It is He who has brought you into being, and given
you ears and eyes and hearts. Yet you are seldom thankful.'

Say: 'It was He who placed you on the earth, and before
Him shall you all be gathered.'

They ask: 'When will this promise be fulfilled, if what
you say be true?'

Say: 'God alone has knowledge of that. My mission is but
to warn you plainly.'

But when they see it drawing near, the unbelievers' faces
will be contorted with woe, and a voice will say: 'This is the
doom which you have challenged.'

Say: 'Consider: whether God destroys me and all my
followers or has mercy upon us, who will protect the
unbelievers from a woeful scourge?'

Say: 'He is the Lord of Mercy: in Him we believe, and in
Him we put our trust. You shall soon learn who is in
evident error.'

Say: 'Consider: if all the water that you have were to sink 67:30
down into the earth, who would give you running water in
its place?'

# THE PEN

*In the Name of God, the Compassionate, the Merciful*

*Nūn.* BY THE PEN, and what they [1] write, you [2] are not mad: 68:1
thanks to the favour of your Lord! A lasting recompense
awaits you, for yours is a sublime nature. You shall before
long see – as they will see – which of you is mad.

Your Lord knows best those who stray from His path, as
He knows best those who are rightly guided. Pay no heed
to the disbelievers: they desire you to overlook their doings 68:9

1. The angels.        2. Muḥammad.

68:10 that they may overlook yours. Nor yield to the wretch of many oaths, the mischief-making slanderer, the opponent of good, the wicked transgressor, the bully who is of doubtful birth to boot. Though such a man be blessed with wealth and children, when Our revelations are recited to him, he says: 'They are but fables of the ancients.' On the nose We will brand him!

We have afflicted them[1] as We afflicted the owners of the orchard who had declared that they would pluck its fruit next morning, without adding any reservation.[2] A visitant from your Lord came down upon it while they slept, and in the morning it was as black as midnight.

At daybreak they called out to one another, saying: 'Hurry to your orchard, if you would pick its fruit.' And off they went, whispering to one another: 'No beggar shall enter the orchard today.'

Thus they went out, fixed in their resolve. But when they saw it they cried: 'We have been wrong. We are utterly ruined.'

The most upright among them said: 'Did I not bid you praise God?'

68:29 'Glory be to our Lord,' they answered. 'We have assuredly done wrong.' And they began to blame one another.

'Woe betide us!' they cried. 'We have been great transgressors. We hope Our Lord will give us a better orchard in its place; to Our Lord we will turn.'

Such was their punishment. But the punishment of the life to come is more terrible, if they but knew it.

With gardens of delight the righteous shall be rewarded by their Lord. Are We to treat alike the true believers and the guilty? What has come over you[3] that you should judge so ill?

Have you a scripture that promises you whatever you choose? Or have We sworn a covenant with you – a covenant binding till the Day of Resurrection – that you

68:40 shall have what you yourselves ordain? Ask if any of them[3] will vouch for that!

---

1. The Meccans.　　　　2. Without saying: 'If God wills.'
3. The unbelievers.

Or have they other deities besides God? Let them 68:41
produce them, if what they say be true!

On the day the dread event unfolds and they are told to
prostrate themselves, they will not be able. Utterly
humbled, they shall stand with eyes downcast; for they had
long since been bidden to prostrate themselves when they
were safe and sound.

Therefore leave to Me those that deny this revelation. We
will lead them step by step to their ruin, in ways beyond
their knowledge. I shall bear long with them: My stratagem
is sure.

Are you demanding pay of them, so that they are 68:46
burdened with debt?

Or have they knowledge of what is hidden? Can they
write it down?

Wait, then, the judgement of your Lord and do not act
like him[1] who was swallowed by the whale when he called
out in despair. Had his Lord not bestowed on him His
grace, he would have been abandoned in the open to be
blamed by all. But his Lord chose him for His own and
made of him a righteous man.

When they hear the Admonition, the unbelievers well-
nigh devour you with their eyes. 'He is surely possessed,'
they say.

Yet it is but an admonition to mankind. 68:52

# THE CATASTROPHE

*In the Name of God, the Compassionate, the Merciful*

THE CATASTROPHE: and what is the Catastrophe? Would 69:1
that you knew what the Catastrophe is!

Thamūd and ʿĀd denied the Last Judgement. By a
deafening shout was Thamūd destroyed, and ʿĀd by a
howling, violent gale which He let loose on them for seven 69:7
nights and eight successive days: you might have seen them

1. Jonah.

lying dead as though they had been hollow trunks of palm-trees. Can you see even one of them still alive?

Pharaoh, and those before him, and the inhabitants of the Ruined Cities, also committed sin and disobeyed their Lord's apostle. With a terrible scourge He smote them.

When the Flood rose high We carried you[1] in the floating ark, making the event a warning, so that all attentive ears might heed it.

When the Trumpet sounds a single blast; when earth with all its mountains is raised high and with one mighty crash is flattened into dust – on that day the Dread Event will come to pass.

Frail and tottering, the sky will be rent asunder on that day, and the angels will stand on all its sides with eight of them carrying the throne of your Lord above their heads. On that day you shall be utterly exposed, and all your secrets shall be brought to light.

He who is given his book in his right hand will say: 'Here it is, read my book! I knew I should come face to face with my account!' His shall be a blissful state in a lofty garden, with clusters of fruit within his reach. We shall say to him: 'Eat and drink to your heart's content: your recompense for what you did in days gone by.'

But he who is given his book in his left hand will say: 'Would that my book were not given me! Would that I knew nothing of my account! Would that my death had ended all! Nothing has my wealth availed me, and I am bereft of all my power.'

We shall say: 'Lay hold of him and bind him. Burn him in the fire of Hell, then fasten him with a chain seventy cubits long. For he did not believe in God, the Most Great, nor did he care to feed the destitute. Today he shall be friendless here; only filth shall be his food, the filth which only sinners eat.'

I swear by all that you can see, and all that is hidden from your view, that this is the utterance of a noble messenger. It is no poet's speech: scant is your faith! It is no soothsayer's

---

1. i.e. your forefathers.

divination: how little you reflect! It is a revelation from the   69:43
Lord of the Universe.

Had he invented lies concerning Us, We would have
seized him by the right hand and severed his heart's vein:
not one of you could have protected him!

It[1] is but an admonition to the righteous. We well know
that there are some among you who will deny it.

It is the despair of the unbelievers. It is the indubitable
truth. Praise, then, the name of your Lord, the Almighty.   69.52

# THE LADDERS

*In the Name of God, the Compassionate, the Merciful*

A SCEPTIC[2] once demanded that punishment be visited   70:1
forthwith upon the unbelievers.

No power can hinder God from punishing them. He is
the Lord of the Ladders, by which the angels and the Spirit
will ascend to Him in one day: a day whose space is fifty
thousand years.

Therefore conduct yourself with becoming patience.
They think the Day of Judgement is far off: but We see it
near at hand.

On that day the sky shall become like molten brass, and   70:8
the mountains like tufts of wool scattered in the wind.
Friends will meet, but shall not speak to each other. To
redeem himself from the torment of that day the sinner will
gladly sacrifice his children, his wife, his brother, the
kinsfolk who gave him shelter, and all the people of the
earth, if then this might deliver him.

But no! The fire of Hell shall drag him down by the
scalp, shall claim him who had turned his back and amassed
riches and covetously hoarded them.

Indeed, man was created impatient. When evil befalls him
he is despondent; but, blessed with good fortune, he grows   70:21
tight-fisted.

1. The Koran.    2. Literally, a questioner.

70:22    Not so the worshippers, who are steadfast in prayer; who
set aside a due portion of their wealth for the beggar and for
the dispossessed, who truly believe in the Day of Reckoning,
and dread the punishment of their Lord (for none is secure
from the punishment of their Lord); who restrain their
carnal desire (save with their wives and slave-girls, for these
are lawful for them: transgressors are those who lust after
other than these); who keep their trusts and promises and
bear true witness; and who attend to their prayers with
promptitude. These shall be laden with honours, in fair
gardens.

70:36    But what has befallen the unbelievers, that they scramble
before you in multitudes from right and left?

Are they each seeking to enter a garden of delight?

No! Let them remember of what We created them!

I swear by the Lord of the East and of the West that We
have the power to replace them by others better than they:
nothing can hinder us from so doing. Let them paddle, let
them play until they face the day they are promised; the day
when they shall rush forward from their graves, like men
70:44 rallying to a standard, with downcast eyes and countenances
distorted with shame.

Such is the day they are promised.


# NOAH

*In the Name of God, the Compassionate, the Merciful*

71:1   WE SENT forth Noah to his people, saying: 'Give warning
to your people before a woeful scourge overtakes them.'

He said: 'My people, I come to warn you plainly. Serve
God and fear Him, and obey me. He will forgive you your
sins and give you respite for an appointed term. When
God's time arrives, none shall put it back. Would that you
understood this!'

'Lord,' said Noah, 'night and day I have pleaded with my
71:6 people, but my pleas have only aggravated their aversion.

Each time I call on them to seek Your pardon, they thrust 71:7
their fingers into their ears and draw their cloaks over their
heads, persisting in sin and bearing themselves with insolent
pride. I called out loud to them, and appealed to them in
public and in private. "Seek forgiveness of your Lord," I
said. "He is ever ready to forgive. He sends down
abundant water from the sky for you and bestows upon you
wealth and children. He has provided you with gardens and
with running brooks. Why do you deny the greatness of
God when He created you in gradual stages? Can you not
see how God created the seven heavens one above the other,
placing in them the moon for a light and the sun for a
lantern? God has brought you forth from the earth like a
plant, and to the earth He will restore you. Then He will
bring you back afresh. God has made the earth a vast
expanse for you, so that you may roam its spacious paths." '

And Noah said: 'Lord, my people disobey me, and follow 71:21
those whose wealth and offspring will only hasten their
perdition. They have devised an outrageous plot, and said
to each other: "Do not renounce your gods. Do not forsake
Wadd or Suwā' or Yaghūth or Ya'ūq or Naṣr." [1] They have
led numerous men astray. You surely drive the wrongdoers
to further error.'

And because of their sins they were overwhelmed by the
Flood and cast into the Fire. They found none besides God
to help them.

And Noah said: 'Lord, do not leave a single unbeliever
on the earth. If You spare them, they will mislead Your
servants and beget none but sinners and unbelievers.
Forgive me, Lord, and forgive my parents and every true 71:28
believer who seeks refuge in my house. Forgive all the
faithful, men and women, and hasten the destruction of the
wrongdoers.'

1. Names of idols.

# THE JINN

*In the Name of God, the Compassionate, the Merciful*

72:1 SAY: 'IT is revealed to me that a band of jinn listened to God's revelations and said: "We have heard a wondrous Koran giving guidance to the right path. We believed in it and shall henceforth serve none besides Our Lord. He (exalted be the glory of our Lord!) has taken no consort, nor has He begotten any children. The Blaspheming One among us has uttered a wanton falsehood against God, although we had supposed no man or jinnee could tell of God what is untrue."'

(Some men have sought the help of jinn, but they misled them into further error. Like you, they thought that God could never resurrect the dead.)

'"We made our way to high heaven, and found it filled with mighty wardens and fiery comets. We sat eavesdropping, but eavesdroppers find comets lying in wait for them. We cannot tell if this bodes evil to those who dwell on earth or if their Lord intends to guide them.

72:11 '"Some of us are righteous, while others are not; we follow different ways. We know we cannot escape on earth from God, nor can we elude His grasp by flight. When we heard His guidance we believed in Him: he that believes in his Lord shall fear neither dishonesty nor injustice.

'"Some of us are Muslims and some are wrongdoers. Those that embrace Islām pursue the right path; but those that do wrong shall become the fuel of Hell."'

If they[1] pursue the straight path We shall vouchsafe them abundant rain, and thereby put them to the proof. He that pays no heed to his Lord's warning shall be sternly punished.

Temples are built for God's worship; invoke in them no 72:19 other god besides Him. When God's servant[2] rose to pray to Him, they pressed around him in multitudes.

1. The Meccans.     2. Muḥammad.

Say: 'I will pray to my Lord and worship none besides 72:20
Him.'

Say: 'I have no control over any evil or good that befalls
you.'

Say: 'None can protect me from God, nor can I find any
refuge besides Him. My mission is only to make known His
messages; those that disobey God and His apostle shall
abide for ever in the fire of Hell.'

When they behold the scourge they are promised, they
shall realize who had the less powerful protector, and who
were fewer in number.

Say: 'I cannot tell whether the scourge you are promised
is imminent, or whether my Lord has set for it a far-off day.
He alone has knowledge of what is hidden: His secrets He
reveals to none, except to the apostles whom He has
chosen. He sends down guardians who walk·before them
and behind them, that He may ascertain if they have indeed 72:28
delivered their Lord's messages. He has knowledge of all they
have, and keeps strict count of all things.'

# THE MANTLED ONE

*In the Name of God, the Compassionate, the Merciful*

YOU[1] THAT are wrapped up in your mantle, keep vigil all 73:1
night, save for a few hours; half the night, or even less: or a
little more – and with measured tone recite the Koran, for
We are about to address to you words of surpassing gravity.
It is in the watches of the night that impressions are
strongest and words most eloquent; in the day-time you are
hard-pressed with the affairs of this world.

Remember the name of your Lord and dedicate yourself
to Him utterly. He is the Lord of the East and of the West:
there is no god but Him. Accept Him for your Protector.

Bear patiently with what they[2] say, and leave their
company without recrimination. Leave to Me those that 73:11

1. Muḥammad.     2. The unbelievers.

409

deny the Truth, those that enjoy the comforts of this life;
73:12  bear with them yet a little while. We have in store for them
heavy fetters and a blazing fire, choking food and
harrowing torment: on the day when the earth shall quiver
with all its mountains, and the mountains crumble into
heaps of shifting sand.

We have sent forth an apostle to testify against you, just
as We sent an apostle to Pharaoh before you. Pharaoh
disobeyed Our messenger, so that with a baleful scourge
We smote him.

If you persist in unbelief, how will you escape the day
that will make your children grey-haired, the day when
the sky will split asunder? God's promise shall be fulfilled.

This is but an admonition. Let him who will, take the
right path to his Lord.

73:20 ·  Your Lord knows that you[1] sometimes keep vigil well-
nigh two-thirds of the night, and sometimes half or one-
third of it, as do others among your followers. God
measures the night and the day. He knows you[2] cannot
tell the length of the vigil, and turns to you mercifully.
Recite from the Koran as many verses as you are able; He
knows that among you there are sick men and others
roaming the land in search of God's bounty; and yet others
fighting for the cause of God. Recite from it, then, as many
verses as you are able. Attend to your prayers, render the
alms levy, and give God a generous loan. Whatever good
you do you shall surely find it with God, ennobled and
richly rewarded by Him. Implore God to forgive you; God
is forgiving and merciful.


# THE CLOAKED ONE

*In the Name of God, the Compassionate, the Merciful*

74:1  YOU THAT are wrapped up in your cloak, arise and give
warning.

1. Muḥammad.          2. The believers.

Magnify your Lord, purify your garments, and keep 74:3
away from uncleanness.

Bestow no favours expecting gain. Be patient for your
Lord's sake.

The day the Trumpet sounds shall be a hard and joyless
day for the unbelievers. Leave to Me the man whom I
created helpless and endowed with vast riches and thriving
children. I have made his progress smooth and easy: yet he
hopes that I shall give him more. By no means! Because he
has stubbornly denied Our revelations, I will lay on him a
mounting torment.

He pondered, and he schemed. Confound him, how he
schemed! Again, confound him, how he schemed!

He looked around him, frowning and scowling; then he
turned away in scornful pride and said: 'This is but sorcery
counterfeited, the utterance of a mere mortal!'

I will surely cast him into the Fire. Would that you knew
what the Fire is like! It leaves nothing, it spares no one; it
burns the skins of men. It is guarded by nineteen keepers.

We have appointed none but angels to guard the Fire, 74:31
and made their number a subject for dispute among the
unbelievers, so that those to whom the Scriptures were
given may be convinced and the true believers strengthened
in their faith; that those to whom the Scriptures were given,
and the true believers, may have no doubts; and that those
whose hearts are tainted and those who have no faith may
say: 'What could God mean by this?' Thus God confounds
whom He will and guides whom He pleases. None knows
the warriors of your Lord but Himself. This is no more
than an admonition to mankind.

No, by the moon! By the departing night and the coming
dawn, it is a dire scourge, a warning to mankind; alike to
those of you that would march on and those that would
remain behind.

Each soul is the hostage of its own deeds. Those on the
right hand will in their gardens ask the sinners: 'What has
brought you into Hell?' They will reply: 'We never prayed,
nor did we ever feed the destitute. We engaged in vain 74:45

74:46 disputes and denied the Day of Reckoning till the inevitable end overtook us.'

No intercessor's plea shall save them. Why then do they turn away from this reminder, like frightened asses fleeing from a lion?

Indeed, each one of them demands a scripture of his own to be unrolled before him. No, they have no fear of the hereafter.

No. This is an admonition. Let him who will, take heed.

74.56 But none takes heed except by the will of God. He is the Lord of goodness and forgiveness.

# THE RESURRECTION

*In the Name of God, the Compassionate, the Merciful*

75:1 I SWEAR by the Day of Resurrection, and by the self-reproaching soul!

Does man think We shall never put his bones together again? Indeed, We can remould his very fingers!

Yet man would ever deny what is to come. 'When will this be,' he asks, 'this Day of Resurrection?'

But when the sight of mortals is confounded and the moon eclipsed; when sun and moon are brought together – on that day man will ask: 'Whither shall I flee?'

No, there shall be no refuge. For to your Lord, on that day, all shall return.

Man shall on that day be told of all his deeds, from first to last. Indeed, man shall bear witness against himself, plead as he may with his excuses.

(You[1] need not move your tongue too fast to learn this revelation. We Ourself shall see to its collection and recital. When We read it, follow its words attentively; We shall Ourself explain its meaning.)

75:21 Yet you[2] love this fleeting life, and are heedless of the life to come.

1. Muḥammad.          2. The Meccans.

On that day there shall be joyous faces, looking towards 75:22
their Lord. On that day there shall be mournful faces,
dreading some great affliction.

But when a man's soul is about to leave him and those
around him cry: 'Will no one save him?' When he knows
it is the final parting and the pangs of death assail him –
on that day to your Lord he shall be driven. For in this
life he neither believed nor prayed; he denied the truth
and, turning his back, went to his kinsfolk elated with
pride.

Well have you deserved this doom; well have you
deserved it.

Well have you deserved this doom: too well have you
deserved it!

Does man think he will be left alone, to no purpose? Was
he not a drop of ejaculated semen? He became a clot of
blood; then God formed and moulded him, and gave him
male and female parts. Has He no power, then, to raise the 75:40
dead to life?

# MAN

*In the Name of God, the Compassionate, the Merciful*

DOES THERE not pass over man a space of time when his 76:1
life is a blank?[1]

We have created man from the union of the two sexes, so
that We may put him to the proof. We have endowed him
with hearing and sight and, be he thankful or oblivious of
Our favours, We have shown him the right path.

For the unbelievers We have prepared chains and fetters,
and a blazing Fire. But the righteous shall drink of a cup
tempered at the Camphor Fountain, a gushing spring at
which the servants of God will refresh themselves: they
who keep their vows and dread the broadcast terrors of
Judgement-day; who, though they hold it dear, give suste- 76:8

---

1. In the womb.

nance to the destitute, the orphan, and the captive, saying:
76:9 'We feed you for God's sake only; we seek of you neither recompense nor thanks: for we fear from our Lord a day of anguish and of woe.'

God will deliver them from the evil of that day, and make their faces shine with joy. He will reward them for their steadfastness with Paradise and robes of silk. Reclining there upon soft couches, they shall feel neither the scorching heat nor the biting cold. Trees will spread their shade around them, and fruits will hang in clusters over them.

They shall be served on silver dishes, and beakers as large as goblets; silver goblets which they themselves shall measure: and cups brim-full with ginger-flavoured water from a fount called Salsabīl. They shall be attended by boys graced with eternal youth, who to the beholder's eyes will seem like sprinkled pearls. When you gaze upon that scene, you will behold a kingdom blissful and glorious.

They shall be arrayed in garments of fine green silk and rich brocade, and adorned with bracelets of silver. Their Lord will give them pure nectar to drink.

76:22 Thus shall you be rewarded; your high endeavours are gratifying to God.

We have made known to you the Koran by gradual revelation; therefore await with patience the judgement of your Lord, and do not yield to the wicked and the unbelieving. Remember the name of your Lord morning and evening; in the night-time worship Him: praise Him all night long.

The unbelievers love this fleeting life too well, and thus prepare for themselves a heavy day of doom. *We* created them, and endowed their limbs and joints with strength; but if We please, We can replace them by other men.

This is indeed an admonition. Let him that will, take the right path to his Lord. Yet you cannot choose, except by the will of God. God is all-knowing and wise.

76:31 He admits into His mercy whom He will: but for the wrongdoers He has prepared a woeful punishment.

# THOSE THAT ARE SENT FORTH

*In the Name of God, the Compassionate, the Merciful*

By THE gales, sent forth in swift succession; by the raging 77:1
tempests and the rain-spreading winds; by your Lord's
revelations, discerning good from evil and admonishing by
plea and warning: that which you have been promised shall
be fulfilled!

When the stars are blotted out; when the sky is rent
asunder and the mountains crumble into dust; when the
apostles are brought together on the appointed day – when
will all this be? Upon the Day of Judgement!

Would that you knew what the Day of Judgement is!
On that day woe betide the disbelievers! Did We not
destroy the men of old and cause others to follow them?
Thus shall We deal with the guilty.

On that day woe betide the disbelievers! Did We not create
you from a humble fluid, which We kept in a safe
receptacle[1] for an appointed term? All this We did; how
excellent is Our work!

On that day woe betide the disbelievers! Have We not 77:24
made the earth a home for the living and for the dead? Have
We not placed high mountains upon it, and given you fresh
water for your drink?

On that day woe betide the disbelievers! Begone to that
Hell which you deny! Depart into the shadow that will rise
high in three columns, giving neither shade nor shelter
from the flames, and throwing up sparks as huge as towers,
as bright as yellow camels!

On that day woe betide the disbelievers! On that day they
shall not speak, nor shall their pleas be heeded.

On that day woe betide the disbelievers! Such is the Day of
Judgement. We will assemble you all, together with past
generations. If then you are cunning, try your spite against Me!

On that day woe betide the disbelievers! The righteous shall 77:41
dwell amidst cool shades and fountains, and feed on such

1. The womb.

77:42 fruits as they desire. We shall say to them: 'Eat and drink, and may every joy attend you! This is the guerdon of your labours.' Thus shall We recompense the righteous.

On that day woe betide the disbelievers! Eat and enjoy yourselves awhile. Surely you are sinners all.

On that day woe betide the disbelievers! When they are bidden to kneel down, they do not kneel.

77:50 On that day woe betide the disbelievers! In what revelation, after this, will they believe?

# THE TIDINGS

*In the Name of God, the Compassionate, the Merciful*

78:1 ABOUT WHAT are they asking?

About the fateful tidings – the theme of their disputes.

But they shall learn; before long they shall learn.

Did We not spread the earth like a bed, and raise the mountains like supporting poles?

We created you in pairs, and gave you rest in sleep. We made the night a mantle, and ordained the day for work. We built above you seven mighty heavens and placed in them a shining lamp. We sent down abundant water from the clouds, bringing forth grain and varied plants, and gardens thick with foliage.

78:17 Fixed is the Day of Judgement. On that day the Trumpet shall be sounded, and you shall come in multitudes. The gates of heaven shall swing open, and the mountains shall pass away and become like vapour.

Hell will lie in ambush, a home for the transgressors. There they shall abide long ages; there they shall taste neither refreshment nor any drink, save scalding water and decaying filth: a fitting recompense.

They disbelieved in Our reckoning, and roundly denied Our revelations. But We counted all their doings and wrote

78:30 them down. We shall say: 'Taste this: you shall have nothing but mounting torment!'

As for the righteous, they shall surely triumph. Theirs 78:31
shall be gardens and vineyards, and high-bosomed maidens
for companions: a truly overflowing cup.

There they shall hear no idle talk, nor any falsehood. Such
is the recompense of your Lord – a gift that will suffice
them: the Lord of the heavens and the earth and all that lies
between them; the Merciful, with whom no one can speak.

On the day when the Spirit and the angels stand up in
their ranks, they shall not speak; except him who shall
receive the sanction of the Merciful and declare what is right.

That day is sure to come. Let him who will, seek a way
back to his Lord. We have forewarned you of an imminent 78:40
scourge: the day when man will look upon his works and
the unbeliever cry: 'Would that I were dust!'

# THE SOUL-SNATCHERS

*In the Name of God, the Compassionate, the Merciful*

BY THOSE who snatch away men's souls, and those who 79:1
gently release them; by those who float at will, and those
who speed headlong; by those who govern the affairs of
this world! On the day the Trumpet sounds its first and
second blast, all hearts shall be filled with terror, and all
eyes shall stare with awe.

They say: 'When we are turned to hollow bones, shall we
be restored to life? A fruitless transformation!' But with one
blast they shall return to the earth's surface.

Have you heard the story of Moses?

His Lord called out to him in the sacred valley of Ṭuwā,
saying: 'Go to Pharaoh: he has transgressed all bounds; and
say: "Will you reform yourself? I will guide you to your
Lord, so that you may have fear of Him."'

He showed Pharaoh the mightiest sign, but he denied it
and rebelled. He quickly went away and, summoning all his
men, made to them a proclamation. 'I am your supreme
Lord,' he said.

God smote him with the scourge of the hereafter, and of 79:25

79:26 this life. Surely in this there is a lesson for the God-fearing.

Are you harder to create than the heaven which He has built? He raised it high and fashioned it, giving darkness to its night and brightness to its day.

After that He spread the earth, and, drawing water from its depth, brought forth its pastures. He set down the mountains, for you and for your cattle to delight in.

But when the supreme disaster strikes – the day when man will call to mind his labours – when the Fire is brought in sight of all – he that transgressed and chose this present life shall have his home in Hell; but he that feared to stand before his Lord and curbed his soul's desire shall have his home in Paradise.

They question you about the Hour of Doom. 'When will it come?' they ask. But how are you to know? Only your Lord knows when it will come. Your duty is but to warn those that fear it.

79:46 On the day when they behold that hour, they will think they had lingered but one evening, or one morning.

# HE FROWNED

*In the Name of God, the Compassionate, the Merciful*

80:1 HE[1] FROWNED and turned his back when the blind man came towards him.

How could you[1] tell? He might have sought to purify himself. He might have been forewarned, and might have profited from Our warning.

But to the wealthy man you were all attention: although the fault would not be yours if he remained uncleansed. Yet to him that came to you with zeal and awe, you paid no heed.

Indeed, this is an admonition; let him who will, bear it in mind. It is set down on honoured pages, purified and exalted, by the hands of devout and gracious scribes.

80:17 Let man perish! How ungrateful he is!

1. Muḥammad.

From what did God create him? From a little germ He 80:18
created him and gave him due proportions. He makes his path
smooth for him, then causes him to die and stows him in a
grave. He will surely bring him back to life when He
pleases. Yet he declines to do His bidding.

Let man reflect on the food he eats: how We pour down
the rain in torrents and cleave the earth asunder; how We
bring forth the corn, the grapes and the fresh vegetation;
the olive and the palm, the thickets, the fruit-trees and the
green pasture, for you and for your cattle to delight in.

But when the dread blast is sounded, on that day each man
will forsake his brother, his mother and his father, his wife
and his children: for each one of them will on that day have
enough sorrow of his own.

On that day there shall be beaming faces, smiling and
joyful. On that day there shall be faces veiled with darkness,
covered with dust. These shall be the faces of the sinful 80:42
unbelievers.

# THE CESSATION

*In the Name of God, the Compassionate, the Merciful*

WHEN THE sun ceases to shine; when the stars fall and 81:1
the mountains are blown away; when camels big with young
are left untended, and the wild beasts are brought together;
when the seas are set alight and men's souls are reunited; when
the infant girl,[1] buried alive, is asked for what crime she was
slain; when the records of men's deeds are laid open, and
heaven is stripped bare; when Hell burns fiercely and Paradise
is brought near: then each soul shall learn what it has done.

I swear by the turning planets, and by the stars that rise 81:15
and set; by the night, when it descends, and the first breath
of morning: this is the word of a gracious and mighty
messenger, held in honour by the Lord of the Throne,
obeyed in heaven, faithful to his trust. 81:21

1. An allusion to the pre-Islamic custom of burying unwanted
newborn girls.

81:22    No, your compatriot[1] is not mad. He saw him[2] on the clear horizon. He does not grudge the secrets of the unseen; nor is this the utterance of an accursèd devil.

Whither then are you going?

This is but an admonition to all men: to those among you 81:29 that have the will to be upright. Yet you cannot choose, except by the will of God, Lord of the Universe.

# THE CATACLYSM

*In the Name of God, the Compassionate, the Merciful*

82:1  WHEN THE sky is rent asunder; when the stars scatter and the oceans merge together; when the graves are hurled about: each soul shall know what it has done and what it has failed to do.

O man! What evil has enticed you from your gracious Lord who created you, and gave you due proportions and an upright form? In whatever shape He willed He could have moulded you.

82:9    Yet you deny the Last Judgement. Surely there are guardians watching over you, noble recorders who know of all your actions.

The righteous will surely dwell in bliss. But the wicked shall burn in Hell upon the Judgement-day: nor shall they ever escape from it.

Would that you knew what the Day of Judgement is! Oh, 82:19 would that you knew what the Day of Judgement is! It is the day when every soul will stand alone and God will reign supreme.

1. Muḥammad.     2. Gabriel.

# THE UNJUST

*In the Name of God, the Compassionate, the Merciful*

WOE betide the unjust who, when others measure for 83:1
them, exact in full, but when they measure or weigh for
others, defraud them!

Do they not think they will be raised to life upon a fateful
day, the day when all mankind will stand before the Lord of
the Universe?

Truly, the record of the sinners is in Sijjīn. Would that
you knew what Sijjīn is! It is a sealed book.

On that day woe betide the disbelievers who deny the
Last Judgement! None denies it except the evil transgressor
who, when Our revelations are recited to him, cries: 'Fables
of the ancients!'

No! Their own deeds have drawn a veil over their hearts.

No! On that day a barrier shall be set between them and
their Lord. They shall burn in Hell, and shall be told: 'This
is the scourge that you denied!'

But the record of the righteous shall be in 'Illiyyūn.
Would that you knew what 'Illiyyūn is! It is a sealed book,
seen only by the favoured.

The righteous will surely dwell in bliss. Reclining upon 83:22
soft couches they will gaze around them: and in their faces
you shall mark the glow of joy. They shall be given pure
nectar to drink, securely sealed, whose very dregs are musk
(for this let all men emulously strive); tempered with
the waters of Tasnīm, a spring at which the favoured will
refresh themselves.

The evil-doers mock the faithful and wink at one another
as they pass by them. When they meet their own folk they
speak of them with jests, and when they see them, they say:
'These are surely erring men!' Yet they were not sent to be
their guardians.

But on that day the faithful will mock the unbelievers as
they recline upon their couches and gaze around them.

Shall not the unbelievers be rewarded according to their 83:36
deeds?

# THE RENDING

*In the Name of God, the Compassionate, the Merciful*

84:1 WHEN THE sky is rent apart, obeying her Lord in true submission; when the earth expands and casts out all that is within her and becomes empty, obeying her Lord in true submission; then, O man, who labour constantly to meet your Lord, shall you meet Him.

He that is given his book in his right hand shall have a lenient reckoning, and shall go back rejoicing to his people. But he that is given his book behind his back shall call down destruction on himself and burn in the fire of Hell; for he lived without a care among his people and thought he would never return to God. Yes; but his Lord was ever watching him.

84:16 I swear by the glow of sunset; by the night, and all that it brings together; by the moon, in her full perfection: that you shall march onwards from state to state.

Why then do they not have faith, or kneel in prayer when the Koran is read to them?

The unbelievers indeed deny it; but God knows best the falsehoods they believe in.

84:25 Therefore proclaim to all a woeful doom, save those who embrace the true Faith and do good works; for theirs is an unfailing recompense.

# THE CONSTELLATIONS

*In the Name of God, the Compassionate, the Merciful*

85:1 BY THE heaven with its constellations! By the Promised Day! By the Witness, and that which is witnessed!

Cursed be the diggers of the trench, who lighted the consuming fire and sat around it to watch the faithful being put to the torture! Nor did they torture them for any reason save that they believed in God, the Mighty, the Praised

85:9 One, who has sovereignty over the heavens and the earth. God is the Witness of all things.

Those that persecute believers, men or women, and never 85:10
repent shall be rewarded with the scourge of Hell, the
scourge of the Conflagration. But those that have faith and
do good works shall be rewarded with gardens watered by
running streams. That is the supreme triumph.

Stern indeed is the vengeance of your Lord. It is He who
brings into being and then restores to life. Forgiving and
benignant, He is the Lord of the Glorious Throne, the
Executor of His own will.

Have you not heard the story of the warriors, of Pharaoh
and of Thamūd? Yet the unbelievers still deny it.

God surrounds them all. Surely this is a glorious Koran,
inscribed on an imperishable tablet.                    85:22


# THE NIGHTLY VISITANT

*In the Name of God, the Compassionate, the Merciful*

BY THE heaven, and by the nightly visitant!              86:1

Would that you knew what the nightly visitant is!

It is the star of piercing brightness.

For every soul there is a guardian watching it. Let man
reflect from what he is created. He is created from an
ejaculated fluid that issues from between the loins and the
ribs.

Surely He has power to bring him back to life, on the day
when men's consciences are searched. Helpless shall he be,
with none to succour him.

By the heaven with its recurring cycles, and by the earth, 86:11
ever bursting with new growth; this[1] is a discerning
utterance, no flippant jest.

They scheme and scheme: and I, too, scheme and
scheme. Therefore bear with the unbelievers, and let them 86:17
be awhile.


1. The Koran.

# THE MOST HIGH

*In the Name of God, the Compassionate, the Merciful*

87:1 PRAISE THE Name of your Lord, the Most High, who has created all things and gave them due proportions; who has ordained their destinies and guided them; who brings forth the green pasture, then turns it to withered grass.

We shall make you recite Our revelations, so that you shall forget none of them except as God pleases. He has knowledge of all that is manifest, and all that is hidden.

We shall guide you to the smoothest path. Therefore give warning, if warning will avail. He that fears God will heed 87:11 it, but the wicked sinner will flout it. He shall burn in the gigantic Fire, where he shall neither die nor live. Happy shall be the man who keeps himself pure, who remembers the name of his Lord and prays.

Yet you[1] prefer this life, although the life to come is better and more lasting.

87:19 All this is written in earlier scriptures; the scriptures of Abraham and Moses.

# THE OVERWHELMING EVENT

*In the Name of God, the Compassionate, the Merciful*

88:1 HAVE YOU heard of the Event which will overwhelm mankind?

On that day there shall be downcast faces, of men broken and worn out, burnt by a scorching fire, drinking from a seething fountain. Their only food shall be bitter thorns, which will neither sustain them nor satisfy their hunger.

On that day there shall be radiant faces, of men well-pleased with their labours, in a lofty garden. There they shall hear no idle talk. A gushing fountain shall be there, and raised soft couches with goblets placed before them; 88:16 silken cushions ranged in order and carpets richly spread.

1. The unbelievers of Mecca.

Do they never reflect on the camels, and how they were 88:17
created? The heaven, how it was raised on high? The
mountains, how they were set down? The earth, how it was
made flat?

Therefore give warning. Your duty is only to give
warning: you are not their keeper. As for those that turn
their backs and disbelieve, God will inflict on them the
supreme chastisement. To Us they shall return, and We will 88:26
bring them to account.

# THE DAWN

*In the Name of God, the Compassionate, the Merciful*

BY THE Dawn and the Ten Nights[1]; by that which is dual, 89:1
and that which is single; by the night, when it comes!

Is there not in this a mighty oath for a man of sense?

Have you not heard how your Lord dealt with 'Ād?[2] The
people of the many-columned city of Iram, whose like has
never been built in the whole land? And with Thamūd,[2]
who hewed out their dwellings among the rocks of the
valley? And with Pharaoh, who impaled his victims upon
the stake?

They had all led sinful lives, and made the land teem with
wickedness. Therefore your Lord let loose on them His
scourge; for from His eminence your Lord observes all.

As for man, when his Lord tests him by exalting him and 89:15
bestowing favours on him, he says: 'My Lord is bountiful
to me.' But when He tests him by grudging him His
favours, he says: 'My Lord despises me.'

No! But you show no kindness to the orphan, nor do you
vie with each other in feeding the destitute. Greedily you
lay your hands on the inheritance of the weak, and you love
riches with all your hearts.

89:20

1. The first ten nights of the sacred month of Dhūl-Ḥajjah.
2. Tradition has it that the tribes of 'Ād and Thamūd were
destroyed on account of their sins.

89:21　No! But when the earth is crushed to fine dust, and your Lord comes down with the angels, in their ranks, and Hell is brought near – on that day man will remember his deeds. But what will memory avail him?

He will say: 'Would that I had been charitable in my lifetime!' But on that day none will punish as He will punish, and none will bind with chains like His.

O serene soul! Return to your Lord, joyful, and pleasing 89:30　in His sight. Join My servants and enter My Paradise.

# THE CITY

*In the Name of God, the Compassionate, the Merciful*

90:1　I SWEAR by this city (and you[1] are a resident of this city), by the begetter[2] and all whom he begot: We created man to try him with afflictions.

Does he think that none has power over him? 'I have squandered vast riches!' he boasts. Does he think that none observes him?

90:8　Have We not given him two eyes, a tongue, and two lips, and shown him the two paths?[3] Yet he would not scale the Height.

Would that you knew what the Height is. It is the freeing of a bondsman; the feeding, in the day of famine, of an orphaned relation or a needy man in distress; to have faith and to enjoin fortitude and mercy.

Those that do this shall stand on the right hand; but those that deny Our revelations shall stand on the left, with 90:20　Hell-fire close above them.

# THE SUN

*In the Name of God, the Compassionate, the Merciful*

91:1　BY THE sun and his midday brightness; by the moon, which rises after him; by the day, which reveals his splendour; by the night, which veils him!

---

1. Muḥammad.　　2. Adam.　　3. Of right and wrong.

By the heaven and Him that built it; by the earth and  91:6
Him that spread it; by the soul and Him that moulded it and
inspired it with knowledge of sin and piety: blessed shall be
the man who has kept it pure, and ruined he that has
corrupted it!

In their presumptuous pride the people of Thamūd
denied their apostle when their arch-sinner rose against
him. God's apostle said: 'This is God's own she-camel. Let
her drink.'

They disbelieved him, and slaughtered her. And for that
crime their Lord let loose His scourge upon them and razed
their city to the ground. He did not fear the consequences.  91:15

# NIGHT

*In the Name of God, the Compassionate, the Merciful*

BY THE night, when she lets fall her darkness, and by the  92:1
radiant day! By Him that created the male and the female,
your endeavours have varied ends!

For him that gives in charity and guards himself against
evil and believes in goodness, We shall smooth the path of
salvation; but for him that neither gives nor takes and
disbelieves in goodness, We shall smooth the path of
affliction. When he breathes his last, his riches will not avail
him.

It is for Us to give guidance. Ours is the life to come,  92:12
Ours the life of this world. I warn you, then, of the blazing
Fire, in which none shall burn save the hardened sinner,
who denies the Truth and pays no heed. But the good man
who keeps himself pure by almsgiving shall keep away from
it: and so shall he that does good works for the sake of the
Most High only, seeking no recompense. Such men shall be  92:21
content.

# DAYLIGHT

*In the Name of God, the Compassionate, the Merciful*

93:1 BY THE light of day, and by the dark of night, your Lord has not forsaken you,[1] nor does He abhor you.

The life to come holds a richer prize for you than this present life. You shall be gratified with what your Lord will give you.

93:6 Did He not find you an orphan and give you shelter?

Did He not find you in error and guide you?

Did He not find you poor and enrich you?

Therefore do not wrong the orphan, nor chide away the
93:11 beggar. But proclaim the goodness of your Lord.


# COMFORT

*In the Name of God, the Compassionate, the Merciful*

94:1 HAVE WE not lifted up your heart and relieved you[1] of the burden which weighed down your back?

Have We not given you high renown?

With every hardship there is ease. With every hardship there is ease.

94:8 When your prayers are ended resume your toil, and seek your Lord with all fervour.


# THE FIG

*In the Name of God, the Compassionate, the Merciful*

95:1 BY THE Fig, and by the Olive!

By Mount Sinai, and by this inviolate city.[2]

We created man in a most noble image and in the end We shall reduce him to the lowest of the low: except the believers who do good works, for theirs shall be a boundless recompense.

1. Muḥammad.     2. Mecca.

What then after this can make you deny the Last Judgement?

Is God not the best of judges?                                    95:8

## CLOTS OF BLOOD

*In the Name of God, the Compassionate, the Merciful*

RECITE IN the name of your Lord who created – created 96:1
man from clots of blood.

Recite! Your Lord is the Most Bountiful One, who by
the pen taught man what he did not know.

Indeed, man transgresses in thinking himself his own
master: for to your Lord all things return.

Observe the man who rebukes Our servant when he prays.
Think: does he follow the right guidance or enjoin true piety?

Think: if he denies the Truth and pays no heed, does he 96:13
not realize that God observes all?

No. Let him desist, or We will drag him by the forelock,
his lying, sinful forelock.

Then let him call his helpmates. We will call the guards of
Hell.

No, never obey him! Prostrate yourself and come nearer. 96:19

## QADR

*In the Name of God, the Compassionate, the Merciful*

WE REVEALED this on the Night of Qadr.[1] Would that 97:1
you knew what the Night of Qadr is like!

Better is the Night of Qadr than a thousand months.

On that night the angels and the Spirit by their Lord's
leave come down with each decree.

That night is peace, till break of dawn.                          97:5

1. Literally, glory.

# THE PROOF

*In the Name of God, the Compassionate, the Merciful*

98:1 THE UNBELIEVERS among the People of the Book[1] and the pagans did not desist from unbelief until the Proof was given them: an apostle from God reciting from purified pages infallible decrees.

Nor did those who were vouchsafed the Book disagree among themselves until the Proof was given them. Yet they were enjoined only to serve God and to worship none but Him, to attend to their prayers and to render the alms levy. That, surely, is the infallible faith.

The unbelievers among the People of the Book and the pagans shall burn for ever in the fire of Hell. They are the vilest of all creatures.

But of all creatures those that embrace the Faith and do
98:8 good works are the noblest. Their reward, in their Lord's presence, shall be the gardens of Eden, gardens watered by running streams, where they shall dwell for ever.

God is well pleased with them, and they are well pleased with Him. Thus shall the God-fearing be rewarded.

# THE EARTHQUAKE

*In the Name of God, the Compassionate, the Merciful*

99:1 WHEN EARTH is rocked in her last convulsion; when Earth shakes off her burdens and man asks, 'What may this mean?' – on that day she will proclaim her tidings, for your Lord will have inspired her.

On that day mankind will come in broken bands to be shown their labours. Whoever does an atom's weight of
99:8 good shall see it, and whoever does an atom's weight of evil shall see it also.

1. Jews and Christians.

# THE WAR STEEDS

*In the Name of God, the Compassionate, the Merciful*

BY THE snorting war steeds, which strike fire with their 100:1
hoofs as they gallop to the raid at dawn and with a trail of
dust cleave a massed army: man is ungrateful to his Lord!
To this he himself shall bear witness.

He loves riches with all his heart. But is he not aware that
when the dead are thrown out from their graves and men's
hidden thoughts are laid open, their Lord will on that day 100:11
have full knowledge of them all?

# THE DISASTER

*In the Name of God, the Compassionate, the Merciful*

THE DISASTER! What is the Disaster? 101:1

Would that you knew what the Disaster is!

On that day men shall become like scattered moths and
the mountains like tufts of carded wool.

Then he whose good deeds weigh heavy in the scales
shall dwell in bliss; but he whose deeds are light, the Abyss
shall be his home.

Would that you knew what this is like!

It is a scorching fire. 101:11

# WORLDLY GAIN

*In the Name of God, the Compassionate, the Merciful*

YOUR HEARTS are taken up with worldly gain from the 102:1
cradle to the grave.

But you shall learn. Then you shall surely learn.

Indeed, if you learned the truth with certainty, you would
see the fire of Hell: you would see it with your very eyes.

Then, on that day, you shall be questioned about your joys. 102:8

431

# THE DECLINING DAY

*In the Name of God, the Compassionate, the Merciful*

103:1 I SWEAR by the declining day that perdition shall be the lot of man, except for those who have faith and do good 103:3 works; who exhort each other to justice and to fortitude.

# THE SLANDERER

*In the Name of God, the Compassionate, the Merciful*

104:1 WOE BETIDE every back-biting slanderer who amasses riches and sedulously hoards them, thinking his wealth will render him immortal!

By no means! He shall be flung to the Destroying Flame.

Would that you knew what the Destroying Flame is like!

It is God's own kindled fire, which will rise up to the hearts of men. It will close in upon them from every side, in 104:9 towering columns.

# THE ELEPHANT

*In the Name of God, the Compassionate, the Merciful*

105:1 HAVE YOU not considered how God dealt with the Army of the Elephant?[1]

Did He not confound their stratagem and send against them flocks of birds which pelted them with clay-stones, so that they became like the withered stalks of plants which 105:5 cattle have devoured?

1. The allusion is to the expedition of Abraha, the Christian King of Ethiopia, against Mecca, said to have taken place in the year of Muḥammad's birth.

# QURAYSH[1]

*In the Name of God, the Compassionate, the Merciful*

FOR THE protection of Quraysh: their protection in their 106:1
summer and winter journeyings.

Therefore let them worship the Lord of this House who
fed them in the days of famine and shielded them from all 106:4
peril.

# ALMS

*In the Name of God, the Compassionate, the Merciful*

HAVE YOU thought of him that denies the Last Judge- 107:1
ment? It is he who turns away the orphan and has no urge
to feed the destitute.

Woe betide those who pray but are heedless in their
prayer; who make a show of piety and forbid alsmgiving. 107:7

# ABUNDANCE

*In the Name of God, the Compassionate, the Merciful*

WE HAVE given you[2] abundance. Pray to your Lord and 108:1
sacrifice to Him. He that hates you shall remain childless. 108:3

# THE UNBELIEVERS

*In the Name of God, the Compassionate, the Merciful*

SAY: 'UNBELIEVERS, I do not worship what you worship, 109:1
nor do you worship what I worship. I shall never worship
what you worship, nor will you ever worship what I
worship. You have your own religion, and I have mine.' 109:6

1. Muḥammad's own clan. Some commentators connect this
chapter with the preceding one.
2. Muḥammad.

# HELP

*In the Name of God, the Compassionate, the Merciful*

110:1 WHEN GOD'S help and victory come, and you see men
embrace God's faith in multitudes, give glory to your Lord
110:3 and seek His pardon. He is ever disposed to mercy.

# AL-LAHAB¹

*In the Name of God, the Compassionate, the Merciful*

111:1 MAY THE hands of Abu-Lahab² perish! May he himself
perish!    Nothing shall his wealth and gains avail him. He
shall be burnt in a flaming fire,³ and his wife, laden with
111:5 firewood, shall have a rope of fibre round her neck!

# ONENESS

*In the Name of God, the Compassionate, the Merciful*

112:1 SAY: 'GOD is One, the Eternal God. He begot none, nor
112:4 was He begotten. None is equal to Him.'

# DAYBREAK

*In the Name of God, the Compassionate, the Merciful*

113:1 SAY: 'I seek refuge in the Lord of Daybreak from the
mischief of His creation; from the mischief of the night
when she spreads her darkness; from the mischief of
113:5 conjuring witches; from the mischief of the envier, when he
envies.'

---

1. This *sūrah* is also known by another title: 'Al-Masad' (Fibre).
2. The Prophet's uncle, and one of his staunchest opponents.
3. A pun on the meaning of Abu-Lahab, 'father of flame'.

# MEN

*In the Name of God, the Compassionate, the Merciful*

SAY: 'I seek refuge in the Lord of men, the King of men, 114:1
the God of men, from the mischief of the slinking prompter
who whispers in the hearts of men; from jinn and men.' 114:6

# INDEX

This index is designed to be of help to the general reader rather than to provide a comprehensive concordance to the text. References are to page numbers; those followed by 'n' are to footnotes. Headings and references in square brackets are mentioned by allusion, not by name. Names beginning with 'al-' are indexed under the letter immediately following.